A GAME AS OLD AS EMPIRE

A GAME AS OLD AS EMPIRE

The Secret World of Economic Hit Men and the Web of Global Corruption

Edited by Steven Hiatt

Introduction by John Perkins,
author of *Confessions of an Economic Hit Man*

BERRETT-KOEHLER PUBLISHERS, INC.
San Francisco
a BK Currents book

Berrett-Koehler Publishers, Inc.
235 Montgomery Street, Suite 650
San Francisco, CA 94104-2916
Tel: (415) 288-0260   Fax: (415) 362-2512
www.bkconnection.com

Ordering Information

Quantity sales. Special discounts are available on quantity purchases by corporations, associations, and others. For details, contact the "Special Sales Department" at the Berrett-Koehler address above.
Individual sales. Berrett-Koehler publications are available through most bookstores. They can also be ordered directly from Berrett-Koehler: Tel: (800) 929-2929; Fax: (802) 864-7626; www.bkconnection. com.
Orders for college textbook/course adoption use. Please contact Berrett-Koehler: Tel: (800) 929-2929; Fax: (802) 864-7626.
Orders by U.S. trade bookstores and wholesalers. Please contact Publishers Group West, 1700 Fourth Street, Berkeley, CA 94710. Tel: (510) 528-1444; Fax (510) 528-3444.

Berrett-Koehler and the BK logo are registered trademarks of Berrett-Koehler Publishers, Inc.

Printed in the United States of America

Berrett-Koehler books are printed on long-lasting acid-free paper. When it is available, we choose paper that has been manufactured by environmentally responsible processes. These may include using trees grown in sustainable forests, incorporating recycled paper, minimizing chlorine in bleaching, or recycling the energy produced at the paper mill.

Library of Congress Cataloging-in-Publication Data

A game as old as empire : the secret world of economic hit men and the web of global corruption / edited by Steven Hiatt ; introduction by John Perkins.
  p. cm.
ISBN 978-1-57675-395-8 (hardcover)
1. International business enterprises--Corrupt practices. 2. Political corruption. 3. Structural adjustment (Economic policy) 4. Dependency. 5. Globalization--Social aspects. I. Hiatt, Steven, 1948- II. Title: Secret world of economic hit men and the web of global corruption. III. Title: Global corruption.

HD2755.5.G36 2006
364.1'323--dc22

2006034244

First Edition
12 11 10 09 08 07   10 9 8 7 6 5 4 3 2 1

Project management, design, and composition by Steven Hiatt / Hiatt & Dragon, San Francisco
Copyediting: Zipporah Collins   Proofreading: Tom Hassett

Contents

**Introduction: New Confessions and Revelations from the
World of Economic Hit Men**   1
John Perkins

Economic hit men serve a small corporate elite whose influence is pervasive,
no matter who wins formal elections, and whose goals are ever more profit
and power: the preservation and extension of an empire. In *Confessions of an
Economic Hit Man* John Perkins told the story of his own journey from servant
of empire to advocate for oppressed and exploited peoples. Here Perkins links
his experiences to new confessions and revelations in this book that reveal the
dark side of globalization.

1 Global Empire: The Web of Control   13
Steven Hiatt

Third World countries pay more than $375 billion a year in debt service, twen-
ty times the amount of foreign aid they receive. This system has been called
a Marshall Plan in reverse, with the countries of the Global South subsidizing
the wealthy North, even as half the world's population lives on less than $2 a
day. How does such an unjust system maintain itself? Steven Hiatt outlines the
web of control—financial, political, and military—that maintains this system
and explains why it's so hard for Third World countries to escape.

2 Selling Money—and Dependency: Setting the Debt Trap   31
S. C. Gwynne
Rising oil prices created an oversupply of petrodollar deposits in international banks, and eager young bankers helped recycle this money into new loans to developing countries to finance dubious projects. Sam Gwynne traveled the globe on behalf of U.S. banks, helping ensnare Third World countries in debt.

3 Dirty Money: Inside the Secret World of Offshore Banking   41
John Christensen
At least $500 billion in dirty money flows each year from poor countries into offshore accounts managed by Western banks, dwarfing the amount those nations receive in foreign aid. The sources of this money range from tax evasion, kickbacks, and capital flight to money laundering and drug trafficking. John Christensen was an offshore banker who found himself managing these secret accounts. He shows how the offshore banking system extracts tribute from countries that can least afford it and explains why this black economy has become essential to the international corporate elite.

4 BCCI's Double Game: Banking on America,
Banking on Jihad   69
Lucy Komisar
The Bank of Credit and Commerce International (BCCI) was a useful tool for many powerful clients, ranging from the CIA and the Medellín cartel to Osama bin Laden, al-Qaeda, and influential figures in both the Republican and Democratic parties. When BCCI was finally shut down, as much as $15 billion had been lost or stolen—the biggest bank fraud in the world. Lucy Komisar reveals why banking authorities looked the other way for so long, and how BCCI's long-time allies in Washington were able to block any meaningful investigation.

5 The Human Cost of Cheap Cell Phones   93
Kathleen Kern
Civil strife in the Democratic Republic of Congo has cost 4 million lives in the last ten years, as militias and warlords fight over the country's resources. The atrocities have been funded, at least indirectly, by some of the biggest Western corporations. They see the country as only a source of cheap coltan—vital

to making semiconductors—and other minerals. Kathleen Kern explores the direct relationship between the suffering of the Congolese people and the low prices Westerners pay for cell phones and laptops.

6 Mercenaries on the Front Lines in the New Scramble for Africa   113
Andrew Rowell and James Marriott
Some 30 percent of America's oil will come from Africa by 2015, and multinational oil companies are increasingly resorting to private armies to protect their operations there. Communities in the Niger Delta have been campaigning for a share of the oil wealth pumped from under their land. In 2006, Nigel Watson-Clark was working as a Shell security officer in Nigeria, protecting offshore oil rigs—a frontline soldier in the web of oil exploitation. Taken hostage during a raid by local militants, he found himself in the middle of the struggle for Nigeria's oil.

7 Hijacking Iraq's Oil Reserves: Economic Hit Men at Work   133
Greg Muttitt
While the Iraqi people struggle to define their future amid political chaos and violence, the fate of their most valuable economic asset, oil, is being decided behind closed doors. Oil production sharing agreements being forced on Iraq will cost the country hundreds of billions of dollars in lost revenue, while funneling enormous profits to foreign companies. Greg Muttitt uncovers a little-known Western foundation, the International Tax and Investment Center, that's providing the hit.

8 The World Bank and the $100 Billion Question   157
Steve Berkman
The World Bank has pushed a debt-based development strategy for Third World countries for decades. Hundreds of billions in loans were supposed to bring progress, yet the programs have never lived up to their promise. Instead, governing elites amass obscene fortunes while the poor shoulder the burden of paying off the debts. A former World Bank staffer, Steve Berkman presents an inside investigator's account of how these schemes work to divert development money into the pockets of corrupt elites and their First World partners.

9 The Philippines, the World Bank, and the Race to the Bottom   175
Ellen Augustine
"Development" and "modernization" became code words for U.S. efforts to prop up the regime of President Ferdinand Marcos, with the World Bank serving as a conduit for the financing of Marcos' dictatorship. Some 800 leaked documents from the World Bank itself tell how the Bank financed martial law and made the Philippines the test case for its export-led development strategy based on multinational corporations—with disastrous results for both democracy and economic development.

10 Exporting Destruction   197
Bruce Rich
Export credit agencies have quietly become the world's largest financial institutions, backing $788 billion in trade in 2004. Secretive and largely unregulated, they pursue a single mission: boost overseas sales of their countries' multinational corporations. In doing so, they've become some of the dirtiest players in the EHM game, financing nuclear power plants in countries that can't manage them and massive arms sales to strife-torn regions—all lubricated by billions of dollars in bribes. Bruce Rich looks at the secretive world of ECAs and the damage they cause around the world.

11 The Mirage of Debt Relief   219
James S. Henry
G8 leaders have proudly announced $40 billion in debt relief for eighteen heavily indebted poor countries in Latin America and Africa—just over 1 percent of the $3.2 trillion that those countries owe. But the actual debt relief granted will be only a fraction of this small amount—and the strings attached to getting it make even this modest amount hardly worth getting: closed hospitals and schools, bankrupted local businesses, and high unemployment. James S. Henry delivers the analysis and outlines steps for an effective relief campaign for Third World debtor countries.

12 Global Uprising: The Web of Resistance   263
Antonia Juhasz
How do you fight—and change—a global system of exploitation? Antonia Juhasz argues that a better world is indeed possible, and finds the power we need to create it in the global justice (anti-corporate globalization) movement. Its

agenda provides direction, empowerment, and—most important—hope that we can and will break the empire's web of control.

About the Authors 283

Acknowledgments 289

Appendix: Resources of Hope 291

Index 303

John Perkins links his experiences to new revelations that expose the drive for empire that lies behind the rhetoric of globalization.

Introduction: New Confessions and Revelations from the World of Economic Hit Men

John Perkins

Economic hit men (EHMs) are highly paid professionals who cheat countries around the globe out of trillions of dollars. They funnel money from the World Bank, the U.S. Agency for International Development (USAID), and other foreign "aid" organizations into the coffers of huge corporations and the pockets of a few wealthy families who control the planet's natural resources. Their tools include fraudulent financial reports, rigged elections, payoffs, extortion, sex, and murder. They play a game as old as empire, but one that has taken on new and terrifying dimensions during this time of globalization.

I should know; I was an EHM.

I wrote that opening paragraph to *Confessions of an Economic Hit Man* as a description of my own profession. Since the book's first publication in early November 2004, I have heard TV, radio, and event hosts read those words many times as they introduced me to their audiences. The reality of EHMs shocked people in the United States and other countries. Many have told me that it convinced them to commit themselves to taking actions that will make this a better world.

The public interest aroused by *Confessions* was not a foregone conclusion. I spent a great deal of time working up the courage to try to publish it. Once I made the decision to do so, my attempts got off to a rocky start.

By late 2003, the manuscript had been circulated to many publishers—and I had almost given up on ever seeing the book in print. Despite praising it as "riveting," "eloquently written," "an important exposé," and "a story that must be told," publisher after publisher—twenty-five, in fact—rejected it. My literary agent and I concluded that it was just too anti-corporatocracy. (A word introduced to most readers in those pages, *corporatocracy* refers to the powerful group of people who run the world's biggest corporations, the most powerful governments, and history's first truly global empire.) The major publishing houses, we concluded, were too intimidated by, or perhaps too beholden to, the corporate elite.

Eventually a courageous independent publisher, Berrett-Koehler, took the book on. *Confessions'* success among the public astounded me. During its first week in bookstores it went to number 4 on Amazon.com. Then it spent many weeks on every major bestseller list. In less than fourteen months, it had been translated into and published in twenty languages. A major Hollywood company purchased the option to film it. Penguin/Plume bought the paperback rights.

Despite all these successes, an important element was still missing. The major U.S. media refused to discuss *Confessions* or the fact that, because of it, terms such as *EHM*, *corporatocracy*, and *jackal* were now appearing on college syllabuses. The *New York Times* and other newspapers had to include it on their bestseller lists—after all, numbers don't lie (unless an EHM produces them, as you will see in the following pages)—but during its first fifteen months in print most of them obstinately declined to review it. Why?

My agent, my publicist, the best minds at Berrett-Koehler and Penguin/ Plume, my family, my friends, and I may never know the real answer to that question. What we do know is that several nationally recognized journalists appeared poised on the verge of writing or speaking about the book. They conducted "pre-interviews" with me by phone and dispatched producers to wine and dine my wife and me. But, in the end, they declined. A major TV network convinced me to interrupt a West Coast speaking tour, fly across the country to New York, and dress up in a television-blue sports coat. Then—as I waited at the door for the network's limo—an employee called to cancel. Whenever media apologists offered explanations for such actions, they took the form of questions: "Can you prove the existence of other EHMs?" "Has anyone else written about these things?" "Have others in high places made similar disclosures?"

The answer to these questions is, of course, yes. Every major incident described in the book has been discussed in detail by other authors—usually lots of other authors. The CIA's coup against Iran's Mossadegh; the atrocities committed by his replacement, Big Oil's puppet, the Shah; the Saudi Arabian money-laundering affair; the jackal-orchestrated assassinations of Ecuador's President Jaime Roldós and Panama's President Omar Torrijos; allegations of collusion between oil companies and missionary groups in the Amazon; the international activities of Bechtel, Halliburton, and other pillars of American capitalism; the unilateral and unprovoked U.S. invasion of Panama and capture of Manuel Noriega; the coup against Venezuelan President Hugo Chávez— these and the other events in the book are a matter of public record.

Several pundits criticized what some referred to as my "radical accusation"—that economic forecasts are manipulated and distorted in order to achieve political objectives (as opposed to economic objectivity) and that foreign "aid" is a tool for big business rather than an altruistic means to alleviate poverty. However, both of these transgressions against the true purposes of sound economics and altruism have been well documented by a multitude of people, including a former World Bank chief economist and winner of the Nobel Prize in economics, Joseph Stiglitz. In his book *Globalization and Its Discontents*, Stiglitz writes:

> To make its [the IMF's] programs *seem* to work, to make the numbers "add up," economic forecasts have to be adjusted. Many users of these numbers do not realize that they are not like ordinary forecasts; in these instances GDP forecasts are not based on a sophisticated statistical model, or even on the best estimates of those who know the economy well, but are merely the numbers that have been *negotiated* as part of an IMF program. . . .[1]
>
> Globalization, as it has been advocated, often seems to replace the old dictatorships of national elites with new dictatorships of international finance. . . . For millions of people globalization has not worked. . . . They have seen their jobs destroyed and their lives become more insecure.[2]

I found it interesting that during my first book tour—for the hardcover edition, in late 2004 and early 2005—I sometimes heard questions from my audiences that reflected the mainstream press. However, they were significantly diminished during the paperback edition tour in early 2006. The level of sophistication among readers had risen over the course of that year. A growing suspicion that the mainstream press was collaborating with the corporatocracy—which, of course, owned much of it or at least supported it through advertising—had become manifest. While I would love to credit *Confessions* for this transformation in public attitude, my book has to share that honor with a number of others, such as Stiglitz's *Globalization and Its Discontents*, David Korten's *When Corporations Rule the World*, Noam Chomsky's *Hegemony or Survival*, Chalmers Johnson's *Sorrows of Empire*, Jeff Faux's *Global Class War*, and Antonia Juhasz's *Bush Agenda*, as well as films such as *The Constant Gardener, Syriana, Hotel Rwanda, Good Night, and Good Luck*, and *Munich*. The American public recently has been treated to a feast of exposés. Mine is definitely not a voice in the wilderness.

Despite the overwhelming evidence that the corporatocracy has created the world's first truly global empire, inflicted increased misery and poverty on millions of people around the planet, managed to sabotage the principles of self-determination, justice, and freedom that form the foundations upon which the United States stands, and turned a country that was lauded at the end of World War II as democracy's savior into one that is feared, resented, and hated, the mainstream press ignores the obvious. In pleasing the moneymen and the executives upstairs, many journalists have turned their backs on the truth. When approached by my publicists, they continue to ask: "Where are the trenches?" "Can you produce the trowels that dug them?" "Have any 'objective' researchers confirmed your story?"

Although the evidence was already available, Berrett-Koehler and I decided that the proper response was to answer such questions in terms that no one could ignore and that only those who insisted on remaining in denial could dispute. We would publish a book with many contributors, an anthology, further revealing the world of economic hit men and how it works.

In *Confessions*, I talked about a world rooted in the cold war, in the dynamics and proxy conflicts of the U.S.–Soviet conflict. My sojourn in that war ended in 1981, a quarter of a century ago. Since then, and especially since the collapse of the USSR, the dynamics of empire have changed. The world is now more multipolar and mercantile, with China and Europe emerging to compete with the U.S. Empire is heavily driven by multinational corporations, whose interests transcend those of any particular nation-state.[3] There are new multinational institutions and trade agreements, such as the World Trade Organization (WTO) and North American Free Trade Agreement (NAFTA), and newly articulated ideologies and programs, such as neoliberalism and the structural adjustments and conditionalities imposed by the IMF. But one thing remains unchanged: the peoples of the Third World continue to suffer; their future, if anything, looks even bleaker than it did in the early 1980s.

A quarter-century ago, I saw myself as a hit man for the interests of U.S. capitalism in the struggle for control of the developing world during the cold war. Today, the EHM game is more complex, its corruption more pervasive, and its operations more fundamental to the world economy and politics. There are many more types of economic hit men, and the roles they play are far more diverse. The veneer of respectability remains a key factor; subterfuges range from money laundering and tax evasion carried out in well-appointed office suites to activities that amount to economic war crimes and result in the deaths of millions of people. The chapters that follow reveal this dark side of globalization, showing a system that depends on deception, extortion, and often violence: an officer of an offshore bank hiding hundreds of millions in stolen money, IMF advisors slashing Ghana's education and health programs, a Chinese bureaucrat seeking oil concessions in Africa, a mercenary defending a European oil company in Nigeria, a consultant rewriting Iraqi oil law, and executives financing warlords to secure supplies of coltan ore in Congo.

The main obstacle to compiling such stories should be obvious. Most EHMs do not think it is in their best interests to talk about their jobs. Many are still actively employed in the business. Those who have stepped away often receive pensions, consultant fees, and other perks from their former employers. They understand that whistle-blowers usually sacrifice such benefits—and sometimes much more. Most of us who have done that type of work pride ourselves on loyalty to old comrades. Once one of us decides to take the big leap—"into the cold," to use CIA vernacular—we know we will have to face the harsh reality of powerful forces arrayed to protect the institutional power of multinational corporations, global banks, government defense and security agencies, international agencies—and the small elite that runs them.

In recent years, the people charged with deceiving ordinary citizens have grown more cunning. *The Pentagon Papers* and the White House Watergate tapes taught them the dangers of writing and recording incriminating details. The Enron, Arthur Andersen, and WorldCom scandals, and recent allegations about CIA "extraordinary renditions," weapons of mass destruction deceits, and National Security Agency eavesdropping serve to reinforce policies that favor shredding. Government officials who expose a CIA agent to retaliate against her whistle-blowing spouse go unpunished. All these events lead to the ultimate deterrent to speaking the truth: those who expose the corporatocracy can expect to be assassinated—financially and by reputation, if not with a bullet.

Less obvious deterrents also keep people from telling the truth. Opening one's soul for public scrutiny, confessing, is not fun. I had written many books before *Confessions* (five of them published). Yet none prepared me for the angst I would encounter while exposing my transgressions as an EHM. Although most of us humans do not want to think of ourselves as corrupt, weak, or immoral, it is difficult—if not impossible—to ignore those aspects of ourselves when describing our lives as economic hit men. Personally, it was one of the most difficult tasks I have ever undertaken. In approaching prospective contributors to a book such as this I might tell them that confessing is, in the end, worth the anguish. However, for someone setting out on this path, that end seems very distant.

I discussed these obstacles and the potential benefits of overcoming them with Steve Piersanti, the intrepid founder and CEO of Berrett-Koehler, who made the decision to publish *Confessions*. It did not take us long to decide that the benefits were well worth the struggle. If my *Confessions* could send such a strong message to the public, it made sense that multiple confessions—or stories about people who need to confess—might reach even more people and motivate them to take actions that will turn this empire back into the democratic republic it was intended to be. Our goal was nothing less than convincing the American public that we can and must create a future that will make our children and grandchildren—and their brothers and sisters on every continent—proud of us.

Of course we had to start by showing journalists the trowels *and* the trenches. We decided that we should also include well-researched analyses by observers who came from a more objective perspective, rather than a personal one. A balance between firsthand and third-party accounts seemed like the prudent approach.

Steve took it upon himself to find someone who could be an editor and also serve as a sleuth: he'd have to ferret out prospective writers and convince them that loyalty to country, family, and future generations on every continent demanded that they participate in this book. After an extensive selection process, he, his staff, and I settled on Steven Hiatt. Steve is a professional editor—but he also has a long history as an activist, first against the Vietnam War and then as a teachers' union organizer. In addition, he worked for a number of years at Stanford Research Institute, a think tank and consultancy organization serving multinationals and government agencies around the world and closely linked to Bechtel, Bank of America, and other players in the EHM world. There he worked on research reports that he describes as essentially "the corporatocracy talking to itself."

Once the process of assembling this anthology began, I started speaking about it. When people asked those questions—"Can you prove the existence of other EHMs?" "Has anyone else written about these things?" "Have others made similar disclosures?"—I told them about the upcoming book. The wisdom of making that decision to publish an anthology was supported on February 19, 2006, when the *New York Times* ran a major article that featured *Confessions* on the front page of its Sunday Business Section. The editors, I am sure, were comforted by the results of a background check confirming my account of my life and the episodes described in *Confessions*; however, the fact that other EHMs and researchers had committed to writing this book was, I suspect, the most important factor in their decision to publish that article.

The contributors to this book uncover events that have taken place across a wide range of countries, all EHM game plans under a variety of guises. Each sheds more light on the building of an empire that is contrary to American principles of democracy and equality. The chapters are presented in an order that follows the flow of money and power in the Global Empire. The chart on page 10 shows that progression: the selling of loans to Third World countries, the flow of dirty money back to First World control via secret offshore accounts, the failure of debt-led development models to reduce poverty, the accumulation of mountains of unpayable debt, the gutting of local economies by the IMF, and military intervention and domination to secure access to resources. Steve Hiatt, in "Global Empire," gives an overview of the web of control that First World companies and institutions use to rule the global economy; each subsequent chapter exposes another facet. In brief summary:

• S.C. Gwynne joined Cleveland Trust and quickly moved into the heady atmosphere of international banking, where he learned that ability to pay had little to do with placing loans. In "Selling Money—and Dependency: Setting the Debt Trap" he describes a culture of business corruption in which local elites and international banks build mutually supportive relationships based on debts that will have to be repaid by ordinary citizens.

• John Christensen worked for a trust company on the offshore banking haven of Jersey, one of Britain's Channel Islands. There he found himself at the center of the EHM world, part of a global offshore banking industry that facilitates tax evasion, money laundering, and capital flight. In "Dirty Money" he reveals the workings of a system that enables the theft of billions from Third World (and First World) citizens; the lures of an opulent lifestyle; and why he decided to get out.

• The Bank of Credit and Commerce International was for two decades a key player in offshore/underground banking. It provided off-the-books/ illegal transactions for a startling range of customers—from the CIA to the Medellín cartel to Osama bin Laden and al-Qaeda. In "BCCI's Double Game," Lucy Komisar recounts the bank's rapid rise and fall—and its $13 billion bankruptcy.

• Congo remains one of the world's poorest countries and is caught in a civil war that has cost at least 4 million lives over the last ten years, with western multinationals financing militias and warlords to ensure access to gold, diamonds, and coltan. In "The Human Cost of Cheap Cell Phones," Kathleen Kern provides an eyewitness account of the high price the Congolese have paid to bring cheap electronics to First World consumers.

• Some 30 percent of America's supply of oil is expected to come from Africa in the next ten years, but U.S. and UK oil companies will be competing with China for access to these reserves. Local communities have been campaigning to gain a share of this new wealth and to prevent environmental destruction of their region. In "Mercenaries on the Front Lines in the New Scramble for Africa," Andrew Rowell and James Marriott tell how a British expat security officer found himself in the middle of this struggle for oil and power.

• According to most estimates Iraq has the world's second largest oil reserves—and access to Iraq's oil has been one of the essential elements of U.S. foreign policy. The occupation regime is planning to sign oil production sharing agreements with U.S. and UK companies that will cost the Iraqi people $200 billion that they need to rebuild their country. In "Hijacking Iraq's Oil Reserves," Greg Muttitt reveals the EHM behind this high-level hit.

• "Have you brought the money?" a Liberian official asked World Bank staffer Steve Berkman, clearly expecting him to hand over a satchel full of cash. In "The World Bank and the $100 Billion Question," Berkman provides an insider's account of how and why the Bank looks the other way as corrupt elites steal funds intended for development aid.

• In the 1970s, the Philippines were a showcase for the World Bank's debt-based model of development and modernization. In "The Philippines, the

World Bank, and the Race to the Bottom," Ellen Augustine tells how billions in loans were central to U.S. efforts to prop up the Marcos dictatorship, with the World Bank serving as a conduit.

• Export credit agencies have a single job: to enrich their countries' corporations by making it easier for poor countries to buy their products and services. In "Exporting Destruction," Bruce Rich turns a spotlight on the secretive world of ECAs and the damage they have caused in selling nuclear plants to countries that cannot manage them and pushing arms in war-torn regions.

• The G8 finance ministers announced before their Gleneagles meeting that they had agreed on $40 billion of debt relief for eighteen Third World countries. In "The Mirage of Debt Relief," James S. Henry, a former international banker, shows how little debt relief has actually been granted—and why dozens of countries remain caught in the West's debt trap.

Feel free to read the chapters according to your interests. Skip around, focus on one geographic area at a time or on one particular discipline, if you wish. Then turn to Antonia Juhasz's "Global Uprising" to learn what you can do to resist global domination by the corporatocracy.

As you read, please allow yourself to think about and feel the implications of the actions described for the world and for our children and grandchildren. Permit your passions to rise to the surface. Feel compelled to take action. It is essential that we—you and I—do something. We must transform our country back into one that reflects the values of our Declaration of Independence and the other principles we were raised to honor and defend. We must begin today to re-create the world the corporatocracy has inflicted on us.

This book presents a series of snapshots of the tools used by EHMs to create the world's first truly global empire. They are, however, a mere introduction to the many nefarious deeds that have been committed by the corporate elite—often in the name of altruism and progress. During the post–World War II period, we EHMs managed to turn the "last, best hope for democracy," in Lincoln's words, into an empire that does not flinch at inflicting brutal and often totalitarian measures on people who have resources we covet.

After reading the chapters you will have a better understanding of why people around the world fear, resent, and even hate us. As a result of the corporatocracy's policies, an average of 24,000 people die every day from hunger; tens of thousands more—mostly children—die from curable diseases because they cannot afford available medicines. More than half the world's population

Global Empire North and South
FLOWS OF MONEY AND POWER

The Global North has for decades sold a model of development based on debt. Loans pushed by First World lenders and eagerly grabbed by corrupt Third World elites have left Global South countries in a debt trap $3.2 trillion deep—often with little real development to show for it. Much of the money simply round-trips back to First World suppliers or offshore banking havens. Meanwhile, a new era of imperial domination has begun with interventions to secure control of scarce resources like oil and coltan.

GLOBAL NORTH

G8 NATIONS · MULTINATIONALS · WORLD BANK · IMF

1. FOLLOW THE MONEY

S.C. GWYNNE
Selling Money—
and Dependency

JOHN CHRISTENSEN
Dirty Money: Offshore Banking

LUCY KOMISAR
BCCI: Banking on America,
Banking on Jihad

4. THE DEBT TRAP

JAMES S. HENRY
The Mirage of Debt Relief

3. INTERVENTION AND DOMINATION: ACCESS TO RESOURCES

KATHLEEN KERN
The Human Cost of Cheap Cell Phones

**ANDREW ROWELL/
JAMES MARRIOTT**
Oil, Mercenaries, and the New Scramble for Africa

GREG MUTTITT
Hijacking Iraq's Oil: EHMs at Work

2. DEBT-LED DEVELOPMENT

STEVE BERKMAN
The $100 Billion Question

ELLEN AUGUSTINE
The World Bank and the Philippines

BRUCE RICH
Exporting Destruction

GLOBAL SOUTH

THE UNDERDEVELOPED WORLD

lives on less than $2 a day, not nearly enough to cover basic necessities in most places. In essence our economic system depends on modern versions of human exploitation that conjure images of serfdom and slavery.

We must put an end to this. You and I must do the right thing. We must understand that our children will not inherit a stable, safe, and sustainable world unless we change the terrible conditions that have been created by EHMs. All of us must look deep into our hearts and souls and decide what it is we can best do. Where are our strengths? What are our passions?

As an author and lecturer, I know that I have certain skills and opportunities. Yours may be different from mine, but they are just as powerful. I urge you to set as a primary goal in your life making this a better world not only for you but also for all those who follow. Please commit to taking at least one action every single day to realize this goal. Think about those 24,000 who die each day from hunger, and dedicate yourself to changing this in your lifetime. Write letters and e-mails—to newspapers, magazines, your local and national representatives, your friends, businesses that are doing the right thing and those that are not; call in to radio shows; shop consciously; do not "buy cheap" if doing so contributes to modern forms of slavery; support nonprofit organizations that help spread the word, protect the environment, defend civil liberties, fight hunger and disease, and make this a sane world; volunteer; go to schools and teach our children; form discussion groups in your neighborhood—the list of possible actions is endless, limited only by imagination. We all have many talents and passions to contribute. The most important thing is to get out there and do it!

One thing we all can—and must—do is to educate ourselves and those who interact with us. Democracy is based on an informed electorate. If we in the United States are not aware that our business and political leaders are using EHMs to subvert the most sacred principles upon which our country is founded, then we cannot in truth claim to be a democracy.

There is no excuse for lack of awareness, now that you have this book, plus many others and a multitude of films, CDs, and DVDs to help educate everyone you connect with. Beyond that, it is essential that every time you read, hear, or see a news report about some international event, do so with a skeptical mind. Remember that most media are owned by—or dependent on the financial support of—the corporatocracy. Dig beneath the surface. The appendix, "Resources of Hope," provides a list of alternative media where you can access different viewpoints.

This may well be the most pivotal and exciting time in the history of a nation that is built on pivotal and exciting events. How you and I choose to react to this global empire in the coming years is likely to determine the future of our planet. Will we continue along a road marked by violence, exploitation of others, and ultimately the likelihood of our self-destruction as a species? Or will we create a world our children will be proud to inherit?

The choice is ours—yours and mine.

Notes

1. Joseph E. Stiglitz, *Globalization and Its Discontents* (New York: Norton, 2003), p. 232.
2. Ibid., pp. 247–48.
3. For more on the corporatocracy as an international, interlinked power elite, see Jeff Faux, "The Party of Davos," *Nation*, January 26, 2006.

1 *Steven Hiatt outlines the pervasive web of control—financial, political, and military—that sustains today's global empire.*

Global Empire: The Web of Control

Steven Hiatt

A never-ending accumulation of property must be based on a never-ending accumulation of power. —*Hannah Arendt*

In June 2003, after declaring "Mission accomplished!" in the wake of Operation Iraqi Freedom, George W. Bush told cheering West Point cadets that America has "no territorial ambitions. We don't seek an empire." Meanwhile, neoconservative pundits like Niall Ferguson and Charles Krauthammer were encouraging him to do precisely that: to "make the transition from informal to formal empire" by acknowledging America's actual role in the world and accepting the reality that "political globalization is a fancy word for imperialism."[1] Had the post-postwar world—the new order emerging since the Berlin Wall came down in 1989—turned full circle to a new Age of Empire?

The victory of the Allies in 1945, confirming the right of peoples to self-determination in their Atlantic Charter declaration, seemed to signal the end for the world's colonial empires. Colonized peoples in Asia, Africa, and the Middle East had seen the armies of Britain, France, and the Netherlands defeated in 1940–41, and knew that the European imperial powers now had neither the military nor the financial resources to enforce their rule for long. Moreover, the two strongest powers, the U.S. and the Soviet Union, seemed to stand on the anti-imperialist side. The U.S. had long pursued an "open door" policy advocating formal independence for developing countries. The Soviet Union had denounced imperialism since its birth in 1917, and the communist movement it led had wide appeal in parts of the colonial world as a result.

Nevertheless, the European colonial powers tried to hang on to their possessions as long as they could. Britain did finally "quit India" in 1947, but fought insurgents in Kenya, Cyprus, and Malaya before granting those countries independence. France fought losing, divisive wars in Indochina and Algeria to retain its bit of imperial *gloire*. Still, around the world the tide of history was clearly running in favor of self-determination. The quandary for Western elites was how to manage this process. Would new Third World leaders attempt to strike out on their own, taking control of their countries' resources in order to build their own national industries? Or—worse—would they ally with the Soviet bloc or would nationalist campaigns prepare the way for takeovers by communist parties?

For Western Europeans, loss of access to colonial resources and markets would be an enormous blow: their weakened economies were only slowly recovering from World War II and they planned to force the colonies to help pay for reconstruction. For its part, the U.S. feared that colonial independence would weaken its European allies and might well lead to the expansion of Soviet influence in Europe. And U.S. business leaders were concerned about a postwar return to the depression that had marked the 1930s and so were eager to preserve access to resources and possible new markets.

Events in Iran, Guatemala, and Egypt in the 1950s marked a new turn in Western policies in what was becoming known as the Third World. In 1951, Iranian prime minister Mohammad Mossadegh nationalized the country's oil industry, which had been run by the Anglo-Iranian Oil Company (since renamed British Petroleum). A democratically elected nationalist, Mossadegh (*Time*'s Man of the Year for 1951) not surprisingly resented the fact that 92 percent of the profits from Iranian oil went to AIOC, a longstanding arrangement reflecting British domination of Persia early in the century. Winston Churchill had recently returned for a second term as prime minister and was determined to restore the UK's finances and prestige in the face of this challenge from a newly assertive client state. Churchill ordered a blockade of the Persian Gulf to prevent Iran from exporting oil to other purchasers, and he was joined in a boycott of Iranian trade by the United States. More muscular action was not possible, however: the Korean War absorbed the attention of the U.S. and Britain, and Soviet intervention in support of Iran was a threat. A more subtle approach was needed, and the CIA devised Operation Ajax, directed by Kermit Roosevelt. The first step was to create political turmoil to undermine Mossadegh's political support: a CIA disinformation campaign worked overtime spreading rumors designed to split secular democrats from Islamic nationalists. Finally, the military made its move in August 1953, and Mossadegh was arrested, a new prime minister was appointed, the Shah was restored to power, and the oil industry was denationalized. The U.S. did demand a price for its help, however: British Petroleum now had to share its access to Iranian oilfields with several U.S. companies. U.S. military and foreign policy leaders were cheered by the success of their plan, recovering Iran at a low cost politically, militarily, and financially.

Guatemala was the next test case for this indirect method of policing empire. In May 1952, President Jacobo Arbenz announced a land reform program that would have nationalized unused land belonging to landlords and, especially, the holdings of Boston's United Fruit Company, the country's largest landowner. His inspiration was Abraham Lincoln's Homestead Act of 1862, with Arbenz hoping to enable peasants and rural laborers to become independent small farmers. But apparently Lincoln was too radical for the Eisenhower administration, especially with Secretary of State John Foster Dulles and CIA Director Alan Dulles sitting on United Fruit's Board of Directors. Kermit Roosevelt gave this description of Alan Dulles' reaction to plans for the CIA's Operation PBSuccess: "He seemed almost alarmingly enthusiastic. His eyes were glistening; he seemed to be purring like a giant cat. Clearly he was not only enjoying what he was hearing, but my instincts told me that he was planning as well."[2] Arbenz was overthrown in a coup in June 1954; some 15,000 of his peasant supporters were killed.

Following the success of covert methods of intervention in Iran and Guatemala, the Suez Crisis of 1956 illustrated the dangers of old-style direct intervention. Egyptian President Gamal Abdel Nasser announced nationalization of the Suez Canal in July 1956; the canal was a key national resource then in the hands of European investors, and Nasser hoped to use canal profits to pay for his ambitious Aswan High Dam project. His plans energized several enemies: Britain, the former colonial power, since a British company ran the canal; France, since Nasser supported the Algerian rebels that France had been fighting since 1954; and Israel, which hoped to settle accounts with a pan-Arab nationalist who supported the Palestinians. Israel invaded Egypt on October 29, 1956, and Britain and France quickly occupied the canal region despite Egyptian resistance. This resort to direct military intervention posed a problem for the United States. The Eisenhower administration was dealing with Soviet intervention in Hungary to depose reformer Imre Nagy. The U.S. hoped to use the Hungarian crisis to undermine the appeal of communism, which had already suffered a serious blow to its prestige earlier in the year with Khrushchev's revelation of Stalin's crimes at the Soviet Twentieth Party Congress. Western intervention in the Suez therefore undercut the U.S. position. The U.S. response this time was creative: Britain was pressured to withdraw, and the intervention collapsed—underlining the weakness of the old colonial powers, speeding decolonization, and enhancing the prestige of the United States in the Third World.

From then on, the United States would have to compete with the Soviets for influence in the Third World as dozens of newly independent countries flooded the halls of the United Nations.

Decolonization vs. Control during the Cold War

For the most part, the newly independent states in Africa and Asia joined Latin America as producers of primary commodities: sugar, coffee, rubber, tin, copper, bananas, cocoa, tea, jute, rice, cotton. Many were plantation crops grown by First World corporations or local landlords, or minerals extracted by First World companies. In either case, the products were sold in markets dominated by European and U.S. companies, usually on exchanges in New York or London, and processed in plants in Europe or North America.

As Third World leaders began to take responsibility for their nations, they emphasized tackling the problem of economic underdevelopment. Their efforts were based on state-led development models, influenced by current thinking in the U.S. and Western Europe. Typically, colonial governments had been heavily involved in economic planning and regulation, and new leaders like Kwame Nkrumah of Ghana, Jawaharlal Nehru of India, and Léopold Senghor of Senegal had been educated in Europe and influenced by socialist and social democratic programs. Moreover, the new states started economic life without their own entrepreneurial class capable of leading economic development.

Not surprisingly, then, many countries concentrated on Big Projects— showpiece government development projects that could be the motor for economic transformation, such as Ghana's Volta River Project, which involved construction of the Akosombo Dam in the early 1960s to form the world's largest artificial lake and building aluminum smelters to take advantage of the country's bauxite resources. And most countries followed policies of import substitution—developing local production capacity to replace expensive imports from Europe and North America. However, these and other industrialization projects all required massive loans, from banks, export credit agencies, or international development institutions such as the World Bank.

Again Western elites faced a problem: how could they preserve their access to Third World resources and markets? Independence offered the West an opportunity to shed the costs of direct rule—responsibility for administration, policing, and development—while maintaining all the benefits of empire. But independence also carried dangers: Asian, African, and Latin American nations might indeed become masters of their own economies, directing them to maximize their own development. And there were alternative models: Cuba and Vietnam, to name the most prominent. After all, the point of empire was not simply to import oil or coffee from Latin America, or copper or cocoa from Africa, but to import these goods at prices advantageous to the West—in effect, a built-in subsidy from the former colonies to their former rulers. Empire, whether based on direct rule or indirect influence, is not about control for its own sake: it is about exploitation of foreign lands and peoples for the benefit of the metropolis, or at least its ruling circles.

At some point, the alternative that Claudine Martin laid out to John Perkins in 1971, as recounted in *Confessions of an Economic Hit Man*,[3] must have become an obvious element of the West's strategy. The U.S. and its allies were competing with the Soviet bloc to provide loans for development projects of a myriad kinds. Why not embrace this burden—and use the debts to bring these countries into the West's web of control economically and politically? They could be lured by economic hit men like John Perkins to take on debt to build grandiose projects that promised modernization and prosperity—the debt-led theory of economic development. Moreover, the large sums flooding in could be useful in winning the allegiance of new Third World elites, who were under pressure to deliver prosperity to their political followers, allies, and extended families. The possibilities for corruption were seemingly endless and would provide further opportunities for enmeshing the leaders in relationships with the West while discouraging them from striking out on their own on what could only be a more austere, and much more dangerous, path.

Debt Boom—and Bust: SAPing the Third World

The Yom Kippur War in 1973 and the subsequent Arab oil embargo led to the stagflation crisis of 1974–76 and marked the end of the postwar boom. As one result, leading First World banks were awash in petrodollar deposits stockpiled by OPEC countries. If these billions continued to pile up in bank

---

Economic Hit Men: Hiding in Plain Sight

Those who serve the interests of global empire play many different roles. As John Perkins points out, "Every one of the people on my staff also held a title—financial analyst, sociologist, economist . . . and yet none of those titles indicated that every one of them was, in his or her own way, an EHM." A London bank sets up an offshore subsidiary, staffed by men and women with respectable university degrees dressed in the same designer outfits you would expect to see in the City or on Wall Street. Yet their work each day consists of hiding embezzled funds, laundering the profits from drug sales, and helping multinational corporations evade taxes. They are economic hit men. An IMF team arrives in an African capital armed with the power to extend vitally needed loans—at the price of slashing its education budget and opening its economy to a flood of goods dumped by North American and European exporters. They are economic hit men. A consultant sets up shop in Baghdad's Green Zone, where, protected by the U.S. Army, he writes new laws governing exploitation of Iraq's oil reserves. He is an economic hit man.

EHM methods range from those that are legal—indeed, some are imposed by governments and other authoritative institutions—through a series of gray areas to those that violate whole catalogs of laws. The beneficiaries are those so powerful that they are rarely called to account, an elite centered in First World capitals, who, together with their Third World clients, work to arrange the world to their liking. And their world is one where only dollars, not people—and certainly not the planet's billions of everyday people—are citizens.

---

accounts—some $450 billion from 1973 to 1981—the effect would be to drain the world of liquidity, enhancing the recessionary effects of skyrocketing oil prices. What to do? The international monetary system was facing its worst crisis since the collapse of the 1930s. The solution was to "recycle" the petrodollars as loans to the developing world. Brazil, for example, borrowed $100 billion for a whole catalog of projects—steel mills, giant dams, highways, railroad lines, nuclear power plants.[4]

The boom in lending to the Third World, chronicled by S.C. Gwynne in "Selling Money—and Dependency," turned into a bust in August 1982, as first Mexico and then other Third World states announced that they were unable to meet their debt payments. What followed was a series of disguised defaults, reschedulings, rolled-over loans, new loans, debt plans, and programs, all with the announced goal of helping the debtor countries get back on their feet. The results of these programs were, however, the reverse of their advertised targets: Third World debt increased from $130 billion in 1973 to $612 billion in 1982 to $3.2 trillion in 2006, as James S. Henry explains in "The Mirage of Debt Relief."

Another result of the crisis of the 1970s was to discredit the reigning economic orthodoxy—Keynesian government-led or -guided economic development—in favor of a corporate-inspired movement restoring a measure of laissez-faire (a program usually called *neoliberalism* outside North America). Its standard-bearers were Ronald Reagan in the United States and Margaret Thatcher in Britain, and international enforcement of the neoliberal model was put into the hands of the International Monetary Fund (IMF) and World Bank. Dozens of countries currently operate under IMF "structural adjustment" programs (SAPs), and despite—or because of—such tutelage few ever complete the IMF/World Bank treatment to regain financial health and independence.

The Web of Control

Payments on Third World debt require more than $375 billion a year, twenty times the amount of foreign aid that Third World countries receive. This system has been called a "Marshall Plan in reverse," with the countries of the Global South subsidizing the wealthy North, even as half the world's population lives on less than $2 a day.[5]

How does such a failed system maintain itself?

Simply put, Third World countries are caught in a web of control—financial, political, and military—that is extremely hard for them to escape, a system that has become ever more extensive, complex, and pervasive since John Perkins devised his first forecasts for MAIN. The chart on page 20 shows the flows of money and power that form this web of control. Capital flows to underdeveloped countries via loans and other financing, but—as John Perkins points out—at a price: a stranglehold of debt that gives First World governments, institutions, and corporations control of Third World economies. The rest of this chapter outlines the program of free-trade, debt-led economic development as preached by the International Monetary Fund and the World Bank, shows how corruption and exploitation are in fact at the heart of these power relationships, and explores the range of enforcement options used when the dominated decide that they have had enough.

The Web of Control
EXTORTING TRIBUTE FROM THE GLOBAL SOUTH

Foreign aid, investment, and development loans to Third World countries are dwarfed by the flow of money for loan service, earmarked goods and services, stolen funds, and flight capital. At least $5 trillion has flowed out of poorer countries to the First World since the mid-1970s, much of it to offshore accounts. Meanwhile, IMF and World Bank structural adjustment programs throttle economic and social development in many countries.

GLOBAL NORTH
G8 NATIONS · MULTINATIONALS · WORLD BANK · IMF

FUNDS FLOWING TO UNDERDEVELOPED COUNTRIES

- Loans for inflated projects
- Structural adjustment loans
- Development loans
- Arms "aid"
- Export credit agency financing
- Offshore production

FLOW OF MONEY BACK TO THE FIRST WORLD

- Contracts, loan payments
- Rigged bids
- Flight capital
- Kickbacks deposited in offshore accounts
- Manipulated commodities markets
- Embezzled funds to offshore accounts
- Arms contracts
- Earmarked services and suppliers
- Tax evasion/money laundering
- Transfer mispricing

CONDITIONS FOR AID, LOANS, AND INVESTMENT

- Resource development concessions
- One-sided production sharing agreements
- "Partnerships" with local elites
- Privatization of public services
- Nonreciprocal elimination of tariffs
- Unnecessary buildup of defense, security forces
- Public investment to enable private corporate projects

ENFORCEMENT

- Rigged elections
- Bribes
- Penetration of military, security forces
- Manipulation of local currency, interest rates
- Manipulation of local ethnic conflicts
- Assassination of uncooperative leaders
- Use of local militias, security forces
- Military intervention

GLOBAL SOUTH
THE UNDERDEVELOPED WORLD

The Market: Subsidies for the Rich, Free Trade for the Poor

If the global empire had a slogan, it would surely be Free Trade. As their price for assistance, the IMF and World Bank insist in their structural adjustment programs that indebted developing countries abandon state-led development policies, including tariffs, export subsidies, currency controls, and import-substitution programs. Their approved model of development instead focuses on export-led economic growth, using loans to develop new export industries—for example, to attract light industry to export-processing zones (firms like Nike have been major beneficiaries of these policies). Membership in the World Trade Organization also requires adherence to the IMF's free trade orthodoxy.

Ironically, as Cambridge economist Ha-Joon Chang points out, the First World countries transformed their own economies from a base of traditional agriculture to urban industry by using an arsenal of protectionist tariffs, subsidies, and controls. Britain became a paragon of free trade only in the 1850s; before then it had pursued highly directive industrial policies (in addition to its forcible extraction of tribute from India and the West Indies).

The U.S. economy developed behind some of the highest tariff walls in the world, President Grant reportedly remarking in the 1870s that "within 200 years, when America has gotten out of protection all that it can offer, it too will adopt free trade." U.S. tariff rates were not significantly reduced until after World War II. In the postwar era, the most successful developing countries have been the East Asian "tiger" economies of Japan, China, Korea, and Taiwan, which have indeed concentrated on export-led development, but have historically prohibited import of any goods that would compete with industries whose products they wanted to nourish. For example, one of today's World Bank teams viewing a Toyota on sale back in 1958 would have advised the company not to bother, since its cars were clearly not competitive on the world market, and West European automakers produced better vehicles at a lower price. Their policy prescription would undoubtedly have been that Japan stick to its relative advantage in the production of toys and clothing. Toyota did not take such advice, and today is the world's most successful automaker. In sum, the First World has "kicked away the ladder," prohibiting Third World countries from using the only economic development strategy proven to work.[6]

The phrase *free trade* suggests images of Adam Smith's marketplace, where equals meet to haggle over the goods on sale and finally arrive at a bargain that meets the needs of both, thus enhancing the general welfare. But these are only images, not reality, and they are images that convey exactly the wrong impression. It is not First and Third World equals who are meeting in the marketplace, and the result of their interaction is not a bargain that benefits both. Ghana, for example, was forced by the IMF to abolish tariffs on food imports in 2002. The result was a flood of imported food from European Union countries that destroyed the livelihoods of local farmers. It seems that the IMF's economic hit men "forgot" to ensure that the EU abolish its own massive agricultural subsidies. As a result, frozen chicken parts imported from the EU cost a third of those locally produced.[7]

Zambia was forced by the IMF to abolish tariffs on imported clothing, which had protected a small local industry of some 140 firms. The country was then flooded with imports of cheap secondhand clothing that drove all but 8 firms out of business.[8] Even if Zambia's clothing producers had been large enough to engage in international trade, they would have faced tariffs preventing them from exporting to EU and other developed countries. And while countries like Zambia are supposed to devote themselves to free trade, First World countries subsidize their exporters through export credit agencies—often, as Bruce Rich explains in "Exporting Destruction," with disastrous results for the environment and economies of the Third World.

There are perverse effects as well—the famous "unintended consequences" that conservatives love to cite. The IMF's structural adjustment program in Peru slashed tariffs on corn in the early 1990s, and corn from the U.S.—whose farmers are subsidized at the rate of $40 billion a year—flooded the country. Many of Peru's farmers were unable to compete, and so turned to growing coca for cocaine production instead.[9]

Meanwhile, the prices that Third World countries receive for many of their traditional exports, from coffee and cocoa to rice, sugar, and cotton, continue to decline. The relative value of their exports has declined even more—for example, in 1975 a new tractor cost the equivalent of 8 metric tons of African coffee, but by 1990 the same tractor cost 40 metric tons.[10] However, it is difficult for these countries to move to production of more complex goods with higher value because they lack capital, access to markets, and workers with sufficient education. In fact, many IMF programs have required sharp cuts in health and education spending, making it harder to improve the quality and capabilities of work forces with low levels of literacy and few technological skills. In some countries, such as Ghana, the percentage of school-age children who are actually attending school is falling because of IMF-imposed budget cuts.[11]

Monopoly: An Unleveled Playing Field

In addition to dominating and manipulating markets, First World elites use extra-market muscle to ensure their control—despite their constant invocation of the magic of free markets. They have insisted on what are called Trade-Related Aspects of Intellectual Property Rights (TRIPS), which they pushed through the Uruguay Round of trade talks in 1994 despite widespread opposition. TRIPS allow patents and other intellectual property monopolies to shut Third World producers out of lucrative markets (thus keeping them trapped in commodity production).

As part of this strategy, the U.S. has insisted on defining genetic material, including seeds, human cells, and microorganisms, as patentable "compositions of matter." First World corporations have used TRIPS clauses to mine the Global South for local plants and other genetic resources that they can then patent, gaining exclusive production and sales rights—a strategy often called biopiracy.[12] In one particularly perverse attempt, RiceTec, a Texas company, applied for, and received, a patent on India's basmati rice, claiming that it had developed "novel" rice lines—genetic lines that had in fact been developed over centuries of plant breeding by Indian and Pakistani farmers.

Debt: Owing Their Souls to the Company Store

Debt keeps Third World countries under control. Dependent on aid, loan reschedulings, and debt rollovers to survive—never mind actually develop—they have been forced to restructure their economies and rewrite their laws to meet conditions laid down in IMF structural adjustment programs and World Bank conditionalities. Unlike the U.S., they do not control the world's reserve currency, and so cannot live beyond their means for long without financial crisis. As Doug Henwood, author of *After the New Economy*, points out:

> The United States would right now be a prime candidate for structural adjustment if this were an ordinary country. We are living way beyond our means, we have massive and constantly growing foreign debts, a gigantic currency account deficit, and a government that shows no interest in doing anything about it. . . . If this were an ordinary country, the United States would have the IMF at our doorstep telling us to create a recession, get the foreign accounts back into balance, consume less, invest more, and save more. But since the United States is the United States, we don't have such a thing happening. If it is not good medicine for us, then why is it such good medicine for everyone else?[13]

Corruption, Debt, and Secrecy

Corruption, always the handmaid of Power, serves as a mechanism of both profit and control—and diverts attention from the real springs of power. Corrupt Third World leaders like Zaire's Mobutu Sese Seko, who stole at least half of Zaire's aid money,[14] are happy to take on additional debt for unnecessary, poorly planned, or inflated projects—debt that must be repaid by their countries' citizens. And the IMF and World Bank were happy to continue lending to Zaire—even though their own investigators warned them that the money was being stolen. Mobutu's support for Washington's African policies during the cold war may have had something to do with their enthusiasm, but the round-tripping of loaned-then-stolen money back to First World banks must have played a role as well. Steve Berkman, in "The World Bank and the $100 Billion Question," gives us an inside investigator's account of how these schemes diverted development money into the pockets of corrupt elites.

More generally, what has been called the "debt/capital flight cycle" has roused the interest of many loan committees: the Sag Harbor Group estimates that "at least half the funds borrowed by the largest debtors flowed right back out the back door, usually in the same year or even the same month the loans arrived."[15] John Christensen describes in "Dirty Money: Inside the Secret World of Offshore Banking" how secret accounts in out-of-control offshore banking havens like Jersey and the Cayman Islands enable Third World elites to hide money they have stolen, embezzled, or derived from kickbacks, bribes, or drug trafficking.

The same offshore institutions enable First World corporations and elites to hide their profits from taxation, leaving rank-and-file citizens to pay the bills. The Bank of Credit and Commerce International, incorporated under Luxembourg's bank secrecy laws, pushed these offshore banking opportunities to new extremes, with as much as $13 billion being lost or stolen in the biggest bank fraud in the world. In "BCCI's Double Game: Banking on America, Banking on Jihad," Lucy Komisar explains why governments and regulatory authorities looked the other way: BCCI accommodated the banking needs of a range of powerful inside players—from the CIA and influential Democrats and Republicans in Congress to the Medellín drug cartel—and, as it turns out, Osama bin Laden's al-Qaeda.

The privatization programs pushed by the IMF offer such rich opportunities for graft that they have been called "briberization." According to Joseph Stiglitz, former chief economist at the World Bank, "national leaders told to sell their countries' water and electricity companies . . . were keen to get commissions paid into Swiss bank accounts. . . . You could see their eyes widen" when they realized the scale of the opportunity in front of them, and "objections to selling off state industries were silenced."[16]

The Enforcers: Carrots and Sticks

But what of the leaders who want to pursue a populist agenda, those whose goals include national control of and profit from their country's resources? Suppose they don't respond to the snares of corruption or the lure of an up-scale First World lifestyle? The EHM game plan includes a full menu of options to ensure compliance, whether willing or not.

Divide and rule is, of course, the time-honored strategy of both conquerors and threatened local elites. Subversion of the political process is one way to rein in a wayward country's leadership. The U.S. and other powers make it a point to establish relationships with key players in the administration, the military, business, the media, academia, and the trade unions. After some quiet meetings and provision of funds to various groups, an uncooperative country might well find political tensions growing. The government encounters resistance from former supporters, and the political opposition becomes more strident. The media raises a state of alarm. Tension grows, and economists increase their assessment of business risk: money starts leaving the country for Miami or London or Switzerland, investments are delayed, and layoffs increase unemployment. If the government gets the message and alters course, the sun comes out: money starts to return, and cooperation suddenly becomes possible. If the government tries to ride out the storm, other, more muscular strategies are brought to bear—from assassination of individual leaders to military coups to fomenting civil war.

Venezuela provides a recent case study. The U.S. government's National Endowment for Democracy in 2002 provided almost $1 million to several business, media, and labor groups, helping finance their noisy campaign against populist President Hugo Chávez in the months leading up to the (unsuccessful) April 2002 coup against him. For example, the NED gave $55,000 to the "Assembly of Education," run by one Leonardo Carvajal—who, coincidentally, was scheduled to be named Venezuela's minister of education had the coup's leaders succeeded in putting Pedro Carmona, a pro-U.S. business-man, in power.[17]

Private or semi-official military forces are often useful as well. Andrew Rowell and James Marriott explore the growing interest in Nigeria's oil on the part of both the West and China. In "Mercenaries on the Front Lines in the

New Scramble for Africa," they uncover another jackal operation: the role of Shell Oil's security agents in making sure that Niger Delta oil profits are safe from the region's people.

Exploiting ethnic or religious divisions within a country has often been a successful strategy. The U.S. was only too glad in 1979 to help support the Islamic fundamentalist mujahadeen in their struggle against Afghanistan's socialist government, which from the *muj* perspective had clearly crossed the line by instituting a program to educate women; Osama bin Laden was a Saudi Islamist recruited by Pakistan's intelligence services to help lead the CIA's campaign.[18] Kathleen Kern, in "The Human Cost of Cheap Cell Phones," describes how ethnic division in eastern Congo and Rwanda has been exploited by Western multinationals to ensure their access to coltan ore and other resources, at the cost of 4 million lives. In Nicaragua, the U.S. used religious and ethnic tensions to turn the Miskitu people on the country's Atlantic coast against the Sandinista government.[19]

And terrorism, though always publicly denounced, is often useful. In December 1981, a Nicaraguan Aeronica jetliner was blown up on the tarmac at Mexico City's airport.[20] The passengers had not yet boarded, so they were luckier than those on Cubana flight 455, which went down over the Caribbean in October 1976 after an explosion, killing all seventy-three passengers and crew. Cuban exile Luis Posada Carriles, who was convicted in Venezuela of having plotted the bombings, later admitted that he had received $200,000 from the U.S. government–funded Cuban American National Foundation for such attacks.[21]

Eliminating uncooperative or ambitious Third World leaders in one way or another is the point, which also serves as an object lesson to any president or prime minister who may be considering resistance. John Perkins provides the backstory leading to the removal of Presidents Omar Torrijos of Panama and Jaime Roldós of Ecuador in 1981.[22] But a long list of popular leaders have met similar fates: Patrice Lumumba of the Congo in 1960; Eduardo Mondlane of Mozambique in 1969; Amilcar Cabral of Guinea-Bissau in 1973; Oscar Romero, archbishop of San Salvador, in 1980; Benigno Aquino of the Philippines in 1983; Mehdi Ben Barka of Algeria in 1965. The career of Craig Williamson, an agent of the South African security services, is typical of the jackals involved in such targeted killings. He was responsible for the death of Ruth First, an African National Congress party activist and writer, killed by a parcel bomb in 1982, and he has been implicated in attacks on a number of other anti-apartheid activists.[23]

The coup d'état is the classical method of eliminating opposition leaders, sweeping their parties out of power, rounding up activists, and clamping down on an entire society to reverse the results of an inconvenient reform program. Perhaps the best known is the overthrow of Chile's Popular Unity government in September 1973 by General Augusto Pinochet, resulting in the deaths of President Salvador Allende and thousands of his supporters. A long list of coups is closely associated with U.S. and Western governments, beginning with the CIA's overthrow of Mohammad Mossadegh in Iran in 1953 and including, notably, the overthrow of Brazil's President João Goulart in 1964, General Idi Amin's overthrow of Milton Obote in Uganda in 1971, and General Suharto's seizure of power in Indonesia in 1965.

Military intervention is an option if the jackals are unsuccessful and no cooperative military officers can be recruited. Intervention sometimes takes the form of civil war by proxy, using a combination of terrorism and guerrilla warfare to overthrow the government or to wear down the population through a war of attrition that can only be ended by electoral defeat or negotiations. The Contra War against Nicaragua's Sandinistas was a classic example, but the U.S. also conducted long campaigns against the governments of Mozambique and Angola with the cooperation of the South African military, wrecking the economies of both countries and killing hundreds of thousands of people.

Direct intervention has been reserved for the most difficult situations, but it is always a possible method of regime change. The lessons of the Vietnam War seemed to make this the least attractive option for exercising First World power, but the collapse of the Soviet bloc and the advance of high-tech weaponry have pushed this method to the fore. In the post–cold war era, U.S. military / strategic theorists have used the advantage offered by the so-called revolution in military affairs, including pervasive surveillance technologies, network-centric command and control of military forces, and precision munitions, to undergird a new assertiveness in U.S. foreign policy. As Belloc remarked about the hegemony of Europeans over their colonies in the heyday of the British Empire: "We have the Gatling gun, and they have not."

In 1992, the neoconservative Paul Wolfowitz, undersecretary of defense in the George H. W. Bush administration, formulated what has since become known as the Bush Doctrine in "Defense Planning Guidance 1994–99." This strategic plan emphasizes three points: the primacy of U.S. power within the New World Order; the right of the U.S. to engage unilaterally in preemptive attacks when necessary to defend its interests; and, in the Middle East, the "overall objective" to remain "the predominant outside power in the region and preserve U.S. and Western access to the region's oil."[24]

The invasion and occupation of Iraq in 2003 followed from these premises. Dick Cheney, now an advocate of the Bush Doctrine, argued against toppling Saddam in the aftermath of the Gulf War in 1991: "I think to have American military forces engaged in a civil war inside Iraq would fit the definition of quagmire, and we have absolutely no desire to get bogged down in that fashion." Times change, however. The lure of Iraq's oil reserves in a world facing future shortages of oil, control of the Middle East as the fulcrum of power in such a world, and prospects of obscenely lucrative contracts and concessions, as Greg Muttitt reports in "The Iraqi Job: Hijacking Iraq's Oil Reserves," seem to have led the U.S. on to a long-term intervention from which it may be difficult to disengage. Andrew J. Bacevich, himself a conservative military theorist, sees the problem: "Holding sway in not one but several regions of pivotal geopolitical importance, disdaining the legitimacy of political economic principles other than its own, declaring the existing order to be sacrosanct, asserting unquestioned military supremacy with a globally deployed force configured not for self-defense but for coercion: these are the actions of a nation engaged in the governance of empire."[25]

Yet, as in 1776, empire is acceptable only as long as its subjects believe they benefit from living under its control and limiting their aspirations to those their rulers deem acceptable. While Third World elites may have ample opportunities to live an opulent First World lifestyle, 2 billion people crowd into urban slums in the cities of the Global South, and mountains of debt continue to shackle economic and social development.[26] In this context, the Bush Doctrine calls for war without end to preserve the empire's web of control. But, as Antonia Juhasz points out in "Global Uprising: The Web of Resistance," the world's peoples seem to be deciding that the struggle to create a democratic alternative to corporate globalization is preferable to living perpetually in the shadow of empire.

Notes

1. Niall Ferguson, "Welcome the New Imperialism," *Guardian*, October 31, 2001.
2. Stephen Kinzer, *All the Shah's Men: An American Coup and the Roots of Middle East Terror* (New York: Wiley, 2003), p. 209.
3. John Perkins, *Confessions of an Economic Hit Man* (San Francisco: Berrett-Koehler, 2004), pp. 14–15.

4. Naomi Klein, "Not Neo-Con, Just Plain Greed," *Globe and Mail* (Toronto), December 20, 2003.

5. *2006 World Data Sheet* (Washington, D.C.: Population Reference Bureau, 2006).

6. Ha-Joon Chang, *Kicking Away the Ladder: How the Economic and Intellectual Histories of Capitalism Have Been Re-Written to Justify Neo-Liberal Capitalism* (Cambridge: Cambridge University Press, 2002).

7. See www.ghanaweb.com/GhanaHomePage/NewsArchive/printnews.php?ID=79568.

8. Lishala C. Situmbeko (Bank of Zambia), and Jack Jones Zulu (Jubilee-Zambia), "Zambia: Condemned to Debt." Accessed at www.africafocus.org/docs04/zam0406.php.

9. Asad Ismi, "Plunder with a Human Face: The World Bank," *Z Magazine*, February 1998, p. 10.

10. Christian Aid, *The Trading Game: How Trade Works* (Oxford: Oxfam, 2003).

11. Asad Ismi, *Impoverishing a Continent: The World Bank and IMF in Africa* (Ottawa: Halifax Initiative Coalition, 2004), p. 13.

12. Vandana Shiva, "North-South Conflicts in Intellectual Property Rights," *Synthesis/Regeneration* 25 (Summer 2001).

13. Doug Henwood, interview with Ellen Augustine, January 21, 2006.

14. John O'Shea, "Paying Aid to Corrupt Regimes No Use to Poor," *Irish Times*, December 9, 2004.

15. James S. Henry, "Where the Money Went," *Fortune,* March/April 2004, p. 45.

16. Quoted in Derek McCuish, "Water, Land and Labour: The Impacts of Forced Privatization in Vulnerable Communities" (Ottawa: Halifax Initiative Coalition, 2004), p. 29.

17. Mike Ceaser, "U.S. Tax Dollars Helped Finance Some Chávez Foes, Review Finds," *Boston Globe*, August 18, 2002.

18. Tariq Ali, *The Clash of Fundamentalisms: Crusades, Jihads and Modernity* (London: Verso, 2002), pp. 209–10. See also Steve Coll, *Ghost Wars: The Secret History of the CIA, Afghanistan, and bin Laden, from the Soviet Invasion to September 10, 2001* (New York: Penguin, 2004).

19. See Roxanne Dunbar-Ortiz, *Blood on the Border: A Memoir of the Contra War* (Boston: South End Press, 2005).

20. Ibid., pp. 119–23.

21. Ann Louise Bardach and Larry Rohter, "Key Cuba Foe Claims Exiles' Backing," *New York Times*, July 12, 1998. See also declassified documents on the National Security Archive website, www.gwu.edu/~nsarchiv/NSAEBB/NSAEBB153/index.htm.

22. Perkins, *Confessions of an Economic Hit Man*, pp. 153–61.

23. See the decision of South Africa's Truth and Reconciliation Commission, available at www.doj.gov.za/trc/decisions/1999/ac990292.htm.

24. Barton Gellman, "Keeping the U.S. First: Pentagon Would Preclude a Rival Superpower," *Washington Post*, March 11, 1992.

25. Andrew J. Bacevich, *American Empire: The Realities and Consequences of U.S. Diplomacy* (Cambridge, Mass.: Harvard University Press, 2002), p. 243.

26. See Mike Davis, *Planet of Slums* (London: Verso, 2006), for an examination of Third World growth without development and the Pentagon's preparations for "low-intensity world war of unlimited duration," previewed by Baghdad's Vietnam Street in the Sadr City district.

2 *An ambitious regional bank and a young banker peddle loans to developing countries to finance dubious projects—leaving ordinary citizens to pay the bills.*

Selling Money—and Dependency: Setting the Debt Trap

S. C. Gwynne

It is an odd business, selling money door to door at the edge of the civilized world. It is odder still when money comes not from out of the anonymous depths of the Eurocurrency market—some dark relay through Nassau, Hong Kong, or Zurich—but from the savings accounts of Americans living in Ohio. Those Americans, like Americans everywhere, are just beginning to realize that their money is no longer being used to build the house next door.

I used to sell their money for a living. I used to travel the world for a medium-sized Midwestern bank with $5 billion in assets. Along the way, I was engaged in some of the startling "business as usual" banking practices that have begun to plague the world financial system.

• • •

It is 1978. Thanks to the venal, repressive regime of President Ferdinand Marcos of the Philippines, I am safely and happily roosting in one of Manila's best hotels, the Peninsula. I am about to set in motion a peculiar and idiosyncratic process that will result in a $10 million loan to a Philippine construction company, a bedfellow of the Marcos clan—a loan that will soon go sour. I am unaware that any of this is going to happen as I enter the lobby of the Peninsula on my way to dinner, still trying to digest the live octopus that a Taiwanese bank served me last night and attempting to remember exactly what it was they wanted and why they had gone to so much trouble.

International banking is an interesting business anyway, but what makes it rather more interesting in this case —both to me and to the hapless Ohioans whose money I am selling—is that I am twenty-five years old, with one and a half years of banking experience. I joined the bank as a "credit analyst" on the strength of an MA in English. Because I happened to be fluent in French, I was promoted eleven months later to loan officer and assigned to the French-speaking Arab countries of North Africa, where I made my first international calls. This is my third extended trip, and my territory has quickly expanded. I have visited twenty-eight countries in six months.

I am far from alone in my youth and inexperience. The world of international banking is now full of aggressive, bright, but hopelessly inexperienced lenders in their mid-twenties. They travel the world like itinerant brushmen, filling loan quotas, peddling financial wares, and living high on the hog. Their bosses are often bright but hopelessly inexperienced twenty-nine-year-old vice presidents with wardrobes from Brooks Brothers, MBAs from Wharton or Stanford, and so little credit training they would have trouble with a simple retail installment loan. *Their* bosses, sitting on the senior loan committee, are pragmatic, nuts-and-bolts bankers whose grasp of local banking is often profound, the product of twenty or thirty years of experience. But the senior bankers are fish out of water when it comes to international lending. Many of them never wanted to lend overseas in the first place but were forced into it by the internationalization of American commerce; as their local clientele expanded into foreign trade, they had no choice but to follow them or lose the business to the money-center banks. So they uneasily supervise their underlings, who are the hustlers of the world financial system, the tireless pitchmen who drum up the sort of loans to Poland, Mexico, and Brazil that have threatened the stability of the system they want to promote.

The system is under severe strain. In 1975, American banks had $110 billion in loans outstanding overseas. By the end of 1982, the figure had risen to $451 billion. The top nine U.S. banks have roughly $31 billion, or *over 112 percent of their combined capital,* in loans to Mexico, Brazil, and Argentina alone, all countries that have had to "reschedule" debt in order to avoid catastrophic defaults.

Manila is heating up as I walk through the lobby of the Peninsula. From the balcony, a Filipino band plays to the crowd of traders, tourists, bankers, local businessmen, and old Asia hands, who sit at small tables waiting for girls or contacts or nothing at all.

Though I don't know yet what is going to happen, I know that something's up. I had arrived in the morning on a China Air flight from Taipei. At the edge of the jet ramp, to my surprise, I was met by an "expediter," an odd creature of the Third World who specializes in facilitating arrivals and departures of important people. The expediter, who introduced himself as "Joy," was an envoy of a client of mine, the Construction and Development Corporation of the Philippines (CDCP), a local Philippine construction company we had been courting for years without success. "Joy" had apparently paid off the security agents at the customs and immigration line. We went through in two minutes what took the other 300 people, sweating and cursing in the tropical heat, an hour and a half. He then took me through the crowd of screaming touts on the arrival deck to a waiting Jaguar, which came equipped with air conditioning, a good stereo system, and a very pretty twenty-year-old girl. The girl was unexpected. Bangkok Bank gives me a silver Lincoln, but no girl. The Saudis give me a stretch Mercedes and a clandestine liter of Johnny Walker Black, but no girl. In the intricate world of Asian business, where the quid pro quo is the essence of every deal, such things are done for a good reason. Yes, I thought, something *is* up. . . .

Now, hours later, I am met again by Joy under the porte cochere of the Peninsula Hotel. He wears an immaculate white uniform. He takes my briefcase, containing $5,000 in traveler's checks, a $9,000 negotiable airline ticket, my passport and credit cards—in short, all that's standing between me and a jail in Intramuros—and disappears. We are playing the "good faith" game. A minute later, the red Jaguar slides up to the entry, my briefcase intact and the girl smiling prettily, and we glide off smoothly in splendid silence into the honking, gridlocked traffic that is Manila on a Saturday night. On the way, the girl tells me that she and the Jaguar are "at my service" for the remainder of my stay.

I am taken to an expensive restaurant in Makati, where the president of the company, whose name is Rudy, is throwing a gala dinner bash in my honor. My bank has been calling on this company for five years. We have bought them twenty dinners. We have taken them golfing and scuba diving. We send them whiskey and cigars at Christmastime. Until now, all we have gotten in return is polite conversation. After eight courses, and enough liquor to intoxicate the Muslim population of Mindanao, the other shoe drops. Rudy announces, in slurred English, that he would like to borrow money. He says he wants to buy earth-moving equipment from my bank's client in the U.S., for a reclamation project on Manila Bay.

"How much were you thinking about?" I ask, in equally slurred English.

"Ten million," he says, and laughs. "My vice president will give you the details in the morning."

Five minutes later, the finance minister of the Philippines "drops by" to meet me. Nothing is said about the loan. But he is unctuous and polite, and makes a point of calling Rudy "my good friend." Maybe I'd like to go to Baguio, they suggest. A nice gesture, I think, unaware that the plane, owned by the company, is gassed up and waiting to take me to a fabulous hotel, which is also owned by the company, in the northern mountain resort.

• • •

The international banker moves in a narrow ambit overseas. Because he is dressed in a suit that costs more than the average native makes in a year, he does not take excessive interest in local people. He does not take a walk down a blind alley or sample local bars on a Tuesday night. He rarely walks anywhere, thus keeping a safe distance from the prospect of physical danger. But danger still lurks, in different, more subtle forms: such as forgetting to hide your "Israeli" passport as you pass through customs in Algiers; or forgetting to leave your bottle of scotch behind when you enter Saudi Arabia. The penalty for these offenses is "detention," usually in an immigration jail, for an indefinite period of time. Then there is the possibility that your driver in one of the strict Muslim countries will have an accident, or run someone down. According to the current exegesis of the Koran, the driver and car would not have had the accident if you had not hired them, and thus you are fully and personally liable for all damages. This accounts for the rather humorous and not infrequent sight of American bankers fleeing from the scene of minor accidents, briefcase in hand, into the relative anonymity of the bazaars and tenements. In Manila you are fairly safe, although if you enjoy too much of your host's hospitality it is likely that you will contract a social disease.

As a loan officer you are principally in the business of making loans. It is not your job to worry about large and unwieldy abstractions, such as whether what you're doing is threatening the stability of the world economy. In that sense, a young banker is like a soldier on the front lines: he is obedient, aggressive, and amoral; his efficiency depends precisely on that very narrow view of the world around him. American banks, through the agency of loan officers like me, have made a considerable number of questionable loans in countries whose balance of payments is so far in arrears that, according to Citicorp's Walter Wriston, "ability to repay" is no longer the main consideration. All that matters now is "access to the marketplace," meaning the ability to borrow even more. This is a convenient rationale, in view of the big banks' exposure in countries that have recently been unable to service their debt. The theory goes something like this: as long as a country can continue to borrow money, it will, in effect, be able to "roll over" its debt indefinitely, in much the same manner as the U.S. government rolls the national debt. As long as the country can roll its debt, the banks will be repaid on schedule and the country will not become insolvent. But the banks are cornered. Unless they pump in more money, they stand to be forced into massive write-offs of bad loans and even more serious chain-reaction consequences, owing to the "cross-default" clauses in many of the loans.

There is another curious aspect to this: even though the banks may allow a country such as Poland to "reschedule" its debt—allowing it twenty years instead of ten to repay, for example—the *interest* payments keep coming. And it is interest that shores up the bottom line of a bank's profit-and-loss statement. This means that Citibank can have a very good year even though many of its loans may be in serious trouble. The banks may have been imprudent in making the loans in the first place, but they are both clever and scrupulous when it comes to protecting the value of their assets.

At the root of this worldwide lending problem is a very simple concept called "security." When you borrow money to buy a car, the bank takes title to the car as security. If you default under the terms of your loan, the bank can sell the car and recoup the rest of its money. But international banks cannot "collect" a power plant in Thailand, or a hospital in Dubai, or even a Caterpillar tractor in the jungles of Kalimantan. They cannot "tag" a banana crop in the Philippines or grab the copper as it comes out of the mine in Chile and sell it in Chicago. In international lending, American banks frequently violate the oldest precepts of lending against security. As a domestic credit analyst, I was taught to develop reasonable asset security for all loans, unless the borrower was of impeccable means and integrity. As an international loan officer, I was taught to forget about all that, and instead to develop a set of rationales that would make the home office feel good about the loan, even though, technically, it was unsecured.

• • •

In Manila, I move dreamily through my appointments, fairly salivating at the prospect of a single $10 million loan. I strike myself as a rather glamorous individual at this point, moving huge sums of money with a stroke of the pen, greasing the vast machinery of international trade. Of course, I cannot personally approve this loan. The bank may be ignorant in certain ways, but it is not stupid. This loan will have to be presented back at the home office to the gray-haired, pink-faced bankers on the senior loan committee. They will peer at me over the rims of their bifocals and ask questions like, "Why is their current ratio declining, in view of increased sales?"

The remainder of my trip includes stops in Hong Kong, Kuala Lumpur, Tokyo, and Seoul. I am able to develop a few prospects—and a severe case of dysentery. But mainly I'm dreaming of that loan, writing pages and pages of pros and cons, imagining what it will be like inside the loan committee. In spite of my enthusiasm, and my growing sense of self-importance, there is a certain con that keeps coming up and is finally given life by a fellow banker from Chase Manhattan, whom I sit next to on the flight into Kuala Lumpur.

"Who do you do business with in Manila?" he asks, after ordering our fifth round of scotch, which is what keeps international bankers happy on their long trips. CDCP, I tell him.

"They're in bed with Marcos," he says. "That's OK. But they're leveraged up to their ears."

When a banker says that a company is "leveraged," he means that the company's debt greatly exceeds the owners' equity in the company. In the United States, bankers are taught early on that leverage is a no-no, that it puts the lender in the high-risk position of having to fight for the company's few capital assets in the event of bankruptcy. I sneak a glance at the leverage ratio of CDCP. It is seven to one. One to one is considered healthy, two to one dangerous. It suddenly occurs to me that it might be pure insanity to make this loan.

"You better have Marcos' signature, *in blood*, on that one," the Chase banker says, laughing.

• • •

Back at the home office, high above the murky winter air of Cleveland, still bleary from four weeks of accumulated jet lag, I begin to sort out my trip. I am trying to remember all those three-hour lunches with five courses and two bottles of wine and what on earth I was talking about.

It is something of a cliché to say that bankers are trained pessimists. While this may be true of the retail banker, what characterizes the international banker nowadays is optimism. For example, when the senior vice president asks you how a certain country is doing in general, you don't say, "Well, Phil, I think it's going down the tubes." Even if it's true, it is not in your interest to say that, because Phil can easily make it impossible for you ever to develop a loan in that country. And your job performance is rated according to how many loans you make. As a credit analyst, I once remarked to the vice president in charge of Mexican loans that in my opinion no amount of petroleum was going to change the fact that 30 million people would be living in Mexico City by the year 2000; and that no amount of social engineering could make all that oil money trickle down to that many people. I was told not to put this in my country report.

"We're concerned about repayment, pure and simple," he said. "Not demographics. They've got so much oil they don't know what to do with it. Play that up."

Ah, optimism. It worked in Mexico, Argentina, Brazil, Poland—all countries that have had to reschedule debt, the current euphemism for "default." If it worked for them, I figure, it can work for me, too, in a volatile, corrupt Asian country with serious balance-of-payments problems and with a company leveraged seven to one.

But before I can develop this specious line of reasoning, my telephone rings. It is the chief financial officer of the earth-moving-equipment company, a subsidiary of a major auto company and an old client of the bank.

"I hear you've been talking to our friends in Manila," he says. He is chatty, as though the difference in our rank means nothing to him.

"They were very hospitable."

"Charming fellows."

"They want us to finance the purchase of your equipment."

"I know," he says. "And we'd like you to give it a good, hard look," he continues, in a voice meant to remind me that his company has a great deal of money lodged with us in the form of demand deposits and pension funds.

I assure him that a good, hard look will be given to his proposal and hang up. Ten minutes later, the president of my bank calls on the same subject. I am told to give it a good, hard look. What he means by that is that he wants to see this thing in loan committee, ASAP, damn the balance-of-payments problems in the Philippines, period.

The instant the wheels begin to turn on this deal, my enthusiasm wanes. I realize that I may well end up the whipping boy. After analyzing the company more closely, I can now see clearly that this is an "undoable" deal. I will take it before the senior loan committee, undergo a thirty-minute grilling, and be thrown out in disgrace. The president of the bank can then tell the client that we gave it a "hard look," in spite of the fact that a young loan officer was made to look like a fool. I therefore undertake to develop one of the handy rationales that I have learned. I attempt, in bankers' parlance, to "cover my ass."

Now we're getting into real international banking, the sort of banking that makes it possible for Citicorp to lend $2 billion to a shaky country like Brazil. We are now in the realm of the "guarantee" and the "standby letter of credit," both nifty ways of shifting the borrower's weakness into some new area of supposed strength and reliability.

Let me explain. When the international loan you are proposing is less than sound, you may secure the guarantee of a third party to shore it up. The third party may be a private commercial bank, a government-owned commercial bank, or a foreign government. A government guarantee is best of all. If the guarantee party looks good on paper, most U.S. loan committees will buy it. Never mind that thousands of bad loans around the world were cheerfully supported by foreign governments, including those in Poland, which don't stand a snowball's chance in hell of being repaid before the millennium. But American banks persist in the decades-old notion that "banks and governments won't default."

Well, that's fine by me, and I set about securing a partial guarantee from the Philippines' largest bank, which has already put its name on more guarantees than it can possibly pay off. It is an easy process. The heads of both the bank and the construction company are wired into the same political terminals. This strategy will not only secure the affection of my president and my client but will also advance my career.

It takes only a month and a few dozen overseas phone calls to get the guarantee from the Philippine bank, which is handing them out these days like free samples. With the help of a cooperative credit analyst, who is three months out of an English degree from Ohio State, we package a stunning little credit report that sweeps through all of the loan committees without even a flesh wound.

I am patted on the head by innumerable vice presidents, given a small raise, taken to the opera by the client, and sent to Hong Kong for the signing of the loan.

Three weeks later, we disburse $5 million, the first in a series of "drawdowns" that will correspond to shipments of earth-moving equipment. Although our transfer bank, Chase Manhattan, manages to lose the $5 million for a few frantic days, the money eventually lands in the right account.

• • •

A year and a half after making this loan—and about a year before this loan went into nonaccrual—I left the bank for a job with one of the big West Coast banks. By the time the borrower suspended its debt payments, all of the loan officers who had worked on it had moved on to other banks. Such rapid job movement is common in banking. The market these days is so hot that, if you have done reasonably well in your job, you can not only double your salary, but you can virtually pick the city in which you would like to live. Thus many of the people who make the big international loans are not around to collect them when they go bad, and, conversely, the people who are collecting the bad loans are not the people who made them in the first place, and therefore feel only vaguely responsible.

My Philippine loan went "bad" very quietly. Interest and principal simply stopped coming one day, without notice. It was impossible to get any sort of recent financial statement from the company, and it was equally impossible to track down the principals, who were ducking a host of other creditors as well. My successor spent several months on the intercontinental telephone lines trying to locate them. When he did, he was assured of immediate payment. The payment never came. There were further negotiations, and the bank deemed it prudent to "reschedule" the loan, in a way that would enable the company to repay over a longer period. As of this date, the bank has received only a fraction of the money owed by the borrower. To my knowledge, the guarantee of the Philippine bank has not been called.

So I move on, someone else is hired to clean it up, and the old boys on the senior loan committee are left to wonder what went wrong. They are doing a lot of wondering these days, with a large Mexican portfolio, 50 percent of which is in technical default, and with millions of dollars in loans to Eastern bloc countries. They are doing nothing "wrong" as they see it, and certainly nothing even remotely as daring as the kind of thing the "go-go" banks in the money centers are up to. It is all just "business as usual," and will continue that way until some catastrophe descends on them, by which time it will be too late to do anything about it.

POSTSCRIPT: By the time Marcos was overthrown in 1986, the foreign debt of the Philippines exceeded $28 billion, including around $675 million in debts incurred by companies run by Marcos' cronies and guaranteed by Philippine government institutions. As Ellen Augustine notes in chapter 9, "The Philippines, the World Bank, and the Race to the Bottom," the Philippine people are still struggling to repay debt accumulated during the Marcos era.

—S.H.

3 *Offshore banking havens enable the extraction of $500 billion a year from the Third World—a flow of dirty money that has become essential to global elites.*

Dirty Money: Inside the Secret World of Offshore Banking

John Christensen

Kuala Lumpur, July 1985: Maybe it was the heat, or perhaps the Guinness and Courvoisier had dulled my senses, but something about what the man next to me was saying didn't quite add up. I was sitting with the chief finance officer of one of Malaysia's largest investment cooperatives, the Koperatif Serbaguna Malaysia; he was a live-wire character and leading light in the Malaysian Chinese Association. I had spent the morning talking with his team and the cooperative's board about the extraordinary growth of its deposit and investment activity. They had gone to great lengths to impress me. After our meeting we took the elevator to the sumptuous penthouse of their downtown office block, where they served me a feast of king prawns and other dishes, washed down with stout and French brandies.

But as lunch progressed and the atmosphere became increasingly relaxed, my neighbor seemed most interested in my childhood roots, thousands of miles away on the island of Jersey, one of Britain's Channel Islands. He was especially fascinated by Jersey's role as an offshore tax haven.

"Is it safe to invest there?" he kept asking. When I told him that I knew very little about how well the island's financial institutions were regulated, he made it clear that this was not at all his concern. Finally it clicked: he wasn't worried about the quality of regulation. Instead, he was up to something that wasn't strictly legit.

Deregulation, Corruption, and Tax Havens

I was in Kuala Lumpur to work on a review of the Malaysian legal and regulatory framework for cooperatives. What I had found was a potentially disastrous mess. A minor loophole intended to help rural savings and loans cooperatives had allowed the boards of directors of a number of deposit-taking cooperatives (DTCs) to offer interest on deposits at a higher rate than those set by Bank Negara, the country's central bank. As a result they were attracting billions in deposits, which they could invest without regulatory control from either Bank Negara or the Association for Banks and Finance Companies. When I visited some of the larger "investment cooperatives" I discovered that they were lending huge sums to their directors, relatives, and associated cronies, often without any collateral.[1] This money had then been directed to secret offshore trusts and companies located in a variety of tax havens, including Hong Kong, London, Singapore, and New York. The funds had been invested in land, property, and stock markets at the peak of the boom, and losses during the subsequent downturn ran to hundreds of millions of dollars. Much of this money was irretrievably lost in a maze of offshore special-purpose investment vehicles, and in 1986 Bank Negara was forced to suspend the trading activities of twenty-four of the largest deposit-taking cooperatives in a move to prevent a total collapse of confidence in the Malaysian banking system.[2]

The lack of investor protection didn't surprise me, since many of the directors of these DTCs were prominent Malaysian businessmen connected to political parties in the governing coalition. What did surprise me, however, was the fact that over a period of years none of the financial intermediaries involved, including banks, law firms, accountants, and auditors, had bothered to report or even question these illicit transfers to offshore tax havens. And I was not alone in noting this extraordinary lack of professional diligence. Many experts on money laundering have noted that the means used to transfer the proceeds of crime, drug trafficking, and terrorist activities are the same financial networks put in place decades ago by Western banks and law firms to facilitate illicit capital flight and tax evasion. When Osama bin Laden taunted in 2001 that al-Qaeda's finances would be secure from U.S. attempts to freeze them, he boasted of exploiting the "cracks inside the Western financial system . . . the very flaws in the Western financial system which are becoming a noose for it."[3]

For a while I struggled to understand more clearly how the money from the DTCs had been spirited away offshore, but I found that this was an impossible task. Offshore trusts are not registered, and there is no way to learn the identities of the people behind them. Faced with this massive wall of secrecy, I was forced to give up. I alerted Malaysian officials to the problems I had uncovered and made recommendations for strengthening the Cooperative Law to overcome them. But my interest had already shifted to the bigger issue of how to stop dirty money from flowing out of developing countries and into the Western banking system.

The Offshore Interface

After completing my assignment in Malaysia, I made a major decision. I would return to Jersey to find out more about how offshore financial systems operate. This was not an easy option, since it meant dropping my career in development economics and starting a new career involving work that I held in considerable suspicion. I also knew that whatever my personal views about the nature of the work, and about tax havens in general, I could not afford to let down my cover even for a moment. In these circumstances, going home to Jersey was a tough choice, and frankly one that I dreaded.

I grew up in Jersey and loved the island's scenery, its coastline, and its fascinating heritage. But, proud as I was to consider myself a Jerseyman, I had felt that I needed to see more of the world and left the island to train in audit and project appraisal in London. I took a break in my mid-twenties to study for a degree in economics and earn a master's degree in economics and law. While studying, I linked up with a network of campaigners associated with Oxfam 2000, a British nongovernmental organization, and started research into how the financial resources of many of the world's poorest countries drain away into secret banking accounts.

This research continued after my graduation, and, while working in India in the early 1980s, I became increasingly aware that the capital market and trade liberalization programs promoted by the International Monetary Fund and the World Bank were making it far easier for wealthy people and corporations to evade taxes. Tax havens were playing a pivotal, but hidden, role in transferring money illicitly into secret bank accounts and offshore trusts—not just benefiting the world's wealthiest and most powerful individuals and companies but also sapping the prospects for economic development in the world's poorest nations. With their wealth disappearing offshore in vast amounts, developing countries take on debt to compensate for falling tax yields. This causes a vicious circle: slower growth rates increase both economic uncertainty and social inequality, further increasing political risks and encouraging more capital flight. Slower growth makes it more difficult for these countries to service their external debts while maintaining public services and infrastructural investment programs. In short, offshore tax havens undermine economic growth and cause poverty.

A few checks through the academic literature of the 1980s confirmed that there were virtually no studies of the role of tax havens or how they were interacting with the emerging globalized financial markets. Offshore finance still scarcely gets a mention in specialist texts on capital markets and world trade, let alone in the mainstream texts studied by economics undergraduates in universities around the world.[4] This is an important omission, especially when you consider that one-half of world trade passes through tax havens, on paper if not in reality, and that trillions of dollars flow daily through the offshore networks.

My work in the early 1980s took me across Southeast Asia and northern Africa, and wherever I traveled there was a widespread perception that wealth, especially wealth from mineral resources like oil, was being expropriated by corrupt political and business elites and exported to offshore bank accounts and trusts in tax havens like Switzerland, Monaco, the Cayman Islands, and Jersey. The corrosive combination of huge inequality and social exclusion in these countries has nurtured deep tensions, most notably in the oil-exporting countries, where fabulous wealth has been accumulated by tiny elites while large numbers are unemployed and live in appalling poverty. Poverty fosters crime, fueling violence and increasing the attraction of terrorism. Viewed from this perspective, the link between dirty money flowing into offshore bank accounts and widespread resentment of the West in so many poor countries becomes easier to understand.

The almost ceaseless looting of Nigeria's assets and that country's slide toward gangsterism and violence vividly illustrate the problem. According to the *Economist*, "When Sani Abacha was dictator of Nigeria at the end of the 1990s, the Central Bank [of Nigeria] had a standing order to transfer $15 million or so to his Swiss bank account every day." Embezzlement on this scale is not possible without a large pinstripe-suited infrastructure of financial specialists and offshore government officials who profit by providing an interface between crime and mainstream financial systems. Some 100 banks around the world were involved in handling Abacha's loot, including major names like Citigroup, HSBC, BNP Paribas, Credit Suisse, Standard Chartered, Deutsche Morgan Grenfell, Commerzbank, and the Bank of India. According to Raymond Baker, an expert on money laundering at the Center for International

Policy, "With [Abacha's] fortune estimated at $3 billion to $5 billion, a feeding frenzy arose to receive, shelter and manage [his] wealth."[5]

About $300 million of Abacha's ill-gotten loot ended up in Jersey-based banks, which would undoubtedly have known the origin of this money and charged top dollar for managing funds for such a politically exposed person (PEP). Needless to say, when international pressure finally forced the repatriation of this looted money to Nigeria after Abacha's downfall, not a cent of the banks' fees was repaid, and not a single white-collar criminal was indicted—let alone punished in any way—for having aided and abetted one of the most flagrant crimes in Africa's recent history. Instead, the Jersey authorities trumpeted loudly how virtuous they had been in repatriating the money.

Put simply, corruption on this scale in the Global South cannot survive without the complicity of wealthy countries' financial institutions. Nigeria has consistently topped Transparency International's world corruption index, but it is hard to disagree with Professor Aliya Fafunwa, a former Nigerian education minister, when he said in 2005 that Switzerland should top the list of most corrupt nations "for harbouring, encouraging and enticing robbers of public treasuries around the world to bring their loot for safe keeping in their dirty vaults."[6]

In most Western countries, banks and other deposit-taking institutions are required to carry out extensive checks to establish the true identity of their depositors and the source of their funds. In practice, compliance officers have privately confirmed to me that "know-your-client" checks are frequently conducted on a check-box basis and that no attention is paid to whether the customer is evading taxes. In recent years these due-diligence checks have been strengthened in the case of PEPs like Sani Abacha. But banks remain reluctant to conduct "enhanced" due-diligence checks, partly because of the expense involved, but also because they prefer to turn a blind eye to the true nature of their clients' activities.

In practice, as I learned from personal experience, many lawyers and bankers sympathize with the tax evaders and earn substantial fee incomes from handling their affairs. What else could explain why the prestigious American company Riggs Bank described one of its PEP clients in its know-your-client documentation as follows: "Client is a private investment company domiciled in the Bahamas used as a vehicle to manage the investment needs of beneficial owner, now a retired professional who achieved much success in his career and accumulated wealth during his lifetime for retirement in an orderly way."[7] The "retired professional" was former Chilean dictator Augusto Pinochet, who from 1979 onward maintained twenty-eight accounts and certificates of deposits with Riggs Bank amounting to between $6 million and $8 million. Pinochet has been accused of involvement in torture and assassinations. Under his command, the Chilean state used death squads to eliminate opposition members and intimidate civil society. He has also been associated with drug trafficking, illicit arms sales, and other forms of corruption. In 2005, Augusto Pinochet and several close family members were placed under investigation for tax evasion and fraud.

Sea, Sand, and Secrecy

Jersey in the mid-1980s was enjoying an extraordinary economic boom. In the previous decade dozens of major banks from around the world had set up offshore subsidiaries to handle the rapid growth of private banking services for their high-net-worth clients. Law firms and major accounting businesses had also set up offshore subsidiaries to provide administration and trust services for their business and private clients. Just a forty-five-minute flight from London, Jersey is well situated to provide offshore services to the City of London, itself a major offshore tax haven. As early as the 1960s, local law firms, keen to follow the examples set by Bermuda and the Cayman Islands, promoted a series of regulatory and statutory changes to Jersey's government that cumulatively created what the business community likes to call "an attractive offshore investment environment." This environment has nothing to do with encouraging research and development or the production of goods and services. Instead, it consists simply of ultra-low or zero taxes and minimal regulation of nonresident business. A great deal of this business is based on illegal tax evasion thinly disguised to look like technically legal tax avoidance.

The growth of demand for offshore services was too great for the island to handle. The banks and finance houses needed staff, but the available workforce was small and experienced people were in short supply. Despite relaxing their hiring requirements, the banks were unable to recruit fast enough to keep pace with growing demand. Within days of returning to Jersey I had several job offers to choose from. Despite my lack of experience in banking or trust management, the salaries offered were far higher than what I had previously earned as a professional economist. I opted for a job with a company called Walbrook Trustees (Jersey) Limited, a subsidiary of what is now Deloitte Touche, a global accounting firm. Walbrook's clients were spread across the globe, and the business was ideal for me to learn about how capital flight and tax evasion work in practice.

From my office window overlooking the Saint Helier waterfront I could watch Jersey's transition to an offshore financial center. Old townhouses and agricultural merchant stores were rapidly giving way to office blocks for international banks and accounting firms, and tourist gift shops were being converted to wine bars and luxury boutiques catering to the high earners of the finance industry. Despite a maximum speed limit of forty miles per hour, the streets outside my window were clogged with cars. Porsches, Jaguars, and BMWs were favorites on an island measuring a mere nine miles by five. In what had previously been a conservative and reserved society, conspicuous consumption had become the order of the day.

By the mid-1980s the island's traditional farming industry was already in steep decline, as was its tourist industry. Both were being throttled by the steep price and wage increases induced by the growth of the offshore financial services industry. The symptoms of economic "crowding out" were evident, and, as the traditional industries were killed off by economic overheating, the island became increasingly dependent on tax haven activity. As this dependency increased, the island's government, which functions largely autonomously from the UK, became more reliant on revenues from a footloose industry that can exert enormous political pressure to ensure special treatment. My initial concerns about this potential "capture of the state" by offshore bankers were borne out a few years later.

Within weeks of starting my job I had a feel for the type of business being done for our clients. Work for the majority of the smaller accounts involved following instructions to make payments or transfer funds from one offshore account to another. The instructions were typically either faxed or mailed from lawyers in London, Luxembourg, New York, or Switzerland. The true identity of the real (beneficial) owner of the funds was kept strictly secret, and ownership of the offshore companies was disguised by nominee directors and shareholders. Very often the companies belonged to offshore trusts, which are wholly secret and not even registered. These procedures, I was told, constituted good practice for almost all offshore transactions, which typically involve at least three vehicles (trusts, companies, and the actual bank accounts) spread across different offshore jurisdictions. Elaborate measures were taken to maintain these walls of secrecy, including programming fax machines to give the appearance that the client companies actually ran functional offices in Jersey and endless precautions to ensure that outsiders would be unable to learn the true identity of the client. This was particularly handy for one client, a syndicate of stockbrokers in London, which used an anonymous offshore company in Jersey as the base for handling its very extensive insider trading racket with almost total impunity. The amounts involved in that company alone ran to hundreds of millions of pounds.

These secret arrangements are put in place solely to deter investigation by legal authorities, but, to further guarantee client security, most of the trust deeds included "flee clauses" that trigger an instruction to their trustees to shift the assets to another jurisdiction and appoint new trustees at the first sign of investigation. Needless to say, these services do not come cheap. But the client's potential earnings and tax savings are far, far larger.

Tax dodging was the principal goal of most of our clients. Publicly, the tax industry makes great play of the distinction between tax evasion, which involves making dishonest and fraudulent claims, and tax avoidance. In practice, however, this distinction is far from clear-cut, being famously described by a former British chancellor of the exchequer as "the thickness of a prison wall."[8] The vast majority of the tax schemes I worked on in Jersey would probably not have survived scrutiny by the tax authorities of the countries in which the beneficiaries lived. Had their tax planning been strictly legitimate, they would have had no need for secret bank accounts and offshore trusts. Of course, anyone asking about this secrecy would be told that depositors from the UK and elsewhere were expected to declare their incomes to their tax authorities, but industry insiders knew that this was unlikely to happen as long as the customers were confident that their finances were kept hidden.

Tax planners justify this extreme secrecy in a number of ways. The most frequent justification is that, in a world of political insecurity and despotism, individuals need protection from rapacious state power. Secrecy, according to half-page advertisements placed in the financial press by members of the Swiss Bankers Association (fighting to restore their tarnished reputations in the wake of the Nazi gold scandal), is "as vital as the air we breathe." One advocate of tax havens from the U.S.-based Heritage Foundation has even linked offshore secrecy to the need to protect the rights of homosexuals in Saudi Arabia![9] My work in international development has made me extremely sensitive to human rights issues, but in thirty years' professional experience I have not encountered a single instance of secret offshore accounts being used by an investigating journalist, dissident intellectual, trade union activist, human rights campaigner, or any person vulnerable to persecution by a totalitarian state of either political extreme. On the contrary, it has been the dictators like Ferdinand Marcos of the Philippines, Suharto of Indonesia, Alfredo Stroessner of Paraguay, Teodoro Obiang of Equatorial Guinea, Augusto Pinochet of Chile, and their families and cronies who have used offshore accounts to hide their stolen loot and evade taxes. The argument that offshore banking secrecy protects human rights simply doesn't stand up to scrutiny.

Oiling the Wheels of Globalized Business:
The Mechanisms of Tax Evasion

Much of the tax evasion by corporations involved trade mispricing. Many of our clients were multinational businesses, which use tax havens to move profits away from higher-tax jurisdictions through what's called *transfer pricing*: the process through which two or more businesses owned by the same people trade with each other. Technically speaking, transfer pricing is legal and necessary because the majority of world trade occurs between subsidiaries of the same company. In practice, however, the international conventions relating to transfer pricing are largely ineffective because there is no market price for goods traded between units of a multinational company. Businesses thus use their tax haven subsidiaries to overprice their imports and underprice their exports, thereby massively reducing their tax bill. Offshore subsidiaries are also used to park intellectual property rights such as patents, which are then licensed at exorbitant levels to onshore operations. While working in Jersey, I encountered subsidiaries of some of the world's largest banks, oil and gas operators, and pharmaceutical firms shifting their profits offshore in this way.

Some of our clients were owners of smaller businesses, many of them based in developing countries, who had set up offshore companies to launder their profits in Jersey through a process known as *re-invoicing*. Re-invoicing involves creating the appearance that goods or services are being sold to a third party, based in a tax haven, which then sells them to the final purchaser. In practice, this arrangement is a scam intended to deceive the tax authorities, and a large proportion of the profit laundered offshore ends up in secret offshore accounts. Some of this money later "round-trips" back to the country of origin disguised as foreign direct investment, which typically receives preferential tax treatment.

In most cases transfer mispricing incurs minimal risk of discovery by the tax authorities. U.S. researchers have uncovered an extraordinary range of mispriced trade transactions, including a kilo (about four rolls) of toilet paper imported from China for $4,121.81; plastic buckets imported from the Czech Republic at an import price of $972.98 apiece; and bicycle tires imported into Russia at a unit price of $364 each.[10] On the export side, examples of prices set at artificially low levels included U.S.-built bulldozers exported to Venezuela for $387.83 per unit and prefabricated buildings sold to Trinidad for $1.20. This research estimated the tax losses to the U.S. government between 1998 and 2001 at $175 billion from transfer mispricing alone.[11]

The consequences are proportionately greater for developing countries, because they lack sufficient resources to pursue lengthy investigations of secret offshore centers. Many African economies, for example, are dominated by multinational businesses operating in strategic sectors such as oil and gas, mining, commodities trading, and pharmaceuticals. Because their tax administrations are unable to investigate transfer pricing schemes, developing countries are unable to raise the money they need to fund their public services. One expert on African tax issues notes that no African country has ever successfully challenged a transfer pricing arrangement, even though such abuses are endemic across the continent.

Some economists actually endorse this type of aggressive tax avoidance. Company directors, they argue, have a duty to minimize costs, including taxes. And by acting in this way they restrain high-tax/high-spend governments, forcing them to comply with the rigors of the market economy. Anyone giving these arguments a moment's serious consideration will recognize how laden they are with political ideology. Taxes are not a business cost in the conventional sense of the term; like dividend payments, they are more correctly termed a distribution from profits, which is how taxes are shown in a profit-and-loss account.

Equally important, the ease with which multinational businesses can structure their trade and investment via paper subsidiaries registered in tax havens like Jersey provides them with a significant tax advantage over their competitors. This creates an uneven playing field, giving multinational businesses an unfair advantage over nationally based businesses, which in almost all cases means favoring large businesses from the Global North over their domestic competitors in developing countries. This bias is exacerbated by the pressures on governments to offer tax incentives to attract investment, a process misleadingly referred to as *tax competition*, which also generally favors multinational corporations over their domestic rivals. None of these issues is considered during international trade negotiations, despite the evidence that tax avoidance and offering tax incentives to encourage foreign investment have played a major role in shaping trade and investment flows in recent decades.

Because of these efforts to rig and distort the market, tax havens actually reduce global productivity and slow economic growth. The fundamentalist advocates of a no-holds-barred approach to free trade have ignored this, and the World Trade Organization has seldom been called on to investigate how fiscal incentives and tax distortions have undermined the concept of free and fair trade. One interesting exception to this rule has occurred: the WTO decided in 2000 to bar foreign sales corporations (FSCs) used by U.S. multinationals to hold profits tax-free offshore; FSCs were a prohibited export subsidy, ruled the WTO. FSCs were withdrawn but were subsequently replaced by a similar extraterritorial income-exclusion tax break, which was again prohibited by the WTO in 2002 after a complaint by the European Union. This issue reveals how much lobbying effort business puts into securing subsidies and tax breaks for itself—while endlessly denouncing welfare programs for the poor.

As my portfolio of clients in Jersey developed, the pattern of abuses became more apparent. Yet, as I developed working relations with my colleagues, I could see that most of them were indifferent to the wider implications of their work. They were simply in it for the money. The junior staff jumped from job to job to secure higher salaries, and the senior partners worked flat out to make their millions as quickly as possible. The atmosphere was marked by almost manic focus on finding new ways of avoiding tax. Anyone who has ever worked in the tax avoidance industry knows how teams of lawyers and accountants are employed to instantly scrutinize new government measures to identify tax loopholes to exploit. Of course, only the very rich can afford to pay $850 per hour to those who devise elaborate tax avoidance schemes, which the majority of small businesses are unable to use. The consequence of this uneven access to tax avoidance is that larger businesses enjoy a harmful competitive advantage—and the tax burden is increasingly being shifted from those who can afford it to middle- and lower-income households.

Not that any of my colleagues cared a damn about the wider consequences of our work. It was remarkable how little interest they paid to the world beyond the coast of our tiny island. Outside work, conversation seldom strayed from local gossip, cars, and house prices. At work, my concerns about the origins of the money flowing into and out of the accounts of offshore trusts and companies, much of it from African states, were simply ignored. One Friday afternoon, before heading out for our thank-god-it's-Friday office binge drinking session, my section supervisor, Sandra Bisson, told me in her characteristically blunt manner that she wasn't interested in discussing these things and didn't "give a shit about Africa anyway." Sandra's attitude was not untypical. Her passions in life focused on convertible sports cars and getting drunk on weekends. She hated her work because it was dull and repetitive, but saw it as the way to get rich quick. Oddly enough, I liked her, and we got along well. I was fascinated by her brutal honesty and the way she felt no empathy, let alone sympathy, for the less-well-off but would unashamedly suck up to wealthy clients. In many respects she epitomized the 1980s, with her devotion to hedonism and utter self-absorption. Like most of my colleagues, Sandra made no connection between what we were doing and criminality and injustice elsewhere. More important, she didn't *want* to make these connections.

Fast and Loose: The Wilder Excesses of Tax Avoidance

"Rules are rules, but rules are meant to be broken." Quoted from a *Guardian* article dated March 2004, these are not the words of a ski-masked antiglobalization activist. Instead, they were taken from an interview with a business tax partner of Moore Stephens, a major accounting business. Commenting on tax proposals in the UK budget, he went on to say that "no matter what legislation is in place, the accountants and lawyers will find a way around it." Confronted with evidence of incitement to criminality, Moore Stephens hastily distanced itself from its partner's comments—but the truth is that the tax avoidance industry has been subverting national tax regimes for decades, and it holds firmly to the view that nothing should stand in the way of making profits.

The multinational accounting and consulting firm KPMG epitomizes this arrogant and subversive attitude. The corporate culture within its tax department was exposed when a U.S. Senate investigating committee revealed internal memos, e-mails, and other correspondence obtained from the accounting business in 2003. In one e-mail, Gregg Ritchie, a senior KPMG tax adviser, alerted Jeff Stein, head of KPMG's tax practice, that, even if regulators took action against the firm's tax strategies for high-net-worth clients, the potential profit from these deals exceeded any possible court penalties. "Our average deal," Ritchie noted, "would result in KPMG fees of $360,000 with a maximum exposure of only $31,000." Another internal document contained a warning that, if the company were to comply with the legal requirements of the IRS relating to the registration of tax shelters, KPMG would "not be able to compete in the tax-advantaged products market." These revelations about the culture of the tax avoidance industry prompted the Senate report to comment that a senior official at KPMG had "knowingly, purposefully, and willfully violated the federal tax shelter law."[12]

Journalists have also played their part in supporting this business culture. They write uncritically about tax avoidance without considering its social and economic impacts, and they echo the Orwellian language of the tax industry practitioners, who talk in terms of "tax-advantaged products," "mitigating tax risks," "proactive asset protection," and "tax efficiency." Working offshore in Jersey showed me that there is no clear-cut distinction between tax evasion and avoidance. The offshore finance industry is also attuned to turning a blind eye to other corrupt and unethical activities such as arms trading, "commissions" paid into offshore accounts for help in securing major contracts, and insider trading operations conducted via offshore companies to disguise the identity of the traders. Complex legal structures and a labyrinth of transactions bouncing between different offshore jurisdictions are used to create misleading trails, and investigators are deterred by nominee directors and uncooperative regulators. As one senior official in the British Serious Fraud Office said: "Tax havens are little more than booking centres. I've seen transactions where all the decisions are taken in London but booked in tax havens. In my experience, all you get in return is obstruction of legitimate investigation."[13]

A culture of "don't tell me, so I won't know" infests the banking and financial services industry. Board directors of many companies claim not to know what tax planning is done on their behalf and profess innocence when their elaborate offshore structures are exposed as fraudulent. In the case of Enron, for example, which used several hundred special-purpose vehicles based in the Cayman Islands to conceal its loss-making assets, CEO Ken Lay and former CEO Jeff Skilling both claimed that they knew nothing about the financial structures put in place by Chief Financial Officer Andrew Fastow. They explain their positions by stating that these structures were approved by lawyers, bankers, and accountants.

Claims such as these are typically pure humbug. The tax director of one very major multinational company confirmed to me in February 2006 how much pressure boards place on their tax departments to stretch tax avoidance to the limits. And in the late 1990s I attended several conferences in London at which lawyers and accountants eagerly promoted Enron as the model company for the 21st century, above all for its innovative financial management, by which they expressly meant elaborate and aggressive tax avoidance in many countries. Enron's published accounts showed net income of $2.3 billion for the period 1996 to 1999, but for tax purposes the firm claimed to have made losses of $3 billion, and it paid no tax over that period. Its financial statements for 2000 reported taxable income of $3.1 billion, but for tax purposes claimed losses of $4.6 billion. This was the model of innovation and entrepreneurship that lawyers and accountants were promoting to boards of directors around the world as the basis for capitalism today.

Enron illustrates the extent to which, even when it remains within the letter of the law, the culture of the financial services industry has become subversive of regulation, taxation, and democratic processes. Senator Joe Lieberman summed up these degraded values when he commented to the U.S. Senate Committee on Homeland Security and Governmental Affairs in November 2003 that "ranks of lawyers and financial accountants have abused the law and their professional ethics simply for the sake of huge sums of money to be made helping their clients evade taxes."[14]

But why pick on the financial and business communities when the rot starts higher up the pecking order? What are we to make of the values of political leaders of democratic states who enforce taxes on their citizens but set up elaborate offshore structures to avoid paying taxes themselves? Take former Canadian Minister of Finance and Prime Minister Paul Martin, whose shipping line was registered in a variety of Caribbean and European tax havens to avoid taxes.[15] Or Silvio Berlusconi, former prime minister of Italy, who is alleged to control his television network Telecinco TV through offshore companies in Monaco and Liechtenstein? How about Thaksin Shinawatra, ex-prime minister of Thailand, who in January 2006 sold control of his telecommunications group, Shin Corporation, for $1.9 billion tax-free and brought hundreds of thousands of Thai citizens out onto the streets in protest at his government's corruption? In a short article entitled "The Department of You Can't Make It Up," British satirical magazine *Private Eye* reported that the Shin Corporation sale was routed via a British Virgin Islands company, suitably called Ample Rich Investments, to avoid paying tax.[16] Or what about Britain's Labour Party, which has held power since 1997 and receives one donation after another from prominent supporters with offshore accounts? This culture of corruption has become the norm.

Her Majesty's Loyal Tax Avoiders

It might seem to casual observers that the offshore world in which I and my colleagues were working is remote from the economy of the "real" world, but in fact offshore banking lies at the core of a globalized financial system that enables businesses and the superrich, known within banking circles as high-net-worth individuals (HNWIs, or "hen-wees"), to operate beyond the reach of onshore public or legal authority. The offshore economy began to emerge as a significant feature in the 1960s when huge volumes of petrodollars started to accumulate in Europe. The globalization of the financial system was catalyzed by a variety of factors, most notably liberalization of financial transactions through the removal of international exchange controls, the demise of the fixed-rate exchange mechanisms conceived at Bretton Woods in 1944, the extensive deregulation of financial markets during the 1980s, and the emergence of new communication technologies that put money transfers into effect at the click of a mouse.

The huge expansion of the financial services industry in the 1980s and 1990s saw the number of offshore tax havens increase from twenty-five in the early 1970s to seventy-two by the end of 2005.[17] More countries are lining up to create their own offshore finance centers. In February 2006, for example, John Kufuor, president of Ghana, announced his government's intention to proceed with legislation to allow offshore financial services to be provided in Accra in a joint venture with British banking group Barclays.[18] Interestingly, thirty-five of the seventy-two havens are linked to the City of London, either through direct constitutional ties to Britain or through membership in the British Commonwealth. Almost all these tax havens have links to the major industrialized countries, with significant clusters of havens located in the Caribbean, around the European periphery, in the Middle East, and in East Asia. The majority are closely tied to the "big three" global financial centers of London, New York, and Tokyo.

Following the international debt crisis of the 1980s, in which a number of highly indebted poor countries reneged on private loans from banking syndicates, major Western banks shifted their marketing efforts to developing "private" banking services for the world's 8 million or so hen-wees. Private banking involves providing "one-stop" financial services to the rich. With about $30 trillion of client assets under management globally, this is a major source of profits, particularly when conducted in a minimal-tax or tax-free environment. At a banking conference in the City of London in 1995, I was told that the industry target was to shift the majority of hen-wee financial assets to offshore trusts and companies within a decade. In Latin America, for example, wealth is highly concentrated, with about 300,000 people holding about $3.7 trillion of personal assets.[19] Over 50 percent of the total holdings of cash and listed securities of rich individuals in the Latin American region is reckoned to be held offshore. Interestingly, even the World Bank, in its 2006 report on Latin America, notes that tax evasion by the wealthy has retarded growth across the region.[20] This has caused a vicious circle of underinvestment, unemployment, and social exclusion, fueling poverty, crime, and extremism.

Research into trends in global wealth management suggests that the off-shore finance industry has made significant progress toward achieving the goal of shifting its wealthy clients' assets offshore. A study published in 2005 showed that about $11.5 trillion of hen-wee assets were offshore, tax-free or minimally taxed.[21] If the income from these assets were taxed at an average rate of 30 percent, government revenue would increase by $255 billion annually, sufficient to allow major tax cuts for the less-well-off or to finance the entire United Nations Millennium Project, which aims to halve world poverty within a decade. The current global aid budget of $78 billion pales to insignificance alongside this estimate of revenues lost, which does not include the additional losses caused by corporate tax dodging—in all its forms—or the harmful impact on developing countries of tax competition, which British aid agency Oxfam estimated at $50 billion in 2000.[22]

Prostituting the Island

Jersey, and other tax havens like it, provides an offshore interface that connects the regulated with the unregulated and the licit with the illicit. Superficially, the offshore banking world appears to mimic the onshore, but the lack of transparency and accountability means that offshore companies are not audited, so there is no way of knowing who owns those companies, who benefits from the offshore trusts, and what purpose they serve. This secrecy provides the ideal setting for criminality and corruption to become indistinguishable from the mainstream economy. Companies do not use tax havens to add economic value to their activities but rather to engage in economic "free riding" or operate financial scams. Operating in a tax haven involves participating in the economy of fraud, corruption, money laundering, tax evasion, arms trafficking, mafia racketeering, insider trading, and other forms of market distortion that tilt the playing field away from genuine enterprise and wealth creation. Almost inevitably, Jersey, labeled "the septic isle" by satirical magazine *Private Eye*, has gained a reputation for dodgy practices, summed up by the City of London joke about "Jersey or jail," which applies to anyone who sails particularly close to the wind in their tax affairs.

Increasingly bored by the work and troubled by the tax avoidance industry, I quit my job at the trust company and applied for a post as economic adviser to the island's government. I was appointed in the autumn of 1987.

Jersey's government, officially known by its feudal title as "The States of Jersey," does not operate on the Westminster model with a government and an opposition, and there is no party system. Legislators have few resources and lack researchers and aides to help them scrutinize the policies of the executive. Local politics are dominated by property owners and business interests. The offices of Chief Judge and president of the States (the legislature) are combined in the post of the island's Bailiff, an appointment made by the British Crown, which means no clear distinction exists between the legislature and judiciary. Jersey's sole newspaper, the *Jersey Evening Post*, was for many years controlled by the island's most senior politician. There are no universities, research centers, or think tanks. Approximately one quarter of the working-age population is directly employed in the island's offshore finance center, and most of the other residents depend on its revenues circulating through the local economy. In such conditions there is little scope for sustained critical scrutiny of what the policy makers are up to. This absence of the checks and balances required of a democratic state creates an ideal environment for incompetence and corruption, especially on a small island with a deeply embedded culture of conformism and secrecy. The *Wall Street Journal* accurately described this polity when it wrote in 1996: "Jersey . . . is run by a group who, although they form a social and political elite, are mostly small business owners and farmers, who now find themselves overseeing an industry of global scope involving billions of dollars. By and large . . . they are totally out of their depth."[23]

The banking and financial regulatory regime in place when I was appointed in 1987 lacked experienced staff and was politically controlled. A minimal number of regulatory measures were in place, and those were largely window dressing. They were intended to give the semblance of regulation, but Jersey lacked the administrative capability for proper enforcement. Lack of enforcement capacity continues to the present day. In January 2006 the *Jersey Evening Post* reported that the lack of police capacity to investigate financial crimes meant that the island risked breaching its commitments to enforce international financial integrity standards.[24] Back in 1987 the situation was made worse by the fact that a number of senior politicians sat on the boards of the companies they were supposed to regulate. For example, Pierre Horsfall, a hotelier, was a director of a subsidiary of Swiss banking giant UBS and simultaneously president of the States Finance and Economics Committee and chair of the Financial Services Department, the authority responsible for regulating banking practices. His successor, Frank Walker, a newspaper proprietor and now the island's chief minister, combined his regulatory duties with a directorship of Barclays Bank. The excuse given for these conflicting roles was that the arrangement gave regulators the opportunity to understand the workings of offshore banks, but in reality these overlapping positions were indicative of a political culture in which conflicts of interest had become institutionalized.

As civil servants we were expected to see no evil, hear no evil, and speak no evil about the tax haven. This "three monkeys" attitude stemmed from constant fears that financial scandals would damage Jersey's reputation. The strategy of leaving no stone turned was highly risky, and it eventually fell apart when the *Wall Street Journal* exposed the trading relationship between Cantrade Bank, a subsidiary of Swiss banking giant UBS, and Robert Young, a British currency trader accused of violating the U.S. Racketeer Influenced and Corrupt Organizations (RICO) Act. In a long exposé of the overlapping political and financial interests, the *WSJ* concluded that Jersey was an offshore hazard "living off lax regulation and political interference." New York Assistant District Attorney John Moscow was even more critical, commenting that "Jersey sees its job as cooperating with criminal authorities when the law requires it, without necessarily keeping the bad guys out."

On the island, anyone asking awkward questions is told to stop "washing the island's dirty linen in public." If they persist, they are advised to "take the boat in the morning." In a small community without effective whistleblower protection and with few alternative job options, this attitude effectively stifles dissent. As a consequence, the people of Jersey, like the populations of many small communities, take care to avoid publicly expressing their inner thoughts. One person who has spoken out against the island's tax haven, Rosemary Pestana, a grandmother employed as a hospital cleaner, says, "Jersey is geared for the rich, and if we talk about it we are putting our necks on the block. If they can't shut you up they will intimidate you." Sadly the levels of divorce, alcoholism, drug abuse, and domestic violence on the island are astonishingly high.

As has happened in other tax havens, Jersey's tax policies have been actively shaped to create a tax environment that is attractive to hen-wees and nonresident corporations. The story told to the outside world is that Jersey attracts offshore business because of its stable and low-tax regime and acts as an important conduit for capital flows into the City of London. This argument ignores concerns about dirty money flows and tax evasion, and, despite all the evidence indicating that Jersey has been used to hide embezzled loot and to evade taxes, the island's senior officials actually deny that the island is a tax haven. In reality, while the headline tax rate of 20 percent has indeed remained stable for decades (having been set at that level by the occupying German military forces in the early 1940s), the tax regime has been continually amended to create new vehicles to attract nonresident business to the island. In 1984, for example, the States finally enacted a trusts law to codify the practice of establishing offshore trusts in Jersey. Later that decade, a law was introduced to create a special category of tax-exempt businesses that were removed from the local economy. In 1993 legislation was introduced permitting the formation of "international business corporations," which allow companies with nonresident shareholders to negotiate tax rates of between 2 and 0.5 percent, depending on the total amount of profit booked in the island. These new forms of companies were "ring-fenced" from the local economy to prevent resident businesses and individuals from taking advantage of them and were purposefully introduced to attract tax haven activity. In 2005 the States decided to reduce the rate of corporation tax on all businesses to 0 percent in order to compete with other tax havens offering the same rate. In January 2006 new legislation came into force to allow "protected cell companies" to engage in offshore insurance activities and conversion of assets into securities for resale.

There is constant pressure from within the tax avoidance industry for tax havens to create new types of offshore corporate entities. Lacking in comparative advantage and politically weak, small island economies can be politically captured by major banks and accounting firms looking for suitable junk states to serve their needs. This explains the ease with which two accounting businesses, Ernst & Young and Price Waterhouse (now known as PricewaterhouseCoopers) managed to persuade Jersey's senior politicians to fast-track legislation to create a variant limited liability partnership. The purpose of this law was to protect the firms from lawsuits by shareholders aggrieved by their failed and negligent audits. The two firms commissioned a City of London law firm to draft the law, at a cost of over £1 million, and arranged with the Jersey legislature's Finance and Economics Committee President Pierre Horsfall to have it presented to the States assembly as a fait accompli. Unexpectedly, however, a small number of politicians complained about the way in which the law was introduced to the States, and a political scandal blew up over conflicts of interest. Opponents of the law argued that the island was being offered up as a "legislature for hire" and expressed broader concerns about how the States of Jersey had become captive to the interests of transnational businesses. Their fears were confirmed by a senior partner of one of the firms involved, who subsequently claimed in the British accounting press that "we were roundly assured that the draft law would go to the States in March, *be nodded through* [emphasis added] . . . and in the statute book by September."[25]

The limited liability partnership law eventually made it to the island's statute book, but not a single business has ever taken up LLP status in Jersey. All along, the real purpose of this exercise had been to force the UK government to reduce the regulatory powers of its own LLP legislation—a strategy that was effective. The rulers of Jersey, most of whom have personally profited from the island's tax haven status, have had few qualms about putting the island's political sovereignty up for sale in this fashion. This process of capture of the state has been gradual and largely ignored by the majority of the islanders, though a handful of politicians have taken a principled stand against some tax haven proposals, and one courageous group of citizen activists was very publicly quoted in the *Guardian* as saying, "We don't need to prostitute our island."

The political crisis created by the way in which the limited liability partnership law was brought to the States in 1997 attracted the attention of politicians in the UK, including senior cabinet members of the incoming Labour government. Jersey found itself at the center of unwelcome attention, not only from the UK government, which appointed Andrew Edwards, a former Treasury official, to conduct a review of its regulatory practices, but also from the Financial Action Task Force established by the IMF to strengthen regulations to combat money laundering by terrorists and the global drug trade. At the same time the Organisation for Economic Co-operation and Development, a think tank for the major industrialized countries, launched its own initiative in 1998 against harmful tax practices. For a short period, tax havens like Jersey came under unprecedented scrutiny.

The Edwards review, published in 1998, identified 153 measures for improving the regulatory systems in place on British Crown Dependencies. However, it fell short of requiring public disclosure of the beneficial ownership of offshore companies and trusts, requiring that offshore trusts be registered, and requiring disclosure of the individuals who set up and benefit from them. I had accompanied a politician to an oral hearing with Andrew Edwards, and we had proposed that, at the very least, offshore trusts settled in Jersey should be required to register details of their settlors and beneficiaries and to file annual financial statements. We were disappointed when even these minimal suggestions were not adopted. An opportunity for increasing transparency had been missed. Unfortunately, the IMF has appeared to legitimize tax havens by endorsing regulatory activities targeted at terrorist and drug funds while ignoring the wider issue of illicit capital flight and tax evasion. This failure to address the fundamentals of offshore secrecy has meant that even today, as I write, it remains pretty much business as usual for tax havens like Jersey.

We Take the Boat in the Morning

Working for over a decade within the political system of a tax haven provided me with numerous insights into political corruption and the subversive activities of the tax avoidance industry. Throughout this period I had fought to maintain a degree of integrity in the face of regular confrontations with politicians and my department head, the chief adviser to the States. The tensions were sometimes unbearable, particularly since my section was hopelessly understaffed and constantly overworked. I also knew that my role as economic adviser was widely seen as legitimizing the illegitimate and that friends outside the island were frequently critical of my involvement. To make matters worse, in 1997 plans were being discussed to reduce my professional independence by restricting the advisory role of my office to only senior politicians rather than members of the entire States assembly. Already in my forties, and with two sons reaching school age, I was entering the stage at which I either committed to staying in the job despite my reservations or followed my conscience and moved on.

Not that I relished the idea of moving on. I was deeply rooted in island life. Being a relatively big fish in a very small pond has its attractions, and despite the heavy workload I managed to keep to a reasonable work/life balance. I was president of the island's film society and did film reviews for BBC Jersey radio. At weekends I raced sailing catamarans in the surf on the island's west coast. My wife was equally busy with her own career in fine arts, and both our sons had been born on the island. Moving and finding new jobs elsewhere was not going to be easy. The temptation to just stay put was enormous, particularly since we had just completed the restoration of a huge Regency townhouse and would have liked some time to enjoy the fruits of this massive task. With secure, well-paid jobs and a relatively easy lifestyle, we had plenty of reasons for staying in Jersey.

After a long period of heart searching, I resigned from the Jersey Civil Service in January 1998 and agreed to serve out a six-month notice period. The day after news of my resignation was published in the *Jersey Evening Post* I was contacted by a firm of headhunters offering twice my previous earnings to join the management team of an offshore company administration business. I knew the company and liked the management team, but I turned the offer down without hesitation. At the end of June we organized a "boat in the morning" party, said good-bye to our many friends in Jersey, and two days later took the ferry from Saint Helier to Weymouth in England. I stood on deck, watching the cliffs on the island's north coast recede into the mist, and reflected that the island I had loved so much as a boy was changed beyond recognition. Whereas I had previously felt proud to call myself a Jerseyman, I now felt a strong sense of shame that the island had been engulfed by the greed and thoughtless self-indulgence of those who abused it as a tax haven. Overcrowded, overpriced, and overrun by cars and ugly office blocks, the island had all but lost its former sense of community and identity. As Jerry Dorey, a former senator of the States of Jersey, described it to me one evening in Saint Helier's Arts Centre: "Jersey has developed the social structure of the lobby of the Hilton Hotel. It has become a collection of alienated individuals chasing after money." My friends on the island thought me insane to leave. Few, if any, ever understood my real motives for taking the boat in the morning. The truth is that I could no longer bear being associated with the offshore economy and did not want my children to grow up thinking that we had earned our money by helping to create poverty and perpetuate injustice elsewhere.

We soon found a new home in the Chiltern Hills between London and Oxford, and I took up a directorship with a publishing and consulting firm that specialized in political and economic risk assessment in developing countries. But my involvement with the offshore tax haven industry didn't end there. In 1999, Oxfam offered me an advisory role as part of a team investigating the impact of tax havens on developing countries. Oxfam's report, *Releasing the Hidden Billions for Poverty Eradication*, generated huge international interest when it was published in June 2000, above all because it estimated that at least $50 billion was being lost annually to developing countries because of the harmful tax practices of multinational companies. Needless to say the politicians and bankers in Jersey were none too pleased about my involvement in what they saw as an "attack on the island." My critical comments about tax havens in international newspapers like the *Financial Times*, the *Guardian*, and *Le Monde*, or on BBC current affairs programs were regarded as outright treachery. The States of Jersey publicity machine went into overdrive to portray me as bitter and twisted. Two BBC journalists in London have separately told me they were contacted by senior officials from Jersey who warned against interviewing me on the ground that I was "personally motivated," whatever that means. A newspaper reporter told me that she was contacted by Phil Austin, a senior executive of Jersey Finance—the marketing arm of the island's finance industry—who tried to insinuate that I was linked to communist and socialist organizations in the UK. A similar nonsensical smear was also tried by Richard Rahn, an adjunct scholar of the Cato Institute, writing in the *Washington Times*,[26] a newspaper that, interestingly enough, is owned by the Reverend Sun Myung Moon, who has been convicted in the U.S. on tax evasion charges. In 2005 I threatened to report Chris Bright, editor of the *Jersey Evening Post,* to the British Press Complaints Commission unless he published an article withdrawing smears against my character and motivation. He quickly capitulated. All of this has been laughable and easily dismissed as a political dogfight, but it illustrates the extremes to which the tax avoidance industry will go to protect itself from legitimate scrutiny. These are not nice people; huge wealth is involved; there are numerous skeletons in many closets.

In November 2002, a large number of civil action groups, academics, journalists, finance professionals, and others converged in Florence, Italy, to discuss the issues raised by the Oxfam report. Attending with a delegation of British academics and campaigners, I was encouraged by the participants' depth of knowledge about the impacts of tax havens and determination to create a civil society network to push our concerns up the international agenda. Within days we had agreed to launch an initiative to coordinate research and campaign activities, and four months later the Tax Justice Network was formally launched at a ceremony in the British Houses of Parliament. National networks have subsequently been launched across Europe, in the United States, and in Latin America, and preparations are under way to launch a network for Africa in January 2007. Six decades after John Maynard Keynes and Harry Dexter White discussed concerns about capital flight and tax evasion at Bretton Woods in 1944, civil society is finally getting to the heart of the problem of persistent poverty in a world of plenty.

The Elephant in the Living Room

Inspired by the civil rights campaigns in the U.S. in the 1960s, I became committed to the cause of global justice in my teens and have retained these ideals despite the mean-spirited behavior I saw firsthand in the offshore economy. Like many in the global justice movement, I am convinced that increasing aid to poor countries or writing off their debts will be ineffective unless accompanied by measures to combat inequality and the root causes of poverty. This means tackling corruption, embezzlement, capital flight, and tax evasion, which will require far more effective regulation of the financial networks that encourage and facilitate these activities. Supported by preferential treat-ment under the Basel I banking agreement, offshore banks have grown at an astonishing rate, but little attempt has been made to regulate their activities in developing countries or to crack down on the use of offshore accounts and trusts for tax evasion. According to one estimate, some $5 trillion of capital has been shifted out of poorer countries to the West in the past decade, and $1 trillion of dirty money flows annually into offshore accounts, approxi-mately half of which originates from developing countries.[27]

The openness of tax havens to proceeds from crime, corruption, and tax dodging might explain why flows of capital have been from South to North, from the poor nations of the world to the wealthy ones, rather than the other way, as economic theory would predict.[28] This largely explains why so many developing countries lack the capital resources they need to finance their own development and instead increasingly rely on external debt and aid to finance services that tax revenue should pay for. With such a large proportion of Latin American assets now held offshore, untaxed and largely untaxable in the cur-rent climate of banking and trust secrecy, it is clear that poverty reduction is not feasible without a major crackdown on tax evasion. This much was conceded by the World Bank in its 2006 report on poverty reduction in Latin America. The situation in Africa and the Middle East is arguably worse, which largely explains the chronic unemployment, crime, and social tensions that have sapped the strength of oil- and gas-rich countries like Algeria, Egypt, Libya, Nigeria, and Saudi Arabia. This particular elephant in the living room has become too large to ignore: $11.5 trillion of assets held offshore is serious money, and the evidence suggests that this sum is increasing at a rising rate.

Alongside tax evasion, corruption, and embezzlement by local elites, international trade and investment flows have clearly been shaped to use tax havens extensively to dodge taxes. Jersey, for example, has been used for many years to import primary commodities like bananas and coffee into Europe. Of course, neither of these tropical crops could actually grow in the cold, windy English Channel, but on paper this trade passes through Jersey, partly to shift the profits offshore and partly to disguise the extent to which these markets have become dominated by only a handful of monopolistic businesses. The British government has estimated that at least half of all world trade now passes—on paper—through tax havens, so the scale of profit laundering is immense.

The experience of countries like Argentina and Brazil suggests that at least some of the money that disappears offshore will be "round-tripped": shifted illicitly to an offshore company in the Caymans or the Channel Islands and subsequently reinvested in the country of origin under the guise of foreign direct investment. This attracts tax breaks, subsidies, and other preferential treatments that distort the local markets to the disadvantage of businesses that follow the rules. In most cases, however, flight capital leaves its country of origin permanently to be invested in Western treasury bonds, or on the major stock exchanges, or in real estate in Switzerland, London, Florida, and the south of France.

Although suitcases full of banknotes remain an option for money launderers, faxes, computers, the Internet, and complex webs of secretive offshore companies and trusts are far more commonly used to morph dirty money into legitimate assets. Faced with a rising tide of dirty money flows, governments are trying harder to regulate international money transfer systems, rogue banks, and tax havens, but their efforts are doomed to failure unless international cooperation in providing effective information exchange is made automatic and extended globally, and comprehensive measures are taken against the parallel economy of tax havens and offshore finance centers. One expert on money laundering quotes a Swiss banker's claim that the failure rate for detecting dirty money flowing through that country is 99.99 percent.[29] This is appalling, though Switzerland is probably no worse in this respect than other major offshore finance centers.

The Revolt of the Elites

The failure to tackle these major flaws in the globalized financial system has generated a spirit of lawlessness and unethical behavior that acts as a cancer attacking the integrity of the market system and the democratic ideal. Company directors committed to good governance and ethical policies find themselves competing on an unfair basis against corporate delinquents prepared to push tax avoidance to the limits. Around the world the tax burden is increasingly shifting from the rich to middle-income earners and the less well off. By a process of stealth the global economy has been reconfigured to serve first and foremost the interests of the superrich. They have become a breed apart, especially in their tax affairs. The majority hold their wealth in offshore tax havens like Jersey, Switzerland, or the Cayman Islands. They live more or less where they choose, and their main preoccupation is staying rich. Their assets are mobile, and they can typically decide where and whether to pay tax.

Taxes, as property millionaire Leona Helmsley said in the 1980s, are for "the little people." At the time, many people were shocked by her remarks.

By now, things have deteriorated to such an extent that most people expect the rich to avoid paying tax. President George W. Bush confirmed as much in August 2004 when he said that trying to tax the wealthy doesn't work because "real rich people figure out how to dodge taxes."[30]

The outcome is an economic and social order that cannot and does not meet the welfare and security needs of the twenty-first century. Throughout the developing world, tax evasion and the looting of resources to fund secret bank accounts has nurtured entrenched popular resentment, widespread unemployment, low levels of public services, and a general lack of economic and social opportunity. But this situation is not irreparable. Most of these problems can be remedied by strengthening international cooperation. Effective information exchange between national authorities would go a long way toward overcoming the problems of capital flight and tax evasion. The barriers posed by banking secrecy could be overcome by override clauses built into international treaties. The secrecy of offshore trusts would be reduced by requiring registration of key details relating to the identity of the settlor and beneficiaries. There is no reason why those who benefit from the privileges conferred by using companies and trusts should not accept the responsibility of providing basic information about their identity. Global frameworks could be adopted for taxing multinationals on the basis of where they actually create their profits. Policies such as these could be implemented in a relatively short time frame. The positive impact on developed and developing countries would be immense. For those who are serious about making poverty history, this is probably the best way to make it happen.

Notes

1. John Christensen, "Current Trends in Cooperative Movement Causing Concern," *Business Times* (Malaysia), December 14, 1985, p. 11.
2. "Malay Bank Fights to Avert Co-op Crisis," *Financial Times* (UK edition), August 12, 1986.
3. Taken from http://al_qaeda.sitemynet.com/alqaeda/id3.htm, accessed September 23, 2002.
4. Mark Hampton, *The Offshore Interface: Tax Havens in the Global Economy* (London: Macmillan, 1996).
5. Raymond Baker, *Capitalism's Achilles Heel* (Hoboken, N.J.: John Wiley & Sons, 2005), p. 62.
6. Quoted in *This Day* (Lagos, Nigeria), June 6, 2005.
7. *Money Laundering and Foreign Corruption: Enforcement and Effectiveness of the Patriot Act—Case Study Involving Riggs Bank*, report prepared by the Minority Staff of the Permanent

Subcommittee of Investigations, U.S. Senate, July 15, 2004, p. 28.

8. From www.economist.com/research/Economics/alphabetic.cfm? February 12, 2006.

9. Press release from the Coalition for Tax Competition, April 7, 2005.

10. Simon J. Pak, Marie E. de Boyrie, and John S. Zdanowicz, *Estimating the Magnitude of Capital Flight Due to Abnormal Pricing in International Trade: The Russia–USA Case,* presentation at workshop on tax competition and tax avoidance, Essex University, July 1–2, 2004.

11. Austin Mitchell and Prem Sikka, *Taming the Corporations* (Basildon, England: Association for Accountancy & Business Affairs, 2005).

12. *The U.S. Tax Shelter Industry: The Role of Accountants, Lawyers and Financial Professionals— Four KPMG Case Studies,* report prepared by the Minority Staff of the Permanent Subcommittee of Investigations, U.S. Senate, November 18, 2003, p. 15.

13. Austin Mitchell, Prem Sikka, John Christensen, Philip Morris, and Steven Filling, *No Accounting for Tax Havens* (Basildon, UK: Association for Accountancy & Business Affairs, 2002).

14. "Lieberman Says Tax Shelters Must Have Economic Substance to Deter Industry Built around Tax Evasion." From a press release by the U.S. Senate Committee on Homeland Security and Governmental Affairs, November 18, 2003; http://hsgac.senate.gov/index.cfm?FuseAction=PressReleases.Detail&Affiliation=R&PressRelease_id=580&Month=11&Year=2003.

15. Alain Deneault, *Paul Martin & Companies: Sixty Theses on the Alegal Nature of Tax Havens* (Vancouver: Talonbooks, 2006).

16. "The Department of You Can't Make It Up," in "In the City" column, *Private Eye,* February 17, 2006.

17. Tax havens by region, from *Tax Us if You Can* (London: Tax Justice Network, 2005).

18. See www.ghanaweb.com/public_agenda/article.php?ID=4824, accessed February 12, 2006.

19. *Institutional Investor,* February 22, 2006; see www.institutionalinvestor.com/default.asp?page=1&SID=614639&ISS=21302&type=12, accessed February 24, 2006.

20. Guillermo E. Perry, J. Humberto Lopez, and William F. Maloney, *Poverty Reduction and Growth: Virtuous and Vicious Circles* (Washington, D.C.: World Bank, 2006).

21. *The Price of Offshore* (London: Tax Justice Network, March 2005).

22. *Tax Havens: Releasing the Hidden Billions for Poverty Eradication* (Oxford: Oxfam Great Britain, June 2000).

23. "Offshore Hazard: Isle of Jersey Proves Less Than a Haven to Currency Investors," *Wall Street Journal,* September 17, 1996, p. 1.

24. Harry McRandle, "Financial Crime: 500-Case Backlog," *Jersey Evening Post,* February 9, 2006.

25. *Accountancy,* September 1996, p. 29.

26. Richard Rahn, "The Injustice of Tax Justice," *Washington Times,* April 2005.

27. Baker, *Capitalism's Achilles Heel,* pp. 172, 173.

28. K. Guha, "Globalisation: A Share of the Spoils: Why Policymakers Fear 'Lumpy' Growth May Not Benefit All," *Financial Times,* August 28, 2006.

29. Ibid.

30. "Rich Dodge Taxes Says Bush: A Flash of Honesty or Another Slip of the Tongue?" Pacific News Service, News Commentary, Lucy Komisar, September 9, 2004. President Bush made this comment when speaking at Northern Virginia Community College in Annandale on August 9, 2004. The full quote goes: "On the subject of taxes, just

remember when you talk about it, we're just going to run up the taxes on a certain number of people, first of all, real rich people figure out how to dodge taxes, and the small business owners end up paying a lot of the burden of this taxation."

4 *How the U.S. used an offshore bank to run guns, finance Islamic jihadists, and launder money. How its Saudi sheikh owners and American insiders defrauded depositors of over $10 billion. And how they all got away with it.*

BCCI's Double Game: Banking on America, Banking on Jihad

Lucy Komisar

CIA Director Robert Gates called it the "Bank of Crooks and Criminals International." It was a cozy partner of arms merchants and drug traffickers. And of Third World dictators and the CIA. It was part of the entourage of the Bush family and other Washington influentials. Its biggest shareholders were Saudi and United Arab Emirates sheikhs. A grand jury would call money laundering BCCI's "corporate strategy," and the money it stole—somewhere between $9.5 billion and $15 billion—made its twenty-year heist the biggest bank fraud in history. Most of it was never recovered. The George H. W. Bush administration, in power when this massive fraud was discovered, went after the bank halfheartedly and only after indictments by New York District Attorney Robert Morgenthau. But its investigation never touched the offshore system that operates in some seventy financial centers around the world where the owners of bank accounts and companies are kept secret from law enforcers. And it never touched the Persian Gulf moneymen who ran the BCCI criminal enterprise. Here's how the Bush family and its allies used and then protected the world's most criminal bank.

The Bank of Credit and Commerce International was founded in 1972 by a Pakistani banker, Agha Hasan Abedi, with the support of Sheikh Zayed bin Sultan al-Nahyan, ruler of the oil-rich state of Abu Dhabi and head of the United Arab Emirates. A quarter shareholder was Bank of America, which got out fairly early but kept its suspicions of wrongdoing to itself. BCCI spent the 1970s building its power in the developing world and then decided to make the jump to the big leagues.

A Passage of Arms

Norman Bailey, a U.S. National Security Council staffer who monitored world terrorism by tracking movements of U.S. money, began seeing references to BCCI in 1981. The NSC learned that BCCI was involved with "terrorists, technology transfers including the unapproved transfer of U.S. technology to the Soviet bloc, weapons dealing, the manipulation of financial markets,"[1] as well as gunrunning, guerrilla movements, and violations of embargoes and boycotts. BCCI routinely provided illicit arms traffickers with counterfeit documents and letters of credit.

Bailey also became aware of a relationship between BCCI and the CIA. BCCI had in fact become one of the agency's secret bankers, handling money for covert ops all over the world. CIA Director William Casey met with Agha Hasan Abedi several times in Washington at the Madison Hotel, across the street from the *Washington Post*.[2] The CIA used BCCI branches in Islamabad and elsewhere in Pakistan to funnel some of the $2 billion that Washington sent to Osama bin Laden's mujahadeen to help fight the Soviets in Afghanistan. BCCI handled the cash that Pakistani military and government officials skimmed from U.S. aid sent to the mujahadeen. It also moved money for the Saudi intelligence services. BCCI was more than a banker for the mujahadeen. It spread cash around to assure the passage of their weapons through Karachi's port and customs. It even organized mule convoys to transport the arms into Afghanistan.

The mujahadeen financed their movement by taking advantage of the multibillion-dollar Golden Crescent arms-for-drugs trade. The North West Frontier Province on the Pakistani side of the border became the main processing and transit site for opium from Afghanistan. When I was in Peshawar in the mid-1980s, the frontier capital was a dusty town where horse carts vied with four-wheel-drives, and local markets sold Russian Kalashnikovs as well as a rainbow of *burkhas*, which salesmen obligingly modeled for foreign buyers. I'd gone to Peshawar to investigate the U.S. proxy war in Afghanistan, then raging just over the border. I discovered that the Americans and their Saudi partners were sending the lion's share of covert money and arms to Gulbuddin Hekmatyar, head and founder of Hezb-i-Islami, the most fundamentalist of the Islamist military factions. I learned that the Pakistani military, the middlemen in the transfers, was skimming large amounts of weaponry and cash intended for the Afghan rebels.

A decade later, as I began to focus on investigating the secret offshore banking system, I learned that, in a reach for market share that American business analysts might marvel at, BCCI had become the central banker for everyone involved in regional black ops, running accounts for the arms and drug traffickers, the mujahadeen, the Pakistanis, and the CIA.

The CIA money passed from the U.S. to the al-Taqwa Bank in Nassau to Barbados to Karachi to BCCI in Islamabad. Al-Taqwa—the name means "fear of God"—was not a real bank with bricks and mortar, depositors, and services. It was a shell bank set up to finance the jihad and in fact was simply a correspondent account in the Banca del Gottardo, the former Swiss subsidiary of the corrupt Banco Ambrosiano ("the Vatican bank"), which collapsed in 1982 after looting customers' accounts of more than $1 billion. (That story famously inspired a subplot of *The Godfather Part III*.) BCCI also handled money from the drug trade and payoffs to Pakistani military and officials.

The BCCI operation gave Osama bin Laden an education in offshore black finance that he would put to use when he organized the jihad against America. And the CIA was well aware of its student's capabilities. After 9/11, U.S. agents headed straight for al-Taqwa's operations in Switzerland, Liechtenstein, and Nassau and shut them down. Swiss police questioned al-Taqwa's president, Youssef Mustafa Nada, who was a member of the radical Islamist Muslim Brotherhood, and Swiss agents searched his home in Campione d'Italia, an Italian tax haven on Lake Lugano.

One day in 2002 I took the ferry from Lugano, on the Swiss side, to Campione. Nada, a man who appeared to be in his sixties, met me at the dock and drove me up the winding road to his hilltop mansion, where luxurious living rooms decorated with ornate carvings and inlaid furniture reminded me of the Blue Mosque in Istanbul. He had a cultured demeanor that went with the elegant surroundings. He called a servant to bring us soft drinks.

I'd been investigating the Banca del Gottardo for several years and had developed sources with intelligence connections. One of them had sent me the confidential Nassau shareholder list of the al-Taqwa Bank, which listed members of the bin Laden family.

I confronted Youssef Nada with the list, and he acknowledged immediately that it was genuine. He said, "You can ask Mr. Nicati [the Swiss deputy federal prosecutor]. He investigated all these things. Even the FBI knew three years ago." Then he corrected himself: "They know since 1997. I talked to them

. . . . The sisters of bin Laden? Ask Mr. Nicati. It is an old story, and they know. The FBI knows it, Treasury knows it. They wrote and brought the photo of the list."

Then the interview was over. Nada drove me over the bridge that connects Campione to Lugano and dropped me at the train station.

Halfway across the globe, the alliance between BCCI and the CIA was equally productive in the Americas. NSC staffer Oliver North set up Panamanian shell companies and secret BCCI accounts to handle payments of $20 million for arms to the Nicaraguan Contras and to Iran in 1985 and 1986. As part of his illegal operation, BCCI provided more than $11 million in financing for 1,250 U.S. TOW antitank missiles sold to Iran's Revolutionary Guards in a deal to buy the release of American hostages in Lebanon. Checks signed by North were drawn on BCCI's Paris branch, which—not surprisingly—had no records of the account when U.S. law enforcement agents later sought them. BCCI also handled Reagan–Bush administration payoffs to Panama strongman Manuel Noriega, who became a BCCI client at the CIA's suggestion. Syrian drug dealer, terrorist, and arms trafficker Monzer al-Kassar made a deal to sell $42 million worth of arms to Iran as part of North's plan, using BCCI's offshore Cayman Islands branch to run the cash.

BCCI also helped Saddam Hussein, again with the complicity of his Washington friends. The bank funneled millions of dollars to the Atlanta branch of the Italian government–owned Banca Nazionale del Lavoro (BNL), which was Iraq's American banker, so that from 1985 to 1989 it could secretly loan $4 billion to Iraq to help Saddam buy arms. Congressman Henry Gonzalez held a hearing on BNL in 1992 during which he quoted from a confidential CIA document reporting that the agency had long been aware that BCCI headquarters was involved in the American branch's loans to Iraq.

Kickbacks from 15 percent commissions on BNL-sponsored loans were channeled into bank accounts held for Iraqi leaders via BCCI offices in the Caymans as well as in offshore Luxembourg and Switzerland. BNL was a client of Kissinger Associates, and Henry Kissinger was on the bank's international advisory board, along with Brent Scowcroft, who would become George Bush Sr.'s national security adviser. In light of that connection, Bush administration indignation at Iraq's "oil for food" payoffs is rather disingenuous. Bush and his friends knew that Saddam was taking payoffs on their watch: their favorite criminal bank was moving the money. In a pre-9/11 incident of imperial blowback, the weapons bought by Saddam with BNL funds were used during the first Gulf War against American troops and their allies.

Another satisfied weapons buyer was terrorist Abu Nidal, Palestinian founder of Fatah and Black September. A BCCI client since 1981, he had a $60 million London account to pay for arms and logistics. A London BCCI bank manager, Ghassan Qassem, discovered that his best customer was the world's most-wanted terrorist when someone showed him Abu Nidal's photo in the French newsmagazine *L'Express*. The manager took the information to BCCI headquarters and was told, "Destroy it immediately, and go back to your branch, and don't you ever mention it to anyone, because the general manager has got enough problems without having to add any more." Qassem alerted agents of MI5, one of the British intelligence services, who traced payments from the BCCI account of a Syrian intelligence operative to an Abu Nidal agent who in 1986 had used his girlfriend in an unsuccessful attempt to smuggle a bomb aboard an Israeli airliner at Heathrow in London. The British warned the CIA, which apparently was not interested—or perhaps already knew.[3]

The bank's drug trade clients were not only politicals. The United Arab Emirates, home of prominent bank shareholders, was a favorite laundering spot for hot cash. By the mid-1980s, the Drug Enforcement Administration (DEA), the IRS, and, of course, the CIA knew that BCCI was laundering cocaine money and had set up numerous branches in Colombia to handle accounts for the Medellín and other drug cartels. According to a classified 1986 CIA report, "Many of BCCI's illicit banking activities, particularly those related to narco-finance in the Western Hemisphere, are believed to be concentrated in the Cayman Islands facility."[4] DEA agents for C-Chase, the operation that first put BCCI in the U.S. dock, discovered $19 million laundered via transfers through BCCI branches in Panama, Geneva, Paris, London, and Nassau.

Offshore Secrets
Abedi moved BCCI's headquarters to London in 1976, but the bank actually operated through a network of offshore centers, especially Luxembourg and the Cayman Islands, as well as in Lebanon, Dubai, Sharjah, and Abu Dhabi, the last three part of the United Arab Emirates. The secrecy of offshore banking and corporations was the key to BCCI's operations and deceptions. Offshore centers—also known as tax havens—allow clients to open bank accounts and companies with hidden or fake owners. They register "shell companies," listed in the names of "nominees," hire front men, and then "layer" them into webs of holding companies, affiliates, and subsidiaries. Records are divided among myriad jurisdictions. The purpose is to move money in a way that

muddies the paper trails. No single government can follow what a crooked company is doing. No one can unravel the series of fictitious transactions. Offshore is used to hide and move money for drug and arms traffickers, dictators, terrorists, corrupt officials, financial fraudsters, tax evaders and other cheats. Offshore exists because the world's big banks want it to exist—they make a lot of money from those secretive branches. BCCI couldn't have invented a better system.

BCCI incorporated in offshore Luxembourg. Then BCCI Holdings was set up, with BCCI SA in Luxembourg to deal with Europe and the Middle East, and BCCI Overseas in Grand Cayman, also offshore, to handle developing countries. BCCI's Caymans "bank within a bank," the International Credit and Investment Company, was just a post office box that by 1990 "held" over $7.5 billion in assets. Audit duties were divided between Ernst & Whinney and Price Waterhouse, which didn't share information with each other. The Bank of England was charged with oversight for fifteen years, and it said that everything was just fine.

By 1977, BCCI had 146 branches in forty-three countries. Its assets rose from $200 million to $2.2 billion. Bank of America smelled a rat because of the poor documentation of loans, and it bailed out in 1978—but without raising any alarms in the U.S. Warnings might have depressed the stock, which BofA sold at a profit, turning a $2.5 million investment into $34 million. Silence was indeed golden.

By 1983, BCCI had 360 offices in sixty-eight countries: 91 in Europe; 52 in the Americas; 47 in the Far East, South Asia, and Southeast Asia; 90 in the Middle East; and 80 in Africa. By the mid-1980s, it was in seventy-three countries and had assets of $22 billion.

Bribes to central bankers and finance ministry officials bought it central bank deposits, or sometimes the right to handle a country's use of U.S. commodity credits, or special treatment on processing money transiting a country with monetary controls, or the right to own a bank in a country where foreigners were not allowed to do so. In Peru, $3 million that moved through a Swiss bank in Panama won BCCI $250 million in deposits from President Alan García's administration.

In all, BCCI corrupted officials in Argentina, Bangladesh, Botswana, Brazil, Cameroon, China, Colombia, the Congo, Ghana, Guatemala, India, Ivory Coast, Jamaica, Kuwait, Lebanon, Mauritius, Morocco, Nigeria, Pakistan, Panama, Peru, Saudi Arabia, Senegal, Sri Lanka, Sudan, Suriname, Tunisia, the United Arab Emirates, the United States, Zambia, and Zimbabwe.

BCCI knew how to collect profits from criminal enterprises, but it wasn't very good at normal business. In 1983, it set up a division to trade in the stock and commodities markets. To cheat countries on taxes, trades would be executed in London but booked in the tax-free, bank-fraud-friendly off-shore Cayman Islands. (Citibank had done the same with currency trades in the 1970s, but, after the Securities and Exchange Commission exposed its tax scam in 1981, the just-appointed Reagan SEC director of enforcement, corporate lawyer John M. Fedders, gave the bank a pass, explaining, "I do not subscribe to the theory that a company that violates tax and exchange control regulations is a bad corporation. . . ."! Abedi must have read the newspaper reports.) BCCI traders lost more than $800 million in speculative trading in U.S. Treasury bonds from 1979 to 1986, but they shifted the losses to hidden records in the Caymans.

Friends in High Places

A bank heavily involved in criminal activity knows the importance of prominent friends. Abedi turned to the Middle East, where he found a few dozen major investors.

Abu Dhabi Sheikh Zayed and his family paid no more than $500,000, but they were the owners of record of almost one-quarter of the bank's shares. A large part of the investment was risk-free—with guaranteed rates of return and buyback arrangements. Sheikh Kamal Adham, head of Saudi intelligence from 1963 to 1979 and brother-in-law of the late Saudi King Faisal, was the CIA's liaison in the area and became one of BCCI's largest shareholders. George Bush Sr. knew Adham from when Bush ran the CIA in 1975. Another investor was Prince Turki bin Faisal al-Saud, who succeeded Adham as Saudi intelligence chief.

With the cash it collected, BCCI made about $2 billion in insider loans to shareholders and others with close affiliations to the bank. For example, Kamal Adham borrowed $313 million, including the money to buy his shares. Ghaith Pharaon, the son of an adviser to King Fahd, was also a BCCI investor as well as a front man for the bank's illegal purchase of three U.S. banks. He got loans of $300 million.

The loans of the Arab backers were written off the books or paid on paper by moving money among offshore banks. BCCI was, in effect, a huge Ponzi scheme. While the Pakistani bankers and their friends took money out, money was paid in by 1.4 million depositors, many of them South Asian small businesspeople or immigrants.

The Arabs' interest in the bank was more than financial. A classified CIA memo on BCCI in the mid-1980s said that "its principal shareholders are among the power elite of the Middle East, including the rulers of Dubai and the United Arab Emirates, and several influential Saudi Arabians. They are less interested in profitability than in promoting the Muslim cause."[5]) The Abu Dhabi princes also enjoyed the favors provided by BCCI's "special protocol department," which, according to the later investigation by Senator John Kerry, provided big investors with prostitutes, especially teenage virgins.

The bank also had American friends.

The Democrats: Jimmy Carter and Associates

Jimmy Carter met Abedi through his former treasury secretary, Bert Lance, who had been bailed out by the banker after he got into hot water in an investment in a Georgia bank. Traveling on BCCI's Boeing 707, Carter accompanied Abedi on trips to Africa aimed at getting officials to deposit foreign reserves with BCCI. In return, the former president got an $8 million donation for health projects. Carter would later defend BCCI when it was charged with criminal acts.

Lance also introduced Abedi to Jackson Stephens, Carter's roommate at the U.S. Naval Academy. Owner of Stephens, Inc., of Little Rock, Arkansas, the largest privately owned investment bank outside Wall Street, Stephens helped smooth BCCI's way in the U.S.

Andrew Young, Carter's UN ambassador and later mayor of Atlanta, took an annual $50,000 consulting retainer from BCCI as well as a line of credit for a loan balance of $150,000 that was later forgiven by the bank. Young earned his fees by introducing Abedi to business and government officials in more than a dozen developing countries and helping him get deposits from their central banks.

The Republicans: The Bushes and Their Associates

The Bushes' links to the bank passed through Texas businessman James R. Bath to major BCCI shareholder Khalid bin Mahfouz. Bath invested money in the U.S. on behalf of bin Mahfouz, and the two, with a third partner, Ghaith Pharaon, shared ownership of Houston's Main Bank. In 1976, when Bush Sr. was head of the CIA, the agency sold some planes from Air America, a secret "proprietary" it had used during the Vietnam War, to Skyway, a company owned by Bath and bin Mahfouz. Bath then helped finance Bush Jr.'s oil company, Arbusto Energy, Inc., in 1979 and 1980.

Harken Energy Corporation, which had absorbed Arbusto, got into financial trouble in 1987, and Carter's friend Jackson Stephens helped it secure $25 million in financing from the Union Bank of Switzerland (UBS). As part of that deal, a place on the board was given to Harken shareholder Sheikh Abdullah Taha Bakhsh, whose chief banker was bin Mahfouz. When George Bush Sr. was elected president in 1988, Harken benefited by getting some new investors, including Salem bin Laden, who was a half-brother of Osama bin Laden, and Khalid bin Mahfouz. Osama bin Laden himself was busy elsewhere at the time—organizing al-Qaeda.

Buying into the U.S.

BCCI had offshore branches scattered throughout the world, but it needed to expand into the U.S. Its money transfers were in dollars, and as an offshore institution without a U.S. charter it had to use Bank of America as its correspondent bank. A correspondent account is an account a bank has in another bank through which it can move money for itself and clients. But BCCI had problems, because it didn't want to supply BofA with the necessary documentation about money transfers. That would have made it difficult to launder criminal cash, an essential part of its business. It tried to buy the Chelsea National Bank in New York but was turned down by state authorities because BCCI's corporate division into two offshore centers meant that no bank regulator could see what was going on worldwide.

So Abedi decided to finesse the regulators and infiltrate the American banking system. Fortunately for him, other U.S. bank regulators were not as stuffy as the New York authorities. BCCI bought banks secretly with the help of prestigious and politically well-connected friends in the U.S. and wealthy friends in the Persian Gulf. By the end of the 1970s, BCCI had four major banks, including National Bank of Georgia and Financial General Bankshares (later renamed First American), operating in the District of Columbia, Florida, Georgia, Maryland, New York, Tennessee, and Virginia: the better to launder money into the American financial system.

Ghaith Pharaon—the Saudi partner of the Bushes' friends James Bath and Khalid bin Mahfouz—was a front man for purchase of National Bank of Georgia and several others. With a loan from BCCI, he bought Bert Lance's shares in the National Bank of Georgia for twice their market value. Lance's friend Jackson Stephens in Arkansas helped organize the stock purchase. Lance, who was in financial trouble at the time, also got a loan from BCCI for $3.4 million—with no collateral or set interest.

Another important friend to BCCI was Clark Clifford, Lyndon Johnson's defense secretary and adviser to several presidents. When I interviewed him in the 1970s, he made a show of taking me to his office window and pointing out how it overlooked the White House. So close to power! Introduced to the conspirators by Lance, Clifford and his protégé Robert A. Altman helped BCCI secretly—and illegally—buy Financial General Bankshares. Clifford became chairman of the bank after it was renamed First American, while Altman became its chief executive. Clifford was legal counsel to both BCCI and First American.

The covert shareholders included Sheikh Kamal Adham, Prince Turki bin Faisal al-Saud, another Saudi intelligence operator, Abdul-Raouf Khalil, and Sheikh Khalifa bin-Salman al-Khalifa, prime minister of Bahrain, whose brother, Bahrain's ruler, gave Harken Energy its famous offshore drilling contract. Five nominee companies controlled by bin Mahfouz and his brothers bought shares in First American Bankshares. Fronting for the clandestine owners were former Missouri Senator Stuart Symington, retired Air Force General Elwood Quesada, and retired Army General James M. Gavin. Symington, who had run in the Democratic presidential primary in 1960 with Clark Clifford as his campaign manager, became chairman of Credit and Commerce American Holdings, a shell company in the offshore Netherlands Antilles that had been set up to buy the U.S. banks with BCCI money.

BCCI's American front men sought government permission to acquire First American, assuring the Federal Reserve, which has authority over federal banks, that they were investing their personal funds supplemented by money borrowed from banks not related to BCCI. The Fed, headed by the Teflon-coated Paul Volcker, had some evidence that BCCI was behind the deal but didn't act on it. The CIA and the State Department told the Fed that they had no concerns about the Middle Easterners behind the purchase. And BCCI's hired guns, Clifford and former Federal Reserve Counsel Baldwin Tuttle, were so reassuring.

The only protest came from Sidney Bailey, Virginia commissioner of financial institutions, who noted that the bank was owned by a series of foreign investors via shell companies registered outside the United States. The money was coming from a small French bank acting as a *prêt-nom* for BCCI. Later Bailey said, "I felt like a voice in the wilderness. The Fed paid little attention to what I had to say."[6]

Clifford spent thirteen years as chairman of First American Bankshares and BCCI's lawyer, but he would later claim that he didn't know that BCCI controlled the bank. Altman also finessed the truth when he was asked if First American's stockholders had borrowed money from BCCI, declaring, "We don't have access here to such information." The records may have been else-where, but BCCI had loaned both Clifford and Altman money to buy and then sell BCCI stock, transactions that made Clifford $6.5 million and Altman $3.3 million.

First American certainly knew how to make friends. It loaned $1 million to Michael Deaver, an official of the Reagan White House, who then became a lobbyist for the Saudis. It gave another loan to conservative journalist Robert Novak. Its board included lobbyist Robert Gray of Hill and Knowlton (which lobbied for the embattled BCCI on Capitol Hill) and Karl G. Harr Jr., an aero-space lobbyist who had served on the National Security Council's Operations Coordinating Board (which oversaw CIA covert operations). The CIA had sev-eral accounts at BCCI and First American,[7] facilitating the movement of at least half a million U.S. government dollars to Panama's Manuel Noriega.

The Kerry Investigation and the Tampa Case

Washington lawyer Jack Blum had been associate counsel to the Senate For-eign Relations Committee during 1972–76 and in that capacity had handled both the committee's investigation of corrupt foreign payments by American corporations and its investigation of the international petroleum industry. Be-fore that he had been assistant counsel to the Senate Antitrust and Monopoly Subcommittee. He was a passionate foe of corruption and knew a lot about criminality inside the U.S. government.

He was hired as special counsel to John Kerry's Subcommittee on Terror-ism, Narcotics, and International Operations to investigate the relationship of narcotics law enforcement to American foreign policy interests. Ever since the Reagan administration had squelched revelations of drug dealing by its Nicaraguan Contra protégés, Kerry had wanted to look at the connections between U.S. foreign policy and drug trafficking. But he'd been blocked in the Senate. Finally, he began hearings in 1987 that lasted into 1988.

Blum explained to me, "The Foreign Relations Committee was looking at the relationship between drug trafficking and arms dealing and the way we run foreign policy. Did we ignore all the stuff going on to support the war in Nicaragua? We got into the issue of money laundering." Blum said that he stumbled across Lee Ritch, who had completed a prison sentence in the U.S. for drug trafficking. Ritch was born in Florida but was a Cayman Islands citizen through his father. He told the panel, "I used to launder my money in the Cayman Islands. The U.S. wised up, and the bankers told me to shift to Panama. In Panama, I'm told the only guy to talk to is Noriega. He sends me to BCCI." Democratic Senator Sam Nunn of Georgia, chairman of the Permanent Subcommittee on Investigations, heard the same information at his own hearing, but he ignored it. So did the Justice Department.

Blum said, "We go poking around. I found a guy who had worked for BCCI. I met him in Miami. He said, 'That's their major line of work. They're a bunch of criminals.' He goes on to say that in addition to handling drug money, they were managing Noriega's personal finances and that the bankers who did that lived in Miami. Noriega even carried a BCCI Visa credit card." So Blum subpoenaed that information.

José Blandón, a former Panamanian diplomat who had turned against Noriega, told Blum that BCCI was Noriega's bank and played a role in major criminal activity, including moving the money of the Medellín cartel. Blum allowed federal customs agents to listen to the testimony from another room and to keep tapes. When Customs Commissioner William von Raab asked the CIA what it knew about the bank, he got lies from Deputy Director Robert Gates. Bush's Treasury Secretary Nicholas Brady told Raab to stay away from the case. Raab was removed from the investigation, and, when he persisted, was told to resign.

Blum heard the same story of BCCI lawlessness from Amjad Awan, head of Latin American operations for BCCI and Noriega's personal banker. He got Awan to admit that BCCI had criminal clients, laundered drug money, and secretly owned and controlled First American Bank.

Tampa, Florida, a sunny port on a bay running into the Gulf of Mexico, is noted for handmade cigars, shrimp, and phosphate shipping. It attracts some of Florida's west coast tourism, personnel from nearby MacDill Air Force Base, and some less savory characters. The BCCI scandal began to unravel with a drug trafficking case that year in Tampa. Blum said, "We find out about coming arrests for money laundering [in the Tampa drug-trafficking investigation, Operation C-Chase]. We started with laundering drug money, but then pursued it much further and got in testimony a pretty good layout of the criminal nature of the bank. Having done that, we wrote a report and said the matter needs further investigation. But the Justice Department doesn't pick up on any of the clues. I talked to them. I got a leading figure in the bank [Awan] to turn evidence to the government, which didn't want to listen. I taped him for three days with undercover agents in a hotel room in Miami; the government didn't transcribe the tapes."

Blum persuaded two former BCCI officials to meet with federal prosecutors in Tampa. Both informants believed and said that BCCI controlled First American. The federal prosecutors issued a few subpoenas but did little else to investigate the allegations or even to give the information to the FBI or other agencies. Blum said, "The feds wanted to make only a limited case in Tampa; they didn't want to investigate other ramifications. Their story is they had their case and didn't want it messed up with extraneous stuff. The notion that the other stuff was extraneous boggles the mind!"

In October 1988, a month before the U.S. presidential election, the bank and eight of its employees were indicted for laundering millions of dollars for the Medellín cartel. The indictment said nothing about Noriega, who was still on the CIA payroll, a relationship that Republican candidate George Bush Sr. had initiated when he headed the agency. Blum alerted Kerry, who released a deposition about Noriega's ties to drug running and BCCI.

But the Justice Department, under Attorney General Richard Thornburgh, made a plea bargain with the bank in which defendants admitted the charges. Five Pakistani bankers got from three to twenty-five years in prison. Curiously, their lawyers did not allow them to plea bargain themselves, which might have reduced the sentences but would also have provided information about BCCI. The Justice Department went for the narrowest case possible. It declined to use the RICO (Racketeer Influenced and Corrupt Organizations) law—invented to aid prosecution of drug traffickers and organized crime—which would have threatened confiscation of the bank's assets.

BCCI's fine was $14 million—about what the undercover agents posing as drug traffickers had deposited! The U.S. attorney's office in Tampa agreed not to charge the bank or any affiliates with other federal crimes "under investigation or known to the government at the time of the execution of this agreement." Justice even wrote letters to state regulators asking them to keep BCCI open! The deal kept the bank alive and discouraged the jailed officials from telling more.

Kerry attacked the pact as a "sad commentary on a country that is supposed to be taking money laundering extremely seriously. . . . When banks engage knowingly in the laundering of money, they should be shut down." When the Justice Department countered that no statute allowed the government to close banks that launder money, he drafted one. It was killed by the Republicans, led by Senator Orrin Hatch, who made a speech declaring BCCI to be a good corporate citizen. Then Hatch asked BCCI to lend $10 million to one of his friends.

Meanwhile, tapes of witnesses talking about the link between First American Bank and BCCI and about payments to American officials disappeared. Blum said, "There's no question in my mind that it's a calculated effort inside the federal government to limit the investigation. The only issue is whether it's a result of high-level corruption or if it's designed to hide illegal government activities."[8]

Federal attorneys later said Justice Department officials told them that BCCI was a "political" case and that Washington decided how to investigate and prosecute it. The CIA needed a dirty bank, and it wasn't going to blow the whistle on this one. When Kerry's investigators tried to find out what the CIA knew, the agency repeatedly lied or withheld information. But Blum discovered the agency's ties to the bank. He found that during the 1980s, the CIA had prepared hundreds of reports that discussed BCCI's criminal connections—drug trafficking, money laundering—and its illegal control of First American Bank. Those in the know, former CIA Directors Richard Helms and William Casey, later lied and said that they hadn't a clue. The CIA blocked investigation of leads in the case. Documents were destroyed, an agent later reported.[9] The CIA provided its reports to Treasury Secretary Donald Regan, who didn't act on them and did not provide information to the prosecutors in Tampa.

The Treasury and Justice Departments also sat on evidence. A report by staff of New York Democratic Rep. Charles Schumer noted that Customs had been tipped off to BCCI's criminality in 1983 by a Jordanian arms dealer and coffee smuggler. In 1984, the Internal Revenue Service was told about BCCI money laundering by the former chauffeur at BCCI Miami. But IRS agents' requests to investigate the bank were turned down by their superiors. In 1986, the IRS got information from India about BCCI money laundering in several countries. No action was taken. A DEA agent taped a BCCI official in a sting telling how he could launder the agent's money. No further investigation. The Schumer report found that there had been hundreds of tips on BCCI to federal agencies.

Robert Mazur, the undercover Customs investigator who ran a sting against the bank in Tampa, found his proposals for more intense investigations led to threats of transfer, so he quit in disgust and went to the DEA. The Justice Department ordered key witnesses not to cooperate with Kerry and refused to produce documents subpoenaed by his subcommittee. Justice tried to gag Mazur, but he finally told the subcommittee that hundreds of leads about BCCI crimes had been ignored, including by Paul Volcker's Federal Reserve. When an agent of the Tampa drug-bust team, David Burris, told a Fed regulator that a BCCI employee had said that the bank controlled First American and a bank in Georgia, the regulator said he couldn't act without documentation.

Ineptitude? Bungling? Or protection of a politically connected criminal bank? Blum told me, "When I first looked at it, I thought there's something nefarious or embarrassing. What is it? Their own incompetence? Worse? You never know the answer." He noted, "This whole collection of people were wrapped up in the Bush crowd in Texas. Prominent Saudis played a key role."

Kerry was a junior senator, and his terrorism and narcotics subcommittee mandate was limited to looking into connections between those two issues. When the subcommittee tried to schedule public hearings on BCCI, it was blocked by the Justice Department and the Senate. He found lack of support from key Democrats, who didn't want to stir up financial scandals after some—including Banking Committee Chair Donald Riegle—had been embarrassed by revelations that they had received contributions from savings and loan crook Charles Keating. Keating and his Lincoln Savings and Loan invested millions of dollars in Trendinvest, an offshore speculator in foreign currencies. One of Trendinvest's board members was Alfred Hartmann, manager of BCCI's Banque de Commerce et Placements and vice chair of Bank of New York–Inter-Maritime Bank, both in Geneva. Lincoln's collapse cost taxpayers $2.5 billion. Embarrassment trumped corruption, so the chair of the Foreign Relations Committee, Senator Claiborne Pell, blocked further hearings.[10]

Blind Oversight: The British Accountants and the Bank of England

The accountants Price Waterhouse UK helped perpetuate the fraud. The fellows running BCCI were not as bright as they thought they were. They were playing with $10 billion in depositors' money, buying and selling currency, trading in commodities; when they lost, they covered up by cooking the books. They hid losses with invented trades through networks of shell companies protected by offshore secrecy. But by 1986 Price Waterhouse had discovered losses of $430 million in commodities trades, the entire cash capital of the bank. By their rules, the auditors had to tell only the managers, who were running the dirty bank, not law enforcement agents who might protect the depositors or creditors. And they didn't tell Price Waterhouse in the U.S., which was auditing BCCI operations stateside.

Until 1987, Price Waterhouse shared accounting duties with Ernst & Whinney, but that firm quit, unhappy at not having access to all the books worldwide. Still, even as sole auditor, PW was blocked by bank secrecy laws from getting information from subsidiaries in offshore jurisdictions such as Switzerland. And PW backed down in surprising cases. The loan files in London were written in Urdu, but when PW sent an Urdu speaker to the bank, he wasn't allowed in. The auditors didn't insist. When BCCI would not identify borrowers, the auditors again backed down.[11] PW may have had other concerns. Price Waterhouse partners in the Caribbean had taken BCCI loans of over $500,000.[12]

In spite of expressions of concern by other countries' regulators, PW kept BCCI's fraud and parlous condition secret. When it learned that BCCI had bought First American Bank illegally through nominees, it didn't tell Price Waterhouse in the U.S. In its audit conclusion, it lied that its picture of BCCI's books was "true and fair."

Price Waterhouse in the U.S. might nevertheless have had a clue. Robert Bench was associate deputy comptroller of the currency in the Treasury Department when he was sent a copy of a CIA report on BCCI. He quit to go to work for Price Waterhouse on the BCCI account.[13] It wasn't until 1991 that Price Waterhouse UK told the full truth. At the request of the Bank of England, PW wrote the confidential *Sandstorm Report,* which detailed the phony records and shell companies, the use of Middle Eastern nominees, the Ponzi schemes.

Another failure in oversight was the work of a committee from eight countries set up in 1987 by the Basel Committee, the central club of the world's big banks, to look at BCCI's operations in the wake of rumors of funny dealings and big losses. The committee was next to useless: It took no action even after the Tampa charges became public knowledge.

In 1988 and 1989, the Bank of England learned of BCCI's involvement in the financing of terrorism and in drug money laundering, but it didn't shut BCCI down. In 1990, when Price Waterhouse reported to the Bank of England about BCCI fraud, the bank still took no action. The bank even tried to keep the accountants from cooperating with agents of New York District Attorney Robert Morgenthau, who was conducting the only serious investigation of BCCI.

England's central bank thought it was just fine for BCCI in 1990 to move its headquarters, officers, and records out of British jurisdiction to Abu Dhabi, where someone else would have to worry about it. When indictments were finally handed down, the government of Abu Dhabi refused to provide the records to criminal investigators in the U.S. or the UK.

Morgenthau: The Tide Turns Against BCCI

With Kerry's support, in 1989 Blum went to see New York District Attorney Robert Morgenthau. Morgenthau had been district attorney for New York County (Manhattan) since 1975. He was the most important financial crimes investigator in the United States. He still is. Blum told him about the Justice Department's refusal to look into BCCI's involvement in drug money laundering and other crimes. Morgenthau opened an investigation and ran into a wall of obstacles from Justice, which refused to cooperate, grant him access to witnesses, or share information. Morgenthau even had to send a fax to the U.S. attorney in Tampa asking him to please answer his telephone.[14] His chief investigator, John Moscow, learned about the tapes that the Tampa prosecutors had made of Blum's informants. However, for months, said Moscow, they had insisted that there were no such tapes.

Then Morgenthau received a gift. The chairman of BCCI's internal review committee in London, Masihur (Arthur) Rahman, told his bosses that the bank's true finances had been distorted by deception and manipulation, and he resigned. He got phone calls threatening him and his family with death. Rahman contacted Morgenthau's office and revealed the Price Waterhouse audit report that, through a series of phony loans, BCCI had gained secret ownership of First American Bankshares, now an $11 billion U.S. interstate bank holding company.

In May 1991, Kerry finally got a one-day hearing before a banking subcommittee, which refused to provide staff for the hearing; Kerry used his own people. Senator Claiborne Pell did his friend Clark Clifford a favor by delaying issuance of subpoenas until the hearing was over. The Justice Department ordered key witnesses not to cooperate, and it refused to supply subpoenaed documents. After Kerry threatened that he would put a permanent hold on the nomination of Robert Gates as CIA director, an agency official testified that the CIA had known about BCCI for years and that it had accounts in BCCI. After Blum told Pell that he had found evidence linking BCCI to First American, Pell had him dropped from the committee payroll.

Blum said the bank's friends prevented more Kerry hearings: "They got it out of Foreign Relations. . . . We later learned that BCCI, between September 1988 and July 1991 when the bank closed, spent $26 million on lawyers and lobbyists trying to keep themselves in business. They hired people on both sides to shut [the investigations] down." Finally banking investigators began to be interested and to discover the BCCI use of front men to buy American banks. In January 1991, after several years of sitting on its hands while receiving damning information about BCCI, the Federal Reserve ordered an investigation into BCCI's control of First American. In March, it announced that BCCI had illegally acquired about 60 percent of First American, and it ordered BCCI to submit a plan for divestiture. It further announced that it would fine Ghaith Pharaon $17 million for his role in the scam acquisitions.

The Bank of England, working with the government of Abu Dhabi and auditor Price Waterhouse, had been trying to reorganize BCCI and cover up the bank's criminality. But in June 1991 the Bank of England notified the Federal Reserve that a new Price Waterhouse audit showed massive fraud at BCCI. Two weeks later, British regulators closed down BCCI's operations in eighteen countries and ordered tight supervision or restrictions in forty-four others. Seventeen branches in the United Arab Emirates and three branches in Pakistan, where BCCI was still politically well connected, remained open.

Years later, documents would show that Bank of England officials had suspected fraud at BCCI for at least seven years. A £850 million ($1.6 billion) willful negligence suit against the bank brought by liquidators Deloitte on behalf of creditors was dropped in 2005 after a negative ruling on the claims by the British High Court.

The Indictments

District Attorney Morgenthau consistently went for tougher indictments that targeted the American and Saudi powers behind BCCI, while the Justice Department sought to limit the scope of prosecutions to the old drug trafficking charge.

In July 1991, a New York County grand jury handed down an indictment that named BCCI, its Cayman Islands subsidiary ICIC (actually several companies, including International Credit and Investment Company Overseas and International Credit and Commerce Overseas, joined under that rubric), and six individuals, including Abedi, Clifford, and Altman. It charged them with a multibillion-dollar scheme that included defrauding depositors, falsifying bank records to hide illegal money, and committing larcenies totaling more than $30 million. It charged that the bank was indeed a criminal enterprise whose corporate strategy had been to seek out flight capital, black market capital, and proceeds of drug sales. It charged that Clifford and Altman had taken millions in fake loans, stock deals, and phony legal fees, and that Khalid bin Mahfouz had stolen as much as $300 million from the bank. It also indicted Ghaith Pharaon and Faisal Saud al-Fulaij, the former chairman of Kuwait Airways. Kamal Adham agreed to cooperate with the investigation.

Morgenthau's revelations moved the New York Federal Reserve Bank (not Volcker's Fed in Washington, which had allowed BCCI front men to buy First American) to coordinate an action to shut BCCI down. John Moscow, who ran the Morgenthau investigation, had persuaded Gerald Corrigan, president of the New York Fed, that BCCI was dirty and had to be closed. The Fed fined BCCI $200 million and took steps to ban its shareholders, including Ghaith Pharaon, Kamal Adham, and Faisal Saud al-Fulaij, from participating in banking in the U.S. It also fined bin Mahfouz $170 million.

Finally, in August, a federal grand jury in Tampa indicted Swaleh Naqvi and five other BCCI officials, as well as a reputed Colombian drug baron, Gerardo ("Don Chepe") Moncada—but not Abedi or the bank. It focused only on drug money laundering and the connection to Noriega (no longer America's friend), not on fraud against the bank's depositors. It used mostly old C-Chase information, extended to some of BCCI's chief executives, and ignored leads, witnesses, and evidence that would have revealed the bank's large-scale frauds (even bribery of the Georgia legislature) or exposed the CIA and Reagan-Bush illegal use of the bank. Attorney General William Barr, who had replaced Thornburgh, formerly worked for the CIA. BCCI pleaded guilty to conspiring with Colombia's Medellín cartel to launder $14 million in cocaine proceeds.

In October 1991, Assistant Attorney General Robert Mueller III oversaw a federal grand jury indictment of Clifford and Altman for conspiring to defraud the Federal Reserve Board by misleading it about BCCI's relationship with First American, obstructing the Fed's inquiries into BCCI, and lying to the Fed about BCCI's loans to First American shareholders, including the loans that the Washington lawyers themselves had taken. But he didn't go after bin Mahfouz or other well-connected oil-kingdom Arabs. And he didn't echo Morgenthau's charge that BCCI had been a criminal enterprise since 1972. Or that the bank had paid millions of dollars in bribes to central bankers or other financial officials in a dozen developing countries. He never got around to interviewing all the witnesses who knew about BCCI dealings or to persuading the CIA to tell what it knew. Kerry's report noted that the Justice Department had repeatedly blocked his own and Morgenthau's investigations into BCCI. The department had lied to other investigators, ignored money-laundering evidence, and refused to provide documents or witnesses that might target Bush friends.

In November, Justice announced an indictment of BCCI, Abedi, Naqvi, and Pharaon. Again the indictment was limited, focusing on BCCI's secret ownership of shares in two banks in California and Miami.

Finally, in December 1991, Justice issued a major indictment against the bank, which pleaded guilty the same day to federal and state charges of racketeering, involving money laundering and the illegal takeover of First American and other U.S. banks. It agreed to pay more than $550 million in U.S. assets, part of which would go to a "victims' fund" and part to bail out First American and Independence Banks. A fine of $10 million would go to New York. But only one of the accused was arrested, in France; by then the others were safely out of reach in the Middle East or Pakistan.

Morgenthau's investigation continued. In July 1992 a New York grand jury indicted Khalid bin Mahfouz and an aide for defrauding BCCI and its depositors of as much as $300 million, using depositors' money to buy his bank shares. The U.S. Federal Reserve alleged that bin Mahfouz had breached banking regulations. But he could not be touched by American criminal law in Saudi Arabia, and Morgenthau dropped the charges in 1993 after bin Mahfouz agreed to settle for $225 million. He and the National Commercial Bank also made a $253 million deal with BCCI's creditors to resolve their claims. Kamal Adham, the former Saudi intelligence chief, agreed to pay a $105 million fine. The fines in the end topped $1.5 billion, but this was a fraction of the amount that had disappeared, and nobody went to jail. The Justice Department didn't go after bin Mahfouz, a Bush family friend and money source, at all.

Clark Clifford evaded trial by using the Pinochet defense: his health. Altman got off after convincing gullible jurors that he—an executive worth millions of dollars in pay and stock benefits—just didn't know who the bank's true owners were. Clifford died in 1998 at the age of 92. Altman is still a lawyer and lives in the Washington suburb of Potomac, Maryland, with his wife, Lynda Carter, the actress of 1970s *Wonder Woman* fame.

What happened to the billions of dollars sucked out of BCCI and never repaid to depositors? International banks' complicity in the secret offshore banking system has effectively covered up the money trail. But in the years after the collapse of BCCI, Khalid bin Mahfouz was still flush with cash, and the former financier of George W. Bush became a financier of Osama bin Laden. In 1992, bin Mahfouz established the Muwafaq ("blessed relief") Foundation in the Channel Island of Jersey, providing it with as much as $30 million. The U.S. Treasury Department called it "an al-Qaeda front that receives funding from wealthy Saudi businessmen."

The $21 billion National Commercial Bank of Saudi Arabia that bin Mahfouz owned was the world's largest private bank. NCB was affiliated with Inter-Maritime Management SA, a subsidiary of the Bank of New York–Inter-

Maritime Bank in Geneva. By coincidence, another Inter-Maritime subsidiary, Unimags Trading, shared a Geneva address with SICO, the Saudi Investment Company run by Yeslam Binladen. SICO is the holding company of the Saudi Binladen Group (SBG), the largest Middle East construction company, which operates through a web of offshore companies and is owned by the extended bin Laden family. Yeslam is the half-brother of Osama bin Laden.

The connections are interesting. Khalid bin Mahfouz was a board member of the Dar al-Mal al-Islami (DMI), the House of Finance of Islam, a Geneva-based bank charged with distributing subsidies by the royal family in the Muslim world. DMI, founded in 1981 and with estimated assets of $3.5 billion, also had connections to the bin Laden family: its twelve-member board of directors included Haydar Mohamed bin Laden, Osama bin Laden's half-brother.

DMI's president, Mohammad al-Faisal, was also an investor and board member of al-Shamal Bank, which held al-Qaeda members' accounts. The U.S. complained to Saudi Arabia in 1998 that the National Commercial Bank was funding Osama bin Laden's activities in Afghanistan and Chechnya. In testimony during U.S. trials of suspects in the 1998 attacks on American embassies in Kenya and Tanzania, an al-Qaeda collaborator, Essam al-Ridi, recounted how bin Laden transferred $230,000 from al-Shamal Bank to a bank in Arizona to buy a plane to fly Stinger missiles from Pakistan to Sudan. Further, al-Faisal's DMI was a major shareholder of al-Taqwa, the shell bank in Nassau used by the CIA and al-Qaeda.

In 1999, American investigators looking into the attacks on U.S. embassies in Africa found suspicious transfers of tens of millions of dollars from NCB to "charities" believed to funnel money to Osama bin Laden. Some of these "charities" were run by the bin Mahfouz family. The Saudis ordered an audit, which confirmed the transfers to bin Laden. Altogether, $2 billion was missing from the National Commercial Bank. The Saudis put bin Mahfouz under house arrest and forced him to sell his shares. But the money he ran still flowed to Osama bin Laden.

Add to the history of derelictions by the Senate and House Intelligence Committees that they did not pursue revelations of involvement by CIA and Saudi intelligence officials in a bank that financed illegal drug and arms trafficking and terrorism. Nor did most other members of Congress seem to care. The Kerry subcommittee report in 1992 revealed that the White House knew about BCCI's criminal activities; that the CIA, which used BCCI for secret banking, had lied to congressional investigators; and that BCCI routinely paid off American public officials. Except for Democrats Schumer of New

York and Henry Gonzalez of Texas, both of whom issued damning reports, the Hill displayed little interest.

Serious investigations with backing by congressional leadership might have turned up answers to some of the questions the Kerry report posed: questions about BCCI and American influentials, including the relationship with late CIA Director William Casey; the use of BCCI by central figures in the "October Surprise" (the Reagan-Bush payoff deal with Iranian militants to keep American hostages imprisoned until after the 1980 Carter–Reagan election); the financial dealings of BCCI directors with S&L fraudster Charles Keating and his front companies; and the nature of financial and real estate investments in the United States by major shareholders of BCCI.

The report wondered about BCCI's international operations, including the extent of the bank's involvement in Pakistan's nuclear program; BCCI's manipulation of commodities and securities markets in Europe and Canada; its relationships with convicted Iraqi arms dealer Sarkis Sarkenalian, Syrian drug trafficker, terrorist, and arms trafficker Monzer Al-Kassar, and other major arms dealers; its financing of commodities and other business dealings of international criminal financier Marc Rich; and the sale of BCCI affiliate Banque de Commerce et Placement in Geneva to the Cukorova Group of Turkey, which owned an entity involved in the Atlanta branch of Italian bank BNL, which handled arms sales to Saddam Hussein, among others.

The Kerry subcommittee said it could not begin to answer such questions without the documents it was denied by authorities in the U.S., the UK, and Abu Dhabi. A large number of the documents the bank controlled were destroyed: after investigations started and the Pakistani chiefs fled, there were seven fires in the fireproof London warehouses where BCCI stored records. In one of them, four firemen were killed. No one was ever charged.

Notes

1. Jonathan Beatty and S. C. Gwynne, *The Outlaw Bank: A Wild Ride into the Secret Heart of BCCI* (Washington, D.C.: Beard, 2004 [1993]), p. 315.
2. *The BCCI Affair: A Report to the Committee on Foreign Relations, United States Senate, by Senator John Kerry and Senator Hank Brown.* December 1992, 102nd Congress, 2nd Session, Senate (the *Kerry Report*).
3. Peter Truell and Larry Gurwin, *False Profits* (Boston: Houghton Mifflin, 1992), p. 135.
4. James Ring Adams and Douglas Frantz, *A Full Service Bank: How BCCI Stole Billions around the World* (New York: Simon & Schuster, 1992), p. 238.

5. Truell and Gurwin, *False Profits*, p. 117.
6. Ibid., p. 57.
7. Ibid., p. 134.
8. Beatty and Gwynne, *Outlaw Bank*, p. 118.
9. Ibid., p. 24.
10. In 1980, Congress, in its orgy of Reaganite deregulation, ended regulation of the savings and loan industry. It allowed S&Ls to invest in risky real estate. It raised the federal insurance limit on S&Ls from $40,000 to $100,000, even though the typical savings account was only around $6,000. Congress had forgotten why regulation was needed. Crooks set up offshore companies and accounts; then they loaned themselves and friends money that they never paid back. A significant number of the crooked banks were in Texas, Colorado, and Florida, all states under Bush family influence. Neil Bush, George Bush Sr.'s son, was on the board of Silverado, a corrupt Colorado S&L. He was fined $50,000 and banned from banking, but he never went to jail. Another son, Jeb Bush (now Florida's governor), was a partner in a Florida building paid for in part by a defaulted loan from Broward Federal S&L. Bush and his partner insisted they didn't owe for the loan, and they were allowed to keep the building; taxpayers paid the cost. The Reagan administration knew about the S&L problem in the mid-1980s, when a bailout would have cost $20 billion, but it waited until after the 1988 election of George Bush Sr. to reveal the scam and shut the banks down. The S&L bailout of nearly 800 banks will cost Americans $500 billion, including $1 billion for Silverado. It is the largest theft in world history.
11. Adams and Frantz, *Full Service Bank*, p. 43.
12. *Kerry Report*, pp. 102–40.
13. Truell and Gurwin, *False Profits*, p. 359.
14. Ibid., p. 287.

5 *Civil war in Congo has cost 4 million lives over the past ten years—strife fueled by Western multinationals seeking cheap supplies of coltan and other minerals.*

The Human Cost of Cheap Cell Phones

Kathleen Kern

Goma's hospital compound has one tent for rape victims awaiting surgery and one for victims recovering from surgery. In the pre-op area, I held a month-old girl who was entranced by the dim electric light hanging from the ridgepole. She arched her back and waved her arms, straining to encounter this exciting new world and oblivious of the atrocity that had created her life.

The mother told me her baby's name was Esther. Clasping her breasts, she said she had no milk. She did not tell me what operation she was waiting for. Perhaps her rapist(s) had caused a fistula, penetrating the wall between her rectum and vagina with penises, guns, or machetes. Hundreds of other injuries are possible. We had seen pictures of women who had been shot in the vagina, who had had salt rubbed in their eyes until they were blind (and thus could not identify their assailants), who had been burned or had limbs amputated after being raped.

A week earlier we had been in Bukavu, where we had visited the office of a human rights organization and seen gory photos of a recent massacre in the nearby village of Kanyola. The assailants were members of the Interahamwe militia that had carried out the genocide in Rwanda. They had hacked their victims to death with machetes or burned them instead of using guns, so that UN peacekeepers at a nearby base would not hear the slaughter. The human rights worker showing us the pictures had recently replaced the previous director of the agency, Pascal Kabungulu Kimbembe. After a local Congolese army officer had threatened him, Kimbembe had been assassinated in front of his home earlier in the year.[1]

These low-tech acts of barbarism engulfing eastern Congo are outgrowths of a global demand for high-tech consumer goods such as cell phones, laptop computers, and PlayStations. Coltan (short for columbite-tantalite), an ore vital for manufacturing these devices, has been a particular concern for those investigating the involvement of multinational corporations in the violence: 80 percent of the known coltan reserves in the world are in Congo, making it potentially as strategically important to the U.S. military as the Persian Gulf.[2] But demand for gold, diamonds, copper, zinc, uranium, cobalt, cadmium, copper, timber, and other resources in which Congo is rich has also contributed to the holocaust that has overtaken the country during the past decade.

Holocaust on the Equator

Since 1996, about 4 million people have died in the Democratic Republic of Congo (formerly Zaire) as a direct or indirect result of civil war.[3] No other conflict since World War II has resulted in such carnage. After the Rwandan genocide in 1994, Hutu soldiers from the Rwandan army and the Hutu militia Interahamwe, who were responsible for the wholesale killings, fled into Congo along with more than a million Hutu noncombatants. Tutsi President Paul Kagame sent Rwandan troops into Congo in 1996, arguing that the Hutus across the border posed a threat to Rwandan security. The army massacred thousands of Hutu noncombatants who had taken refuge in Congo when Kagame came to power. Rwanda, Burundi (which also had a Tutsi government), and Uganda sent troops in 1997 to aid a Congolese rebel group under Laurent Kabila, who was attempting to overthrow Zaire's dictator, Mobutu Sese Seko.[4] The fighting forced civilians off their lands and into mining areas, where they dug for gold, diamonds, and coltan in order to survive.

In 1997, the rebels deposed Mobutu and installed Kabila. Citing an assassination attempt against him and the Rwandan army's slaughter of Hutu refugees, Kabila expelled Rwandan and Ugandan forces from Congo in 1998. Rwanda again invaded, claiming that it needed to pursue Hutus threatening its security. The Ugandans, in turn, attempted to combat Ugandan rebel groups based in Congo by creating a buffer zone like the one Israel had created when it bombed and subsequently occupied southern Lebanon in the 1980s.[5] In planning their invasion, Rwandan President Kagame and Ugandan President

Yoweri Museveni agreed to install a new president in Congo while maintaining control over the eastern part of the country near their borders. Kabila called on Angola, Namibia, and Zimbabwe for help, and by 1998 eastern Congo was left in a stalemate. Uganda held the northern territory, while Rwanda controlled the southeast. Rwandan, Burundian, and Ugandan soldiers pillaged banks, factories, farms, and storage facilities in the region, loading their contents onto vehicles and shipping them back to their home countries.

The Rwandan government shipped seven years' worth of Congo's coltan stockpiles—about 1,500 tons—from warehouses to Kigali in 1998.[6] At the time, coltan was fetching about $18 a pound ($40 a kilo). Over the next few years, often using Rwandan prisoners as indentured laborers, the Rwandan military systematically stripped coltan from mines in eastern Congo and sent it back to Rwanda. The international price of coltan climbed to $30 a pound in January 2000 and then spiked to $380 the following December. (A shortage of coltan resulted in a shortage of the Sony PlayStation 2 during the 2000 Christmas season.) Since the ore requires only a pick and shovel to mine, military, political, and corporate elites could make a huge profit from the labor of Rwandan prisoners or impoverished Congolese.

The brother of Ugandan President Museveni, Salim Saleh, controlled three airlines, which he leased to the Ugandan military to fly troops and supplies into Congo. With the cooperation of Ugandan army officers, Congolese rebel groups, and private entrepreneurs, Saleh ensured that the planes returned to Uganda loaded with gold, timber, and coffee. He also cashed in on the lucrative coltan mines and worked with Lebanese businessman Khalil Nazeem Ibrahim to smuggle diamonds out through the company known as the Victoria Group—free of tax, thus depriving Congo of revenue it desperately needed.

Uganda's and Rwanda's export histories reveal the extent of the looting. Between 1996 and 1997, Rwanda's coltan production doubled, giving Rwanda and its Congolese rebel allies up to $20 million a month in revenue.[7] The Rwandan government claimed that the country was producing all of the coltan it was exporting—1,440 metric tons a year. However, the 2001 report by a UN Panel of Experts (discussed later) cites official government statistics that put the production at 83 metric tons a year.[8]

Rwanda has no diamond mines, but its diamond exports increased from 166 carats in 1998 to 30,500 in 2000. In 1999, Uganda produced no coltan but exported 69.5 tons. In 2000, Uganda received more than $1.25 million from exporting diamonds, despite having no diamond mines. It produced 0.0044 tons of gold, but exported 10.83 tons.[9]

A "peace" deal signed in 2002 left President Joseph Kabila, who had replaced his assassinated father, in power. His vice presidents were four of the
warlords whose militias had wreaked havoc in Congo. Over the next several years, Rwanda and Uganda continued to make incursions into the country. Rwanda sent 6,000 troops into eastern Congo in December 2004, again
claiming it was dealing with Hutu rebels who posed a threat to its security.[10]
Rwandan troops committed massacres in North Kivu province, burning and
looting everything in their path. Our delegation saw the result of this pillaging when we visited a students' association in the university town of Bukavu
almost a year later. A young man took us through bare rooms and showed
us that everything—furniture, computers, phones, and fax machines—had
been stolen by Rwandan troops. Because students had spoken out against
the human rights abuses of the Rwandan military, the young man told us,
the Rwandan military and the Congolese militia it backs had targeted their
student center.

Rape as a Weapon of War

I first came to eastern Congo in October 2005 as part of a Christian Peacemaker Team (CPT) delegation, to explore the possibility of setting up a vio-
lence-deterring project similar to the ones CPT has had in the Middle East
and the Americas. The delegation quickly realized that the situation in Congo
presented challenges our organization had not faced before. We also noted
that the widespread practice of rape by all armed groups was something that
most of the world, including our church constituency, was not aware of. With
an eye toward publicizing these rapes, we began to focus on this issue as we
met with pastors and civic leaders trying to nurture a fragile social order in
their devastated country.

For many Congolese women, rape is only the beginning of their trauma.
Their assailants infect from one-fourth to one-third of the women with HIV,
and often rape the women in front of their husbands and children. The husbands or husbands' families then view the women as "contaminated," even
when they do not contract a disease, and drive them and their children out
of the village. Sometimes they tell the women that they may stay if they kill
children born as a result of the rape. Those not killed often become street
children, an unknown phenomenon in this area before 1996, several Congolese told us.

Deprived of their social supports, many women become burden-bearers in
order to feed themselves and their children. We saw them in every commu-

nity we visited: bent double, carrying loads of produce or building materials supported by straps that cut deep grooves into their foreheads.

Congolese churches and civic groups have attempted to provide medical care, counseling, and job training for the rape survivors and to challenge social practices that marginalize them. But the staggering numbers of raped and displaced women overwhelm these efforts. The UN Fund for Women and human rights groups estimate that hundreds of thousands of women and girls have been raped since 1998, although the vast majority of rapes have gone unreported because of the social stigma. The head of a women's organization in Bukavu told us that in 2004 a small grant from the Danish Lutheran church had enabled her to help 1,200 women in the area who had been raped. She had to stop the program when funds ran out and now lacks the means even to document the rapes.

The use of rape as a weapon of war has had broader ramifications for the people of eastern Congo. Since armed groups often attack women when they are working in their fields, many women are afraid to leave their homes. Thus, in fertile lands with a year-round growing season, people are going hungry.

Violence perpetrated by armed groups has also led to an increase in violence among the civilian population. "Something in our society is unhinging," reported Jeanne Muliri-Kabekatyo, the head of the Protestant Women's Society of North Kivu. Her organization documents stories of rape and sexual assault unheard of before the wars. She told us of girls—some as young as eighteen months—raped by neighbors, brothers, taxi drivers, and teachers. Her organization has responded by training 36,000 children to resist rapes and teaching parents never to let their daughters go anywhere alone or be alone with a man, even a teacher.

Some stories seem especially to haunt her. One young woman delivered a stillborn baby the day after her three-year-old child had died. The cadaver of the newborn was still in the room when five armed men entered the house, and her husband fled. She was too weak to move, let alone resist the men who gang-raped her. She needed five operations and will never have more children. The husband married someone else.

Then there was the girl raped by two brothers and their father. When her mother saw she was pregnant, she sent her daughter to the men who had raped her, saying it was their job to take care of her. "She is mentally ill now and cannot stand to be touched," Muliri-Kabekatyo told us. "We can't bring a case against the rapists because she has stopped speaking. She is in a deplorable state."

After relating these stories, she paused and said, "You can get sick your-self."

With so many millions of people dead of starvation and disease, with mas-sacres continuing despite the presence of 15,000 UN peacekeeping troops, with government employees having received no wages for ten years, these hundreds of thousands of rapes get lost in the chaos.

Western Complicity in Congo's Wars

Westerners telling stories like these need to be mindful that we have benefited from a colonialism that stereotyped Africans as savages. For too long, people in the First World have known about Africa chiefly through atrocities such as the Rwandan genocide or "famine pornography"—fly-covered children with bloated bellies.

We asked the pastors, human rights workers, and women activists who were working with rape victims how they wanted these stories told. Most agreed that the situation was so dire that spreading the news was more im-portant than other considerations. "Christ said to keep telling the truth even up to the death," said the director of a women's organization in Goma. How-ever, she told us, if we wanted to provide balance, we ought to publicize how Western countries are facilitating and profiting from Congo's misery. "We are treated like the wastebasket of the world," she said, referring to the enormous numbers of weapons being dumped in the region. The Rwandan government uses the military aid it receives from the U.S. to fund the Congolese Rally for Democracy army (RCD-Goma), which rampages through the eastern Congo. The U.S. also funds President Kabila and his Congolese army, which fights against the RCD. A representative of the human rights organization CODHO spoke to our delegation of an "Anglophone conspiracy" by the U.S., UK, and South Africa to distribute arms to militias and armies. By doing so, he said, they keep the region destabilized and thus open to exploitation of its resources.

Nearly all the Congolese with whom we met cited these resources as the key to understanding Congo's desperate situation and as the smoking gun in the hands of the West. Rwanda and Uganda might be the pirates, but multi-national corporations based in the First World have equipped them to do their plundering.

An April 6, 2001, hearing held by U.S. Congresswoman Cynthia McKinney exposed the involvement of Western nations, and the corporatocracy appears in almost every stage of the conflict in the region. Rwandan President Paul

Kagame was trained by the U.S. military at Fort Leavenworth in 1990.[11] The United States wielded its power to prevent UN peacekeeping troops from entering Rwanda to stop the genocide in 1994 but promptly provided the country with $75 million in military aid after Kagame took control.[12] U.S. Special Forces began training the Rwandan army in 1994, three months before the April 6, 1994, missile attack on the aircraft carrying the Rwandan and Burundian presidents—the event that precipitated the genocide in Rwanda. The Special Forces training included counterinsurgency, combat, psychological operations, and instructions about how to fight in Zaire.[13] In August, before ordering the 1996 invasion, Kagame visited the Pentagon to get U.S. approval. Rwandan and Ugandan troops who were trained at Fort Bragg participated in the 1996–97 invasions to topple Mobutu.[14] Military contractor Brown & Root, a subsidiary of Halliburton, reportedly built a military base on the Congolese/Rwandan border, where the Rwandan army has trained.[15] The Bechtel Corporation provided satellite maps and reconnaissance photos to Kabila so that he could monitor the movements of Mobutu's troops.[16] Bechtel is a particularly good example of collusion between corporate and political interests. Former Secretary of State George Schultz sits on Bechtel's board and former Secretary of Defense Casper Weinberger served as legal counsel. Jack Sheehan, senior vice president, is a retired U.S. Marine Corps general and a member of the Defense Policy Board at the Pentagon.[17]

During 1996–97, many corporations began negotiating with Kabila for access to the minerals in eastern Congo. He sent a representative to Toronto early in 1997 to speak to mining companies about "investment opportunities." The trip resulted in $50 million for Kabila, which he used to march on Kinshasa, capital of Congo. In May 1997, American Mineral Fields (AMF) cut a $1 billion deal with Kabila immediately after his forces captured Goma (near the Rwandan/Congolese border). Kabila's U.S.-trained finance commissioner handled the negotiations, giving AMF exclusive exploration rights to zinc, copper, and cobalt mines in the area. Mike McMurrough, a friend of U.S. President Bill Clinton, was the chair of AMF. Tenke Mining announced in the same month that it had signed a contract with Kabila that it had previously signed with Mobutu's government in 1996. Planeloads of representatives from other corporations like Bechtel also began arriving to do business.

The *Washington Post* reported that U.S. soldiers (probably Special Forces) were sighted in the company of Rwandan troops in Congo on July 23 and 24, 1998—about a week before the "official" Rwandan invasion of Congo. The Canadian mining firms Barrick Gold (whose board members include former

U.S. President George H. W. Bush, former Canadian Prime Minister Brian Mulroney, former U.S. Senator Howard Baker, and Clinton adviser Vernon Jordan) and Heritage Oil and Gas arrived with the Ugandan and Rwandan militaries when they invaded Congo in 1998 and secured lucrative oil contracts. In 1999, the financial arm of RCD-Goma (the Congolese militia allied with Rwanda) received $5 million in loans from Citibank NY. It also received financing from the Belgium company Cogecom.[18] Belgium, Denmark, Japan, Switzerland, and the United States doubled their aid to Rwanda from $26.1 million in 1997 to $51.5 million in 1999, which helped Rwanda finance its intervention in Congo.[19]

As Rwanda and Uganda continued to enrich themselves with the plunder, they received praise from the International Monetary Fund and the World Bank for increasing their gross domestic product. An unintentionally ironic IMF press release in 2002 noted that its representatives in Rwanda "urged the authorities to pursue peace relentlessly," even though the rise in the GDP the IMF had applauded occurred precisely because the Rwandan government had exacerbated violence in eastern Congo and had used the instability to exploit the area economically. In 2006, the IMF offered this praise of Uganda: "Fiscal restraint, coupled with prudent monetary management, have supported Uganda's robust growth and helped contain inflation to single digit levels over most of the past decade. In recent years, these policies have contributed to a very comfortable level of international reserves." Again, it chose to ignore how Uganda had come to accumulate these reserves.[20]

In 2001 the World Bank committed itself to reforming Gécamines, the decrepit Congolese state-owned mining company. Workers laid off because of the privatization of Gécamines were supposed to receive training as a part of this reform. The Bank's second important goal was drawing up a plan that would rebuild the mines to benefit the Congolese state. Instead, the transitional government sold off most of Gécamines and its plants to private interests, despite recommendations by the consultants the World Bank had hired.[21] The World Bank, which was supposed to be scrutinizing the mining sector and rebuilding Gécamines, thus allowed foreign interests to strip Congo of what was once its most important source of revenue.[22]

The UN Panel of Experts and the OECD Guidelines

Although the misery that engulfed Congo from 1996 to 2004 caused little outcry among Western nations, the UN Security Council, beginning in 2000, sought to address the underlying causes for the violence. It set up a Panel of

Experts that issued a series of reports over the next three years describing how networks of high-level politicians, military officers, and businesspeople from Congo and surrounding countries collaborated with armed groups to gain control over Congo's resources. The panel noted that the militias and warlord armies then used these resources to buy weapons that fueled the war.

As their reference point, the Panel of Experts used the Organisation for Economic Cooperation and Development (OECD) "Guidelines for Multinational Enterprises." Established in 1976, these guidelines were intended to facilitate trade and define what constitutes responsible corporate behavior.[23] Governments adhering to the guidelines set up "National Contact Points" (NCPs) whom they charged with promoting the guidelines and solving problems that might arise when corporations did not adhere to them.

Based on the Panel of Experts' October 2002 report, the nongovernmental organization (NGO) Rights and Accountability in Development (RAID) put out its own report in 2004, noting the violations of the OECD guidelines committed by corporations in Congo that are shown in Table 1.

The Panel's 2002 report listed eighty-five multinational companies that, it charged, had profited from the war in Congo, including six U.S. companies. With the exception of the Belgian Senate, governments in the countries where these corporations were based made little attempt to hold the corporations accountable for the contributions they had allegedly made to the violence in Congo. Indeed, in most cases, it appears the reports caused the opposite to happen. Some of the companies lobbied their governments and the Security Council to have their names removed from the Panel's list of culprits.[24]

The process through which companies interacted with their governments to get their names off the Panel's list lacked transparency. One member of the Panel noted that he had no direct knowledge of which of the eighty-five companies listed had insisted that their governments intervene on their behalf. However, of five Canadian companies that appeared on the list and then were removed, he said, "It seems only to be expected that one or more of them contacted Foreign Affairs, Marc Brault in particular, who was Canada's envoy to the Great Lakes Region at the time."[25] First Quantum Minerals, a Canadian company, told various news outlets that it was pushing for a "full retraction."[26]

Appendices to documents from the 2005 annual meeting of the National Contact Points provide an insight into the responses of two UK companies to the UN Panel of Experts' report and the UK NCP's intervention. The diamond company DeBeers claimed that the panel offered no details to back up

Table 1   Corporate Violations of OECD Guidelines in Congo

OECD Guidelines	Violations of Guidelines in Congo
Corporations should hold the human rights of those affected by their activities in other countries to the same standard of human rights held by the countries where they are based.	Corporations benefited from armies and proxy militias who traded in minerals mined by forced labor. They also used armed groups to protect their assets.
The human rights provision in the Guidelines implies that corporations should not facilitate the human rights abuses of the armed groups.	Corporations supplied arms to rebel and government forces, even participating in some of the military actions.
Corporations must adopt accounting and auditing practices that truthfully record transactions.	Corporations engaged in the smuggling of diamonds, money laundering, and illegal currency transactions.
Multinational organizations must hold local business partners, suppliers, and subcontractors accountable to the conduct mandated by the OECD guidelines.	Corporations bought minerals from foreign- or rebel-controlled areas without investigating where the minerals came from and who was profiting from sale of these minerals.
Even if corporations do not buy resources directly from regions where armed groups are controlling the mineral resources, they are responsible for following the supply chain. For example, a company buying diamonds in Belgium needs to ask where those diamonds originally came from.	Corporations bought minerals from suppliers outside of Congo without asking where these resources came from.
Corporations should not give or demand bribes to obtain or keep business. They should also not enter into anti-competitive agreements or see exemptions from laws and regulations.	Knowing that regions were unstable, corporations chose to deal with shady middlemen to secure contracts and concessions.
Corporations should contribute "to economic, social and environmental progress with a view to achieving sustainable development."	Companies profited from joint ventures with representatives of the DRC government to exploit natural resources. Few, if any, of the benefits from these ventures went to the Congolese people.
All enterprises, including banks, need to "uphold good governance principles." Banks and financiers need to make sure the corporations and individuals using their services are complying with the OECD guidelines.	Banks enabled companies to profit from their misconduct by offering services to individuals and corporations who were pillaging Congo.

Source: Rights and Accountability in Development (RAID), *Unanswered Questions: Companies, Conflict and the Democratic Republic of Congo: Executive Summary,* report, April 2004, p. 2, www.raid-uk.org/docs/ UN_Panel_DRC/Unanswered_Questions_Full.pdf.

its allegations, despite requests for this information from the company in 2002 and 2003. The UK NCP wrote, "In the circumstances and on the basis of the information provided, the UK NCP concludes that the allegations made by the UN Expert Panel against De Beers are unsubstantiated." The NCP also ended up sharing the view of the Avient Corporation that its aviation business operations in Congo had been legitimate.[27]

In the face of protests by the corporatocracy, the UN Security Council recommended a six-month renewal of the Panel's mandate in its Resolution 1457 of January 23, 2003. The resolution stipulated that the extension was intended to "verify, reinforce and, where necessary, update the Panel's finding and/or clear parties named in the Panel's previous reports with a view to adjusting accordingly the lists attached to these reports."[28]

The Panel of Experts' fourth and final report in October 2003 concluded that no further investigation was required into the activities of most of the corporations it had cited in the previous reports. Many of the corporations that had protested their appearance on the list were moved into an ambiguous "resolved" category. According to the Panel, "resolved" indicated that the company had acknowledged inappropriate behavior and had proposed or taken remedial action; *or* had ceased trading with unethical Congolese partners; *or* had initially shown lack of transparency, which led the Panel to find its ethical conduct suspect, but had later shown that it had not participated in unethical ventures; *or* had been working in Congo many years before 1998; *or* had done nothing unethical even though it had been working in conflict zones; *or* had only a tangential connection to the pillage.

The 2003 report did not explain precisely into which "resolved" category each company fell. Thus, theoretically, a company that had knowingly bought coltan mined by Rwandan military–controlled slave labor and then stopped had the same culpability as a company that had behaved more or less ethically but had not initially provided records to prove that its conduct was aboveboard. Indeed, the Panel never provided any information describing how each case was "resolved." Some companies who had not responded to the Panel ended up in the "resolved" category. Other companies listed under "for further investigation" did not appear to merit that designation any more than some listed under "resolved." Companies listed as simply not having responded to the Panel's allegations appeared to escape further scrutiny.

Although the 2003 report clearly stated that resolution should not be interpreted as absolution, most corporations on the list and their governments claimed that it *had* absolved them.[29]

After the UN Panel of Experts charged in 2002 that Western corporations were complicit in pillaging Congo's resources, U.S. Ambassador Richard S. Williamson (Alternative Representative for Special Political Affairs to the UN) told the UN Security Council that the "United States Government will look into the allegations against these [American] companies and take appropriate measures." However, Friends of the Earth (FoE), which had been following up on the Panel's allegations against American companies, noted in October 2003 that "to date, the Bush administration has placed a greater emphasis on exonerating U.S. companies than on undertaking a meaningful examination into how U.S. companies might have contributed to the conflict in [Congo] via supply chains."[30]

Because the American government did not take appropriate action regarding the behavior of U.S. corporations listed in the Panel of Experts' report, Friends of the Earth and the UK-based group Rights and Accountability in Development filed a complaint with the State Department on August 4, 2004, against Cabot Corporation, Eagle Wings Resources International (EWRI), and OM Group, Inc.

Boston-based Cabot allegedly purchased coltan mined in Congo during the war. Cabot denied these allegations, but a report by the Belgian Senate confirmed that EWRI (a subsidiary of Trinitech Holdings) had a long-term contract to supply Cabot with coltan. The Panel asserted that EWRI received privileged access to coltan sites and captive labor because of its close ties to the Rwandan military. Ohio-based OM Group's joint relationship with a Belgian national, George Forrest, made its activities suspect. The Panel had specifically designated Forrest in its 2001 report as having profited from the violence in eastern Congo. The Panel accused his company, Groupement pour le Traitement des Scories du Terril de Lubumbashi, Ltd. (GTL), of deliberately ignoring technical agreements that provided for the construction of two electric-powered refineries and a converter for germanium processing in Congo, to be built next to existing stockpiles of cobalt and copper. Instead, semi-processed ore from the mine was shipped to OM Group's processing facility in Finland, thereby depriving the state mining company, Gécamines, of revenue.[31]

Wesley S. Scholz, the National Contact Point for the United States, declined to investigate the companies further, citing the Panel's conclusion in its October 2003 report that the issues involving the U.S. companies were resolved. However, in January 2005, he notified the three companies that FoE and RAID still had issues they wished to discuss, and he offered to facilitate an informal dialogue between the two organizations and the corporations. His official position, however, was that "the real focus of the Guidelines is not to focus on past behaviours, but to try and improve future behaviour. We do not sit in judgment and conclude whether companies met their obligations under the Guidelines. Making judgments is about past behaviour and saying you did something wrong." When RAID contacted Scholz in September 2005 to follow up, he said that the companies had confirmed receiving his letter but had not responded.[32]

The U.S. was not alone in its laissez-faire attitude to the OECD Guidelines for Multinational Enterprises. Instead of addressing the substance of the Panel's allegations, several governments questioned whether a UN-appointed panel could even allege violations of the OECD guidelines and whether the guidelines applied to companies' suppliers.

Changing the Guidelines

Given the ineffectual efforts of the NCPs in following up on the charges of corporate misconduct in Congo, RAID suggested revising the OECD Guidelines. Something extra was needed to compel First World governments to investigate abuses committed by the corporations based in their countries. The report also stressed that governments must find means to enforce corporate compliance with the guidelines. Their strictly voluntary nature meant that corporations faced no consequences for behaviors that cause staggering amounts of human suffering.[33]

These conclusions were also affirmed in a September 22, 2005, report by the organization OECD Watch, *Five Years On: A Review of the OECD Guidelines and National Contact Points*. The organization noted pessimistically, "There is no evidence to suggest that the Guidelines have helped reduce the number of conflicts between local communities, civil society groups and multinational companies." Key to failure of the guidelines was the fact that NCPs had generally adopted a narrow interpretation of when the guidelines ought to apply to corporations' activities. The NCPs argued that relationships between multinational businesses and their suppliers were trade-related rather than investments—and thus not subject to the guidelines. The corporations cited by the UN Panel were therefore at fault for buying plundered resources only if they actually owned the companies doing the plundering. These proponents of a narrow interpretation argued further that multinational corporations had little control over the other companies in their supply chains and so could not be blamed for the illegal and unethical behavior of companies more directly involved in extracting resources.

The NGOs argued that the text of the guidelines clearly showed that they applied to both investment and trade. They also argued that corporations must "readily accept responsibility for product quality in the supply chain and engineer their management practices to ensure product quality." Companies hire subcontractors in other countries to produce goods of a specified design and quality and could easily choose to hire people who do not violate the guidelines.

The OECD Watch report suggested ways to make the OECD Guidelines for Multinational Enterprises stronger by enhancing the power of NCPs, governments, and NGOs to address corporate abuses. For example, it suggested appointing NCPs who were more independent of their governments and of business interests and who had more power to investigate violations of the guidelines. These NCPs would present annual reports to parliaments and have their decisions scrutinized by parliamentary committees or ombudsmen. Governments could provide subsidies, export credits, and political-risk insurance for corporations only if corporations observed the OECD guidelines. NGOs could have the power to challenge NCPs who were interpreting the guidelines too narrowly. In countries that were not signatories to the OECD guidelines, NGOs could present complaints directly to NCPs through the diplomatic staff from the corporations' home countries.[34]

If national and international governing bodies do not mandate such reforms, the corporatocracy and its local suppliers will continue to shirk responsibility for funding wars and human rights abuses.

Testimony

When I first came to Congo in October 2005, I tried to understand the situation there using other projects that my NGO, Christian Peacemaker Teams, has established over the years as frames of reference. In both Haiti and Chiapas, we had lived among people targeted by paramilitary violence. We had accompanied rural and urban Palestinians facing violence by Israeli soldiers and settlers.

At the time of the invasion of Iraq in 2003, we had set up camps near water-treatment plants and hospitals in order to protect the infrastructure when the U.S. began bombing. (Destruction of these plants in the first Gulf War and the imposition of sanctions caused a grave humanitarian crisis in subsequent years.) After we began hearing stories of U.S. forces abusing Iraqi families during home raids and torturing Iraqi detainees (almost all of whom never had charges brought against them), our team began documenting these abuses. We sent reports to all relevant U.S. military and civilian authorities three months before the story of Abu Ghraib broke.[35]

Of all the Christian Peacemaker Team projects I have worked on, Colombia struck me as bearing the most resemblance to the situation in Congo. Colombia is also a resource-rich country. Its resources fuel military, paramilitary, and guerrilla groups whose victims are mostly civilians. Acts of terror—kidnapping, torture, and mutilating bodies—enable armed groups to control the resources. Multinational corporations have a vested interest in preventing meaningful democratic change.

However, Colombia has a more or less functioning government, judicial system, and press—even though government representatives, prosecutors, judges, and reporters are often murdered. (A Colombian church leader once told us, "In Colombia you are free to say whatever you want, and anyone else is free to kill you for saying it.") Colombian church and civic groups, and small settlements of *campesinos* in the Magdalena Medio region we visited, immediately saw ways that a CPT presence might open some political space for them to work for social reforms. About a hundred families displaced by paramilitary groups moved back to their farms with the promise of CPT accompaniment.

In contrast, few Congolese saw any use for the work that CPT has done traditionally in the Americas and the Middle East. We asked about accompanying women when they cultivated the fields and were told that we would inevitably meet the same fate as the Congolese in an attack by armed groups. "Of course you would be raped," said a woman who works with the Department of Women and Children in Bukavu. Indeed, we were told, the presence of white people might actually cause militias to target the Congolese communities hosting us (although black internationals *might* be able to travel surreptitiously into the countryside and document atrocities there, several women told us).

So we were left feeling helpless. We could refuse to use technology made cheap by the pillage in Congo. But the corporatocracy has millions of consumers lined up to take our places. Besides, cell phones, laptops, and digital cameras have dramatically enhanced the ability of human rights workers to document abuses by governments and individuals.

In the end, once they found out that we were not aid and development workers, most of the Congolese we met said that they just wanted their stories told. So I am telling you about fifty or sixty rape survivors who clapped and sang for us as we entered the Lutheran meeting hall in Bukavu. About the Lutheran laywoman who told us, "When they are singing they can forget what happened." About the dejected pastor who brightened only when we talked about bringing delegations of women from North America to meet the 250 survivors under his care. About the university student who said of Western nations, "They denounce things and nothing happens, so the international community must want it to happen."

And I will proclaim the tragedies of baby Esther and her mother. The first is the rape that forced them to the margins of a devastated society. The second is the reality that Congo has more than enough wealth for Esther and the millions of other Congolese children to have an abundance of nutritious food, clean water, education, and decent medical care for the rest of their lives. But its resources go instead to adorn the wealthy with jewelry and to manufacture PlayStations, cell phones, and weapons systems for affluent First World societies.

John Perkins' term *economic hit man* seems almost too tame for the behavior of the corporatocracy and its minions in Congo. An unflinching look at what they have done to the Congolese makes *economic war criminals* seem more apt.

And like all unrepentant hit men and war criminals, they belong in prison for the protection of society.

Notes

1. In this chapter, *Congo* refers to the Democratic Republic of Congo (DRC), the nation once called Zaire, whose capital is Kinshasa—as opposed to the Republic of Congo, which borders the DRC and whose capital is Brazzaville.

2. Testimony in a congressional hearing conducted by Representative Cynthia McKinney, April 16, 2001, www.house.gov/mckinney/news/pr010416.htm.

3. The International Rescue Committee estimated in 2004 that approximately 3.9 million people have died since 1998 because of the instability: 38,000 deaths occur in Congo every month above what is considered a "normal level" for the country, translating into 1,250 excess deaths every day. Over 70 percent of these deaths, most due to easily preventable and treatable diseases, occur in the insecure eastern provinces. "Less than two percent of the deaths were directly due to violence," Richard J. Brennan points out. "However, if the effects of violence—such as the insecurity that limits access to health care facilities—were removed, mortality rates would fall to almost normal levels." The British medical journal *Lancet* confirms the IRC statistic of 3.9 million war-related deaths between 1998 and 2004. It also notes that every few months "the mortality equivalent of two southeast Asian tsunamis [referring to the December 2004 catastrophe] ploughs through its territory." *Lancet* declares that the high mortality rates are ongoing: "Preemptive War Epidemiology: Lessons from the Democratic Republic of Congo." The

primary article discussing the procedure by which the IRC and the *Lancet* came up with their statistics is Benjamin Coghlan, Richard J. Brennan, Pascal Ngoy, et al., "Mortality in the Democratic Republic of Congo: A Nationwide Survey," *Lancet 367* (January 7, 2006), www.thelancet.com.

4. In 1961, the U.S. installed Mobutu, who had, with the support of the U.S. and Belgium, assassinated Patrice Lumumba, the first prime minister of Congo/Zaire after Belgium granted the country independence. Lumumba was a Pan-Africanist and populist, unwilling to ally with either the U.S. or the Soviet Union. After he publicly advocated using Congo's resources to benefit the Congolese, the diamond corporation DeBeers feared it would lose access to Congo's diamonds; Lumumba's stand no doubt hastened his demise. Once Lumumba was out of the way, acting Prime Minister Adoula approved a deal with DeBeers's negotiator Maurice Tempelsman and telegrammed the news to U.S. President John F. Kennedy. A 1961 State Department memo headed "Congo Diamond Deal" concluded that the U.S. ought to support the proposal: "How US Foreign Policy over Decades Was Influenced by the Diamond Cartel," www.minesandcommunities. org/Company/diamonds1.htm. This Web site contains a partial transcript from an April 6, 2001, discussion held by Congresswoman Cynthia McKinney at which Janine Farrell Roberts testified. Roberts's research appears in *Blood-Stained Diamonds: A Worldwide Diamond Investigation* (Bristol: Impact Media, 2001). Over the next decades, Mobutu pillaged the country, as the Belgians had before him, depositing billions of dollars in foreign banks. Tempelsman and his staff helped Mobutu run Congo/Zaire and secured funding for Mobutu from the United States. Mobutu, however, had begun to limit Western access to Congo's resources, and this may also have been a motive for the U.S. to support Kabila, Rwanda, and Uganda in their quest to overthrow Mobutu. Tempelsman is a major donor to the Democratic Party. During the presidency of Bill Clinton, he stayed at the White House several times and went sailing with the Clintons when they vacationed at Martha's Vineyard: Susan Schmidt, "Tempelsman Plan Got the Ear of U.S. Aides," *Washington Post*, August 2, 1997.

5. Madeleine Drohan, *Making a Killing: How and Why Corporations Use Armed Force to Do Business* (Guilford, Conn.: Lyon's Press, 2004), pp. 302–3.

6. "Report of the Panel of Experts on the Illegal Exploitation of Natural Resources and Other Forms of Wealth of the Democratic Republic of Congo," 2001, www.un.org/Docs/sc/letters/2001/357e.pdf; Asad Ismi, "Congo: The Western Heart of Darkness," *Canadian Centre for Policy Alternatives Monitor*, October 2001, posted on the Mines and Communities website, www.minesandcommunities.org/Country/congo1.htm.

7. Small coltan deposits have been mined for some time in Rwanda, Burundi, Uganda, and Zaire, where it is often found as a byproduct of cassiterite in industrial tin mining: Pole Institute, "The Coltan Phenomenon: How a Rare Mineral Has Changed the Life of the Population of War-Torn North Kivu Province in the East of the Democratic Republic of Congo," January 2002, www.pole-institute.org/documents/coltanglais02.pdf.

8. All Party Parliamentary Group on the Great Lakes Region and Genocide Prevention, "Illegal Minerals and Conflict," Parliamentary Briefing, March 2003, www.appggreat lakes.org/cgi-bin/site/index.cgi?back=&pid=27&keywords=&topic=Briefing_Papers. See also the official Rwandan response to the "Report of the Panel of Experts," 2001, at www.gov.rw/government/04_22_01news_Responce_To_UN_Report.htm.

9. "Report of the Panel of Experts," 2001. See also Dena Montague and Frida Berrigan, "The Business of War in the Democratic Republic of Congo," *Dollars and Sense*, July/August 2001. The report covers plunder by Congolese and Zimbabwean political, military,

and commercial interests, noting this network had transferred as much as US$5 billion of assets from the state mining sector to private companies. From 1998 to 2000, none of these transactions benefited Congo's treasury. The report notes that the rates of malnutrition and mortality in the government-held areas were a result of diverting resources from state companies such as Gécamines to corrupt Zimbabwean and Congolese officials.

10. "Report of the Panel of Experts," 2001, on the plunder of Congo, casts doubt on Rwanda's assertions that it was invading Congo for its own security. The Panel had a letter dated May 26, 2000, in which the Military High Command for RCD-Goma (a Rwandan-backed Congolese militia group) urged its units to maintain good relationships with their Interahamwe "brothers." A 30-year-old Interahamwe combatant living in Bukavu told United Nations personnel in 2002, "We haven't fought much with the RPA [Rwandan Patriotic Army] in the last two years. We think they are tired of this war, like we are. In any case, they aren't here in the Congo to chase us, like they pretend. I have seen the gold and coltan mining they do here, we see how they rob the population."

11. In an April 16, 2001, hearing Congresswoman Cynthia McKinney investigated charges that Kagame had orchestrated the April 6, 1994, assassination of the presidents of Rwanda and Burundi, shooting down their plane with surface-to-air missiles obtained from the U.S. via Uganda. Cameroonian journalist Charles Onana made similar claims in his book *The Secrets of the Rwandan Genocide.* Kagame sued him for defamation, but a Paris court found in favor of Onana. Sympathy for Tutsis in the West after the Rwandan genocide has given Kagame carte blanche to commit egregious human rights abuses in much the same way that the world does not hold Israel accountable for human rights abuses because of Germany's attempt to slaughter all the Jews during World War II. The Congolese resent this indulgent attitude toward Rwanda. At a guest house in Goma where our delegation stayed, the manager, discovering our intent to understand the roots of violence in the region, told us, "The Tutsis are a cruel people." He then described abuses committed by Tutsis in Rwanda before the genocide.

12. Montague and Berrigan, "The Business of War."

13. McKinney hearing, April 16, 2001.

14. Ismi, "Congo: The Western Heart of Darkness."

15. McKinney hearing, April 16, 2001.

16. Dena Montague, "Stolen Goods: Coltan and Conflict in the Democratic Republic of the Congo," *SAIS Review* 22, no. 1 (Winter–Spring 2002).

17. Amy Goodman and David Goodman, *The Exception to the Rulers: Exposing Oily Politicians, War Profiteers and the Media That Love Them* (New York: Hyperion Press, 2004).

18. Montague and Berrigan, "The Business of War"; Ismi, "Congo: The Western Heart of Darkness"; "Report of the Panel of Experts," 2001; *Five Years On: A Review of the OECD Guidelines and National Contact Points*, September 22, 2005, www.oecdwatch.org/docs/OECD_Watch_5_years_on.pdf; All Party Parliamentary Group, "Illegal Minerals and Conflict."

19. "Report of the Panel of Experts," 2001.

20. "IMF Concludes 2002 Article IV Consultation with Rwanda," September 20, 2002, www.imf.org/external/np/sec/pn/2002/pn02104.htm; "Rwanda Laying Foundations for 'Robust Growth,' " *afrol News,* www.afrol.com/html/News2002/rwa023_econ_growth.htm; "IMF Executive Board Completes Final Review of Uganda's PRGF Arrangement and Approves 16-Month Policy Support Instrument," Press Release No. 06/14, January 24, 2006.

21. One of these corporations was Kinross Forrest. Not surprisingly, it was headed by Belgian war profiteer George Forrest, whose past mineral piracy in the Congo had earned him censure by the UN: "Congo Asset Strip," *Mines and Communities Website,* February 27, 2006, www.minesandcommunities.org/Action/press949.htm.

22. Rights and Accountability in Development (RAID) press releases, "Group Calls on World Bank to Investigate Mining Contracts; Bank's Failed Reform Project in DR Congo," February 27, 2006; Letter to Paul Wolfowitz, President, World Bank Group, February 27, 2006, www.raid-uk.org/news.htm; "Congo Asset Strip," February 27, 2006. The World Bank also proved true to John Perkins's assessment of its morality in its dispersal of insurance money to corporations in Congo. The Multilateral Investment Guarantee Agency (MIGA), the insurance arm of the World Bank, approved "political-risk" insurance for Australian-owned Anvil Mining's copper and silver mine in Dikulushi in September 2004. One month later, Anvil provided logistical support to the Congolese army during its violent suppression of a small-scale rebel uprising in the nearby town of Kilwa. The offensive killed as many as 100 civilians. The World Bank investigated the matter, under the orders of Paul Wolfowitz, but delayed releasing the report until nongovernmental organizations protested. The Australian police are currently investigating Anvil, which has claimed that the army commandeered its vehicles and food. "World Bank Buries Internal Report on Controversial Congo Mining Project," January 31, 2006, http://www.choike.org/nuevo_eng/informes/3933.html.

23. Rights and Accountability in Development (RAID), *Unanswered Questions: Companies, Conflict and the Democratic Republic of Congo: Executive Summary,* report, April 2004, p. 2, www.raid-uk.org/docs/UN_Panel_DRC/Unanswered_Questions_Full.pdf.

24. Human Rights Watch, "The Curse of Gold: IX. International Initiatives to Address Resource Exploitation in the DRC," http://hrw.org/reports/2005/drc0505/12.htm#_Toc102992181; RAID, *Unanswered Questions*; All Party Parliamentary Group on the Great Lakes Region, "The OECD Guidelines and the DRC," February 7, 2005, www.appggreatlakes.org/cgi-bin/site/index.cgi?back=&pid=75&keywords=2005&topic=.

25. E-mail to the author, April 7, 2006.

26. See, for example, http://www.cbc.ca/story/news/national/2002/10/24/mining_congo021024.html0.

27. "OECD Guidelines for Multinational Enterprises: 2005 Annual Meeting of the National Contact Points," https://www.oecd.org/dataoecd/20/13/35387363.pdf.

28. See www.un.org/News/Press/docs/2003/sc7642.doc.htm. The Panel of Experts member cited wrote in his e-mail to the author, "It was clear that its purpose was not to do further research but rather to find some way to exonerate a large number of those companies who had been named."

29. Some corporations that had acquired cheap coltan from Rwanda during the coltan boom of 1999–2000 claimed that the fact that they had stopped buying it from Rwanda after 2001 meant that they were responsive to ethical considerations. For example, the U.S.-based Kemet Corporation announced in 2003 that it would require its suppliers to "provide a Letter of Certification that they do not or will not, (a) illegally mine any tantalum material from the Congolese mines, (b) purchase any illegal material containing tantalum, including coltan, from the Congolese mines and (c) sell any illegal material to KEMET from such mines": www.kemet.com/kemet/web/homepage/kechome.nsf/weben/KEMET%20Supports%20Avoiding%20Tantalum%20Mined%20in%20Restricted%20Areas%20of%20Congo. However, piracy might again serve as a useful analogy: pirates who had spent several years raping and pillaging their way up and down

a seacoast would not be absolved by the argument that "We haven't done that for at least two years."

30. See www.foe.org/camps/intl/unreportmemo.pdf. Copies of the UN reports and letters that FoE and the UK group RAID (Rights and Accountability in Development) have sent government officials regarding corporations' lack of compliance are available at www. foe.org/new/releases/84drccomplaint.html.

31. Friends of the Earth, "Groups File Complaint with State Department against Three American Companies Named in UN Report," August 4, 2004, www.foe.org/new/ releases/84drccomplaint.html. See also paragraphs 22–64 of the UN Panel of Experts' October 16, 2002, report, which covers the Congolese and Zimbabwean government networks in the illegal resource exploitation from Congo. Interestingly, the report from the 2005 annual meeting of National Contact Points noted, under a section entitled "Follow-up by NCPs," that "Finnish and U.S. NCPs have been exchanging views on a U.S.-based company and its Finnish subsidiary with reference to the deletion of the companies from the final Report of the UN Panel." The fact that the report does not mention the OM Group by name contributes to the impression that the role of the NCPs involves protecting corporations. "OECD Guidelines for Multinational Enterprises: 2005 Annual Meeting of the National Contact Points," www.oecd.org/dataoecd/20/13/35387363.pdf. FoE and RAID also brought up OM Group's environmental record as cited in a World Bank report. The report questioned whether the measures in place at OM Group's plant in Lubumbashi were sufficient to prevent radioactive contamination of the Congolese workforce and whether the local population was exposed to an unacceptably high level of pollution from operation of the plant.

32. Colleen Freeman, phone and e-mail interviews, December 2005–January 2006. Freeman worked with Friends of the Earth prior to taking a job with RAID. See also the report *Five Years On: A Review of the OECD Guidelines and National Contact Points,* September 22, 2005, available at www.oecdwatch.org/docs/OECD_Watch_ 5_years_on.pdf.

   I contacted the U.S. companies mentioned in the third UN report. Two of them, Cabot and Kemet, supplied links to Web pages responding to charges that they had profited from illegally obtained coltan. Cabot's page has a link to a PDF file stating, "Cabot will not purchase any tantalum supplies from any unlawful source in any part of the world." However, the 2001 UN Panel of Experts report noted, "In fact, no coltan exits from the eastern Democratic Republic of Congo without benefiting either the rebel group[s] or foreign armies." During the period covered by the report, 60 to 70 percent of the coltan in eastern Congo was mined under the surveillance of the Rwandan military, using the forced labor of prisoners. George W. Bush's secretary of energy (appointed in 2005), Samuel Bodman, was CEO and chair of Cabot Corp. in 1997–2001, when large quantities of illicit coltan from Congo hit the market and Cabot allegedly acquired them.

33. RAID, "Unanswered Questions," report, April 2004. Human Rights Watch echoes RAID's final suggestion in the report, writing, "The international community may want to consider a permanent roster of experts who can investigate these issues throughout the world, rather than ad hoc panels." Arvind Ganesan and Alex Vines, "Engine of War: Resources, Greed and the Predatory State," www.hrw.org/wr2k4/14.htm.

34. For more on this point, see http://www.raid-uk.org/news.htm.

35. Seymour Hersh, who broke the Abu Ghraib scandals in the American media, cited CPT as a source in his May 5, 2004, *New Yorker* article "Chain of Command." After the kidnapping of four CPTers in Baghdad, Hersh told *Democracy Now*'s Amy Goodman that the work of CPT was "cutting edge": www.democracynow.org/article.pl?sid=05/11/30/153252.

Private armies are increasingly part of corporate operations in the Third World. How one officer found himself defending Shell's grab for oil against the people of the Niger Delta.

6

Mercenaries on the Front Lines in the New Scramble for Africa

Andrew Rowell and James Marriott

"I like Nigeria. I like the pulse of Africa. It is very stimulating. I will miss it."[1] Nigel Watson-Clark always had a flair for excitement and a challenge. For twelve years, he saw active military service as a British Royal Marine, but he also had a passion for skydiving. A British national skydiving coach, he spent six years competing in championships.

Like many ex-service personnel, after leaving the Marines he took a variety of jobs, such as running a sky-diving school in Spain and working as a close protection officer—more commonly known as a personal bodyguard—in the UK. One of his friends worked on maritime security, and so Watson-Clark ended up working with Chevron in Angola. Then, in 2002, a job in Nigeria came up.

For the next three and half years, he coordinated the security needs of Shell in a strategic offshore oil field. His official job was security liaison officer for the Echo Alpha Field. His main concern was protecting Shell's orange-colored floating oil platform, the *Sea Eagle*, some seven miles offshore.[2] He was stationed on a dedicated 250-foot-long security vessel called the *Liberty Service* that was owned by a subsidiary of the American company Tidewater. Based in Louisiana, Tidewater owns the world's largest fleet of vessels serving the oil and gas industry.[3]

There was a simple reason for Watson-Clark to be there. The creeks and shallow waters of Nigeria's Niger Delta are strategically important to both the oil industry and the Nigerian government. In fact, oil is the lifeblood of the government, accounting for more than 80 percent of its revenues, 90 percent of the country's foreign exchange earnings, and 40 percent of its gross domestic product.[4]

Nigerian oil and gas are core assets for Shell as well as for the American companies Chevron and ExxonMobil.[5] Currently the Delta represents over 10 percent of the Shell Group's production. Meanwhile Shell controls over 50 percent of the oil and gas reserves in the country.[6] Shell's corporate fate and that of Nigeria are thus intertwined.

Vessels such as Tidewater's *Liberty Service* are an essential part of the oil industry web that stretches across continents. Shell is part of this web, and its operations in Nigeria could not exist without the web's structure of subsidiary companies, subcontractors, and consultants.

Shell's International Web

The web of control is truly international: Royal Dutch Shell's global operations are controlled from the Hague and London. Its Hague-based Exploration and Production Division controls its Nigerian arm, Shell Companies in Nigeria, based in Lagos. One of several subsidiaries of Shell Companies in Nigeria is SNEPCO, the Shell Nigeria and Exploration Company. SNEPCO had engaged the company Ecodrill (itself a subsidiary of the larger Expro Group) to assist in its oil production operations. It was Ecodrill that employed Watson-Clark, who worked on one of Tidewater's vessels. Tidewater itself, though based in Louisiana, runs its West African operations not from Nigeria, but from Aberdeen, the oil capital of Scotland.

To operate effectively in a country as corrupt as Nigeria, Shell, its subsidiaries, and its contractors have to maintain extremely close contacts with several layers of government and different branches of Nigeria's military. That is the only way of doing business. Sometimes this closeness manifests itself as a revolving door between corporation and government. At other times it takes the form of a financial relationship between the corporation and the Nigerian military or Mobile Police Force (MPF). For years Shell denied that any such financial relationship existed but now admits it. Nigerians often see no difference between the government and Shell or between Shell and the military, just as they see no difference between Shell and its contractors. To the people they are all part of a governing alliance of interests.

Hostages Taken

January 11, 2006. On board the *Liberty Service* were the ship's sixty-one-year-old American skipper, Patrick Landry, and two engineers: Milko Nichev, fifty-four, from Bulgaria, and Harry Ebanks, fifty-four, from Honduras. Also stationed on the vessel were twelve men from the Nigerian navy, who were being paid by Shell. It was Watson-Clark's job to oversee Shell's security, to look after the *Liberty Service* crew, and to train the Nigerians, who had two inflatable dinghies, known as *ribs*. "Their job was securing the field in the case of any incursion or invasion," said Watson-Clark. "We were patrolling 24/7 on the *Liberty Service*. It was quite a unique role—we never went to port, we never left the field."

Watson-Clark was essentially a front-line soldier in the web of oil exploitation—a soldier working for a private company rather than a state. Colonizing powers have always used armed forces to protect their commercial assets in the Delta. The role he was playing had changed little from that of an English mariner in the 1660s. Then soldiers were employed by the Royal Navy and sent to protect the ships of the Royal African Company, which were transporting slaves from the creeks of the Delta to the American colonies. For 150 years Britain played a pivotal role in the Atlantic slave trade. After slavery came palm oil plantations. Now the exploited resources are oil and gas.

The security liaison officer was about to be caught up in the vortex of violence that has swirled over the Niger Delta for the past four decades. The heart of the crisis is oil—who controls it, who benefits, and who suffers as a result.

For forty years the communities of the Niger Delta have been campaigning for a greater share of the oil wealth that has been pumped from under their land. They have benefited very little from it. Some people have grown rich, but rampant Nigerian corruption has meant that they were a very small elite. The oil companies have grown rich, too, but complicated tax maneuvers steered much of their profit quietly out of Nigeria before anyone realized just how much money they had made. Ordinary people have nothing to show for the oil extraction, and the communities of the Delta have remained extremely poor.

Currently the Nigerian federal government is supposed to return 13 percent of oil revenue to the Niger Delta states where the oil is extracted. In reality, a far smaller percentage makes it back to the communities. Living in the underbelly of the oil world, these states have suffered from oil's unglamorous excesses: routine air and water pollution and twenty-four-hour-a-day gas flaring that roars into the African night, rots corrugated roofs, and burns the backs of people's throats.

For forty years, the communities have complained about their plight. Often their protests have been met with ruthless military force that has left thousands dead and countless others injured or homeless.[7] Children as young as ten have been raped or tortured. Whole villages and towns have been destroyed. It is difficult to summarize the suffering of the Delta people in words. After one attack on the town of Odi in 1999, Nigerian Senate President Chuba Okadigbo said simply: "The facts speak for themselves. There is no need for speech because there is nobody to speak with."[8]

As the simmering bitterness has grown over the last ten years, the young people of the Delta have become more radical, turning to new tactics to fight back and increasingly using violence and hostage taking. Because of the violence, Watson-Clark's role was dangerous—contractors like him are often the targets of community anger in the Delta. Shell's senior executives are powerful but far away and invisible, but the contractors are very visible and extremely exposed. And using contractors, not direct employees, gives Shell a useful level of deniability.

On January 11, tensions were high. The security level on the *Liberty Service* had been increased. Just how exposed Watson-Clark and his crew were became clear that afternoon, when he spotted three speedboats with forty men on board approaching fast. The occupants wore the traditional symbols of Ijaw warriors. One of the naval ribs was sent out to intercept them. "We intercepted the three boats, but, as the navy approached, they saw that they were outmanned and out-gunned, and they retreated," recalled Watson-Clark. "There was a tactical withdrawal."

Some Nigerian navy security men were still on board the *Liberty Service*. "To be quite honest I thought we were on top of the situation, although they [the rebels] were heavily armed. I thought we would be able to handle it," said Watson-Clark. All the practice drills were put into place.

He managed to get the other supply vessels out of the area and the floating storage vessel, the *Sea Eagle*, "locked down." Then those under Watson-Clark's command began shooting with live rounds. "I believe our navy opened fire first, and then they [the rebels] opened fire with everything they had. We took heavy rounds." Bullets used against the *Liberty Service* included armor-piercing rounds. "It was very dramatic, very violent, and it overwhelmed our navy."

Watson-Clark was on the bridge. All around him instruments exploded as they were hit by bullets. Miraculously no one was hurt apart from Watson-Clark, who received only a cut on his chin. But the Nigerian navy could not repel the rebels—the men in the ribs refused to fight and those on board just hid. "Once that happened, the militants just started to board. There was no one left. We had to surrender. It was then that I thought, 'This is not good.' I don't know why, but I wasn't scared. I had never been in a firefight like that before, even in the Marines. It was like being in the middle of a movie."

Only after being taken captive did Watson-Clark realize that the attackers might not have intended to take hostages. A massive argument broke out among the rebels about whether to attack the *Sea Eagle* with rocket-propelled grenades. Within three hours the hostages had been taken into the myriad creeks that make up the Niger Delta. To the outside world, they had disappeared into the swamps. News of the attack sent the global price of oil skyrocketing.[9]

For Watson-Clark and the other hostages, captivity was just beginning. "They identified me as the Shell representative straight away," he recalled. "They always addressed everything to me. Some of the military guys did not like what I stood for. To them I represented what they were fighting against: Shell and the federal government."

Enter China: A New Economic Competitor

That same day—January 11—China's foreign minister, Li Zhaoxing, flew to Africa to begin a weeklong tour aimed at supplying China's growing needs for African oil and gas—a trip that, of course, included Nigeria. A seasoned diplomat—China's former ambassador to the United States—Li was sent to Africa's capitals for one reason: the continent's rich resources. China, like many countries, needed more African oil. China's consumption had risen exponentially in the past decade. By 2005 China was dependent on imports for 40 percent of its oil needs,[10] making it the world's second largest oil importer after the United States.

Two days into Li Zhaoxing's trip, China released its first-ever white paper on the continent. "Africa is abundant in natural resources which are urgently needed by China's economic development," assistant Foreign Minister Lu Guozeng told the press.[11] On his trip, Li outlined how China's plans to boost its ties with Africa were based on a "win-win" concept of economic and military cooperation.[12] China intended to access the resources and give military cooperation in return.

His visit did not go unnoticed in the oil capitals of the world. The week before, the Chinese state-controlled oil company, CNOOC, had announced that it was paying $2.3 billion for a 45 percent stake in an offshore Nigerian oil block. The decision had analysts perplexed: this block had been shunned by Shell and other Western oil majors, and even the acquisitive Oil and Natural Gas Corporation of India had refused to buy it because of the dubious legality of its ownership. China's purchase showed just how much risk it was prepared to take in its desire to buy overseas energy assets.[13]

The deal was heralded by China and Nigeria as mutually beneficial. "China is a giant market with giant needs, and we can fulfill them," said Ngozi Okonjo-Iweala, the Nigerian finance minister and a former World Bank vice president.[14] "The [Nigerian] deal gives CNOOC its first base in Africa. We will explore further opportunities in the continent," said Fu Chengyu, president of CNOOC.[15] In just six months, Chinese firms had signed oil deals worth $7 billion in Kazakhstan, Nigeria, and Syria.[16] Six weeks later CNOOC signed another oil agreement in Equatorial Guinea.

Washington's Interest in the Delta

Nowhere was China's interest in African oil being more closely monitored than in Washington. Ever since 9/11, the U.S. had been looking to protect its economic security through diversifying its sources of energy. For the last five years, the Bush administration and a whole host of influential right-wing think tanks had seen West Africa, and Nigeria in particular, as a counterbalance to dependence on Middle Eastern oil. Africa was the "next Gulf"—a reservoir of oil away from such troublesome countries such as Iraq, Iran, and Saudi Arabia.

Nigeria currently supplies 10 percent of America's oil, but U.S. government officials expect that amount to increase rapidly. Some 30 percent of America's oil will come from Africa in the next ten years.[17]

If West African oil is increasingly important to the U.S., its protection needs to be increasingly strengthened. Since 9/11, in conference after conference and report after report, analysts have argued that the Gulf of Guinea should be declared an area of "vital interest" to the U.S., to be protected by American military power. For example, Republican Congressman Ed Royce told an oil conference in January 2002, "I think that African oil should be treated as a priority for US national security post-9/11."[18]

Attending the same conference as Royce was Lieutenant Colonel Karen Kwiatkowski from the Department of Defense's Office of African Affairs. She, too, emphasized how "important Africa is to US defense policy and US security" and explained how the U.S. had recently developed "International Military Education and Training" in Nigeria. The number of defense attachés to Africa had doubled in the past three years. Kwiatkowski asserted that the military was keen to understand the challenges of U.S. energy companies and investors in sub-Saharan Africa: "The more we know, the more we might be able to help."[19]

Out of the symposium a working group was formed called the African Oil Policy Initiative Group. Its report was handed to the House Energy and Commerce Committee on June 12, 2002. The committee's chair, Republican Billy Tauzin from Louisiana, said, "9/11 has reawakened the awareness of the American public to our extraordinary dependence on energy from the Middle East. It has taught us the value once again of diversifying energy supplies. It is important for us to build new relations with new sources of supply . . . and to look toward Africa and other regions of the world."[20] One of the report's key recommendations was that "Congress and the Administration should declare the Gulf of Guinea an area of 'Vital Interest'" to the U.S.[21]

Since then, other think tanks have touted similar conclusions: "The United States has vital—indeed rising—national interests in West and Central Africa, concentrated in, but not restricted to, Nigeria and Angola," reported a task force from the Center for Strategic and International Studies (CSIS) in March 2004. This "complex, unsteady zone" was critical to the "security and diversification of U.S. energy supply."[22] In July 2005, a new CSIS task force recommended that the U.S. should "make security and governance in the Gulf of Guinea an explicit priority in US foreign policy."[23]

The same month that Watson-Clark was taken hostage, the influential Council on Foreign Relations published a report by its Independent Task Force on Africa. Once again the importance of African oil to U.S. national security was recognized. But now the threat of China competing for that oil was also realized. "By the end of the decade," said the report, "sub-Saharan Africa is likely to become as important a source of U.S. energy imports as the Middle East. China, India, Europe, and others are competing with each other and with the United States for access to oil, natural gas, and other natural resources."

One of the co-chairs of the task force was Anthony Lake, former assistant to the national security adviser in the Clinton administration and in 2002 chair of the U.S. Committee for UNICEF working on humanitarian aid. At a seminar discussing the report, Lake outlined how U.S. interests in Africa went beyond "humanitarian" concerns into three major issues: oil, China, and terrorism. "Africa will provide the largest incremental increase in oil production over the next two or three years anywhere in the world. By 2010, Africa could be providing us with as many oil imports as the Middle East."

A second interest, Lake continued, "is China. China now gets 28 percent of its oil imports from Africa. It owns 40 percent of the oil industry in Sudan. Because its government is so involved in supporting its companies, it is able to compete with American companies in very effective, not to say unfair, terms. For example, recently it made a $2 billion loan to Angola, secured by future oil deliveries, to win a bid for oil exploration there. And it is competing in similar ways for the oil resources that we need so desperately throughout the oil-rich Gulf of Guinea, including notably in Nigeria."[24]

Although Lake asserted that China was not America's enemy in Africa, it *was* "undercutting" efforts for greater transparency, better business practices, and less corruption on the continent.

Another chair of the task force was Stephen Morrison, who is also the director of the Africa Program at CSIS and another former Clinton official. Morrison was a central figure in the debate on African oil exploitation and the need for transparency in business dealings. Agreeing with right-wing think tanks in Washington that African oil should be labeled an area of vital U.S. interest, Morrison also asserted that these dealings needed to be transparent and to promote development and human rights.

A cynical observer might argue that this stance is clever: there have been so many decades of corrupt deals with little money going to the local population that the status quo cannot continue. If U.S. energy security can be guaranteed only by African oil, exploiting that oil can be guaranteed only if America can claim that Africans are benefiting from oil development. Transparency in oil deals then becomes a tool to make exploitation of African oil acceptable to the wider community.

Just as Washington and European capitals were wielding these new tools of exploitation, however, here came China advocating the same old tools: the raw power of money, with little or no regard for human rights, let alone transparency. "China has come to advance its own commercial and strategic interest on the basis of unsentimental, hard-headed logic," wrote Rory Carroll in the *Guardian*. "They have come to make money, and as much as possible."[25]

China's moves into Africa had certainly ruffled feathers in Washington. "America and its allies and friends are finding that their vision of a prosperous Africa governed by democracies that respect human rights and the rule of law and that embrace free markets is being challenged by the escalating Chinese influence in Africa," wrote the right-wing Heritage Foundation in Washington. "China's burgeoning relationship with Africa is alarming not only because it has facilitated Chinese energy and weapons dealings, but also because it is competing with U.S.-African trade."[26] A right-wing think tank that had spawned the ruthless era of Reagan economics was now bemoaning the unscrupulous behavior of China, the new economic power on the block! Just as the old hit men of Africa—the U.S. and Europe—were sporting a veneer of conscience toward the continent, the new hit man—China—was not only muscling in on their patch but also doing so with a business attitude that the old hit men had belatedly declared amoral and out of date.

At the end of the day, though, both sets of hit men are advocating exploitation no matter how it is presented. One scholar at the Chinese Academy of Social Sciences argued in an interview with the *Economist* that China's behavior was actually reminiscent of that of the old colonial powers. "Since we are mainly there to make money and get hold of their resources," he said, "it's hard to see the difference."[27]

The Militarization of Commerce

"They made it brutally clear that we weren't going anywhere for a long time. I knew we were in a very difficult situation," recalled Nigel Watson-Clark. He and the other hostages had been taken to a village somewhere in the Niger Delta. "Between the four of us there was a feeling that we were in a lot of trouble and that it was going to be very difficult to find our way out."

After two days of captivity, Watson-Clark was instructed to phone the Reuters news agency. Reading from a script, he spelled out a list of the militants' demands. These included control of oil by the local region; payment of £1.5 billion by Shell to compensate for its pollution of the area; release of Alhaji Asari, the Ijaw leader of the Niger Delta People's Volunteer Force; release of former Bayelsa State Governor Chief Diepreye Alamieyeseigha; and expulsion of foreigners from the region.

"The main demands were more control of the resources, all ex-pats to leave, and the £1.5 billion to the Bayelsa State," Watson-Clark said. "At no point did they suggest that they wanted money themselves. They were not asking for the normal hostage-release terms." For the better part of a decade, "normal" hostage taking in the Delta had been a means of raising cash—but this was different. As soon as he read the demands, Watson-Clark's heart sank; he realized that there was no way they would be met.

He soon had another problem to deal with. His captors were monitoring CNN and the BBC to find out how much publicity their hostage taking had generated. They were annoyed at how little coverage they received. Bizarrely, the world's press was fixated at the time on a whale stuck in the River Thames in London: "That whale really, really made them angry."

Watson-Clark's captors identified themselves as MEND, the Movement for the Emancipation of the Niger Delta. They were labeled "pirates," "guerillas," and "shadowy" by the world's press but were young men from the Delta whose lives had been so blighted by oil that they had resorted to violent rebellion to raise awareness of their plight. MEND may have been a new name, but their demands were rooted in the oil conflict. To the people of the Niger Delta, particularly the Ijaw people, the demands made perfect sense. As one MEND member told a British journalist: "We have no water to drink, no schools, no electricity, no jobs." Another said: "We are not terrorists; we are freedom fighters."[28]

According to people close to the conflict, MEND represents different groups of Ijaw youth who have become increasingly radicalized over the last few years. The Ijaw are one of the largest ethnic groups in the Delta and one of the most vocal communities fighting the oil industry, along with the much smaller Ogoni. Both communities, like others in the Delta, have long demanded greater control of the wealth from the oil drilled on their land. They have also campaigned for just compensation for the pollution and degradation of their region.

It was the Ogoni who won the attention of the global media when their leader, Ken Saro-Wiwa, was murdered by the Nigerian military after a sham trial in 1995. Two of the chief prosecution witnesses at that trial later testified that they had been bribed by Shell and others to give evidence against Saro-Wiwa,[29] a claim that the company vehemently denies.[30]

The first recorded protest by the Ogoni against Shell took place in 1966, just eight years after Shell found oil in the Delta. The following year, an Ijaw named Isaac Boro, equipped with £150 and a red flag, formed the Niger Delta Volunteer Service and staged a revolt. "If we do not move," he wrote, "we would throw ourselves into perpetual slavery." He took issue with the oil companies and "their continued atrocities to our people and their wicked reluctance to improve the lot of the people." Soldiers were transported to the scene of the revolt on Shell's boats. Soon after, Boro surrendered, and the first Ijaw revolution was over.

Boro's short revolution inspired Alhaji Dokubo Asari to form the Niger Delta People's Volunteer Force in 2004 and to threaten an all-out war in the Delta. His threat sent shock waves through the oil industry, and world oil prices surged. Unsurprisingly he was arrested and charged with treason. There remains a wide-spread demand among the Ijaw people that Asari be released.

A further demand from MEND was release of Bayelsa State Governor Chief Diepreye Alamieyeseigha, who is a hero in Ijawland for demanding a greater share of oil revenue. But he had also been arrested on charges of corruption and money laundering. The final demand was that Shell comply with a recent Nigerian court order and pay $1.5 billion in compensation for pollution in the Niger Delta, especially in Ijawland. So MEND was asking for what the courts had already decreed. Indeed, the following month a Nigerian federal court upheld the judgment,[31] but Shell still refuses to pay.

Although Boro's revolution put poverty and pollution on the country's political map, the response to it set a precedent that has continued ever since: oil companies collude with the army to repress any dissent. The deadly pattern has been repeated as the people have asked for a fairer share of the oil revenues and an end to pollution. In the early 1980s the people of Iko in Andoniland were arrested and mistreated after a demonstration. In 1987 two people were killed and nearly forty houses destroyed after the Mobile Police Force (MPF), locally dubbed the Kill and Go Force, were called in.[32] In 1990, eighty died and 495 houses were destroyed when the MPF attacked the community of Umuechem; Shell had specifically requested the MPF after another demonstration against the company.[33] The list goes on. Thousands of Ogoni were killed in the early 1990s in security force retaliation for their campaign against Shell.

In May 1994 the local military commander, Major Paul Okuntimo, wrote: "Shell operations still impossible unless ruthless military operations are undertaken for smooth economic activities to commence."[34] And so ruthless military operations happened. Shell later admitted that on at least one occasion it had paid the field allowances of Okuntimo and his men.[35]

Conflicts involved not just the Ogoni and not just Shell. In the late 1990s two Illaje youths were killed after unarmed young men occupied a Chevron oil platform. Once again the MPF had been called—and arrived in Chevron helicopters. Months later, Nigerian forces, this time paid by Chevron, killed four, and some sixty-seven protesters went missing. The late Nigerian academic Claude Ake called this government–company interdependence "the militarization of commerce," the blurring of private oil company and state in oppression and violence.[36]

In December 2003, a leaked report noted that when Shell staff "and particularly senior staff, visit the community they are typically escorted by the Mobile Police." The same report noted that the way Shell operated "creates, feeds into or exacerbates conflict" and that "after 50 years in Nigeria" Shell had become "an integral part of the Niger Delta conflict system."[37]

But other players are also poised to become part of the conflict. As Watson-Clark and the other captured contractors suffered from diarrhea and fatigue in the swamps,[38] the red carpet was rolled out at Abuja's airport for China's Foreign Minister Li Zhaoxing. In a move of diplomatic quid pro quo, Li added China's weight to Nigeria's campaign for Africa to be given a seat on the UN Security Council: "China is in support of Africa's aspirations for UN reforms," he said, forgetting to mention that China had consistently blocked UN resolutions condemning Sudan for the genocide occurring in Darfur. Now China wanted African oil.[39]

"China and Nigeria are good friends," he said. "We've a lot in common in the fields of politics, economics, sports and the exchange of students."[40] Trade, sports, and students are not all the Nigerians are looking for from the Chinese. When, in the same month, Nigerian Vice President Atiku Abubakar was interviewed by the *Financial Times*, he expressed frustration with the slow response of the U.S. to the fight against rebels like MEND. He explained that, in the absence of U.S. support, Nigeria was increasingly looking to the Chinese government to supply weapons systems. In 2005 the Chinese won a $250 million deal to supply Nigeria with twelve fighter jets, and there were reports that China would provide dozens of patrol boats to secure the creeks of the Delta.[41]

Although the Americans have increased their military presence in the Gulf of Guinea in recent years to protect their interests, once again the Chinese moved with a swiftness that surprised many. It may have been a British foot-soldier who was still hostage, but his captors could soon be facing Chinese weapons. The more China invests in oil assets in the Delta, the more it will become involved in the militarization of those assets.

As the days went on, Watson-Clark's captors came back with tales of killings and gunfights. "It became very, very difficult," he recalled. "Things became more and more desperate as every day went by. I am quite optimistic by nature, but pessimism, and this overwhelming feeling of sadness that we weren't going to get out, dominated the mood. It was real."

In the Media Spotlight

The hostage crisis could not have come at a worse time for Dr. Edmund Daukoru. The Nigerian minister of state for petroleum resources, Daukoru had become the president of OPEC on January 1, 2006. Every New Year's Day, the oil cartel rotates the presidency, and now it was Nigeria's turn. As the minister responsible for oil, it was Daukoru who wore the coveted crown.

This was set to be his year of global fame, and the youthful-looking sixty-two-year-old had been looking forward to his first two major appearances as OPEC's president. The humble boy from the Delta had come a long way, most of it with Shell Oil Company. "I have been an oilman right from the beginning," said Daukoru. "After acquiring primary and secondary education, I was picked by Shell to go abroad for my studies; I studied geology at the Imperial College in London. On finishing my doctorate degree program, I came back to join Shell. I have thus been a Shell man right from the beginning: first as a scholar, then an employee."[42] Daukoru had worked for the company in the Netherlands, Italy, Spain, France, Switzerland, Tunisia, and, of course, Nigeria.

This Shell man "went through the ranks and became the first indigenous chief geologist in the industry, then first indigenous general manager and director of exploration." At the time this was the highest position a Nigerian could reach in Shell. Daukoru was then seconded by Shell to become the managing director of the Nigerian National Petroleum Corporation (NNPC) for eighteen months in 1992–93.[43]

However, soon after the dictator General Sani Abacha came to power in 1993, Daukoru was sacked at NNPC.[44] He retired, only to be asked six years later by President Olusegun Obasanjo to be his presidential adviser. On his appointment as minister of state for petroleum resources in 2005, Daukoru declared, "We must take our destiny in our own hands."[45]

He is not the only oil man to move from Shell to government. Chief Rufus Ada George, an ex–Shell Petroleum Development Company (SPDC) employee, was governor of Rivers State in the Delta during the Ogoni uprisings in the early 1990s. Godwin Omene, a deputy managing director of SPDC, was appointed head of the Niger Delta Development Commission in 2001. Ernest Shonekan, who briefly became Nigeria's president in 1993, was an SPDC director.

This revolving door of senior Shell staff to positions in government only adds to the belief in the Delta that Shell and the government are one. Indeed, the Ogoni activist Ken Saro-Wiwa once remarked about a forthcoming community protest, "It is anti-Shell. It is anti-Federal government, because as far as we are concerned the two are in league to destroy the Ogoni people."

Saro-Wiwa's fight against Shell cost him his life, whereas Daukoru's career within Shell took him to the heights of the oil industry. Two men born in the Delta, two men whose destiny was shaped by oil, but two very different outcomes. Both men became international news. For Saro-Wiwa the news-making event was his death; for Daukoru, his appointment as president of OPEC.

Daukoru's story personifies how the revolving door between company and state allows a tiny elite to benefit from oil exploitation. But Daukoru, as a black, is one of the few exceptions to the rule within the oil industry. Shell managing directors had all been white until 2004, when Basil Omiyi became the first Nigerian to head Shell's main subsidiary in Nigeria—Shell Petroleum Development Company.

On his OPEC appointment, Shell man Daukoru changed from having national Nigerian prominence to having international importance. He was hailed in the Nigerian press: "The move will bolster international commercial confidence in investing in Nigeria," proclaimed *Business Day*.[46]

His first appearance as OPEC president was at the World Economic Forum at Davos, Switzerland, the annual get-together of the world's business and political elite. Davos nestles snugly in the Swiss Alps; outside the conference hall, clear, crisp blue skies formed the backdrop to chalets laden with snow. Inside the hall, some 2,300 delegates had come to the ultimate exclusive net-working event.

OPEC had been represented at Davos for over a decade, but this year it was putting on a special program featuring an "Energy Summit" with the theme of "Managing Tectonic Shifts." Dr. Daukoru was in high-powered company. Bill Gates, the world's richest man, was there; so, too, were political giants such as Bill Clinton, UN Secretary Kofi Annan, President of the World Bank Paul Wolfowitz, and UK Chancellor of the Exchequer Gordon Brown. Hollywood stars such as Michael Douglas whisked in and out; sports legends such as Pele and Muhammad Ali and rock star Bono all made appearances in Davos.

Inside the hall, there was heavyweight business to attend to. The growing importance of China and India featured heavily on the agenda. Having just recorded GNP growth of 9.9 percent, China was grabbing headlines. Zeng Peiyan, China's vice premier, was quick to assure the audience that the expected surge in Chinese energy consumption would not put a strain on oil and gas prices. "China is not only a major energy consumer, it is also a major energy producer," he said.[47]

Daukoru, too, was keen to soothe frayed nerves over the energy market. At a working lunch on the second day of the conference he gave his address. He started by examining the last two years of the market. "There has been the challenge of meeting exceptionally high levels of growth in oil demand from large emerging economies, especially China and India, as well as from some developed economies, such as the USA."

Daukoru continued by arguing that if there was one outstanding challenge it was the need to prevent rapid upheavals in the energy market in the future. "The century began with three years of high market stability, which was to the satisfaction of all responsible parties," he said. "But, since then, we have been experiencing a very different and much more volatile situation."

If he meant the crisis unfolding back home, he did not say. But the issue of the hostages was making other news at Davos, too. The chair of Royal Dutch Shell, Jeroen Van der Veer, talked about the hostages. Funsho Kupolokun from the Nigerian National Petroleum Corporation assured delegates that "the Niger Delta is safe." The latest unrest was just a periodic flare-up—something oil companies such as Shell were accustomed to in the Delta.

"What you are seeing now is just another round. It will be dealt with very rapidly," Kupolokun said. If anything, the hostage taking had diverted attention away from the fact that Nigeria and West Africa were developing new production faster than OPEC. "With advancing technology, reserves are not the issue," he said. "The challenge really is developing the reserves fast enough."[48] So community grievances such as grinding poverty and murderous pollution were annoyances. The real challenge was to get the oil out of the ground as fast as possible.

CNN beamed pictures of the Davos meeting to the Delta, where Watson-Clark was being held hostage. After broadcast of a meeting between Obasanjo and Brown, MEND members were delighted: "They liked that, they thought it must have something to do with them. So they would say, 'Things are working,' but then we would never get released."

Welcome News

Finally, on Monday, January 30, Watson-Clark's parents were awakened by a morning phone call from their son. Nigel had been released. "He said he's fine. We're just happy he's alive and well," his father said. The British High Commissioner in Nigeria, Richard Gozney, told the BBC Radio 4 *Today* program:

"We learnt late in the night that the negotiations by the governor of Bayelsa State in the Niger Delta had been successful. We saw the hostages very early this morning, at first light, and they seemed to be safe and well."[49]

The following morning Watson-Clark flew to Heathrow, where his partner, Briony Tomkies, and their four children were waiting for him. "It is absolutely wonderful to be home. I feel great. I've got my family around me, which is very nice," he told the waiting press.[50]

Ironically Watson-Clark did not feel a huge sense of relief, just gratitude. "I was humbled by the various agencies that were there in Lagos that did get us out," he recalls. Asked who these agencies were, he replied Scotland Yard, the FBI, his bosses at the Expro Group, the Nigerian arm of Tidewater, and "there were other people involved as well who I would prefer not to go into." He added that "the whole collective effort was fantastic." If secret service agents were involved, Watson-Clark did not say. It would not be the first time that British or American agents had meddled in the affairs of Nigeria. Still Watson-Clark was glad that his moment in the media spotlight was over and that he was home.

For Dr. Daukoru, public attention was just beginning. The same day, January 31, he was in Vienna to chair the 139th Extraordinary Meeting of the OPEC Conference at the organization's Secretariat there. It was his first official meeting in charge of OPEC. The flags of the cartel's nations hung behind the delegates like silent guards watching the proceedings. Bouquets of orange, yellow, and white flowers on the main conference table added color to the otherwise drab room decor. Again concern was expressed about the "high degree of price volatility" in the oil market. Dr. Daukoru looked calm and relaxed, stylishly dressed in a gray suit with an upturned collar. If the ongoing violence in Nigeria was worrying him, he did not show it.

Asked by the press whether OPEC would increase output in the course of 2006, Daukoru said, "We have always maintained that we have more spare capacity than the market was willing to take." He revealed that OPEC had at least 2 million barrels of spare capacity, and noted that Nigeria was working to bring onstream by the first half of the year an additional output of 600,000 barrels per day on top of a base of 2.5 million barrels per day. Afterward he was mobbed by the world's oil press, eager to hear more from the most important oil leader of the moment. The price of a barrel of oil hung on his every word.

Someone else whose words can move the oil market also had a say on that day. Alhaji Dokubo Asari, the imprisoned Ijaw leader of the Niger Delta People's Volunteer Force, said that the release of the hostages was a "goodwill gesture to the international community," but he added that the attacks would continue. He singled out Britain for special mention: "We, the Ijaw and Niger Delta people, want to remind the people of the world that Great Britain has facilitated the illegal, criminal and inhuman occupation and exploitation of our lands for 112 years."[51]

It is interesting that Asari blamed the old colonial power for the problems of the Niger Delta, just as the new powers—America and China—were beginning to fight over Nigeria's oil. There is no doubt that Shell benefited from British colonial rule in Nigeria, and its continuing dominance of the Nigerian oil industry is a colonial legacy. Its monopolistic position means that, ironically, for Shell, Nigeria remains a lethal legacy, too.

In February 2006, Citigroup released an in-depth study on Nigeria. "Our analysis," it said, "suggests that Nigeria is *the* major growth region for Shell to the turn of the decade." Although much of Shell's growth will be from deepwater offshore oil fields, Watson-Clark's experience shows that operating offshore does not insulate the industry from community grievances. Citigroup concluded that Shell was "the most exposed of its peers to Nigeria. We estimate that by 2010 Nigeria will account for almost 17% of group production, up from 11% currently." More importantly, the report concluded that the region accounts for a significant proportion of Shell's expected volume growth to 2010.[52]

So the spiral of violence seems set to continue, with Shell at its center. In February, MEND took more hostages, although they, too, were later released unharmed. Two weeks after Nigel Watson-Clark was released, Nigerian military helicopters attacked the area, killing an estimated twenty people. The government claimed that it was targeting barges used for smuggling oil. MEND accused the military of targeting civilians instead. Once again, Shell was intertwined with the violence—information emerged that the helicopters had used a company airstrip—and Shell again tried to distance itself from the military action. "Armed intervention is always a decision for the proper authorities and not for private companies such as Shell," a spokesperson said.[53]

However, the following month, Charles Dragonette, a senior analyst at the U.S. Office of Naval Intelligence, admitted that Shell had asked the U.S. military for protection. Dragonette cited the Ijaw insurgency and conflict stemming from President Obasanjo's attempt to hold on to power as reasons why "Nigeria's Delta situation is not going to improve, certainly not anytime soon," and concluded that "the production of oil in Nigeria will hang precariously in the balance for the foreseeable future."[54] Forty years after Shell provided boats to put down Isaac Boro's rebellion, the company remains as intertwined with the military and oil conflicts in Nigeria as ever.

China's involvement is only just beginning. Interestingly, the Citigroup report argued that, should "Shell wish to diversify its portfolio risk" in Nigeria, potential buyers would be the Brazilian company Petrobras and CNOOC, the Chinese state oil company.

Just how important Nigeria is to China's energy plans was reconfirmed when President Hu Jintao made a state visit to Abuja as part of a weeklong tour in April 2006. To mark the occasion, Nigeria granted China four drilling licenses in exchange for a commitment to invest at least $4 billion in oil and infrastructure projects.[55]

As the red carpet was once again rolled out for a Chinese dignitary, MEND issued a warning. "We wish to warn the Chinese government and its oil companies to steer well clear of the Niger Delta," MEND wrote in an e-mail. "Chinese citizens found in oil installations will be treated as thieves. The Chinese government by investing in stolen crude places its citizens in our line of fire."[56]

One person who will no longer be in the line of fire is Nigel Watson-Clark. He handed in his resignation to Ecodrill on his return to Britain, since the only security job the company would offer him was back on the Echo Alpha field. "Everyone in Nigeria knows that there is an imbalance between what is happening in Abuja and the fabulous wealth that is coming out of Nigeria and where they are getting it from—the coastal states," he says. "I don't have a lot of sympathy for what MEND did to us, but they have been driven to that. They have been driven to doing what they are doing. There are an awful lot of people who are not benefiting from that country's wealth. They have absolutely nothing." In Africa, he points out, oil is known as the black curse.

Notes

1. Nigel Watson-Clark, telephone interview with Andy Rowell, April 21, 2006; all quotes attributed to Watson-Clark are from this interview unless otherwise stated.
2. See www.news24.com/News24/Africa/News/0,,2-11-1447_1865650,00.html.
3. See www.news.moneycentral.msn.com/ticker/article.asp?Feed=BW&Date=20060130 &ID=5457691& Symbol=US:TDW.
4. Shell Petroleum Development Company of Nigeria Limited, *2004 People and the Environment Annual Report*, May 2005.

5. M. Enfield, *The Oil Industry in the Delta*, PFC Energy, presentation to the Conference on Nigeria's Delta Region, Meridian International Center, February 15, 2005.

6. J. Bearman, "Shell Set to Rise Again with Nigerian Gas," *African Energy*, June 2005, pp. 8–9; Enfield, *The Oil Industry in the Delta*.

7. Michael Fleshman, "Report from Nigeria 2," *Nigeria Transition Watch* no. 9 (New York: Africa Fund, 1999).

8. Karl Maier, *This House Has Fallen: Nigeria in Crisis* (Harmondsworth: Penguin, 2006), p. 142.

9. "Kidnappings, Sabotage Slash Nigerian Oil Output," Agence France Presse, January 12, 2006.

10. See the Web site http://english.aljazeera.net/NR/exeres/5F9B91A6-C289-446B-A08E-FF9A2BA73791.htm.

11. Xinhua Financial Network News, "China Defends African Policy, Touts Mutual Benefits following CNOOC Oil Deal," January 13, 2006.

12. "China Unveils New Partnership Plan for Africa," AFX News, January 16, 2006.

13. T. Pitman, "Chinese Foreign Minister Heads to Africa on Weeklong Tour of Oil-Rich Continent," Associated Press, January 11, 2006.

14. A. R. Mihailescu, *U.P.I. Energy Watch*, February 7, 2006.

15. See www.cnooc.com.cn/defaulten.asp.

16. J. McDonald, "China Spending Billions on Foreign Oil but Trying to Curb Appetite," Associated Press, Beijing, February 6, 2006.

17. See http://api-ec.api.org/filelibrary/BacAprr5.pdf.

18. See www.israeleconomy.org/strategic/africatranscript.pdf.

19. Ibid.

20. See his comments at http://usembassy.state.gov/nigeria/wwwhp061402b.html.

21. See www.israeleconomy.org/strategic/africawhitepaper.pdf.

22. The report is available at www.csis.org/africa/GoldwynAfricanOilSector.pdf.

23. Available at www.csis.org/africa/0507_GulfofGuinea.pdf.

24. See www.cfr.org/publication/9371/more_than_humanitarianism.html.

25. Rory Carroll, "China's Gold Mine," *Guardian*, March 28, 2006.

26. P. Brookes and J. Hye Shin, *China's Influence in Africa: Implications for the United States*, Heritage Foundation Backgrounder no. 1916, February 22, 2006.

27. "No Questions Asked: China and Africa," *Economist* (U.S. edn.), January 21, 2006.

28. K. Houreld, "My Rendezvous with the River Rebels," *Daily Mail*, March 22, 2006.

29. M. Birnbaum, *Nigeria: Fundamental Rights Denied: Report of the Trial of Ken Saro-Wiwa and Others*, Article 19, in association with the Bar Human Rights Committee of England and Wales and the Law Society of England and Wales, Appendix 10: Summary of Affidavits Alleging Bribery, June 1995.

30. S. Buerk, e-mail to Andy Rowell, July 11, 2005.

31. See www.guardian.co.uk/oil/story/0,,1717598,00.html.

32. Environmental Rights Action, *Hell in Iko: The Story of Double Standards*, July 10, 1987; Andrew Rowell, *Green Backlash: Global Subversion of the Environment Movement* (London: Routledge, 1995), pp. 294–95.

33. Hon. O. Justice Inko-Tariah, Chief J. Ahiakwo, B. Alamina, Chief G. Amadi, *Commission of Inquiry into the Causes and Circumstances of the Disturbances That Occurred at Umuechem in the Etche Government Area of Rivers State in the Federal Republic of Nigeria*, 1990; J. R. Udofia, "Threat of Disruption of Our Oil Operations at Umuechem by Members of Umuechem Community," Letter to Commissioner of Police, October 29, 1990.

34. Lieutenant Colonel Paul Okuntimo, "RSIS Operations: Law and Order in Ogoni Etc.," Memo from the Chair of the Rivers State Internal Security Task Force to His Excellency, the Military Administrator, Restricted, May 12, 1994.

35. A. Rowell, "Shell Shock," *New Zealand Listener,* December 14–20, 1996; A. Rowell, "Shell Cracks," *Village Voice,* December 11, 1996.

36. A. Rowell, J. Marriott, and L. Stockman, *The Next Gulf: London, Washington and Oil Conflict in Nigeria* (London: Constable, 2005).

37. WAC Global Services, *Peace and Security in the Niger Delta—Conflict Expert Group,* Baseline Report, Working Paper for Shell Petroleum Development Company, December 2003.

38. Available at http://news.biafranigeriaworld.com/archive/bbc/2006/01/21/nigerian_rebels_vow_new_oil_raids.php.

39. "China Backs Africa for Seat on UN Security Council," Agence France Presse, FM, Abuja, January 16, 2006.

40. Ibid.

41. Reported in www.defenseindustrydaily.com/2005/09/nigeria-spends-251m-for-chinese-f7-fighters-after-oil-deals/index.php; D. Mahtani, "Nigeria Accuses US of Failure to Help Protect Its Oil Assets," *Financial Times,* February 28, 2006.

42. Quoted at www.winne.com/nigeria/topinterviews/edmund_daukoru.php.

43. Ibid.

44. P. Adams, "Nigeria's Burden of Proof: Arrests Have Been Made But the State Oil Business Has Still to Satisfy the Industry that Its Reforms Are Working," *Financial Times,* November 3, 1993, p. 34; *Economist,* "Oiling the Big Wheels," November 6, 1993, p. 107.

45. See these Web sites: http://allafrica.com/stories/200507150045.html; www.odili.net/news/source/2005/jul/17/201.html; and http://allafrica.com/stories/200507250536.html; "Oil Exploration: 'We Must Take Our Destiny in Our Hands,'" *This Day,* July 24, 2005.

46. M. Umar, "Stakeholders Applaud Daukoru's OPEC Presidency," *Business Day,* February 13, 2006.

47. Reported at www.weforum.org/site/homepublic.nsf/Content/China+Will+Rely+On+Domestic+Demand+For+Economic+Growth%2C+Says+Zeng.

48. See the Web site www.weforum.org/site/knowledgenavigator.nsf/Content/_S15722?open&event_id=1462&year_id=2006.

49. See www.timesonline.co.uk/article/0,,3-2016701,00.html.

50. Nigel Watson-Clark, quoted in www.newsandstar.co.uk/news/viewarticle.aspx? id=326757; http://news.bbc.co.uk/1/hi/england/somerset/4666186.stm.

51. Alhaji Dokubo Asari, www.timesonline.co.uk/article/0,,3-2017164,00.html.

52. Citigroup Global Markets, "Delta Force," *The Pump,* February 27, 2006.

53. "Shell Defends Use of Nigerian Airfield by Attack Chopper," Agence France Presse, February 16, 2006. Also see www.coanews.org/tiki-read_article.php?articleId=738; http://quote.bloomberg.com/apps/news?pid=10000006&sid=aEmm3EpJnEh4&refer=home; www.theallineed.com/news/0602/16185243.htm.

54. Reported at www.fin24.co.za/articles/markets/display_article.asp?Nav=ns&lvl2=markets&ArticleID=1518-25_1903224.

55. See www.voanews.com/english/2006-04-27-voa13.cfm.

56. See www.washingtonpost.com/wp-dyn/content/article/2006/04/30/AR2006043001022.html.

7   *It's all about the oil. Production sharing agreements being forced on Iraq will cost the Iraqi people hundreds of billions of dollars. Greg Muttitt takes a look at the men behind the hit.*

Hijacking Iraq's Oil Reserves: Economic Hit Men at Work

Greg Muttitt

The Ultimate Prize

A year before he became vice president, Dick Cheney, CEO of Halliburton, outlined the U.S. strategic landscape in an era of constrained oil supplies: "By 2010 we will need on the order of an additional fifty million barrels a day. So where is the oil going to come from? . . . While many regions of the world offer great oil opportunities, the Middle East, with two-thirds of the world's oil and the lowest cost, is still where the prize ultimately lies."[1]

Cheney's problem was that the prize has been beyond the reach of Western oil majors since the 1970s, when most Middle Eastern countries nationalized their oil industries. Saudi Arabia remains out of bounds to foreign oil company investment. Iran's constitution forbids foreign control of the country's oil. The Kuwaiti government has been trying to bring foreign companies into its northern oil fields but has consistently been blocked by its parliament. Iraq, with 10 percent of the world's reserves, seemed to be the easiest to turn around. And if Iraq could be reopened to multinationals, perhaps its neighbors could be pressured to follow suit.

This was a prospect that Western oil companies longed for. Shortly before the 2003 U.S. invasion of Iraq, U.S. oil company ConocoPhillips stated that "we know where the best [Iraqi] reserves are [and] we covet the opportunity to get those some day."[2] Shell has said that it aims to "establish a material and enduring presence in the country."[3]

Spearheading this drive is Dan Witt, an unlikely looking economic hit man. A short, enthusiastic American with round spectacles and neatly combed hair, he would look almost schoolboyish if it weren't for his sharp suits. One colleague describes him as "a bundle of energy." It is not unusual for him to visit three or even four countries in a week, shuttling between his home in Washington, D.C., his second office in London, and projects in Kazakhstan, Russia, Libya, and elsewhere.

Witt heads the International Tax and Investment Center, an organization that lobbies for corporate-friendly tax and investment policies in developing and transition countries. As he puts it, "Our thesis is that open economic policies that attract investment are better for prosperity than closed policies."

Now with eighty-five corporate sponsors, ITIC has a turnover of $2.5 million. Yet despite representing these business interests, ITIC describes itself as a "research and education foundation" and is registered with the U.S. Internal Revenue Service as a tax-exempt, not-for-profit organization. "We create [a] neutral table to bring guys to share their knowledge with the policymakers," Witt explains, portraying ITIC as a facilitator between investors and legislators. However, the organization is accountable only to its corporate sponsors, who together provide 90 percent of ITIC's income, and its board of directors is populated by executives of some of the world's largest multinational corporations.

Insofar as ITIC is an "education foundation" at all, corporations are clearly the educators and governments the educated. Like many Western governments, corporations, and institutions such as the World Bank, Witt shares the view that what developing countries need is "expertise" to assist their reform processes, bringing them in line with "best international practice." Their assumption is that decisions on the economy and infrastructure are no longer political issues but instead simply technical ones—and that radical economic reform is achieved not by lobbying but simply by advising.

At times, this can be a euphemism too far. Apologizing that he's never been to Iraq, Witt sheepishly told one interviewer that "I'm not completely comfortable not having been. I mean, who the hell are you to be sharing stuff if you've not been there. It's a bit hypocritical."[4] The phrase that stands out is "sharing stuff"—not an activity one would normally be embarrassed about. However, in the case of Iraq, when the offers of advice and sharing are backed up by 150,000 troops, they become harder to refuse.

ITIC does not engage in public education, focusing its efforts instead on officials and politicians. "Public is always hard," Witt explains. "We don't, you know, do a lot of mass media stuff."

However, ITIC's approach is thoroughly systematic and politically sophisticated, not stopping at current governments but also targeting potential future members of governments. This work is most advanced in the former Soviet Union. According to ITIC's ten-year review, "Senior tax officials in the Commonwealth of Independent States usually do not have to learn about ITIC when they take office, because they have already known us in their positions as Duma deputies, as lower-level officials in the ministries, or as auditors in a regional administration."[5] Kent Potter, vice president of Chevron Overseas, captures ITIC's role by commenting, "In many ways, ITIC is like a private-sector version of the OECD [Organisation for Economic Co-operation and Development] or IMF [International Monetary Fund]."[6]

ITIC's role may indeed be similar, but Dan Witt is dismissive of many of his public-sector counterparts. "All too often these advisers that come in as part of a World Bank project or a DFID [Department for International Development] project haven't really worked in industry. I mean, if they did, they wouldn't be working for £45,000 [$85,000] a year in one of these donor agency jobs."

Witt's contempt for those on mere $85,000 salaries makes one wonder about his attitude to those in the countries he claims to be trying to help.

Oil Workers in Iraq

"Iraq is a rich country, but its people are poor," Hassan Juma'a told me as we sat in the sparse living room of his crumbling rented house in Basra. I had only to look around me to agree. Although meticulously tidy, the house was barely furnished. A few walls bore peeling paint; most were bare plaster, some with growing cracks. Hassan is relatively lucky. Having worked in the oil industry for thirty-two years, he earns around $200 a month, which is just enough to pay the rent and feed his family of six. More than 50 percent of Iraqis are now unemployed, according to Iraq's Planning Ministry.[7] Meanwhile, a February 2006 study by the Labor Ministry found that one fifth of the population— 2 million families—live below the poverty line, defined as having income of less than a dollar a day.[8]

Hassan, a thickset oil worker now in his mid-fifties, speaks with a calm authority that makes you want to listen. He is right about Iraq's richness. The former Mesopotamia—the land between the rivers—is known as the "cradle of civilization." Built on the fertile areas around the Tigris and Euphrates

rivers, present-day Iraq was where human beings first learned to write, practice agriculture, administer cities. Whereas once it was water that Iraq was
rich in, now it is oil, the commodity on which all modern-day economies
are built.

That richness puts Iraq in the target sights of the West. But Iraq's oil workers will be one of the major obstacles to a Western takeover and indeed to
Dan Witt's intentions. Hassan Juma'a leads a trade union, formed just days
after the fall of Saddam Hussein, and it already represents more than half of
the oil workers in southern Iraq. Now, the General Union of Oil Employees is
on the front line of trying to defend Iraq's natural resources against predatory
multinational corporations. Sovereignty over its oil reserves is vital to Iraq's
future development, Hassan believes. "Oil must stay in the hands of Iraqis,
because oil is the only national resource that we have which is of great value,
and our economy depends on it."

Witt's Rise and the Birth of ITIC

In spite of their key strategic interest in Iraqi and Middle Eastern oil reserves,
acknowledged in numerous policy documents,[9] the governments of the U.S.
and the UK are sensitive to accusations that oil was part of their reason for going to war. As a result, they have had to be cautious about being seen lobbying
for changes in oil policy in postwar Iraq—something their partners in the private sector, and indeed foundations, do not need to be so concerned about.

Dan Witt himself made the transition from the constraints of working in
government to a career in right-wing foundations and think tanks, where he
could push stronger views more assertively.

Armed with an MBA from Western Michigan University in 1984, Witt
started out in New Zealand as a visiting economist at Victoria University of
Wellington and made his name as an advocate for deregulation. On his return to the U.S. two years later, he got a job with the Reagan administration,
first in the Office of Management and Budget and then with the President's
Commission on Privatization. That commission marked a turning point in
policy on providing public services through government in the U.S. While its
recommendations did include some traditional privatizations of state companies and assets—including Amtrak and two Naval Petroleum Reserves—and
opening the Postal Service to competition, it went much farther, effectively
converting citizens into consumers. The commission's report recommended
that the market, rather than the state, provide schools, public housing, and
Medicare, with users given vouchers to pay for them. It also called for the U.S.

Agency for International Development to promote privatization in developing countries.

Although the political contacts Witt made in the Reagan administration would later prove useful to him, it seems that even Reagan's economic policies were not strong enough for him. One commission member, Richard Fink, offered Witt a job as vice president of Citizens for a Sound Economy, an anti-regulation lobbying group, and Witt gladly accepted. Fink had set up CSE in 1984, with money from the Koch family, owners of the diversified oil company Koch Industries, the second largest privately owned corporation in America.

Two years into the job at CSE, Witt spotted a new opportunity. The Tax Foundation, a corporate-led organization that had, since 1937, called for lower domestic taxes, was in financial trouble—about $500 million in debt. Witt persuaded CSE to make a "friendly buyout," and he moved over to the foundation, where he became executive director in April 1991.

At the time, the Soviet Union was on its last legs, with its constituent republics declaring de facto independence. It was this that propelled Witt from targeting U.S. domestic taxes onto the international stage.

Just seven months after Witt became its executive director, the Tax Foundation "organized the substantive part of" the U.S.–USSR Conference on Trade and Bilateral Economic Relations, held in Moscow in December 1991. The conference was attended by both Soviet President Mikhail Gorbachev and Russian President Boris Yeltsin. American delegates included Ambassador Robert Strauss, Secretary of Labor Lynn Martin, and Deputy Secretary of the Treasury John Robson, as well as numerous corporate CEOs invited by the Tax Foundation. This conference marked the start of Witt's new direction. Coming just three weeks before the final collapse of the Soviet Union was declared, the conference marked a change in direction for the newly independent former Soviet states, a direction over which Witt and his colleagues had extensive influence.

In the summer of 1992, the Tax Foundation sent a delegation of eleven corporate executives—"vice presidents of tax at Citibank and Exxon and Philip Morris, the guys who were interested in going to these crazy places at that time"—to Russia to advise Russia's State Committee on Taxation and Ministry of Finance on the taxation of foreign investment.

The Tax Foundation commissioned Charles McLure of the Hoover Institution at Stanford University to coauthor a statement to be delivered by the delegation. McLure had been deputy assistant secretary of the treasury from

1983 to 1985. He was responsible for developing proposals that ultimately became the basis of Reagan's Tax Reform Act of 1986, which cut the top rate
(from 50 to 28 percent) and increased the bottom rate (from 11 to 15 percent)
at the same time, to orchestrate a massive transfer of the tax burden from the
rich to the poor.

McLure's statement offered a range of prescriptions for Russia's tax systems,
including lower tax rates, and urged Russia to consult with foreign investors
before passing any new legislation. Witt commented in the Tax Foundation's
newsletter that he was "gratified to see that three days after we submitted
our statement, the Russian Supreme Soviet voted to reduce the maximum
personal income tax rate from 60 percent to 40 percent."[10]

A series of visits followed to Russia and Kazakhstan, and in 1993 the Tax
Foundation signed cooperation protocols with both countries' finance ministries. These newly independent governments were keen to shake off old
Soviet ways, and Witt was eager to fill the policy vacuum in ways that would
serve U.S. corporations.

Witt and McLure decided that the time had come to set up a new organization, the International Tax and Investment Center, which would be spun off
from the Tax Foundation, with Witt as its president. Funding was not hard to
find, and the initiative quickly attracted twenty of America's biggest companies as sponsors, including Bechtel, Chevron, Citibank, Boeing, Nestlé, and
Philip Morris.

The next step was to build political infrastructure on both sides of the newly parted Iron Curtain. To chair ITIC jointly, they selected John Robson and
Lord Peter Walker. Robson, a lawyer who had been head of the Civil Aero-
nautics Board in the 1970s, was renowned for his toughness and his role as an
architect of airline deregulation. Subsequently, he became a protégé of Donald Rumsfeld at the Searle pharmaceutical company before joining George
Bush Sr.'s administration as deputy secretary of the treasury.

Peter Walker also knew how to be tough. As energy secretary under Prime
Minister Margaret Thatcher, he had taken on—and beaten—the National
Union of Mineworkers. While Witt and McLure had both played key roles in
the Reaganomics of privatization and low taxes, Walker's confrontation with
the miners union was the decisive struggle that allowed Thatcher to break the
power of the British trade union movement.

In both Russia and Kazakhstan, ITIC had major success in influencing tax
policy. ITIC claims that the principles it pushed in Russia became "the basis for the nation's tax law."[11] In 1999, Russia introduced Part I of a new tax

code abolishing progressive income taxes and replacing them with a flat 13 percent tax for all citizens, regardless of wealth. In Kazakhstan, ITIC's reach went even farther, since Charles McLure wrote the white paper on which the country's 1995 tax code was based. The code was implemented without parliamentary scrutiny, for the simple reason that Kazakhstan President Nursultan Nazarbayev had dissolved parliament. Like the Russian code, it targeted both individual and corporate taxes, cutting income tax from 60 percent to 40 percent and abolishing export tariffs. "It's simple, broad-based, business-oriented, and we're certainly pleased with it," applauded Gene Handel, a senior financial officer at Chevron.[12]

Handel and his colleagues at Chevron were no doubt at least as pleased with ITIC's successes about specific oil and gas taxation. In 1998, six of the eleven recommendations of ITIC's Kazakhstan Minerals Taxation Committee were enacted as tax code amendments or instructions.

Focus on Oil and Gas

Oil and gas have always had a special place on ITIC's agenda. For more than ten years, three of the four corporate members on ITIC's Executive Committee have been representatives of Chevron, BP, and British Gas.

In this emphasis, ITIC shares a strategic interest with the U.S. and British governments, whose foreign policies have for nearly a hundred years been geared to securing the flow of oil. In the first half of the twentieth century, oil was prized for its military value—the technological advantage that oil-derived fuels brought first to ships, then to tanks and other land vehicles, and then to aircraft. In the Second World War, oil played an important role. One prong of Hitler's ill-fated march into Russia was headed for the oil fields of Azerbaijan, while on the other side of the world, the Japanese attack on Pearl Harbor was motivated by a desire for control over the Pacific Ocean and oil supply routes from Indonesia. Military leaders on all sides knew that if they could not secure their oil supplies, their war machines would grind to a halt.

Since then, the military significance of oil has not declined: during the invasion and occupation of Iraq, the U.S. military used 1.4 million gallons of fuel per day.[13] But since the middle of the twentieth century, oil's military value has been matched by an economic role, becoming *the* commodity that markets respond to. In the words of Daniel Yergin, official historian of the oil industry, "Whatever the twists and turns in global politics, whatever the ebb of imperial power and the flow of national pride, one trend in the decades following World War II progressed in a straight and rapidly ascending line—the consumption of oil. . . . Oil emerged triumphant, the undisputed King, a monarch garbed in a dazzling array of plastics."[14]

For most of the twentieth century, the U.S. was the world's largest oil producer. However, as U.S. supplies declined and oil consumption in North America, Europe, and later Asia increased, the geographical gap between oil-consuming and oil-producing countries has widened. Oil is a central factor in international geopolitics—and nowhere more than in the Middle East, which holds more than 60 percent of the world's oil reserves.

This was perhaps most forcefully seen in the Carter Doctrine of 1980. In his State of the Union address, President Jimmy Carter announced, "Let our position be absolutely clear. An attempt by any outside force to gain control of the Persian Gulf region will be regarded as an assault on the vital interests of the United States of America, and such an assault will be repelled by any means necessary, including military force." Although he referred to "outside force," the policy has equally applied to actors within the Middle East itself—as was seen in the Gulf War of 1991 and the Iraq invasion of 2003—and it is playing out now in the crisis over Iran.

I first visited Iraq two years after the 2003 invasion. Hosted by Hassan Juma'a and the General Union of Oil Employees, I spent a week in the searing heat of a Basra summer, meeting his fellow oil workers and visiting their work sites. Working for a London-based NGO called PLATFORM, I had been studying the impacts of British oil companies around the world for about eight years—and watching what had been happening to Iraqi oil policies since 2003.

One of the sites I visited in May 2005 was the Basra refinery. Like any other, it is a maze of pipes connecting odd-shaped buildings, pervaded by a sulfurous smell. Towering above is the giant flare tower, spewing flames whose heat can be felt on the ground. But what is different about Basra is the look of age in all the equipment. The computer screens of the control room look like something from a 1970s movie. The buildings are worn and corroded. The pipes are all rusty.

As I walked round the plant, I began to feel nervous. I knew that in refineries in Britain and America old pipes and valves under high pressure have failed, causing accidents. At this thought, I involuntarily hunched and almost cowered as I walked.

I asked the Basra refinery manager if the plant had a lot of safety problems. He looked quite surprised by the question. Accidents are very rare, he said, because everything is constantly checked. "For the operator, the refinery is part of him," he explained. I contrasted this with the appalling safety record in British and American refineries, where asset managers see workers as a cost to be minimized. In many refineries, the workforce has been cut back so much that equipment is rarely checked, and faulty parts are not repaired or replaced. One example is BP's Grangemouth refinery in Scotland, which I visited in 2002. Two years earlier, the plant had had a string of near misses, including explosions, gas leaks, and fires, for which it received the largest health and safety fine in Scottish history. Fifty firefighters with fourteen fire engines fought for seven hours to bring one blaze under control; the effort was hampered in the crucial early stages when one of the two on-site fire engines broke down. Both financial analysts and the local member of Parliament blamed lack of skilled staff for the incidents.[15] In 1998, the refinery had cut back staff levels by 200 people, and a further 400 in 1999. Before the ink had dried on a safety review of the June 2000 fire, BP cut its workforce again—by an enormous 40 percent, from 2,500 to 1,500.

In comparison, the Basra refinery had not had a fire since 2003, Faraj Rabat Mizban, a firefighter at the refinery, proudly told me. During the invasion, however, there were twenty-three fires, one of them a major explosion of a storage tank caused by an F-16 jet.

A quiet, wiry man with a wicked grin, Faraj has worked in the refinery since 1976. In the early 1980s, he was a musician, playing the kanan, a Middle Eastern stringed instrument. His band was successful and was frequently invited on international tours. But he could never join them—having refused to join the Ba'ath party, he was not given permission to travel.

Faraj's experiences capture the persistent tragedy of the Iraqi people. Situated in southeastern Iraq, his refinery was on the front line of Iraq's three recent wars. In the 1980–88 war with Iran, Faraj lost several colleagues to the continual shelling. Just two years after the end of that war, Saddam Hussein invaded Kuwait. The subsequent 1991 Gulf War, Faraj recalls, "was a really terrifying war, because we saw in that war arms that we'd never seen before—F-16s, stealth planes, Tornados, cruise missiles. So that man, woman, child, even animals—they would hear the sound of the plane coming and they would be dead scared."[16] For Faraj, disaster struck. An allied missile landed near his house, crippling his son, who was playing nearby. His son remains bedridden, fifteen years later, and needs constant care.

After the U.S.-led coalition drove Saddam's forces out of Kuwait, Shi'a Muslim groups in the south of Iraq started to mobilize against Saddam, having received a signal that the Americans would support an uprising—a hope that never materialized. Saddam responded with some of the most brutal repression of his reign. Faraj was arrested for having attended a demonstration. He was kept in prison for three months, in terrible conditions.

Throughout the 1990s, Iraq was subjected to international sanctions. Hundreds of thousands of people, especially children, died because there were no medicines and not enough food. A study by the United Nations children's agency UNICEF found that between 1991 and 1998, half a million more children under five died than would be expected by comparison with preceding trends;[17] many died because clean water was unavailable, since chlorine was considered a "dual use" commodity and its import was prohibited under the sanctions. When the U.S./UK force invaded in March 2003, most people in the south of Iraq, and many across the country, welcomed the move because it meant the end of Saddam.

But that hope soon soured as the realities of occupation set in. Faraj recalls one incident. As he and his colleagues were going home after a shift, they met with some American soldiers, whom they greeted. The Americans, very nervous and aggressive, locked the gates, refusing to let the workers go home. When one of the senior workers went to ask them what was going on, he was thrown to the ground and a boot placed on his head.

Many of the American soldiers, barely adults, have been taught that any Iraqi is a potential terrorist. But this kind of stereotyping is not limited to the eighteen-year-olds. It extends deep into the ranks of senior bureaucrats of the occupation and consultants who are desperate to offer the Iraqis "advice" on how to develop their economy.

Much of this advice is peppered with a subtext that Iraqis are not capable of running their own oil industry—that only multinational oil companies have the skills to do so. My experience at the refinery in fact suggested the opposite conclusion. As Hassan Juma'a commented about the multinationals, "Although their equipment is impressive, the same cannot be said for their technical know-how."

The General Union of Oil Employees began with a meeting, organized by Hassan Juma'a, on April 20, 2003, just days after Saddam fell. Trade unions had been illegal since 1987, when the dictator had outlawed all except his own union—which was really part of his security apparatus. The workers' purpose was not just to defend their rights. "From the start of the occupation some union activists found it was very necessary to form an oil workers' union because such a union would protect the national economy, because we knew very well that the Americans and their allies came for the oil," Hassan says.

From that first meeting, a nine-member committee was formed. At first, many workers were reluctant to form a union, because they associated the idea with Saddam's instrument of repression. At the time, the country had just been invaded, and the Americans had come in without any plan for how to run the country once they got there. So one of the first roles of the committee was to organize workers to resume basic production and repair some of the war damage. Once these efforts started to prove effective, workers were attracted to the committee, which then established the South Oil Company Union and organized elections. Hassan Juma'a was voted president, and Faraj gained a place on the Executive Committee.

The union's next task was to address workers' treatment by the occupiers. For the first two months of the occupation, workers were not paid. By June 2003, they had had enough. Faraj, Ibrahim Radhi (another refinery worker in the union), and about 100 other workers blockaded the fuel collection point for the British army's tankers by moving a crane into the road and sitting underneath the trucks.

Armored vehicles arrived, and the soldiers aimed their guns at the protesters. But the workers bravely sat firm and called their bluff, telling the soldiers to shoot if they wanted to. The protest spurred frantic negotiations, and within hours all salaries were paid; the British military commander recognized that the workers had control of the fuel supply that was the lifeblood of the occupation. Following that protest, the union became the subject on everyone's lips, and membership leapt from 100 to 3,000.

Still, Iraqi oil workers continued to be marginalized, as occupation forces tried to assert control over the oil industry, through Halliburton. The oil services company, like its political and military masters, was ill-prepared for the task, and its efforts to run and rebuild the sector were largely failing.

In August 2003, the union called a strike, which for two days completely shut off Iraq's oil production. Like the refinery protest, this strike played a key role in the union's subsequent success. The following month, U.S. administrator Paul Bremer proposed a table of wages for Iraqi workers, starting from just 69,000 Iraqi dinars ($40–$45) per month, on which workers simply would not be able to survive. The threat of further strikes forced a negotiation, in which the bottom two levels were abandoned, leaving a minimum level of 100,000 dinars. Since then, the union has had other dramatic successes, including pressuring a Halliburton subcontractor to replace its 1,200 imported foreign workers with Iraqis, lobbying for the construction of housing for workers, and forcing the creation of jobs for the latest crop of graduates of the oil academy. Meanwhile, the union has grown to more than 23,000 members and consolidated into the General Union of Oil Employees, combining ten trade union councils in nine Iraqi oil companies in Basra, Amara, Nasiriyah, and Samawah—the four southernmost of Iraq's eighteen provinces, where most of the country's oil is.

But Hassan knows that the biggest fight is yet to come. "There are two stages of this war. First, the military occupation. Then the economic war and the destruction of Iraq's economy."

ITIC in Iraq

In summer 2003, Dan Witt decided to move into Iraq. Witt saw an opportunity in the political and economic restructuring of Iraq and a parallel to how ITIC had been working in the former Soviet Union, where the organization had entrenched itself at a time of rapid political change, with essentially a blank sheet on which to work. "My original thinking was, why don't we just try to see if what we started in '93, '94 with the Kazakhs—let's take some pages out of that playbook with the Iraqis."

Witt's board thoroughly approved. In strategy planning meetings in late 2004 and early 2005, ITIC's directors and sponsors—almost all of them representatives of large multinational companies—argued that the goal should be to go beyond Iraq itself and regain oil companies' access to the region's other oil-rich countries. In making this case, the ITIC board selected an unfortunate military metaphor, that the Iraq work "should be continued and considered as a 'beachhead' for possible further expansion in the Middle East."[18] Specifically, they mentioned the oil-rich states of Iran and Libya.

Witt approached some of ITIC's sponsors, who willingly agreed to fund the Iraq project on top of their normal contributions to ITIC. Six oil companies participated in the project: BP, ChevronTexaco, ExxonMobil, Shell, Total, and Eni SpA.

To lead the project, Witt hired Brian O'Connor, a former economist at BP and later an energy adviser to Britain's Department for International Development. O'Connor had been petroleum tax adviser to ITIC since 2000, when he led a European Union project to reform Russia's tax system. Although the EU project was publicly funded, ITIC had enthused in its newsletter, "The legislative areas to be addressed in this project will include many of the priorities identified by ITIC sponsors, including: transfer pricing, oil and gas taxation, VAT, and environmental taxation, and profits tax. . . . As the project moves forward, we will be regularly seeking input and guidance from our sponsors."[19]

O'Connor and Witt formed an "expert group" of nine other economists to work on the Iraq project. Only one, Muhammad Ali Zainy, was Iraqi. He now works at the Centre for Global Energy Studies (CGES), a London-based think tank founded by former Saudi Oil Minister Sheikh Ahmad Zaki Yamani. Another CGES member of the ITIC Iraq expert group, Leo Drollas, was O'Connor's former colleague and fellow economist at BP.

The group's main job was to write a report that would make the case for major multinational oil company involvement in Iraqi oil production—which had been in the public sector for more than 30 years.

This was not the first time the West had tried to grab control over Iraq's oil. As the First World War was drawing to a close in 1918, Britain identified Iraq as a crucial source of oil. Sir Maurice Hankey, secretary to the War Cabinet, wrote in a letter to Foreign Secretary Arthur Balfour, "The only big potential supply that we can get under British control is the Persian [Iranian] and Mesopotamian [Iraqi] supply. . . . Control over these oil supplies becomes a first-class British war aim."[20]

Following the war, Britain occupied Iraq under a League of Nations Mandate and achieved Hankey's aim of controlling oil supplies. In 1925, Iraq's British-installed monarch, King Faisal, awarded a concession contract to a consortium of Western companies named Turkish Petroleum Company (renamed Iraq Petroleum Company, IPC, in 1929). After a few changes of membership, the consortium consisted of the companies that later became BP, Shell, Total, and ExxonMobil.

The concession contract followed a model widely applied in the British colonies. It was for a period of seventy-five years, during which terms were frozen. Combined with two further concessions granted in the 1930s, IPC obtained rights to all the oil in the country. Even the Iraqi call for a 20 percent stake in the concession was denied, although that had been specified in earlier agreements.

As Iraqi frustration grew at the unfair terms of the deal, the contract came under pressure during the 1950s and 1960s. Key issues were whether the split of revenues between company and state was a fair one, and whether foreign companies had too much control over oil development: they restricted production to boost their other producing areas and used their monopoly on information to fix prices so as to deprive Iraq of income. The same charges were echoed in all the major oil-producing countries at the time, most of which had similar deals with multinational companies. The conclusion to these disputes was the nationalization of many oil industries—in Iraq's case in two stages, in 1961 and 1972.[21] This was the situation that Dan Witt and his oil company sponsors now wanted to reverse.

The 1970s was the most successful period in the history of Iraq's oil industry. Freed from the control of the multinational companies, between 1970 and 1979 the Iraq National Oil Company increased production from 1.5 million to 3.7 million barrels per day, and more than doubled the country's reserve base through exploration. This success came to an end in 1980, when Saddam Hussein invaded Iran, starting an eight-year war that caused a million casualties.

The Iraqi oil industry briefly recovered in the late 1980s, before the second of Saddam's disastrous military incursions, into Kuwait in 1990. During the subsequent twelve years of sanctions, the industry was badly damaged as infrastructure collapsed. By 2003 when the U.S./UK forces invaded, the industry was ripe for foreign takeover under the cloak of much-needed investment.

Things would get even worse for the Iraqi oil industry. At the start of the occupation, oil facilities, like much of the rest of the country's assets, were looted. The Iraqi Drilling Company is a good example. I visited one drilling rig in the giant South Rumaila field, in the baking desert two hours southwest of Basra. Nasir Mohsin Mohan, the site manager, described it to me as I sat in the site portacabin, straining to feel some breeze from the fan. "The equipment was all looted—they just left the skeleton of the rig." This was not just a couple of days of post-invasion chaos—the looting went on for four months, until July 2003. "All the looting happened with coalition forces present," said Nasir. "They did nothing to prevent it." The total cost to the IDC was $240 million.

Contrast this with the Oil Ministry building in Baghdad, which was heavily defended by U.S. troops, while other public buildings in the city were ransacked. Unlike the physical equipment—cables, motors, instruments—which could all be replaced by capital investment, the Oil Ministry contained irreplaceable geological data on the oilfields.

Even after the looting, Iraqi oil workers were determined to rebuild their industry themselves. Iraqi Drilling Company workers began to rebuild their equipment in August 2003. Cobbling together spare parts from wherever they could be found, the workers had the first drilling rig up and running within forty-five days. Weeks later, they had twelve rigs in operation.

Sitting next to Nasir in the portacabin, Hassan Juma'a applauded this success. "The Iraqi Drilling Company [workers] are the warriors of the sector. They rebuilt from scratch, in the face of a conspiracy to do away with IDC." Another oil worker commented that this was the third time Iraqi oil workers had rebuilt their industry following its destruction in a war, in the face of extreme adversity. As a result, the workers have a strong sense of ownership over the oil sector, which they will not willingly relinquish.

Dan Witt's challenge was to give his sponsors the control they wanted, against this background of Iraqi pride in the national ownership and development of the country's most important natural resource. "It's a very politically sensitive matter, to have foreigners come in and extract hydrocarbons," he admitted.[22]

The solution was to make it *look* as if the Iraqis were maintaining control of their oil.

Production-Sharing Agreements

Witt and his team completed their report in autumn 2004. They recommended that Iraq's oil be developed by foreign companies, using a form of contract called a production-sharing agreement (PSA). PSAs were first developed in the late 1960s in Indonesia, when nationalism was surging through oil-producing countries. Although the oil companies in Indonesia were initially skeptical, they managed to avoid the nationalizations that took place elsewhere. The ingenious PSAs define the resource as the legal property of the state and even describe the foreign company as a "contractor." But in practice the foreign company maintains control over development and access to a large share of profits. In fact, PSAs can be written to be almost exactly equivalent to the old-style concession agreements.

The point is explained by Thomas Wälde, one of Dan Witt's favorite academics. Wälde, a specialist in oil and gas law and contracts at Dundee University in northeast Scotland, sees the approach as "a convenient marriage between the politically useful symbolism of the production-sharing contract (appearance of a service contract to the state company acting as master) and the material equivalence of this contract model with concession/license regimes in all significant aspects. . . . The government can be seen to be running the show—and the company can run it behind the camouflage of legal title symbolizing the assertion of national sovereignty."[23]

To Dan Witt, PSAs must have sounded perfect.

I first came across Dan Witt on the radio. The BBC's World Service broadcasts a weekly program called *World, Have Your Say*, in which panelists discuss a topical issue and listeners are invited to e-mail in their opinions. One Tuesday evening in November 2005, the subject was the future of Iraq's oil industry, and I was invited to the studio in Bush House, a grand, courtyarded building just off the Strand, to be on the panel. Witt, another panelist, was in London at the time but declined to go to the studio, instead participating by phone.

Although I didn't know him, I knew of his organization. I had read his 2004 Iraq report that summer and found myself disagreeing with almost everything it said.

For a start, the ITIC report claims that production-sharing agreements are now the "norm in most countries outside the OECD."[24] Although it is true that PSAs are used in many countries—generally ones where oil reserves are small or expensive to extract, or where exploration risk is high—they are not used in countries like Iraq, which has enormous, known, simple- and cheap-to-access reserves. In fact, when one looks at share of world reserves rather than number of countries, International Energy Agency figures show that PSAs are used in only about 12 percent of the total, whereas 67 percent is developed solely or primarily by national oil companies.[25]

But perhaps the most misleading element of ITIC's report was that its economic models ran up to only 2010. In this period, the models showed the foreign oil company investments, and hence growth in the Iraqi economy. However, the models stopped before oil was due to start flowing, and thus before revenues began to be divided.

If this had not played so neatly into the short-term goals of Iraqi politicians anxious to see some quick results, I would have considered it an elementary error. The time frame masked the fact that oil company investments would be paid back in oil revenues once the oil started flowing. It is as if I took out a bank loan that had to be paid back starting in five years' time, and then looked at my finances over just the next four years. Before the loan has to be repaid, of course, I am better off.

I raised this point with Witt on the radio, and asked him to explain. He ducked the question, giving a general answer about the importance of investment. I replied that of course Iraq needs investment—the real questions were in what form and on whose terms. "Dan Witt, how do you respond?" asked the presenter. Silence. "Er . . . well . . . David Horgan, you're still on the line, aren't you?" So the third panelist, the head of an Irish company that had recently won a minor oil contract in Iraq, and I were left to continue the discussion without Daniel Witt.

I was amazed. Here was a man who spends half his time in the company of finance ministers and represents some of the most powerful corporations in the world. And he'd walked out because I asked him a simple question!

As I reflected on what had happened, I realized that I shouldn't have been surprised. In fact, I began to see, it was precisely *because* he deals with ministers and chief executives that he was thrown. Throughout the discussion, he kept stating simply, "This is how Iraq can bring in investment." So normally he is not challenged on the cost of that investment—and that's why he can't explain it to ordinary members of the public.

The story of the emperor's new clothes seemed quite appropriate.

The revenue that ITIC didn't mention could hardly be more significant. Oil accounts for more than 90 percent of the Iraqi government's income. To sacrifice a significant chunk of that would undermine the whole country's development.

Working with Ian Rutledge, a respected energy economist from Sheffield in the north of England, I set out to correct ITIC's omission. I had been an admirer of Rutledge's work for several years. During the late 1990s, oil companies had lobbied hard against any increase in Britain's rock-bottom taxation of its North Sea oil production, claiming that an increase would make the North Sea economically unviable and they would have to pull out altogether. Rutledge's research had shown that, for some of the companies making these claims, the North Sea was in fact their most profitable region in the world, even after tax. More recently, Rutledge wrote *Addicted to Oil*,[26] one of the best books available on international energy dynamics and the strategic context of the Iraq War.

By constructing economic models of the cash flows on Iraq's oil fields, we could project how oil revenues would be divided. The result depends on the precise terms of the PSA contract—some PSAs are very profitable for companies, while others are less so.

We used a range of different PSA terms that have been applied elsewhere in the world—from the quite strict terms of Libya to the generous (for the oil companies) terms of Russian contracts. Based on an oil price of $40 a barrel, we estimated that these PSAs for just the twelve oil fields that have been prioritized for development (out of more than sixty known but undeveloped fields) would rob Iraq of between $74 billion and $194 billion, compared to keeping oil in the public sector.[27] To put this amount in perspective, it could be as much as six times Iraq's current gross domestic product. If the price of oil were to stay high (as I write, it is around $70), the loss to Iraq would be correspondingly higher.

PSAs generally last for between twenty-five and forty years and fix their terms for this period. When I interviewed Dan Witt about PSAs in summer

2006, he admitted that the deals are often seen as unfair in retrospect: "Another thing is the time inconsistency of these things; I mean it's really easy to sit here today—and I have these discussions with Kazakhs, with Azeris—'Oh, well, maybe we gave too much away, maybe we didn't get enough government take, maybe the foreign investors aren't paying fair share.'" But, he argues, "You've got to really look at the political risk and what other industries are prepared to invest in an unstable risky environment?"

I pushed him on this point. If the risk situation improves, shouldn't the Iraqi government be able to renegotiate the terms? In principle, he had no choice but to agree. "Sovereign's always sovereign. . . . If it becomes politically untenable on the government side, they're going to force the other party to the table to talk."

However, in Kazakhstan, Witt has lobbied for precisely the opposite. Throughout 2001 and 2002, as the Kazakh government sought to adjust the terms of its PSA deals to reflect the new realities in the country, Witt's ITIC put extensive pressure on them to stick with the agreements. ITIC's efforts included marshaling foreign company threats to pull out and leave the Kazakh government high and dry, lobbying Kazakh ministers and parliamentarians at every opportunity, and mobilizing pressure from other external actors, such as the European Bank for Reconstruction and Development. "The contract stability question is hanging over Kazakhstan like a black cloud—affecting existing investors with respect to their future development investments, and, of course, new investors," Witt threatened the Kazakh government in 2002.[28] Eventually Witt won; the PSAs were not renegotiated.

Thus, long-term PSA contracts could be signed in Iraq while the government is new and weak, the security situation dire, and Iraq still under military occupation. In such circumstances, oil companies would insist on large profits to justify their risks, and a weak Iraqi government would not be in a position to drive a hard bargain. The prospect of such an unfair deal lasting for decades would strike many Iraqis as a blatant theft, repeating other such thefts from Iraq's colonial past.

Furthermore, PSAs often exempt foreign oil companies from any new laws that might affect their profits, through what is known as a "stabilization clause." And the contracts often stipulate that disputes are to be heard not in the country's own courts but in international investment tribunals, which make their decisions on commercial grounds and do not consider a country's national interest or other national laws. Iraq could thus be surrendering more than its ability to decide the rate of depletion of its assets, one of the most important economic decisions in an oil-dependent country. It could also lose the ability to regulate the oil sector and even to pass new laws. In effect, Iraq would be deprived of democratic control of its most important industry.

The Goal: Democracy or Plunder?

Despite the U.S. government's rhetoric about bringing democracy to the Middle East, Dan Witt seems unconcerned about such issues. In an article in late 2005 about the much-criticized elections in Azerbaijan, where ITIC has an office, he opined, "Western leaders must accept that in these emerging democracies some local opposition does not have an equal opportunity to win [elections]. Even a free press has little interest in reporting on opposition. The *real challenges* come once voting is completed. These reforms—economic, social and political—must continue. . . . The West must embrace countries and not alienate them with fair and free election lectures."[29]

In line with Witt's cynical attitude toward democracy, his next step after completing his Iraq report was to take it directly to those in power. The obvious route to Iraqi decision makers was through the occupation forces, and the British government was especially helpful.

As the report was being completed in September 2004, ITIC staff met with officials of Britain's Foreign Office and Treasury, to discuss the most effective strategy for persuading the Iraqis of its contacts. When the then finance minister (now vice president), Adil Abdul-Mahdi, received the ITIC report, it was sent not by Daniel Witt but by Edward Chaplin, Britain's ambassador to Iraq. With Britain's 8,500 troops still in Iraq, this was an envoy whom Abdul-Mahdi and his colleagues would not ignore.

The British government also repeated ITIC's prescriptions in its own advice to the Iraqi Oil Ministry. In Britain's "Code of Practice for the Iraqi Oil Industry," the opening paragraph copied ITIC's arguments almost word for word, stating that "the revitalization and development of the Iraqi oil sector will require a substantial injection of international capital investment. . . . Iraq would need to engage with the International Oil Companies to provide appropriate levels of Foreign Direct Investment to do this."[30]

Then, in January 2005, ITIC presented its arguments to ministers and officials of the Iraqi Ministries of Finance, Oil, and Planning, at a meeting in Beirut. The meeting was combined with an event organized by the International Monetary Fund and the World Bank. Although Witt plays down the role of the IMF and World Bank in his meeting—"technically speaking, they were two completely separate and distinct things that were held in the same place, back to back"—the presence of the two institutions no doubt sharpened Iraqi minds.

Iraq under Saddam Hussein acquired the world's largest per capita foreign debt, comprising both reparations owed to Kuwait for the 1990 invasion and unpaid loans from other countries. For the most part, these were Saddam's debts, used to build his palaces and purchase arms, and the funds did not benefit the Iraqi people. Still, when the Paris Club of industrialized creditor countries agreed in November 2004 that it would cancel 80 percent of what Iraq owed those countries, the agreement set the condition that the IMF would give Iraq a clean bill of economic health in 2005 and 2008. On top of the need to get this seal of approval, Iraq may also need the World Bank's and IMF's support to secure concessional finance in the future. In any case, the involvement of these two organizations made Witt's advice difficult to refuse.

The British government also stepped in again to help ITIC with the conference, in particular enlisting a diplomat in Britain's embassy in Baghdad. Chris Brown was First Secretary (Economic) at the embassy, and his brief included energy issues. Witt describes him as "an excellent guy—perhaps one of the most knowledgeable people in terms of what was going on in the Ministry of Oil, and helping to bring them best practice."[31] Brown advised Witt on which Iraqi officials to invite to the meeting and helped with communication with the authorities in Baghdad.

After the Beirut meeting, Witt kept his project on hold through much of 2005, waiting to see which politicians emerged from Iraq's transition process. But Witt's work was already taking effect. In November 2005, Ahmed Chalabi announced that PSAs were the way forward for Iraq. The former confidant to the Pentagon was now deputy prime minister and chair of the Energy Council, the most influential person in shaping major decisions about the structure of Iraq's oil industry. "In order to make major quantum increases in oil, we need to have production-sharing agreements," he said.[32]

In early 2006, Witt geared up his efforts again, now coordinating more with the U.S. government—in the form of the Trade and Development Administration—than the British.

In all his advocacy work, Witt claims not to represent any particular interest but rather to be advancing "best practice." He also insists that the supplementary funding for the Iraq project was "unrestricted" for accounting purposes—although sponsors understood that it would be spent on the Iraq project, there was no legal requirement for ITIC to do so. This is important for

Witt, because if ITIC were seen to be representing companies, its tax-exempt status would be undermined.

However, while Witt's work in Iraq did not favor any *one* company, it clearly advanced the interests of Western oil companies in general. And the six companies involved in the work already seemed to be benefiting. In summer 2005, the Oil Ministry announced that it was already in early discussions with four of those companies—BP, ChevronTexaco, Eni, and Total—about future contracts.[33]

Dan Witt is enthusiastic about his results so far: "I'm confident that the report has had an impact because there continues to be a sustained appetite for there to be a role for PSAs in Iraq."[34]

The decisions he wants to influence are soon to be made—decisions the oil companies eagerly await. No major oil company will start putting its cash into Iraq until the proper legal framework is in place, for fear that it could lose its assets in the international courts. First, a constitution is required: although approved in a referendum in October 2005, the Iraqi constitution is subject to six months of review in 2006 and 2007. Once that is finalized, the Iraqi government can write an Oil Law, which will set out the future structure of the oil industry and the terms on which any foreign investment can take place. Only after such a law is passed can long-term contracts be signed.

In December 2005, the Iraqi government signed a Standby Agreement with the IMF, which gave Iraq a financing facility and also allowed the next step in reducing Iraq's foreign debt. In exchange, the agreement set out the IMF's economic conditions for Iraq. The agreement was most controversial for forcing the government to slash public subsidies on fuel—including cooking gas, lamp oil, and the diesel and gasoline that are crucial for keeping generators running, since electricity is often available for only four hours a day. Prices tripled, suddenly and without alternative social protection programs in place, leading to protests on the streets and resignation of the oil minister, Ibrahim Bahr al-Uloum. Largely unnoticed in the small print of the agreement was a deadline at the end of 2006 for passing an Oil Law and a requirement that the IMF be involved in drafting the law.

Witt plans to play a key role in this process: to "hopefully contribute to the fruitful negotiations between investors and the Iraqis, so that they can be guided by best international practices, and hopefully our contribution will accelerate this process."[35] But his success is far from guaranteed. Throughout the history of the global oil industry, there has been a shifting balance of power between oil-producing countries and Western corporations, where what happens in one country is influenced by what is happening in others. As Iraq's oil future is being decided, the tide may be flowing away from the Western companies. Venezuela, with the world's sixth-largest oil reserves, has twice forced foreign companies to renegotiate their deals on fairer terms—or to leave the country. Smaller Bolivia copied this move more spectacularly in May 2006, moving troops into its gas fields. Russia, which has the world's seventh-largest oil reserves, may be starting to reverse the rapid liberalization and privatization of the 1990s, with government pressure currently focused on the oligarchs who got rich grabbing the nation's companies. And in Kuwait, the situation is finely balanced between a government that wants to bring in foreign companies and a parliament that refuses. Clearly, Western interests hope that, if Iraq can be pushed to let multinational companies control its oil industry, that will put pressure on Iran, Kuwait, and oil producers in general. Conversely, events in those other countries will play on Iraqi minds.

As Witt increases his efforts in Iraq, he is hoping for renewed support from the British government. Once again, this may give him access to high-level decision makers in the new Iraqi government. But what he has not factored in is the reaction of ordinary Iraqis, many of whom are strongly opposed to handing control of their oil back to the corporations who ripped them off so badly in the past.

Not the least of these obstacles to Witt's ambitions are the oilworkers. While Dan Witt courts politicians and government officials in expensive hotels, Hassan is on the drilling rigs and in the pumping stations, constantly working to educate his union's 23,000 members about the challenges they face. He has earned their loyalty, and he knows that if the union calls a strike it can stop all of Iraq's oil exports, with the potential to send the international oil price rocketing. The union has assiduously built support and solidarity among trade unionists and the antiwar movement around the world, who will all act to help the union when needed.

It is clear that the union will do everything in its power to stop foreign companies from grabbing Iraq's resources. The struggle over Iraqi oil is set to be one of the most important—and toughest—economic battlegrounds of the early twenty-first century.

As Hassan Juma'a says, "The opinion of all [Iraqi] oil workers is that they are against privatization. We see privatization as economic colonialism. The authorities are saying that privatization will develop our sector and be useful, but we do not see it as development at all: we view any plan to privatize the oil sector as a big disaster."

Notes

1. Dick Cheney, speech at the Institute of Petroleum Autumn Lunch, London, November 15, 1999.
2. Carola Hoyos, "Big Players Anticipate Iraq's Return to Fold," *Financial Times*, February 20, 2003.
3. *Shell in the Middle East*, Shell corporate magazine, April 2005.
4. Andrew Rowell, "Undue Influence," in *al-Khaleej*, June 4, 2006 (UAE) (in Arabic).
5. "ITIC 10-Year Review, 2003" (Washington, D.C.: International Tax and Investment Center, 2003), p. 4.
6. "ITIC Annual Report 1997."
7. Deepa Babington, "About Half of All Iraqis Unemployed—Govt. Official," Reuters, February 9, 2006.
8. "One Iraqi in Five Living in Poverty," Agence France Presse, January 25, 2006.
9. See, for example, (U.S.) National Energy Policy Development Group, *National Energy Policy*, report, May 2001, p. 8-5; Jack Straw, UK secretary of state for foreign and commonwealth affairs, speech, "Strategic Priorities for British Foreign Policy," January 6, 2003; UK Ministry of Defence White Paper: *Modern Forces for the Modern World* (Strategic Defence Review), July 1998, chapter 2, paragraph 40; Foreign and Commonwealth Office, *UK International Priorities: A Strategy for the FCO*, December 2003; U.S. Department of Commerce, Memorandum for the President, Transmittal of the Report on the U.S.–UK Energy Dialogue, July 30, 2003.
10. Dan Witt, "Applying the Principles of Taxation to the Russian Economy," *Tax Features*, September 1992, p. 7.
11. "ITIC 10-Year Review, 2003," p. 3.
12. Eduardo Lachica, "New Kazakh Tax System Is Applauded by Investors," *Asian Wall Street Journal*, May 7, 1995.
13. U.S. Department of Defense, "Pipeline Sustains Operations," press release, September 4, 2003.
14. Yergin, *The Prize: The Epic Quest for Oil, Money, and Power* (London: Simon & Schuster, 1991), p. 541.
15. "BP, UK Investigate Grangemouth's Woes," *Octane Week*, July 24, 2000; Fiona O'Brien, "BP Amoco Safety under Spotlight after UK Mishaps," Reuters, June 15, 2000.
16. Interview by David Bacon and Martha Mundy, international delegation to Basra, May 2005.
17. UNICEF, *Child and Maternal Mortality Survey—Iraq*, July 1999.
18. ITIC, *Strategic Questions for Our Future* (Washington, D.C.: International Tax and Investment Center, undated [2004]).
19. *ITIC Bulletin*, January 2003, p. 3.
20. Sir Maurice Hankey, letter to Arthur Balfour, 1918, cited in Yergin, *The Prize*, p. 188.
22. The last remnants of concessions were nationalized in 1975.
23. Rowell, "Undue Influence."
24. Thomas W. Wälde, "The Current Status of International Petroleum Investment: Regulating, Licensing, Taxing and Contracting," *CEPMLP Journal* 1, no. 5 (July 1995), published by the University of Dundee.
25. ITIC, "Petroleum and Iraq's Future: Fiscal Options and Challenges," Fall 2004, p. 10.
26. Dunia Chalabi (International Energy Agency), "Perspective for Investment in the Middle East/North Africa Region," presentation to the OECD, Istanbul, February 11–12, 2004, p. 7.

27. Ian Rutledge, *Addicted to Oil: America's Relentless Drive for Energy Security* (London: I. B. Tauris, 2005).

28. These figures are in real terms (2006 prices), *undiscounted*. The calculation is based on data from the Iraqi Ministry of Oil and industry sources, for the fields Halfaya, Nahr Umar, Majnoon, West Qurna, Gharaf, Nasiriya, Rafidain, Amara, Tuba, Ratawi, East Baghdad, and Ahdab. Cash flow models were constructed for these fields, applying PSA terms that are used in Russia, Libya, and Oman. A range of standard modeling assumptions were made; full details of the assumptions and methodology are given in Greg Muttitt, *Crude Designs: The Rip-off of Iraq's Oil Wealth* (London: PLATFORM, November 2005), available at www.carbonweb.org/crudedesigns.htm. Economists use a concept called *discounting* to take into account that having money now is worth more than having the same amount later—because money now in your possession can be invested and grow. Using this concept, amounts can be expressed as *net present values*—the equivalent amount now that "later money" would be worth. In these terms, the *net loss* (that is, the total expenditure minus the total revenue) to the Iraqi state would be in the range of $16 billion to $43 billion, expressed in 2006 net present value, at a 12 percent discount rate. This methodology is further explained in the report "Crude Designs."

29. Daniel Witt, speaking at the Second Eurasia Investment Summit, Almaty, Kazakhstan, April 2002; reported in *ITIC Bulletin,* special edn., April 19, 2002, p. 1.

30. Daniel Witt, "Take Democratization Slowly, So that Everyone Wins," *Arizona Daily Star,* November 12, 2005.

31. Foreign and Commonwealth Office (FCO), "Code of Practice for the Iraq Oil Industry," undated (Summer 2004), pp. 4–5.

32. Rowell, "Undue Influence."

33. "Iraq Exports Could Hit Pre-War Levels in '06—Chalabi," Reuters, November 12, 2005.

34. "Iraq Fast-Tracks Upstream Contract Talks with IOCS," *Middle East Economic Survey* 48, no. 25 (June 20, 2005).

35. Rowell, "Undue Influence."

36. Ibid.

8 *The World Bank has pushed debt-led economic development, and hundreds of billions of dollars in Bank loans were supposed to bring progress to the developing world. Where did the money go?*

The World Bank and the $100 Billion Question

Steve Berkman

Fostering a culture of lending without regard for results, the management of the World Bank has built a wall of misinformation around its lending operations, creating the illusion that all is well in the world of development. They have created the myth that they are at the "cutting edge" of development, while they hide the appalling number of failures within the Bank's portfolio—failures that enrich the governing elites of the Third World, while creating mountains of debt that cannot be repaid. Singing their own praises, they lead the Bank ever farther from its primary mission, ignoring their professional and fiduciary obligations as they advance their individual careers, while the people they have promised to help continue to live in poverty.

What Happened to the $100 Billion?

> The International Bank for Reconstruction and Development (IBRD):
> Cumulative Lending: $394 billion
> The International Development Association (IDA):
> Cumulative lending: $151 billion

So states the World Bank in its Annual Report for 2004. These figures are the focus of recent debates questioning the purpose and integrity of Bank loans and credits to Third World governments to fund economic development and alleviate poverty.[1] The Bank's critics charge that roughly $100 billion of the more than $500 billion it has lent since its creation has disappeared through ill-conceived loans to corrupt governments. Citing the Bank's lending operations to notoriously corrupt regimes in the Philippines, Zaire, Indonesia, Nigeria, and Haiti, they paint a picture of an institution obsessed with lending, no matter to whom, and no matter with what results. World Bank loans were supposed to bring progress to the underdeveloped nations of the Third World, yet somehow the programs have never lived up to their promise. Instead, the poor remained mired in poverty while their governing elites amassed obscene fortunes.

Countering these allegations, the Bank's management claims that its fiduciary safeguards keep lending losses to a minimum. But before we go any further, let me be clear about the Bank's management, for it is important to separate the institution from those who manage it. The Bank has long been saddled with an entrenched bureaucracy more concerned about its own well-being than about the success of the Bank's mission. Hiding behind the Bank as they disburse billions to corrupt and dysfunctional Third World regimes, these managers are accountable to no one as they advance their careers in an institutional culture that places lending above results. Management may approve bad loans, but it is the Bank that gets blamed. Management may be responsible for supporting failed projects, ignoring the theft of Bank funds for decades, and burdening the Third World with enormous debts, but the Bank's managers are never held personally responsible. And so the institution is called to task for its failures, while those who acted on its behalf are rewarded.

Management, in its attempts to demonstrate that it is fiscally responsible, tells us that the conditions stipulated in loan agreements, the procurement guidelines to control the use of funds, the supervision of lending operations, and periodic audits are all proof of the integrity of the Bank's portfolio. Management also says that its anticorruption programs have accomplished much during the past decade. The creation of a Department of Institutional Integrity to conduct fraud investigations, a hotline for reporting fraud and corruption, an investigation unit to pursue allegations, and a debarment process to deal with firms found guilty of paying bribes and kickbacks are often cited to demonstrate the Bank's commitment to fighting corruption. Management also presents numerous academic exercises with an anticorruption focus and its lending for anticorruption projects to refute the Bank's critics. But the Bank has yet to demonstrate that these actions have had any measurable impact on the cancer of corruption within its portfolio.

While the debate between the Bank and its critics has become heated at times, neither side has provided adequate evidence to support its claims. Critics refer to the failure of Bank loans to achieve their objectives and the obvious risk of lending to corrupt regimes, but they have presented little hard evidence to support their allegations. And while it is quite logical to conclude that the Marcos, Suharto, Abacha, Aristide, and similar regimes must have stolen Bank funds entrusted to them, until such allegations are proven, they are only conjecture.

So the question remains unanswered. Has the Bank lost $100 billion to fraud over the past several decades, or is this just a frivolous claim by critics who do not have all the facts? Sadly, having spent sixteen years in Bank lending operations and anticorruption investigations, I have become convinced that $100 billion or more may well have been lost to fraud, and that the critics' claims may not be all that frivolous. In this chapter, I offer a sample of the many cases of fraud and embezzlement I have observed and investigated in Bank-funded lending operations over the years. Real-life proof of the extent to which corruption permeates the Bank's lending portfolio, and the extent to which this has compromised the Bank's mission and credibility. Real-life proof that the Bank may indeed have lost $100 billion, possibly more, to fraud and embezzlement over the past several decades.

Liberia: Did You Bring The Money?

What seemed like an endless flight on Pan Am had brought me to Monrovia the previous evening, and now, as we climbed the steps of the city hall in the warm morning sun, my adrenaline picked up as the reality of it all began to sink in. It was November 1983, and I was on my first field mission for the World Bank. I was eager to begin work, for after several years of knocking on doors, networking, and generally making a nuisance of myself, someone, in their great wisdom, had at last been desperate enough to hire me. I had no background in international banking, nor was I an economist, but I did have some experience with overseas project operations and technical training that seemed to coincide with some of the Bank's staffing needs. Within a few days of signing a one-year consulting contract with the Bank's West Africa Region, here I was entering the decaying portals of the City Hall in Monrovia, the capital of Liberia, a small West African nation ruled at the time by Samuel Doe and his brutal, corrupt, and dysfunctional regime.

The white stone steps showed the effects of time and neglect, with broken treads and missing sections of balustrade. As we entered the lobby I saw more decay and deterioration, and I imagined how it must have looked in earlier times. It had been well built and was reminiscent of a bygone era, but sadly it had gone to ruin through mismanagement, corrupt government, bad politics, and God knows what else. I would see similar scenes many times during the coming years, scenes that would always stir feelings of frustration at the futility of trying to get anything accomplished on projects the Bank had financed in Africa, and at the inability of our African counterparts and the well-meaning donor community to bring some sanity to this great continent.

As I walked across the empty lobby with Benny di Zitti and two consultants, we were beckoned by someone on the balcony above us. Benny, the "mission leader," would be my supervisor, mentor, and, for many years after, good friend. Fortunately for me, he was an old hand in the business, and this calmed the trepidations I'd had when hired only a few days before without any briefing on the nature of the Bank's business or the mission itself. A Canadian citizen of Italian descent who grew up in Uganda and spoke English, French, and Swahili in addition to his native Italian, Benny was at home in any environment and had a wonderful way of getting the job done in a very low-key manner. There were others like Benny at the Bank, dedicated, hard-working individuals who struggled to make things work under extremely difficult conditions. Unfortunately, I would soon learn that dedication and hard work did not always translate into positive results for Bank-funded projects in Africa.

We were there to supervise implementation of the Monrovia Urban Development Project (MUDP), which was financed by the International Development Association (IDA), the lending arm of the World Bank that provides interest-free credits to the world's poorest countries. This particular credit of $10 million was provided to the government of Liberia to improve conditions for the urban poor living in and around Monrovia. The local population did not have access to clean water, many roads were impassable, and sanitation and drainage were nonexistent, while garbage accumulated throughout the city. This project was going to change at least some of that, and my part was to help the local authorities develop training programs to ensure that municipal administrators, supervisors, and employees could perform their duties effectively.

We climbed the stairs to the second-floor balcony and walked past a number of offices. The whole place was strangely quiet, and I filed away mental images of workers in various states of lethargy as I passed each office. It appeared that sleeping at their desks or listening to music on the radio were the only tasks on their agendas. At the end of the hall we were ushered into the mayor's office, where I somehow wound up at the front of our little team. As we entered, the mayor came out from behind his desk. Short, a bit on the portly side, he was dressed in crisply pressed fatigues with a colonel's insignia pinned on his collar and had a pearl-handled revolver strapped to his side, cowboy style. Looking quite serious, he walked toward me and I found that I couldn't take my eyes off his revolver. Suddenly, he stretched out his arms, broke into a big smile, and said, "World Bank, World Bank, welcome, welcome." As he grabbed me by the shoulders, his face became serious again. He eyed our leather bags filled with project documents: "Did you bring the money? Where is the money?"

I began to say nervously that all we had were our travel advances, but fortunately Benny came to the rescue. He quietly explained that the Bank pays project costs directly to suppliers as they are incurred and that we do not bring cash with us. The mayor, obviously disappointed, just stared at us blankly for a few seconds before he asked us to be seated. We then sat down to discuss what we planned to do during our mission, and I began to focus seriously on the work at hand.

With some rare exceptions, all Bank-financed projects in Africa operate on the assumption that local government personnel at all job levels will need training to perform their jobs properly. My job was to ensure that the training programs would accomplish this objective, and I would come to understand very quickly that things were not quite as simple as they appeared. Over the coming years, I would learn that the real motivation for training, especially overseas training, was often merely a perquisite to enable civil servants to profit from stipends and other arrangements that were considerably more than they earned at their jobs. It was not unusual for a government official with a $300 monthly salary to obtain thousands of dollars in tuition and stipend payments that would never be accounted for; excess payments to high-level officials could easily run to tens of thousands of dollars.

Later that morning, along with the Liberian project director, we visited the Department of Public Works to see how things were progressing. As we passed through various offices, I noted more of the same lethargy among the workers that I had noticed at City Hall. They made no attempt to hide the fact that they were not working—some were asleep at their desks or sprawled on benches, while others just sat idly at their desks. I also noted the appalling physical environment: poor lighting, broken windows, broken furniture, and office equipment that obviously did not work. We then toured the motor pool or, more appropriately, the vehicle boneyard, where the same apathy and physical conditions were equally evident. Workers were sleeping, or chatting in small groups, while occasionally one could be found supervising a young apprentice at tire repair, greasing vehicles, or other semi-skilled tasks in the workshop.

Achieving some of the project objectives connected with road improvement, drainage, and garbage collection required trucks, graders, tractors, and other moving equipment in good working order. One of the key problems faced by the project was that none of the equipment was working. The motor pool consisted of some vehicles up on blocks with their wheels off, others with their engines removed, and still others in various states of disrepair. We discussed these problems with the works supervisor, who ran down a list of the reasons why work was not under way. They had no funds for operating expenses. They had no spare parts. The local fuel supplier had not been paid for some time and would not give them fuel on credit. The employees had not been paid in several months. The few vehicles that were still operating had been "borrowed" by the minister. And so on. Although project funds provided by the Bank were to be used, among other things, to purchase spare parts, none had yet been ordered, and, while the government was to provide counterpart funding for daily operational expenses, that, too, had not been forthcoming. The result: total inertia.

I gradually realized that inertia was only a tiny part of the problem when I returned to Liberia four months later for the final appraisal of the Second Water Supply Project. Still very new, and still very much in awe of what the Bank was doing in Africa, I was slowly learning to read between the lines to decipher the differences between what was said and written and what was actually done. The Liberia Water and Sewer Corporation (LWSC) had received an $8 million IDA credit in 1978, and the Bank was now preparing to approve a second credit for about $5 million. Again, my job was to ensure that the funds to be provided for staff training would be used effectively. But where to start? Despite assistance from the Bank and other donors on the previous project, LWSC's institutional problems seemed insurmountable.

As a government institution designed to be self-supporting from the service fees it collects from the public, LWSC was supposed to operate on a quasi-commercial basis. But this was clearly not the case, and our mission team found serious financial problems in the billing and collection process:

> Although LWSC consistently bills about 13,000 private consumers each month, only about 3,000 actually pay. Fortunately, the larger private con-

sumers pay fairly consistently, so that on a volume basis approximately 50% of the amounts billed to private consumers are collected. One apparent cause of LWSC's poor collection ratio is the lack of reliable accounts receivable records. Although LWSC's service bureau produces a report purporting to be an accounts receivable aging, the report carries some 22,000 accounts, while current active customers are estimated at 13,000. Furthermore, the aging report carries cumulative arrears totaling over US$17 million.[2]

The arrears owed to LWSC were more than three times the new credit the Bank was planning to provide. And the arrears did not include roughly $4.6 million owed to LWSC by the government for service to the various ministries and public corporations. In addition, our report noted that

The grim financial picture of LWSC is partly attributable to inefficient operations. Overstaffing is the most obvious drain on the budget, but the mission was informed of several others. These include:

a) Poorly monitored chemical dosage, with attendant likelihood of excess chemical use;

b) Set-rate pumping and operation at the treatment plant, disregarding reduced demands at night. This leads to excess consumption and waste;

c) Cumbersome purchasing procedures leading to extended waits for repairs of vehicles, machinery, etc. necessary for leak repairs;

d) Excessive purchase prices for chemicals, in part for failure to assure payments;

e) Private use of vehicles.

Now all this might seem mundane, but it was difficult to grasp how in hell we could expect LWSC to get its act together. Why were we lending the agency more money when it couldn't collect what was due from its customers? And how would this new credit help them when the last one had been such a dismal failure? I was still very new to all this, and I decided to keep my concerns to myself, since these problems had nothing to do with the project training programs I was responsible for.

The credit was, of course, approved, and three years later I visited the ongoing project to find LWSC more mismanaged and inefficient than before.

While some of this condition could be attributed to the deteriorating political situation within the country, much of it was due to incompetence and corruption within the institution—a condition the Bank kept conveniently ignoring.

My one-year contract was renewed for another three years, and I continued working on projects in Liberia. In June 1985, I was asked to look at the progress being made at the Monrovia Vocational Training Center (MVTC), which was being financed as part of the Fourth Education Project. This $12.6 million project was the last in a series of education credits totaling $30 million from 1972 through 1988, with the objective of improving the quality of vocational training.

I met with the project manager at the Ministry of Education, and we drove to the MVTC on the outskirts of town. It was housed in a school building set on a large parcel of land and appeared to be in reasonably good physical condition. After meeting with center administrators and faculty to discuss curriculum development, apprenticeship programs, equipment procurement, and staff fellowships, I toured the facilities to review repairs and improvements that had been made with project funds. Having spent some of my earlier career in the construction industry, I was interested in seeing how the work was carried out and what local construction costs were.

Two separate contracts had been awarded for the installation of burglar-proofing on the doors and windows and construction of a barrier wall around the campus. I chose to review these items because they appeared to be much less critical than other priorities that were already short of funds and because the costs of the contracts were high compared with many of the others. The burglar-proofing contract exceeded $60,000—for installing steel bars on all ground floor windows and doors. According to the project director, this was necessary to prevent theft of school equipment. Over the years I would observe that although burglar-proofing of public buildings was a common practice in West Africa, looting was usually done by people already inside.

After inspecting the iron window bars and door grills and noting the quantities of materials used, I visited a few local metalworking shops to compare costs. Posing as an expatriate who would be moving into the area with a private firm, I used specifications identical to the items installed at MVTC. Surprisingly, with the prices I obtained "off the street," I estimated that the MVTC installation could have been done for less than $15,000, or about one quarter of the price actually paid. If anything, I would have expected, as an obviously well-off foreigner, to get price quotes much higher than the MVTC costs. But when I discussed all this with the project director, he smiled and assured me that the administration had awarded the contract to the lowest bidder. He also explained that, since the government was notoriously slow to pay, contractors increased their prices to compensate for payment delays. This seemed to contradict what had actually occurred: project records indicated that the contractor had been paid immediately upon submission of his invoice. When I pointed this out, the director smiled weakly and said nothing. Where the extra $45,000 went, only God, the contractor, and a few civil servants would ever know.

The contract for the perimeter wall was even more interesting. The MVTC was located along a road from Monrovia and situated on several hectares of land that, except for the building itself, was vacant and covered with scrub brush. Behind the campus boundary was a small settlement of huts. For some unexplained reason, it had been decided that a wall had to be built around the campus both to prevent the local inhabitants from walking through the property on their way to the road and to prevent their goats from grazing there. The concrete block wall was about two meters high, with electric lights along the top every twenty meters. Extending around the perimeter of the campus, it cost over $250,000. The wall itself was poorly constructed and incomplete, and the electrical work had never been finished. Despite this, the project accounts indicated that the contractor had been paid in full immediately on submission of his invoice. When I told the project director my observations, he dismissed my concerns, saying that there was no problem—he would have the contractor come back to finish the work.

Again, I did my research at a local building materials supplier and talked to some local masons. Again, I was quoted prices considerably lower than the "low bid" contract awarded for the project. Using the "off the street" prices, I estimated that the true cost of the contract, had it been completed, should have been somewhere around $75,000, leaving an unexplained difference of roughly $175,000. The highlight of my review was the fact that the contractor had left a ten-meter gap in the wall where the path used by the local inhabitants ran through the property. It seems that, because the terrain around the sides of the campus was very marshy, there would have been no way for people to get to the road if the wall had been constructed across the pathway. And so, people still passed freely through the campus while the goats continued to graze—one more lesson in my ongoing education about economic development in Africa.

The last of my four missions to Liberia occurred in September 1987, when conditions in the country had deteriorated to such an extent that the Bank was no longer lending to the Doe government. Why it took the Bank's management so long to realize the hopelessness of dealing with this corrupt regime is something I could never understand, and whether the halt to lending was due to that realization or to some bureaucratic requirements that the government had been unable to meet, I do not know. As someone still relatively new to the Bank, I believed that we were making a difference and that some good would come from the work we were doing. I believed that our counterparts, the civil servants and politicians we were working with were, by and large, trying to do the best they could under extremely difficult circumstances, and that the instances of fraud and corruption I had seen on Bank projects were the exception, not the rule. In the coming years, I would come to understand that, in most cases, if you looked closely into Bank projects, you would find that they were more about the personal enrichment of government officials than about alleviating the poverty and deplorable living conditions of the average African citizen.

These snapshots of my early observations and perceptions of Bank operations in Liberia show the glaring contradictions between the glowing pictures painted by the Bank in describing its African development efforts and the chaos and corruption that existed on the ground. Despite all indications to the contrary, at no time would the Bank admit that its lending operations were achieving nothing. At no time would it admit that perhaps its money and advice might have been wasted, through untenable politics, incompetence, or corruption—most likely all three. And, despite the ever-increasing debt burden placed upon the African people, at no time would the Bank reduce its lending in the face of incontrovertible evidence that these factors would negate all well-meaning efforts to nurture economic progress. And so the game would continue to be played, year after year, in country after country.

Corruption: "Greasing the Wheels"

My early missions to Liberia were just the beginning of my education into the world of economic development. Each country that I worked in on the African continent brought with it growing awareness that the whole business was a facade—smoke and mirrors put up by the Bank and its local counterparts to convince everyone that good things were being accomplished with the billions being loaned to alleviate poverty in the Third World. For it was seldom that the money we were providing for development ever accomplished anything of substance that truly benefited the poor. Yet year after year, and despite glaring evidence to the contrary, the Bank would produce glowing reports of success in one sector after another, in one country after another, as its managers sought to protect themselves from criticism.

What lay underneath those glowing reports? Was life improving for the average man or woman in the streets, or was the Bank's management covering up the obvious failures of its policy of lending to corrupt and dysfunctional governments? Was it being honest about its clients' concern and commitment to improve the lot of their citizens, or was it content to let sleeping dogs lie, as long as the Bank could feed its appetite for lending? Sadly, the Bank's penchant for lending has blinded it to the simple truth that placing money in the hands of corrupt government officials is a recipe for disaster: there is no end to the creative ways in which those officials will steal from Bank-funded projects.

From big multimillion-dollar contracts to daily transactions through general cash accounts, project officials have concocted all sorts of scams to embezzle Bank funds. With or without the aid of accomplices on the outside, they establish shell companies, facilitate bid rigging, create fraudulent procurement documents, establish hidden project accounts, authorize payments for overpriced goods and services, and commit other fraudulent acts to enrich themselves. While some Bank apologists dismiss these criminal acts as "the cost of doing business," or "just greasing the wheels," in reality they severely hinder project operations far beyond the actual dollar loss. Ignoring the fact that a hundred dollars stolen may cause a thousand dollars in economic damage, Bank proponents pretend that corruption has not prevented the Bank from achieving its mission. Whatever the percentage of funds stolen from project accounts, the process is like stealing $20 worth of fuel from a new $20,000 vehicle. You may have a car, but you're not going anywhere.

Nigeria: A Small Commission

While filling in for a colleague on vacation, I was contacted by someone from the British Embassy regarding a matter that had been referred to the embassy by a British distributor of textbooks. The matter concerned a contract for approximately $25 million worth of university textbooks in a Bank-funded project in Nigeria. It seemed that the distributor had been approached by an individual claiming to represent certain government officials in the National Universities Commission (NUC) who were in a position to award the contract to whomever they pleased. The "representative" presented confidential project documents to prove his relationship with the NUC officials and said that he could ensure the contract award in exchange for a commission. The commission was to be 15 percent ($3.75 million) of the contract amount and would be shared among the project officials. The distributor said that it would not pay such a fee, and soon after that the representative contacted the distributor again to say that the officials would be willing to accept 10 percent ($2.5 million) but nothing less. Still refusing to cooperate with this extortion attempt, the distributor sought help from the Bank through the British Embassy.

Knowing that there were only a few international firms qualified to bid on such a large book order, and anxious to win the award, the distributor had submitted a very competitive bid. Nine days after learning of this situation from the British Embassy, I was contacted by the representative of a U.S. distributor, who said that it had also submitted a bid and had been informed by an unnamed consultant that the company would soon be invited to Nigeria to "negotiate" the award of the bid. Ten days after that, I was again contacted by the U.S. distributor, who passed on information it had received from an unidentified person. The distributor had been told that "Bank procedures had prevented the negotiation of the bid award," but, since only three bidders were short-listed, the Nigerians had decided to split the procurement into three awards.

The whole business sounded suspicious, and I passed on this information to my colleague and to Bank management, who in turn intervened to get the bid award back on a transparent track. But the Nigerian officials, ever determined, had other plans, which centered on a divide-and-conquer scheme using subcontracts as a vehicle for enriching themselves and their accomplices.

This award was to be made through international competitive bidding in which the lowest-priced technically qualified bid would receive the contract. If, in the course of providing goods and services, a winning bidder decided to use subcontractors, this fact and the qualifications of the subcontractors were to be disclosed at the time of bid submission. But that was not how it would be in this case. Soon, both the British and the U.S. distributors received identical letters dated February 15, 1991, from NUC stating the following:

> I am pleased to inform you that as a result of the bid evaluation made on your bid as procurement agent for Books under the above credit facility, **your company has been successful**. A meeting of a representative of your organization with the Executive Secretary of the National Universities Commission has therefore been scheduled for Monday, 25th February, 1991, to discuss this development.
>
> It is very important that a representative of your organization to this crucial meeting is senior enough to take on-the-spot decisions on behalf

of the company as there may not be time for any representative to consult his/her organization on any issues that may be discussed at the meeting before agreements are reached.

And so the scam was put into motion. With only ten days' notice, both distributors went to Lagos thinking they had won the $25 million book contract. Upon arrival at NUC, both were handed letters dated February 15, 1991, that were nearly identical to the letters of the same date they had received earlier—identical, but with one exception: instead of stating "your company has been successful," the second letter stated that "your company has been shortlisted." What a difference one word can make! Now in the same room with the NUC officials and two unqualified Nigerian bidders, the British and U.S. distributors quickly learned that, if they wanted any business with NUC, they would have to share the award with all the other bidders.

The two international distributors tried in vain for two months to win the award honestly while pleading for assistance from the World Bank. The Bank made an initial effort to keep the procurement transparent, but in the end allowed the officials to succeed in their scheme by not pursuing the obvious fraud they committed after the award was made to the British distributor.

This is how it played out: The British distributor had clearly submitted the winning bid, and NUC reported to the Bank that it had been awarded the $25 million contract. The award was approved by the Bank. But the Bank was not told that the award was made on condition that the other three "bidders"—the U.S. firm and the two Nigerian firms—would share in the business as subcontractors. The British firm would get 50 percent, the U.S. firm would get 15 percent, and the Nigerian firms would get 20 percent and 15 percent, respectively. And so it was that 35 percent ($8.75 million), or more than twice the original "commission" solicited by the NUC officials, was awarded to two unqualified Nigerian firms. In the end, much of what the Nigerian firms were to deliver to the universities was never accounted for, and neither was the money that was paid to them.

Argentina: Oxygen and Money

Africa is not the only place where World Bank funds are stolen, for corruption has been the bedfellow of all Bank-funded projects I have encountered over the years. And while I have found differences in the sophistication of the various scams perpetrated by government officials and their associates, all constituted fraud and embezzlement. For example, the sophistication of a scam involving a $100 million health project in Argentina was in a different league from the blatant attempts to extort kickbacks by officials of NUC in Nigeria.

The Argentine project was created to improve health services in several provinces and the city of Buenos Aires. It was managed through the national Ministry of Health. Bank funds were to be used to rehabilitate hospital facilities and provide consulting services to improve health policy and administration. Project operations were managed by provincial project units that reported to a central coordinating unit in the ministry. Contracts were awarded by the provincial units with the approval of the central unit, which handled the disbursement of Bank funds. This created a multilayered contract award process that officials at both levels manipulated to suit their own agendas.

The hospital rehabilitation program involved numerous civil works contracts and the procurement of medical equipment. Among the equipment awards was a $750,000 contract for medical oxygen generating plants for two of the hospitals. After a complaint by a losing bidder, Bank investigators learned that the contract had been awarded to a newly established local company that claimed to be the exclusive representative of a reputable U.S. manufacturer of oxygen plants. The complainant alleged that the winning bidder had inside contacts with the central project unit and should have been disqualified, since it did not provide three years of financial statements as required under the terms of the bidding.

The Bank, through its then newly formed Anti-Corruption and Fraud Investigation Unit, investigated the allegations and found the following:

> The local firm winning the bid had been formed specifically to obtain the oxygen plant contract, and was not officially incorporated until one month *after* the bid was submitted. The principals of the company had no prior experience in the specialized field of medical oxygen, and evidence linked them to officials within the project unit.
>
> The winning bidder's claim that it was the exclusive representative of the US manufacturer was false, since the manufacturer confirmed that it would sell its products through any distributor in the country. The manufacturer's only involvement in the bidding process was to submit a discounted price to the local firm.
>
> Although the Bank was notified that the award had been made to the local firm, the project unit made the contract out to the US manufacturer. When queried about this deviation from the Bank's procurement guidelines, the project officials offered the lame excuse that the US firm was able

to comply with the three-year financial record requirement and that was why the contract had been sent to them. Although this excuse merely confirmed that the local bidder had not been qualified to receive the award in the first place, it was apparently not contested by Bank management.

Included within the contract award was a $100,000 component for civil works to construct two small buildings to house the oxygen-generating equipment at the hospitals. In effect, the US manufacturer, with no presence in Argentina, and no construction background, was being asked to carry out this activity. When the US firm objected to this contractual obligation, they were told by the project officials that "it was the way the World Bank wanted the contract written." The manufacturer was told that the local firm would take care of the construction, payment would be made to the manufacturer, and the manufacturer was instructed to then transfer the $100,000 back to the local firm.

Bank investigation into other contract award anomalies revealed that the construction of the oxygen plant buildings had been embedded in hospital civil works contracts awarded to other Argentine firms that actually did the construction. The resultant double invoicing of the civil works was done with the full knowledge of certain project officials in collusion with the principals of the local "representative" of the US manufacturer, providing them with a $100,000 windfall profit for which no services had been performed.

Although the oxygen plants were shipped from the US manufacturer and installed in the newly constructed buildings, it was found that the equipment did not fully comply with the technical requirements of the original request for bids. Due to the lack of technical knowledge of the local "representative" who supplied the plant specifications to the US manufacturer, and the complicity of the project officials in the scam, it would cost an additional $180,000 to modify the equipment to comply with the original requirements.

Several years after the contract was awarded to this shell company, the equipment remained inoperative at the two hospitals. Government officials had failed to force the local "representative" and the U.S. manufacturer to comply with the bid specifications. Despite considerable evidence of collusion between the local firm and certain project officials, the government made no effort to prosecute the individuals involved.

A Cascade of Scams Uncovered

It would be naive to think that the oxygen plant scam was just an anomaly in this $100 million project. The temptation of all that money was too much for project officials to resist. This investigation alone exposed several other cases involving consulting contracts and civil works that showed the creativity of project officials in embezzling funds from the project:

A $216,000 consulting contract to supervise the civil works at one hospital was to be awarded to a local consultant. Although the award had already been approved by the Bank, the consultant was advised by a project official that he would have to pay a 10% "commission" to get final approval. At a meeting with the official in a local bar, the consultant secretly taped the attempted shakedown, and agreed to pay the bribe once he got the contract. After being awarded the contract, the consultant refused to pay the 10% and subsequently had his contract terminated. Despite bringing the tape recording to the Bank's attention, and that of Government authorities, his contract was never re-instated.

In the course of investigating the consultant's allegations above, it was revealed that the consulting contract for the architectural work at the hospital had been awarded to a close associate of the project director. Evidence was found pointing to strong indications that the integrity of the bidding and award process had been compromised. Subsequently, serious defects in the quality of the architectural work resulted in extensive change orders costing an additional $600,000 above the original civil works contract. The same architecture consultant was also awarded a contract in connection with a $2.5 million civil works undertaking at another hospital. This, too, resulted in an additional $800,000 in highly questionable change order payments that were never fully accounted for.

During the investigation of the architectural consulting contract, it was learned that a local construction company had been awarded a $5.1 million contract for civil works at one hospital. The award went to the lowest qualified bidder and had been made prior to a change in government and the election of a new president. Before signing the contract, the project officials took deceptive measures to disqualify the winning bidder and the second lowest bidder. They then awarded the contract to the third highest bidder for $5.9 million, or $800,000 over the original winning bid. Although there was no evidence of direct involvement, information was obtained linking the president of the winning firm and the project director to the newly elected president of Argentina.

Such questionable contract awards were also found in other investigations carried out in Argentina's health sector. Bid rigging, extortion, fraudulent invoicing, manipulation of tax exemptions, and every other form of embezzlement imaginable were practiced by government officials and their accomplices. While the amounts were relatively small in the context of a $100 million project, we must not forget that thousands of contracts were awarded for various Bank-funded projects in Argentina each year, and it would be the rare exception to find one that had not been abused in some way.

From One Scam to $100 Billion

How do these few examples of fraud on Bank-funded projects translate into losses of $100 billion over the past few decades? The cases I've just described are only a small picture of what is going on every working day as the Bank disburses billions of dollars each year through the hands of Third World government officials who consider those funds their personal piggy banks. I have seen firsthand much more than I can squeeze into this brief chapter: millions of dollars for roads that could not be found, millions paid for the rehabilitation of infrastructure that could not be verified, millions to improve social services that somehow never reached the poor, millions to facilitate better economic policies, and millions to improve governance. All in the name of economic development. All in the name of alleviating poverty.

Some will dismiss the cases of fraud I have cited above as merely anecdotal evidence and insufficient to prove the extent of corruption within the Bank's portfolio. But they do a disservice to themselves and the Bank by refusing to see this evidence for the reality it exposes. The reality is that a disproportionate percentage of the procurement transactions occurring on Bank-funded projects hide rampant fraud and embezzlement perpetrated by the government officials entrusted to manage those funds. Just what might that percentage be, and just how much would it come to in dollars?

While I am sure that the Bank's apologists would prefer theoretical analyses and detailed studies to prove that corruption robs the poor of even one dollar, I submit that the cases I have described, and the many more I have not discussed, are ample proof of the extent of the problem. I have seen entire projects looted from one end to the other. I have discovered payments made at over 1,000 percent of actual value, for goods or services that might not have been delivered at all. I have witnessed every sort of chicanery imaginable in the perpetration of fraud on Bank-funded projects. Such rampant corruption can lead only to the conclusion that fraud and embezzlement are more the rule than the exception in the Bank's portfolio.

And so, the big question. Has the Bank lost $100 billion to corruption over the past several decades, or hasn't it? Even those most supportive of the Bank's historic "see no evil, hear no evil, speak no evil" approach to the issue will admit to annual losses averaging 10 percent. Although extremely conservative, that proportion translates into $2.0 billion per year,[3] no small amount even for the World Bank. And while I would be happy to provide evidence that the figure could be as high as 30 to 40 percent in some countries, there is no doubt that, at the very least, 20 percent is lost each year, a figure no one has seriously disputed with me. While still on the conservative side, this figure, applied to the $500 billion dollars loaned by the Bank over the past decades, gives us $100 billion, supporting in broad terms the claims of the Bank's critics. Yes, the World Bank has lost $100 billion from its portfolio through fraud and corruption, and it may possibly have lost even more.

And so, despite the Bank's rhetoric, corruption remains alive and well. Government officials and their accomplices continue to plunder billions of dollars each year with impunity, while the Bank and the other donor institutions nibble at the edges pretending that they are making a difference. The poor continue to live in abject poverty, while their leaders continue to live in luxury.

We must insist upon a different course of action. The individuals who manage the Bank, and the donor community in general, must honor their fiduciary responsibilities and ensure that the money provided for economic development is used to bring direct benefits to the poor. They need to lend less and supervise more. They need to study less and act more. They need to report honestly and completely about the failures in their lending program. They need to use the full power of their institutions to press governments to investigate, prosecute, and punish corrupt officials, as they would any other criminals, and to recover stolen funds and assets wherever possible. The Gods of Lending can do no less if we are to keep our promise to all those who are struggling to survive in what we still call the developing world.

Notes

1. *Loans* are made at interest rates established by the Bank, while *credits* are provided to the poorest nations interest-free. For purposes of brevity, loans referred to in this article will include credits.
2. Back-to-Office-Report, dated March 13, 1984, Appendix A, Paragraph 2.
3. Based upon recent averages of $20.0 billion disbursed annually.

9 *The World Bank made the Philippines a test case in its loan-based, export-led development strategy—and the results were dictatorship, poverty, and a crushing debt burden.*

The Philippines, the World Bank, and the Race to the Bottom

Ellen Augustine

The early 1970s. The Vietnam War is in the headlines daily. Mass demonstrations are rocking the world. Policy makers think in terms of the domino effect in the bitter struggle between communism and capitalism. In the Philippines, strongman Ferdinand Marcos holds power, but there's a growing insurgency in the countryside. In the eyes of the United States and the World Bank, Marcos is the only thing standing between one more country falling to the Reds in the Cold War. Direct aid is one way to keep him in power. The other and more potent means: World Bank loans, with their oversight and conditionalities. With an American always the president of the Bank, the United States got what it wanted—with disastrous results for the Philippines. But this time, thanks to whistle-blowers inside the World Bank, we can get an insider's view of how the development game is played and why the results are usually far different from official rhetoric.

America's Hidden Colonial Past

The U.S.–Philippines relationship goes back a long way, though few remember the Spanish-American War from History 101. The U.S. "purchased" the Philippines after defeating Spain in 1898. The Philippines had been under Spanish control for 300 years, and Filipinos did not welcome another master. In fact, a provisional government led by Emiliano Aguinaldo had been set to take power after assisting the U.S. forces. Instead, the Filipinos were swept aside and a bloody insurrection ensued, which was finally defeated after several years and the loss of 250,000 Filipino lives. The U.S. established a typical colonial relationship, with the Philippines exporting agricultural commodities such as sugar and importing American manufactured goods. In 1946 the U.S. granted independence—keeping twenty military bases, however, including Clark Field and Subic Bay.

During its rule, the U.S. had allied itself with the country's wealthy land-owning elite, which maintained political power after independence. Coming from this strata, Ferdinand Marcos assumed the presidency in the 1960s. In a particularly corrupt and violent election, he secured a second term in 1969, in the process using up the government's foreign exchange reserves. Without reserves, the country was unable to cover a huge trade deficit and pay interest on mounting external debt.

Marcos turned for help to the World Bank. One of its conditions for assistance was a 60 percent devaluation of the peso. In the 1970s, currency devaluation was the standard Bank prescription for Third World countries needing loans. In theory, this would bring the trade account into balance by increasing foreign exchange earnings from cheaper Philippine goods while decreasing outward cash flow for now more expensive imports. Devaluation in fact brought disaster to businesses and workers alike. Scores of Filipino entrepreneurs were thrown into bankruptcy when suddenly confronted with more expensive imported components for their products.[1] The wages of urban workers dropped as much as 50 percent. Years later the first draft of the Poverty Mission report, leaked by whistleblowers, identified this Bank-imposed devaluation as the key factor precipitating decline in Filipino living standards—though this admission was excised from the final version of the report.[2]

They Came, They Saw, They Liberalized

The collision of the World Bank's macroeconomic policy and real people's lives was bloody and left a multitude of casualties. Currency devaluation is part of the broader policy of *liberalization*—sometimes called *neoliberalism*—which is both the standard precursor to structural adjustment loans and a continuing part of the structural adjustment package. Liberalization is at the core of World Bank trade policies, for the Philippines as well as most other developing countries.

Liberalization can be a very confusing word. In common usage, *liberal* means "progressive, imbued with compassion for the less fortunate, and a willingness to put government resources into redressing past harms and creating social and economic equality." But in modern economics, liberalization is quite different. Doug Henwood, economist and publisher of the *Left Business Observer*, explains it this way:

"Liberalization means removing any barriers to the efficient functioning of the market. That would mean eliminating trade barriers, eliminating obstacles to foreign investment, reducing the size of government domestically, and reducing the regulation of an economy. Basically it means Reaganism: "unleashing the magic of the marketplace." This might sound attractive to Americans, especially a lot of Americans who are opposed to state intervention and distrust welfare states."[3]

The problem with the World Bank/International Monetary Fund model is that no country using it has ever developed successfully.

"The countries that have developed successfully over the last forty years have been those primarily in East Asia, whose governments took a very active planning role. They regulated imports, limited capital flows, regulated interest rates, and directed capital into preferred areas for development. China, the current star, has developed under the very skillful hand of the state, and it followed *none* of the standard policy prescriptions. So liberalization has a very poor track record. It's highly unusual for a country to develop successfully without some degree of protectionism."[4]

Not so long ago, the United States itself was a developing nation. Did its rise to prosperity follow the path recommended by the World Bank? Henwood recaps U.S. history:

"We violated all the laws we impose on countries today. We depended on protective tariffs into the early twentieth century. We also violated all the intellectual property rights we now hold sacred. The U.S. chemical industry got started during World War I, when we stole the German patents. In the nineteenth century, U.S. publishers were notorious for republishing works of foreign authors without permission or royalties. Orthodox economics insists on letting the market work and subjecting domestic producers to foreign competition. But this is also the ideology of the strong. You want to prescribe free competition and liberalization when you're the big guy on the hill, because no one can compete with you. So on the way up, everybody's a protectionist. But once you get to the top, you're a free trader. For rich countries like Japan, Western Europe, the United States, Canada, open trade is fine. But poorer countries that are trying to develop cannot afford a regime of free trade. There's no way they can develop their own industries facing competition from the developed countries. It's just impossible. It's not going to make the poor less poor."[5]

Export Processing Zones: Subsidies for the Multinationals

Another condition imposed by the World Bank for the loans Marcos sought was opening up the Philippines to foreign investment in the form of export processing zones (EPZs). A major zone was created across the bay from Manila. Incentives for foreign corporations included:

- Permission for 100 percent foreign ownership
- Permission to pay a wage lower than Manila's minimum wage
- Tax exemptions
- Low rents for land and low charges for water
- Government financing of infrastructure and factory buildings, which could be rented or purchased at a low price
- Accelerated depreciation of fixed assets[6]

These projects did not come cheap for the Philippines. One site alone, the model Bataan EPZ, cost $150 million to develop, including a dam and water-treatment plant. Overall, the government spent billions of borrowed money on energy, transportation, communications, water, and construction to entice foreign corporations.[7] Companies that made hefty profits in these EPZs included Texas Instruments, Fairchild, Motorola, and Mattel.[8] While the cost of export-oriented development was high for the Philippines, the commitment was low for the multinationals. Such an arrangement made it relatively easy for them to pick up and leave when workers demanded a more realistic wage—and that is exactly what the multinationals did.

Play by the Rules—and Lose

Export-oriented development is a key component in the World Bank's standard prescription for developing countries. Yet targeting the bulk of a country's borrowed money to support export-oriented development means that little is left to address pressing domestic needs. Doug Henwood explains how this plays out in a country such as the Philippines:

"Export-oriented development is still the absolute centerpiece of orthodox development theory. Countries like the Philippines have dire domestic needs that should take precedence over export-oriented development. There's just no way that they can meet the needs of their populations under this model.

It's economically unwise, but it's also a crime against humanity to put exports ahead of the needs of a very hungry and unhealthy, ill-educated population.

"What you would ideally want—and what is not happening—is for the multinationals to do some degree of skills and technology transfer, such as using Philippine engineers instead of importing their own engineers from home. They would start training the workers to do more and more skilled work rather than just routine assembly tasks. They would develop suppliers locally; components would be made where they're assembled. That's the way a country could use foreign investment as a real development strategy. This would also provide hard currency to service the loans—since World Bank loans cannot be paid back in a country's own currency. Local governments can't get much in the way of tax revenue out of these multinationals because they're getting tax holidays and paying very low wages.

"That's why, despite opening up to foreign investment and doing everything they're supposed to, so few countries succeed in this game. It's pretty much stacked against them. There are 120 to 150 countries competing on this model. They can't all export their way to solvency, much less prosperity. It's a very nice arrangement for the richer countries, because they have all these poor countries desperately competing with each other to see who can produce goods most cheaply. There's no way you can get more than a minority of winners out of this kind of model."[9]

Clearly, the Philippines is *not* one of the winners.

The Dark Side of Globalization

For those who work in the export industry, conditions are brutal:

Workers in the electronic industry tend to suffer from eye defects after three years of employment. Others complain of acid burns, skin rashes from epoxy resins, and other reactions due to solvents like trichloroethylene. Even if they are given gloves and masks, they do not use them because that slows them down and makes it difficult to reach their quota. They are not required by the company to use them, and, in fact, are not taught about the need for protective devices.[10]

In the tuna canning export industry, 95 percent work under temporary contracts, and 85 percent are women. When orders are high, workers are forced to work twelve-hour days; when demand is low, they get few hours of work. Work is very tightly controlled. Workers are not allowed to speak to each other during work hours, they are not provided with drinking water, they do not receive sick or holiday pay, and wages are very low.[11]

Confidential documents show that the World Bank steadfastly propound-
ed that the "comparative advantage of the Philippines lies in the utilization
of skilled, low-wage labor."[12] Bending to Bank pressure to keep wages low,
Marcos instituted a new Labor Code that allowed employers to pay new employees only 75 percent of the minimum wage during a six-month probation-
ary period. It's therefore common practice for employers to fire workers just
before the end of their probation.[13] By keeping workers on short contracts
rather than as permanent employees, employers avoid paying legislated benefits such as health care and pensions.[14] According to the World Bank's own
report, from 1972 to 1978 the real wages of unskilled workers declined by 30
percent, and those of skilled workers by 25 percent.[15]

Martial Law: Good for Whom?

In addition to the economic turmoil caused by liberalization and wage repression, the Philippines was rocked by massive middle- and lower-class demonstrations, strikes, and rallies against Marcos and his elite and against U.S. domination.[16] Marcos' response was to declare a state of martial law in September
1972. U.S. business gave its stamp of approval in the form of a congratulatory
telegram: "The American Chamber of Commerce wishes you every success
in your endeavor to restore peace and order, business confidence, and economic growth. . . . We assure you of our confidence and cooperation. . . . We
are communicating the feelings of our associates and affiliates in the United
States."[17]

The American public did not share that sentiment. Polls in the early 1970s
showed 87 percent in favor of cutting aid to repressive regimes.[18] But Marcos'
authoritarian rule suited American foreign policy interests, and, exerting its
controlling interest, the World Bank supported Marcos. As U.S. government
aid dropped (reflecting public sentiment) from $125 million in 1972 to $72
million in 1979,[19] confidential Bank statistics show that the Bank funneled $2.6
billion into sixty-one projects between 1973 and 1981.[20] This massive inflow
allowed Marcos to shift domestic resources to more than triple his defense
budget.[21] Repressive measures increased both at home and abroad, particularly in the United States—including the assassination of anti-Marcos activists
Silme Domingo and Gene Viernes in Seattle.[22]

The early martial law years brought accomplishments that impressed Bank
bureaucrats. GNP rose by 10 percent in 1973. Major efforts by the government to attract foreign investment brought in $55 million. High prices for ag-
ricultural exports shifted a $120 million trade deficit in 1972 to a $270 million

surplus in 1973. Over the next three years economic growth leveled off, however, and during 1977 to 1981 "the program began to unravel in spectacular fashion."[23] A major reason for the decline was protectionist barriers put up by Australia, Canada, Europe, Japan, and the United States. In two years alone, from 1978 to 1980, thirty-three barriers were erected to Philippine exports.[24] Did the World Bank assess this trend and stop promoting export-led development to poor countries? Not at all. Did the Bank pressure developed countries to drop their barriers to Philippine goods? Of course not.

A Billion Here, a Billion There . . .

As the economy plummeted, the country's foreign debt skyrocketed. But, while life was becoming more difficult for poor and middle-class Filipinos, Ferdinand Marcos and his wife, Imelda, were siphoning off billions from development projects. The amount they stole is not known precisely because of banking secrecy laws in the countries where they hid their money, but most accept the $10 billion estimate by the Commission on Good Government, established to recoup the losses. In 1966, when Marcos came to power, Philippine foreign debt was $1 billion; at the time of his ouster twenty years later, it was $28 billion.[25] The Marcos legacy lives on: Filipinos are still struggling to pay off many of these loans.

The Marcos clan used every possible avenue to amass wealth. Cronies were installed at the highest levels of government to broker deals. One particularly egregious deal, the Bataan Nuclear Power Plant, was handled by Marcos' buddy Herminio Disini. Disini, a regular golfing partner of Marcos', claimed that "he had the authority to arrange the deal in any way he wished."[26] This nuclear power plant was to be sited at the base of a volcano on an active earthquake fault. Marcos chose Westinghouse to build the reactor, even though its plan was nearly twice as expensive as General Electric's. Disini then collected $80 million from Westinghouse for "assistance in obtaining the contract and for implementation services." He passed on 95 percent of this fee to Marcos.[27] The Philippine Atomic Energy Commission refused to give a permit until the plant was already under construction. At that point, Commissioner Librado Ibe issued the permit and then moved to the United States. As he later told *Fortune* magazine, it was unsafe to resist Marcos' lieutenants for too long.[28]

Imelda meanwhile was in charge of development in the Greater Manila area, the locus of most foreign investment. So pervasive was the corruption that she was nicknamed "Mrs. 10 Percent" for the cut she allegedly took off the top of government contracts. As minister of human settlements, she administered vast sums, including aid from the U.S. Agency for International Development.[29]

The Spark That Started the Prairie Fire
While Ferdinand and Imelda were busy padding their own fortune, they also made sure that the Bank-mandated policy of wage suppression was strictly adhered to. Strikes were banned, and labor leaders were imprisoned, tortured, and murdered. Repression had its price, however: increasingly bolder resistance by workers who felt they had nothing to lose.[30]

Many middle-class people also joined the struggle. Anita was a graduate of the University of the Philippines whose interest in issues turned into direct participation after the declaration of martial law:

"People in the National Democratic Front asked me to help set up a church-based organization. Actually, this was a new idea—channeling the support of middle-class people to poor workers in the metro Manila area. We were teaching trade unionization courses and organizing factories at a time when strikes and organizing were illegal. Our two lawyers handled legal cases. We thought it would take a long time before the terror effect of martial law would wear off. But in 1975, we were approached by a group of workers from a factory that made gin. They had people who had been in the company for years and were not being upgraded to regular workers. They wanted to go on strike. We discouraged them, because one union going on strike alone would be open to all sorts of attacks. We thought it would be better for them to bide their time, wait until other unions would also go on strike to create a coordinated movement. But they said, 'If you don't want to help us, we'll go ahead alone.' At that point we thought we might as well support them rather than leave them hanging!

"So we mobilized all our contacts—the priests and nuns, seminarians, deacons, deaconesses, and the community. This factory was located in the Tondo, where people fought against the World Bank project intending to remove squatter families to enlarge the port for multinationals. The workers went on strike October 24, 1975. They were really bold, locking the gates and refusing to let management inside. On the second night, the Metropolitan Command came with twenty buses. They broke down the door and dragged all the workers out and started putting them in buses. In response, the community people lay down in front of the buses. But the buses started moving, so we had to get out of the way. Two Filipina nuns and an Italian priest held on to the doors and were being dragged along the road. Everyone was screaming. Finally the buses stopped, and they put the two nuns and priest inside.

"To our extreme surprise, in the next morning's *Daily Express*, the administration newspaper run by Marcos' brother-in-law, there were pictures! The photos were very dramatic: the nuns and priest hanging on, being dragged, and the people crowding around. This was the spark that set off the prairie fire. Only a few days after that, people started going on strike. This lasted through January. One day there were six strikes—the unions started flooding into our office."[31]

Actions such as these by Anita, union workers, and community people proliferated across the country.

Rural Poverty Reduction—for Landlords

Rural areas were also hotbeds due to extreme poverty and unequal benefits of World Bank projects. The World Bank funded rural projects as part of its stated mission to reduce poverty, but the underlying goal was to quell rural unrest.[32] Most project benefits eluded the poor. "So as not to antagonize privileged groups, Bank projects were consciously designed to make sure that the benefit of the projects also went to these sectors. Supervision reports and post-project evaluations revealed that a number of projects, like the Smallholders Tree Farming Project and rural credit projects, were actually benefiting mainly big landlords, medium and big commercial farmers, and foreign agricorporations."[33] According to the World Bank's own *Rural Development* policy paper, "It is normally optimistic to expect that more than 50% of the project benefits can be directed to the target group; often the percentage will be considerably less."[34]

The Green Revolution was touted as the best way to address the needs of farmers, but only half the story has been told. "The cost of the Bank's basic prescription for upgrading small farmers' productivity—the adoption of a mechanized chemical-intensive and fertilizer-dependent rice technology—drove many small farmers to bankruptcy, while bringing windfall profits to farm machinery manufacturers, the fertilizer cartel, and the U.S. pesticide industry."[35] Promoting mechanization in a labor-surplus country is not a strategy geared to increase the well-being of the people.

Structural Adjustment and Corruption

As the economy deteriorated and turmoil increased, it became clear to many World Bank officials that their anti-poverty effort had collapsed.[36] At the same time, Marcos was coming under increasing pressure to abandon martial law. After nine years of dictatorship, Marcos lifted martial law on January 17, 1981, but not before he had issued several presidential decrees to ensure that he retained sweeping powers.[37]

The Bank also tightened its control. By June its most trusted agent, César Virata, had been installed as the Philippine prime minister; by August, a cabinet dominated by Bank-sponsored technocrats was in place.[38] Marcos' reward for compliance was receiving a new type of loan: the structural adjustment loan. In contrast to previous *project* loans, the structural adjustment loan was a *program* loan. "It involved restructuring the industrial sector through tariff reform, formulating more attractive incentives for foreign investors and export producers, and planning more export processing zones where multinational firms enjoying tax breaks could gain access to cheap Filipino labor."[39] It essentially "formalized World Bank surveillance and control over a wide swathe of the economy."[40]

One commentator noted, "The Bank was perfectly aware of the fact that most loans were transferred into the bank accounts of Marcos and his generals; nevertheless, the Bank considered these as necessary bribes for paying the political staff in power."[41]

Though Marcos had to heed Bank directives in order to get the money to keep his country afloat, he also had to deal with domestic needs. To address the virtual absence of a heavy industrial base, he proposed an $11 billion package of eleven capital-intensive projects, including a steel plant, a petrochemical complex, and a copper smelter. This caused the Bank to "issue a stern warning that many of the projects 'do not harmonize well with the policy reforms.'"[42] If the Philippines developed its own industrial base, the country would no longer be such a good customer for the multinationals. What finally brought the demise of the projects was the "cold shoulder given by prospective financiers who had learned of the Bank's veto."[43]

Opposition to Marcos continued to mount. Despite this, "the World Bank decided to maintain its support to the dictator. . . . It strongly raised loan amounts: $600 million in 1983 (more than double the previous year's $251 million)."[44]

In the end, even the support of the World Bank was not enough to keep Marcos in power. Hundreds of thousands of Filipinos from all classes came into the streets in a display of "People Power" in February 1986. The Marcos family fled to Hawaii, and Corazon Aquino, widow of assassinated opposition leader Senator Benigno Aquino, was sworn in to office. While some details changed, however, the essential policies and structures put into place by Marcos under World Bank–mandated liberalization and structural adjustment have continued to reverberate through the Philippines.

The Face of the "Cheap Labor Pool"

One of the key sectors that had been targeted for restructuring by the Bank under the structural adjustment loan imperatives was the textile industry.[45] By the Bank's own estimates, roughly 100,000 workers in the "inefficient" garment and textile firms would lose their jobs.[46] This amounted to 46 percent of the workforce in the industry.[47]

What is life like for those "lucky" enough to still have a job? Meet Elvira:

"Job orders became fewer, and our union was not able to ask for additional pay and other benefits. The company owner told us many clients had transferred their orders to China and Taiwan. When the factory closed, it was difficult to find another job. Almost all the job openings were with subcontractors for twelve to sixteen hours a day of piece-rate work with very low pay. I worked in three of these subcontractors before I finally found a regular job. I was supporting the studies of my younger siblings then. The job I found paid higher, but the prices of goods had also gone up.

"I used to be a favorite of my supervisor. I was even once commended by the plant manager because the quality of my work passed their standards. Later, I realized this was not an asset. The standard means you agree on ten centavos for each garment, you do overtime and overnight work, you are never absent, and you do not ask for any kind of benefit. I refrained from going to the toilet and eating during break time just to reach my quota. I had to come to work even if I had the flu so there would be no deductions in my salary.

"The workplace is hot and dusty. Employers say, 'If you do not like what is being asked of you, you can leave anytime. There are plenty of people looking for jobs.' Piece-rate garment workers get 500 to 1,000 pesos per week. A kilo [a little over two pounds] of fish costs 150 pesos, tomatoes are 80 pesos per kilo, papayas are 25 pesos. Even if I want to support Filipino products I cannot do so. Prices of goods from other countries are cheaper. If you have little money, you no longer think of the effects on local farmers or the local economy."[48]

Elvira's experiences are corroborated by another worker, Marivic. She is a widow whose husband died when she was pregnant with her second child. Despite the fact that Marivic has had to raise both her children alone, she has freely given hundreds of hours to strengthening her community and her union. She shares an insider's view of the global Code of Conduct Agreement highly touted by the multinationals:

"The Code of Conduct is posted on the board but usually not followed. The management tells the workers to "behave" when representatives from the parent company come to check if the Code provisions are being followed. The supervisor tells the worker, "If you are asked how much you earn, tell them this much." Workers are forced to lie, and, if you do not "cooperate" with them, management finds ways to punish you until you are terminated. The majority of workers whom I know are not given the minimum wage. We are experts in sewing but management classifies us as apprentices so we can be paid below the minimum standard. Corporate globalization is a nightmare for workers in the garment industry. It has brought greater poverty, displacement of workers, contract work instead of regular jobs, and threats to unionism. This is in contrast to how the government treats employers in the garment industry—they are wooed and supported."[49]

As Marivic and Elvira noted, there is now a very large unemployed sector. Because of this, unions are very weak. A lot of people are desperate and will work for less than minimum wage under subhuman conditions. While strikes are no longer prohibited, workers must notify authorities several weeks in advance.[50] The lowest possible wages remain a key driver to export-led growth, a central theme in the World Bank policy of liberalization.

$13 vs. $15,000—A Level Playing Field?

For peasant farmers in the countryside, the details are different but the struggle is the same. Riza Bernabe is the program coordinator of the Small Farms and Agricultural Trade Center of Centro Saka. The center works with small farmers and focuses on how agricultural policies and trade, including the General Agreement on Tariffs and Trade (GATT) and the World Trade Organization (WTO), affect them. In the mid-1990s, most governments signed on to GATT. The World Bank was a strong proponent of GATT, which reflects the imperatives of liberalization. Citizen outrage against the treaty was particularly fierce in many Third World countries. The WTO is the administrative arm of GATT. Riza explains the conditions farmers face:

"When you talk to small farmers, the general feeling is that life has gotten worse. When we joined GATT, most of our government officials and the WTO were saying that this will be good because it will open up export markets and create new employment. They had actual figures in terms of forecast: 'We will have 500,000 new jobs every year.' Before, we had an agri-trade balance. But ten years later, our imports are much bigger than our exports. Many countries found ways not to open their markets to us.

"The Safety Nets Adjustment Survey found that most of the support services, like irrigation facilities, are still the same ones built during Marcos' time. Secretary Luis Lorenzo said that the typical Filipino farmer gets $13 in subsidies, while a farmer from the U.S. or European Union gets $15,000 to $20,000. How can our farmers compete with such a disadvantage? Limited public investment and opening our markets has been a deadly combination for a lot of small farmers."[51]

The WTO is "a very contradictory animal," according to Walden Bello, executive director of Focus on the Global South. "It is supposed to be an organization that moves the world to free trade through the elimination of trade quotas and lowering of tariffs, but many of its central agreements, like those on agriculture, intellectual property rights, and investment measures are, in fact, not free-trade-oriented. It talks free trade but really protects subsidies and monopolies held by Northern corporations. And ever since the Bush administration came to power, the U.S. has been more aggressively protectionist for its corporations. The Bush administration policy is a double standard: protectionism when it comes to the United States, but free trade for the rest of the world."[52]

Expendable National Industries

Local businesses were also sacrificed on the altar of liberalization. Joy Chavez notes: "The oft-mentioned industry is steel, through both liberalization and lack of government support. While imports are coming in, the government has scrapped industry support programs, and they're not very good at building infrastructure that's not just for the export industries but for everybody. The steel industry is virtually dead. For any country that has some industrial ambition, the absence of a steel industry is a big handicap. The other industries that are dying are petrochemicals, the glass industry, and auto assembly. We used to have a quite vibrant auto assembly sector. There also used to be a thriving shoe industry in metro Manila."[53]

The textile industry, also severely affected, shrank from 200 firms in the 1970s to less than 10 in 2003.[54]

Domestic food processing felt the sting of liberalization, too. Helen and Jimmy Lim owned a small canning business, the Maranatha Company, that sold fresh and canned baby corn and asparagus. They brought the vegetables from the outlying area to Manila for packaging and delivered them to assorted stores that stocked their goods. With higher prices for gasoline and fertilizer, they could not sell at the old prices. When they raised prices, people who had bought their products in the past could no longer afford them. In addition, they couldn't compete with the canned baby corn that came in duty-free from Thailand. They then opened a neighborhood hardware store. Though the store did relatively well, they were never able to own their car or house. Helen and Jimmy sold the hardware store and emigrated to New Zealand with their three children because they felt they could never make it in the Philippines.[55]

Another casualty of Bank-mandated liberalization is the rubber industry. Freddie de Leon's family business was rubber, which is grown in the Philippines. After he got his MBA at Wharton, he came back to the Philippines in 1969. He began working in his family's business and eventually became head of the company, which ceased operations in 2003. Why did the business fail?

"Labor costs went up, and the costs of imported materials went up, especially with devaluation—that's the cost side. Now, on the market side, cheap imports of tires came in, and our business competed directly with brand-new tires. Our business was in tire retreading. When old tires get chewed up and abraded, we retreaded them and made them look and function like new. Cheap imported tires came in because of trade liberalization. We lost market share, and we couldn't raise our prices as much as we should have. Even without the imports, the market was already very competitive here. There were many tire retreading companies—a few big ones, and many small ones. Especially after we joined the WTO in 1995–96, the industry started to have real problems.

"Then with the Asian financial crisis of 1997, there was devaluation, and the price of imported goods went up. At first we thought that devaluation would help us, that imported tires would become expensive, but that never happened. The prices of imported tires remained low—and our costs went up! We got caught in operating losses that accumulated over the years, and the business failed. In fact, the whole industry failed—many retreading companies closed shop. It's really too bad, because our industry is a form of recycling. If you manufacture a brand-new tire, you use more petroleum than if you just retread it. It reduces the number of tires that are thrown into dump sites. That's the environmental impact our industry has.

"It was hard to let people go who had been with us a long time. We employed 250 people. But that's what is happening to industry as a whole in the Philippines. The WTO has hollowed out the productive enterprises of this country. It's discouraged people from going into business. Everybody now just wants to leave the country. We're exporting people and importing goods.

These policies have to be reversed. Any sensible country, any country with wisdom, would go into production. In fact, that's what China, India, Korea, and Malaysia are doing. We have to rethink this WTO globalization program. If the poor countries are not benefiting from these policies, then they should consider resigning en masse. They should form another organization that would be more beneficial to developing countries."[56]

What is Freddie doing now? "Some friends and I are trying to put up a business that will service overseas foreign workers. We hope to help them invest their funds in the Philippines."[57]

Far, Far Away

Freddie will have a large potential market. As Walden Bello explains: "One in ten Filipinos has gone overseas to find employment. They're in Europe and the Middle East as domestics, and they're the largest number of seamen. Eight million households subsist on remittances sent by these workers. The combination of economic stress plus the possibility of working outside the country has had a dampening effect on the political struggle in the Philippines. Many people would rather leave the country than stay and fight for a better social and political deal."[58] Filomeno Sta Ana III, the coordinator of Action for Economic Reform, adds: "The combined unemployment and underemployment rate is about a third of the workforce. Quality jobs cannot be found, so people just move out. This has led to a lot of losses, not only in terms of human skills that our country needs but also the breakdown of families."[59]

Mini-Size Me

The poverty that overseas workers are escaping is severe. According to a survey by the nonprofit organization Social Weather Station, the proportion of Filipino households experiencing hunger hit 16.7 percent in the fourth quarter of 2005. Self-rated poverty rose to 57 percent, having fluctuated between 46 percent and 58 percent since the beginning of 2004.[60] In some parts of the Philippines, the human development index is almost the same as that in sub-Saharan Africa.[61] The Philippine Center for Investigative Journalism revealed a new "Mini-Size Me" phenomenon. "Procter & Gamble unit manager Jonathan Chua explains: 'Package downsizing is in response to consumer coping behavior.' With the disposable income of Filipinos shrinking almost daily, canned food in 100- to 200-gram size (100 grams equals approximately 4 ounces) eats up more than half the market volume share."[62] Poor people can now afford to buy food only in very small quantities.

Why doesn't the Philippine government put more money into poverty alleviation or supporting its own industries? The country's money is going to service its foreign debt. After Marcos was ousted in 1986, President Corazon Aquino relinquished the opportunity to renegotiate illegitimate debts. Instead, she assured the U.S. Congress, "We will pay all debts."

90 Percent Means "Moderately Indebted"?

Lidy Nacpil is international coordinator for Jubilee South, a network of NGOs addressing the debt issue. She is dedicated to helping ordinary people understand how economic policies affect them and empowering them to fight for alternatives. Her passionate commitment has been tested by fire: her husband, also an activist, was assassinated by the military in 1987 when their daughter was six months old.

"The amount of tax revenue that goes to debt payment ranges between 80 and 90 percent. With only 10 to 20 percent left, the rest of the government budget is financed through new loans from domestic banks and multilateral institutions. The Philippines is still paying back some Marcos-era loans, including [those for] the Bataan Nuclear Power Plant. The Philippines is not in line for any debt forgiveness. At the Annual Meeting of the World Bank in September 2005, [the Bank] agreed to debt cancellation for eighteen countries that have already complied with structural adjustment policies [liberalization, privatization, deregulation] under the Heavily Indebted Poor Countries program. This is a small drop in the ocean of debt of the South.

"The creditors are saying that only the poorest and the most indebted need debt forgiveness. The Philippines are considered 'middle income, moderately indebted'—at 90 percent of revenue spent on debt service we're called 'moderately indebted'! They're saying that the answer is better tax policies. We have to increase our taxes and borrow more. We're considered a sustainable debtor, a 'viable market economy,' because we have a law making debt service automatic—it doesn't matter that only 10% of our revenue is left to pay for everything else. They don't care that it has cost us so much in terms of health service and education—so long as they're getting their money.

"From the point of view of the creditors and big international investors, the definition of 'viable market economies' is exactly expressed in the paradigms and policies of the World Bank. What they see as viable market economies are economies that are open in terms of trade and capital accounts, and where government does not play a big role in the economy. This, of course, translates to privatization. They want government to pull out of especially potentially highly profitable areas like power or water—because they're a vital commodity and there's no alternative."[63]

Electric power and water have already been privatized in the Philippines. How did that come to pass and what are the consequences?

The Tsunami of Privatization

In the early 1990s the Philippines had widespread shortages of electrical power. Because the bulk of its resources were going to service the debt, there was no money to invest in power infrastructure. Joy Chavez of Focus on the Global South was engaged in this issue:

"Power-sector reform was pushed very aggressively by the World Bank. The Philippine government entered into contracts with independent power producers, including Enron. This essentially privatized power, because the state-owned National Power Corporation no longer invested in new generation plants. Electricity costs in 1990 averaged 1.83 pesos per kilowatt hour. By 2004 it was 5.58 pesos. Water has been privatized in metro Manila, and they're targeting other areas as well. The rates of private water companies are 400 percent higher than pre-privatization levels. The quality of service has also deteriorated in many areas because private companies refuse to make the necessary investments to maintain services. Water and power are considered the second wave of privatization.

"The first wave consisted of government-owned and -controlled corporations. This included Petron Corporation [oil refining and marketing—and among the top-performing corporations in the country], the National Steel Corporation, the Philippine National Bank, Philippine Airlines, Philippine Shipyard and Engineering Corporation, and Philippine Associated Smelting & Refining Corporation. A number of mining, cement, and sugar companies have also been privatized. Public/private partnerships in health, education, and pension funds are the next (third) wave of privatization."[64]

It Only Works in Books

Though the Philippines is not now under a formal World Bank/IMF program, it is still following the same economic policies. Riza Bernabe of the Small Farms and Agricultural Trade Center explains:

"There are many pressures on the Philippine government to liberalize. First, we have GATT. Second, the World Bank usually comes up with studies saying that liberalization is part of the economic management formula that countries have to adopt. And most of our economists are educated in Western universities, where the current mode of thinking is the neoliberal frame-work that says that when you liberalize, producers become more efficient, consumer prices will go down, etc. But in reality, consumer prices have not gone down. The Philippine producers lose their jobs, and our productive base is being eroded by imports. It only works in books."[65]

Lidy Nacpil of Jubilee South elucidates the underlying dynamic: "The most important point about the lending relationship is that it's necessary for maintaining a power relationship, so they are able to push other policies from which they earn more than what they earn from the profits from debt. It's not just the financial interest that we've paid. It's also the wealth extraction from the policies that we were forced to implement because we were in debt. How much did we lose from tariff reductions alone? Since 1995 it's over 100 billion pesos! In the end we ask, who owes whom? You made so much wealth from us—it's the whole history of colonization."[66]

Today the World Bank is no longer forcing structural adjustment loans on Third World countries. By the late 1990s, the loans had gotten a bad name because it was clear that they were not really helping countries to move out of poverty. Were they abandoned as a terrible mistake? Hardly. They were rechristened "poverty reduction strategy programs," with new language like "good governance" and "consultations with communities affected" added to the mix. But the essentials are the same.[67] Nor is it just populist NGOs who believe that Bank policies are not mainly designed to reduce mass poverty. The U.S. Treasury Department's own report, "U.S. Participation in the Multilateral Development Banks," concluded that the World Bank is "an institution solidly dominated by the United States, faithfully promoting not only strategic U.S. economic goals, but short-term political objectives as well."[68]

Glimmers of Hope

Is there hope for the Philippines to gain a greater measure of self-determina-tion and be able to put more resources into education, health care, infrastruc-ture, and support of national industries? Joy Chavez sees people being "more proactive now and more ready to take up their cause. They're more ready to take action and demand support from the government. There's more com-munity organization and collective action."[69]

A new progressive political party, Akbayan, has three members in Congress and is rooted in sixty-four of seventy-nine provinces. It is built on social move-ments, and its leaders are young (in their early thirties). They are crafting a new kind of politics, based on programs, not personalities.[70]

Lidy Nacpil is very much encouraged by what is happening in South America: "A relatively more progressive block of nations is emerging between Venezuela, Brazil, Bolivia, Ecuador, Cuba, and Chile. We can't do alternative policies separately. We have to band together. It's a global problem. We need global solutions."[71]

What could this new reality look like? Elvira, the garment worker, has this dream: "A society where basic needs are provided, there is enough food, there is housing for everyone, all children can go to school, hospitals are for everybody, and there is a job for everyone—a job that helps people to develop their potential as human beings."[72]

Notes

1. Walden Bello, David Kinley, and Elaine Elinson, *Development Debacle: The World Bank in the Philippines* (San Francisco: Institute for Food and Development Policy, 1982), p. 22.
2. Ibid., p. 59.
3. Doug Henwood, economist and founder of *Left Business Observer*, interviewed by Ellen Augustine, January 21, 2006. Hereafter cited as Henwood interview.
4. Ibid.
5. Ibid.
6. Bello et al., *Development Debacle*, pp. 140–41.
7. "Manila Export Zones Lure Business," *Christian Science Monitor*, September 18, 1980.
8. Bello et al., *Development Debacle*, p. 146.
9. Henwood interview.
10. "Testimony of a Worker," in Permanent Tribunal for the Rights of Peoples, Session on the Philippines, *Philippines: Repression and Resistance* (London: KSP, 1981), pp. 89–90.
11. Mylene, Philippine organizer, interviewed by Ellen Augustine, February 2006.
12. Bello et al., *Development Debacle*, p. 142.
13. Ibid., p. 143.
14. Filomeno Sta Ana III, coordinator, Action for Economic Reforms, interviewed by Ellen Augustine, January 20, 2006. Hereafter cited as Sta Ana interview.
15. *The Philippines: Domestic and External Resources for Development* (Washington, D.C.: World Bank, 1979), p. 12.
16. Bello et al., *Development Debacle*, p 20.
17. Quoted in Sam Bayani, "What's Happening in the Philippines," *Far Eastern Economic Reporter,* November 1976.
18. Severina Rivera and Walden Bello, "The Anti-Aid Campaign after 4 Years," in *Logistics of Repression* (Washington, D.C.: Friends of the Philippine People, 1972), p. 4.
19. Bello et al., *Development Debacle*, p. 21.
20. World Bank confidential statistics for 1976, 1979, 1980, and 1981.
21. Bello et al., *Development Debacle*, p 37.
22. Chong-suk Han, Sue Chin, Ron Chew, Robert Shimabukuro, and David Takam, "Unknown Heroes," *Colorlines* 4, no. 3 (Fall 2001).

23. Ibid., p. 43.

24. Ibid., pp. 48–49.

25. Available at the Web site www.probeinternational.org/probeint/OdiousDebts/Odious Debts/chapter13.html.

26. Ibid.

27. Ibid.

28. Ibid.

29. Ibid.

30. Bello et al., *Development Debacle*, p. 54.

31. Anita, Philippine organizer, interviewed by Ellen Augustine, February 18, 2006.

32. Bello et al., *Development Debacle*, p. 15.

33. Ibid., p. 45.

34. *Rural Development: Sector Working Paper* (Washington, D.C.: World Bank, 1975), p. 40.

35. Bello et al., *Development Debacle*, p. 45.

36. Ibid., p. 92.

37. Ibid., p. 183.

38. Ibid.

39. Ibid., pp. 59–60.

40. Ibid., p. 166.

41. Eric Toussant, "The World Bank and the Philippines," www.cadtm.org/article.php3?id article=1732. Hereafter cited as Toussant.

42. "Working Level Draft CPP [Country Program Paper]," memorandum from Bruce Jones, Washington, D.C., Aug. 29, 1980, p. 7.

43. Bello et al., *Development Debacle*, p. 61.

44. Toussant.

45. *Industrial Development Strategy and Policies in the Philippines*, Report no. 2513-PH (Washington, D.C.: World Bank, October 29, 1979), vol. 2, chap. 7.

46. *Report and Recommendations of the President of the IBRD to Executive Directors on a Proposed Structural Adjustment Loan to the Republic of the Philippines*, Report no. P-2872-PH (Washington, D.C.: World Bank, August 21, 1980), p. 31.

47. Bello et al., *Development Debacle*, p. 170.

48. Elvira, Philippine trade union organizer, interviewed by Ellen Augustine, February 12, 2006. Hereafter cited as Elvira interview.

49. Marivic, Philippine trade union organizer, interviewed by Ellen Augustine, February 12, 2006.

50. Sta Ana interview.

51. Riza Bernabe, program coordinator of the Small Farms and Agricultural Trade Center of Centro Saka, interviewed by Ellen Augustine, February 5, 2006. Hereafter cited as Bernabe interview.

52. Walden Bello, executive director of Focus on the Global South, interviewed by Ellen Augustine, January 22, 2006. Hereafter cited as Bello interview.

53. Joy Chavez, senior associate, Focus on the Global South and Coordinator of the Philippines Program, interviewed by Ellen Augustine, February 5, 2006. Hereafter cited as Chavez interview.

54. *Stop De-Industrialization: Re-Calibrate Philippine Tariffs Now* (Manila: Fair Trade Alliance, 2003), p. 16.

55. Family of Madge Kho, interviewed by Ellen Augustine, January 30, 2006.

56. Freddie de Leon, businessman, interviewed by Ellen Augustine, February 12, 2006.

57. Ibid.
58. Bello interview.
59. Sta Ana interview.
60. Social Weather Station Survey, 4th quarter 2005.
61. Sta Ana interview.
62. Avigail Olarte and Yvonne Chua, "Mini-Size Me," Philippine Center for Investigative Journalism, Jan.–March 2005, www.pcij.org/i-report/1/mini-size.html.
63. Lidy Nacpil, international coordinator for Jubilee South, interviewed by Ellen Augustine, February 17, 2006. Hereafter cited as Nacpil interview.
64. Chavez interview.
65. Bernabe interview.
66. Nacpil interview.
67. Bello interview.
68. Bello et al., *Development Debacle*, p. 198.
69. Chavez interview.
70. Joel Rocamora, co-founder, Akbayan, interviewed by Ellen Augustine, January 29, 2006.
71. Nacpil interview.
72. Elvira interview.

10 *Export credit agencies have quietly become some of the biggest and dirtiest players in the EHM game, financing arms sales, nuclear power plants, and environmental disasters.*

Exporting Destruction

Bruce Rich

Imagine the following fantasy set in a dystopic future: The industrialized countries decide to create ruthless agencies whose only goal is national economic aggrandizement. These agencies keep most information on their activities secret—not just from the public that pays for them through taxes but often from their own national legislatures and ministries as well. Their job is to enrich their countries' corporations by making it easier for poor countries to buy their products and services, with little regard for the environmental and social disruption such purchases may cause.

They ignore international environmental conventions, and the various UN meetings and summits on sustainable development of the past fifteen years may just as well have occurred on another planet. They support nuclear power plants, massive arms purchases, and huge white elephant schemes no private bank alone or international development agency will touch. Their financing enables the forced displacement of millions of poor people worldwide. They support half of all new greenhouse gas–emitting energy-intensive infrastructure being built in the developing world, with total disregard for the impacts on climate. And to facilitate all this, they subsidize billions of dollars of bribes annually, undermining democracy and development by corrupting governments and businesses in poor countries.

Unfortunately, this is no fantasy. It is an accurate description of the typical export credit agency (ECA). ECAs are publicly funded or publicly guaranteed financial institutions operated by the richer industrialized nations and, increasingly, a few of the most dynamic emerging economies, such as China and Brazil. Collectively, ECAs have become key players in the global economy, annually pouring more money into the developing nations than all development aid worldwide, both bilateral and multilateral, including aid from UN agencies and the World Bank. But they are not foreign assistance agencies. They are designed to be *domestic* assistance agencies. Their mission is to boost the overseas sales of their countries' multinational corporations. Their method is to provide direct loans, and guarantees for private bank loans, so that poor countries can buy the products and services of First World multinationals.

How ECAs Operate

A typical ECA transaction might involve the sale of turbines and engineering services to build a dam in a developing nation, let's say Bangladesh. A Bangladeshi government agency receives a loan from the United States Export-Import Bank (which is subsidized by American taxpayers) to buy the turbines and engineering services from a U.S. company. If there are no problems, the American company makes a hefty profit from the transaction, and the loan is repaid by the Bangladeshis, partly subsidized by American taxpayers. If there are problems in the project, and the Bangladeshi government defaults on payments, or wants to renegotiate the terms of the loan, the U.S. Ex-Im Bank has U.S. government backing in its attempts to pressure Bangladesh to pay the American company as originally agreed. There are numerous and more complicated permutations of this game, but the basic mechanism is quite simple. ECAs have been attacked as the world's biggest purveyors of global corporate welfare—for good reason.

While ECAs now account for about 9 percent of world exports, this figure understates their impact in the poorer developing countries, where private banks will not lend, particularly for large environmentally and socially disruptive projects, unless First World taxpayers assume the financial risk through ECAs. According to the World Bank, in the early years of this decade ECAs accounted for 80 percent of gross capital market financing in the world's seventy poorest countries; between 1997 and 2002 every private international commercial bank loan larger than $20 million to those countries was made with the backing of an official, industrialized country government ECA guarantee.[1]

But unlike bilateral development agencies and international development banks like the World Bank,[2] most of which now screen loan projects to minimize their potential for environmental and social disruption, until recently most ECAs stoutly asserted they didn't even care. They often flout international environmental treaties and mandates for sustainable development. It is no exaggeration to state that ECAs are rogue agencies that make the World Bank, the International Monetary Fund, and even the World Trade Organization seem like models of benevolence and accountability.

ECAs are now collectively the world's biggest public financial institutions. In 2004 they financed, guaranteed, and insured $788 billion worth of international trade and investment, of which longer-term loans and guarantees totaled about $76 billion. Probably 70 to 80 percent of the longer-term loans went to support big infrastructure projects in developing countries. Indeed, ECAs are the single largest public financiers of such projects. Very serious environmental and social effects flowed from a significant number of the projects, particularly large dams, coal and nuclear power plants, mining operations, roads in both pristine and densely populated areas, oil pipelines, chemical and other industrial facilities, and logging and plantation enterprises. At the end of the 1990s, ECA credits accounted for 24 percent of Indonesia's debt—about $28 billion—and were concentrated in the power sector (building large coal-fired plants) and the paper and pulp industries (constructing huge paper mills and conducting massive logging operations to feed them).[3]

A growing number of ECA projects are so problematic for environmental, social, and economic efficiency reasons that even the World Bank now refuses to finance them. In effect, ECAs have taken over the funding of projects that much of the world community has rejected as intrinsically inimical to the well-being of developing countries. And the mandate of ECAs is not even the growth-through-globalization trumpeted by free trade advocates as the best route to economic and social development. It is solely to subsidize exports to promote the economic welfare of their home countries.

Over the past two decades ECA finance has more than quadrupled, while foreign aid from the industrialized nations has hardly increased in inflation-adjusted terms. Foreign aid from the world's richer governments and international public agencies over the past five years has averaged some $65 billion a year—about the same amount that the ECAs have been lending for large projects in developing countries over the same period. In the early 2000s, ECA transactions accounted for 40 percent of the indebtedness of all developing countries to official creditors (governments and government-supported agencies), far exceeding the combined debt they owed to the World Bank and IMF. Certain developing nations, such as Nigeria, Iran, and Algeria, and several unstable economies in transition—Uzbekistan, Turkmenistan, and Azerbaijan—owe more than half their total debt to ECAs.[4] What has really occurred in the past two decades of ECA ascendancy has not been the triumph of open markets but rather a "new mercantilism"—the revival of alliances between the more powerful and richer governments and large corporations to secure new markets in the face of growing international competition, no matter what the consequences.

By definition, export credit agencies subsidize transactions that corporations will not undertake and private banks will not support because of financial or political risk. Classical economics does not dictate that rich country ECAs should assume risk for private sector investments. On the contrary, that assumption of risk clearly interferes in the workings of the market. As a result, the actions of ECAs have frequently led to economically perverse results with important environmental consequences. Indonesia provides a classic example, particularly because of its shaky, corrupt governments and civil strife in regions like Aceh and West Papua. In the face of the civil unrest risk, over the past decade and a half ECAs, working with multinational corporations to funnel payoffs to the children and cronies of former President Suharto, subsidized huge excess capacity in key sectors such as pulp production. That industry in turn catalyzed massive, illegal destruction of rainforests and protected areas, and brought pollution from poorly managed mills. ECAs have thus played a significant role in despoiling Indonesia's environment, distorting its economic development, and undermining public pressure for democratic reforms.

The net result is an enormous—and obscene—policy joke at the expense of the world's poor. The rich nations solemnly sign environmental conventions and clothe themselves in politically correct rhetoric by their taxpayer-supported bilateral aid agencies and multilateral institutions like the World Bank and UN Development Program. But their ECAs not only ignore the policies and goals but actually work against them. The rich countries preach free markets and increased transparency in governance to developing nations. In contrast, their ECAs work surreptitiously to subsidize trade at home, their most important transactions are excluded from the requirements of the World Trade Organization, and they use the pretext of commercial confidentiality to remain opaque themselves—most refuse to release even the most basic information about what they do.

Many countries have, in addition to ECAs, public investment insurance agencies to provide political and financial risk insurance to their domestic multinationals for overseas ventures. Examples of such agencies include the U.S. Overseas Private Investment Corporation and the Japan Ministry of International Trade and Industry Investment Insurance Department (the legendary MITI). In some countries both functions—export lending and guarantees, and investment insurance—are combined in the same agency.

The oldest ECA is probably the UK's Export Credits Guarantee Department, founded after World War I to promote British exports. The U.S. Export-Import Bank was founded in 1934. Most of the others, such as the Canadian Export Development Corporation, French COFACE, German Hermes Guarantee, Italian SACE, and Japanese Export-Import Bank (now part of the Japan Bank for International Cooperation), were established after World War II. Each institution has a unique mix of loans, loan guarantees, and (sometimes) risk insurance. The largest ones, such as the ECAs of Japan, Germany, and the United States, in recent years have each been approving new loans and guarantees averaging $15 billion to $20 billion annually.

The Record: Social Disruption, Environmental Destruction, and Corruption

Highlights of the ECAs' record of environmental, social, and indeed economic negligence in recent years include their disproportionate contribution to global political instability through massive subsidies of corruption, environmentally and socially destructive projects, and arms sales.

The support of the Three Gorges Dam on the Yangtze River in China is a case in point. In 1996, several ECAs approved financing for the project after both the World Bank and the U.S. Ex-Im Bank rejected it on environmental grounds. The largest construction project on earth, the dam is displacing over a million and a half people. Despite large-scale corruption, massive construction flaws, and the protests of Chinese scientists, engineers, and journalists, the ECAs of Canada, Germany, Sweden, and Switzerland, among others, are supporting the project with hundreds of millions of dollars of export loans and guarantees. In addition, resettlement is in shambles because over 100 Chinese officials have embezzled millions of dollars from the resettlement budget. Corruption from the project budget is enormous—with one official alone diverting more than $40 million.[5]

ECAs are undermining exporting nations' commitments to sustainable development under the UN Framework Convention on Climate Change and the

Convention on Biological Diversity, both adopted by most nations at the Rio Earth Summit in 1992. For example, ECAs and national investment insurance agencies are supporting large-scale expansions of fossil fuel power production without considering the global climate impacts. In fact, nearly half of all new trade and project finance in the developing world in energy-intensive sectors is being financed with, and because of, ECA support.[6]

Loans and guarantees by ECAs distort normal market supply and de-mand—and risk—encouraging massive expansion of environmentally de-structive industries in some countries. For example, ECAs have kept the Ca-nadian, French, German, and U.S. nuclear power construction industry on life support by subsidizing reactor exports to developing and former communist countries. In contrast, even the World Bank has always refused to support nuclear power on purely economic grounds—it is a bad investment.

The massive environmental and economic problems in Indonesia's pulp and paper sector were mentioned earlier, and similar problems arose in its pow-er-generating industry. In the 1990s, ECAs from Canada, Denmark, Finland, Germany, Japan, and Sweden financed three giant pulp plants in Sumatra, for over $4 billion. The result, according to the Center for International Forestry Research in Bogor, Indonesia, was both overcapacity in relation to interna-tional demand and immense pressure to supply the mills with wood. Failure to develop forest plantations to supply the mills adequately meant that be-tween half and two-thirds of the wood supply came from illegal clear-cutting of natural forests in one of the world's great biodiversity reserves. In turn, the increase in pulp production capacity put downward pressure on prices, which then further increased pressure to engage in unsustainable logging.[7]

The direct community impacts are disastrous. Built on rivers, the mills dump effluents that would be illegal in rich countries, poisoning tens of thou-sands of people nearby. The children of the villagers living downstream are covered with ulcerous scabs and sores from being washed in the rivers, the only water supply for most remote communities in Sumatra. Ancestral lands of indigenous peoples have been seized for construction of the mills and plan-tations without compensation.

In the case of power generation, the coal-fired Paiton I and II plants in Java involved over $3.7 billion in investment covered by loans and guarantees from German, Japanese, and U.S. ECAs. They provide an illuminating example of the way ECAs subsidize private profits and corruption but invoke govern-mental muscle to enforce one-sided, in this case blatantly corrupt, deals when things go wrong. Even the World Bank refused to finance the power project, noting in its own technical reviews both that there was insufficient demand for the electricity and that the Paiton plants and their Western investors had made agreements that would charge the Indonesian state power utility exorbitant rates. According to the *Wall Street Journal,* adjusted for local purchasing power the Paiton power cost 60 percent more than power in the neighboring Philippines and twenty times rates paid by U.S. consumers.[8] The Paiton plants and power purchase agreements were negotiated under the corrupt cronyism of the deposed Suharto regime, with no competitive bidding. They included, among other things, giving Suharto cronies a 15 percent equity share in Paiton and one of Suharto's daughters a 0.75 percent share, all at no cost. These equity shares amounted to gigantic bribes, in effect financed through "loans" from the ECA-backed investors that would be repaid out of the project's profits. The coal supply for the plants was also negotiated with no competitive bidding with a company that was also owned by Suharto cronies, who received a 15 percent equity interest—and the cost of the coal, not surprisingly, was 30 to 40 percent above world market prices.[9]

After Suharto was overthrown in 1998, the Indonesian government asked for an independent financial review of Paiton by Canadian auditors, who concluded that project costs were inflated by as much as 72 percent. The post-Suharto government tried to renegotiate the power purchase agreement, arguing it was a corrupt, noncompetitive transaction facilitated by huge bribes to the Suharto family. The agreement required the Indonesian government to pay 8.6 cents per kilowatt hour—for thirty years—whereas Indonesian consumers could afford only 2 cents per hour. Representatives of the U.S., German, Swiss, and Japanese ECAs actually traveled to Jakarta to browbeat the new, struggling post-Suharto regime into not reneging on the agreement, threatening that the major G7 governments that backed their respective ECAs would declare Indonesia an international debt pariah and limit its access to new loans from the international financial system. The Indonesian government caved in, and a compromise more acceptable to the ECAs and Western investors was reached.[10]

Mining is another major sector rife with ECA negligence, often on the part of the Australian and Canadian ECAs, since overseas mining is an important export sector for both countries. One of the more notorious examples occurred in 1995 in Guyana, where a tailings dam burst at the huge Omai gold mine financed by Canada. One billion gallons of cyanide-laced waste spilled into the country's most important river, killing millions of fish, endangering human lives, and threatening the water supply of the country's capital. The

UN Development Program criticized the lack of environmental monitoring in the project, and lawsuits from the spill continue to this day.

The Australian ECA, Export Finance and Investment Corporation (EFIC), has backed mining operations in Papua New Guinea that have had disastrous environmental and social impacts. EFIC financing of $243.8 million supported construction of a giant copper and gold mine by a consortium led by the Australian mining giant BHP in Papua New Guinea, near the Ok Tedi tributary of the Fly River. The U.S. and Japanese export-import banks also supported the project with smaller loans. The mine had one of the world's worst environmental disasters of the past quarter-century. Following the collapse of a tailings retention dam in 1984, BHP has dumped over 30 million tons of toxic mine tailings and 40 million tons of waste rock annually into the Ok Tedi and Fly rivers, resulting in the virtual biological death of the rivers and severely disrupting the livelihoods of 50,000 people in 120 downstream villages. In 2000, the World Bank recommended that the Ok Tedi mine be shut down immediately, but BHP transferred its equity to a Papua New Guinea government entity. BHP paid indemnities to settle a lawsuit brought by affected villagers—and obtained legal immunity from any future damage claims.[11]

In the mid-1990s EFIC guaranteed $250 million in private bank loans for the mining giant Rio Tinto Zinc, assisted by a $29.6 million guarantee from the Canadian EDC, to subsidize one of the world's largest gold mines on Lihir Island off the northeast coast of Papua New Guinea. The mine is annually dumping 110 million cubic meters of cyanide-contaminated waste into the sea, in addition to 20 million tons of rock waste a year, creating a toxic submarine waste plume several miles long—all in apparent violation of the London Dumping Convention prohibiting marine disposal of toxic waste. This project was so bad that even the U.S. Overseas Private Investment Corporation—whose environmental record is certainly problematic—refused to finance it on environmental grounds.[12]

Perhaps the most notorious EFIC deal of all was its $80 million guarantee in the 1980s for the notorious Rio Tinto Zinc Panguna copper mine on the island of Bougainville, Papua New Guinea, which contaminated major rivers and bays on the island, destroying the land, forests, and fish resources of many tens of thousands of villagers. The social and political instability provoked when a large portion of the island's population lost its subsistence livelihood directly catalyzed a civil war that led to the deaths of 15,000 people.[13]

The massive involvement of major European ECAs in arms exports is another aspect of their operations that follows logically from the "exports über alles" approach. ECA arms exports have become a campaign target for church and human rights groups in Europe, who rightfully see an international tragedy in the billions that their governments lavish annually to subsidize such purchases. Some 30 percent of the UK ECA's budget in the 1990s and a third of export credits granted by France's ECA went to subsidize arms exports. In 1999 the Indonesian military used British Aerospace fighters purchased with UK ECA credits in its battle for East Timor, leading to outraged protests in Parliament. The Indonesian government had bought the aircraft after promising that they would not be used for domestic repression. As UN forces prepared to move into East Timor, the Indonesians defaulted on $250 million in loans used to purchase the aircraft, and the private UK banks pressed the ECA to pay them immediately. The $250 million is only a fraction of nearly $1.3 billion of this ECA's support of arms sales to Indonesia since the mid-1990s.[14]

Not to be outdone, Germany's ECA offered $407 million in export guarantees to enable a $1 billion purchase of thirty-nine obsolete East German PT boats. The Suharto government closed several newspapers and threw students into prison for protesting the purchase. Even Indonesian generals protested the waste of money for obsolete technology, but the deal went through because the science and technology minister at the time was a personal friend of then German Chancellor Helmut Kohl's. Kohl also attempted to sell an obsolete fleet of East German diesel submarines to the Indonesians, backed by another $387.3 million in ECA guarantees, but that deal fell through.[15]

The U.S. Ex-Im Bank is able to claim, somewhat hypocritically, that it does not finance military arms exports—but only because other agencies of the U.S. government specialize in doing so.

The corruption involved in the PT boat transaction is but a small example of ECA ethical abuses. Given the lack of transparency surrounding ECA operations, it's not surprising that they are probably the single biggest official financers of bribes and other corruption in the developing world. Transparency International has published a working paper and other documents revealing that major European ECAs have as a matter of course systematically insured and guaranteed financial transactions rife with corruption and bribery. Transparency International estimates that corruption amounts to at least 10 percent of many transactions. The ECAs have done nothing to address this issue effectively, despite the OECD's anti-bribery convention, which came into force in early 1999.[16]

This witches' brew of social and environmental irresponsibility would not be complete without nuclear power, which has been one of the biggest export finance sectors for Canada, France, Germany, and the United States. For two decades virtually no new nuclear power plants have been built in any of these industrialized countries. In defiance of the economic (and environmental) logic that led to this stoppage, their ECAs have kept the builders alive by financing lucrative export deals for new and refurbished nuclear plants in the developing world and former communist states.

Canada's ECA supported the purchase and construction of two nuclear reactors by China in 1996, two proposed reactors to Turkey in 1997, and $1 billion of additional financing to complete the Cernavoda nuclear reactor in Romania in 1998. The reactor was financed by earlier export credits and left half-finished under the communist Ceausescu regime. It had been partly constructed by conscripted forced labor living in unheated barracks with limited food rations. Even more disturbing, in April 2000, when Germany's Green Party was at the height of its power as part of a governing Social Democrat–Green coalition, its leader, Vice-Chancellor and Foreign Minister Joscka Fischer, approved export credits for a new nuclear plant to be built in China—despite the Greens' platform against nuclear power for the past decade and a half. Clearly, the new mercantilism trumps political and environmental principles.

The opening of India to nuclear exports through President George W. Bush's visit in March 2006—revoking an international nuclear embargo that had been in force for many years—is certain to provoke a feeding frenzy of activity by the U.S., French, Canadian, and German ECAs.

In theory at least, U.S. ECAs have appeared more environmentally responsible. The Ex-Im Bank and its sister agency, the Overseas Private Investment Corporation (OPIC), are required to perform limited environmental assessments for major projects (including assessment of major impacts on indigenous peoples) and to mitigate serious impacts (including compensating populations for forced resettlement), in large part as a result of lobbying by U.S. environmental groups over the years. OPIC also has a development mandate, because of its origin in the U.S. Agency for International Development. The Ex-Im Bank is required by law to conduct environmental assessments for sensitive projects and has been more transparent than other ECAs. However, finding the most transparent ECA is a bit like finding the least promiscuous prostitute in a bawdy house. Ex-Im does post on its Web site lists of upcoming projects that require environmental assessments and descriptions of transactions in its annual report—hardly breathtaking openness for a tax-payer-supported agency. But many European ECAs to this day do not disclose even descriptions of projects and deals they have already approved, making it difficult to get a clear view of their activities.

The actual record of Ex-Im and OPIC in mitigating environmental and social harm associated with their investments is more questionable. In fact, one of the arguments cynically put forth by the German ECA Hermes has been that the allegedly more rigorous U.S. environmental and social assessment criteria have not actually resulted in a "cleaner" environmental and social record than that of the Germans.

The record of OPIC suggests that the German view is well informed. OPIC is relatively small compared to Ex-Im and, unlike most public export and investment insurance agencies, has not only "do no harm" environmental guidelines but also a positive mandate to report on "development benefits" in host countries. The 2002 OPIC Annual Report contains a great deal of rhetoric about OPIC's commitment to those development benefits. However, over 57 percent of new OPIC insurance and loan commitments in fiscal 2002 went for giant projects by big multinationals in the oil and gas sector. This was a huge focus on big oil, some $685 million out of total commitments of $1.2 billion. Almost 30 percent of the 2002 portfolio consisted of a $350 million loan for a huge UNOCAL operation for offshore oil and gas development in Indonesia adjacent to an onshore oil and gas terminal in the Indonesian province of East Kalimantan (Borneo). UNOCAL operations there have been the subject of massive nonviolent protests about environmental and social abuses inflicted on Indonesian community and human rights activists in a devoutly Muslim area.

How about the other 43 percent of OPIC commitments? Here are some examples from 2002: $15 million to Diamond Fields International for mining offshore diamond deposits in Namibia; $168,000 to B&C Management Inc. for a gravel quarry in Ghana; $250,000 to Lee Cashell and his firm Mongolian Resorts for "Tourist Camps to provide adventure tourist activities" in Mongolia; $600,000 for "underwater submarine tourism" in Thailand; $4.349 million for the Marriott Tbilisi and Marriott Courtyard hotels in Georgia; $56 million to El Paso Energy (some of whose former management were under federal indictment for fraud in the California energy-trading debacle) for two gas power plants in Pakistan; $1.219 million to expand the Wend-Rey restaurant franchise in Mexico; and $150,000 to an advertising firm, Colite Outdoors, LLC, for outdoor advertising billboards in Nicaragua.

Environmental, worker and human rights, and corruption issues may mark many OPIC projects because OPIC has to some extent been "captured" by some of its most powerful clients. A 2002 *Washington Post* front page exposé of Enron's Cuiabá Brazil–Bolivia pipeline, supported by $200 million in OPIC loans that were approved in 1999, alleged that lobbying and U.S. loans put the project on a "damaging path" that scarred South America. According to the *Post*,

> The pipeline . . . and its service roads have opened the [Chiquitano] forest to the kind of damage environmental groups had predicted: Poachers travel service roads to log old-growth trees. Hunters prey on wild game and cattle graze illegally. An abandoned gold mine reopened and its workers camp along the pipeline right-of-way.
>
> Perhaps most stunning, however, to many federal employees who reviewed the project, was how Enron persuaded a U.S. agency, the Overseas Private Investment Corp., to support the pipeline, even though the agency was charged with protecting sensitive forests such as the Chiquitano.
>
> "It shouldn't have been done," said Mike Colby, a former Treasury Department senior environmental advisor and now a corporate consultant. "The forest has already been declared by the World Bank . . . one of the two most valuable forests in Latin America. And OPIC chose to ignore that. They were so driven to reach these unsupportable conclusions because they wanted to finance the project at all costs."[17]

OPIC did withdraw its approval for loans to the pipeline in December 2001, but its initial involvement and financial commitment at critical stages of the project helped promote and accelerate the work.

The Enron Dabhol gas-fired power plant in India is another example. OPIC and the U.S. Ex-Im Bank together provided $460 million in loans and $200 million in insurance for an undertaking involving major human rights and corruption abuses, prompting the U.S.-based organization Human Rights Watch to prepare a 166-page report documenting beatings, attacks, arbitrary arrests, and other abuses against villagers protesting the illegal seizure of their lands by Enron and its contractors and the massive bribery of the Maharastra state government by Enron. The World Bank again rejected financing the project as too large, too costly, and not economically viable because of extremely one-sided terms granted to Enron by the state officials.[18]

Overall, according to the Institute for Policy Studies, OPIC provided some $2.6 billion in loans and insurance for fourteen Enron-related fossil-fuel projects between 1992 and the end of 2001. This represents a very substantial proportion of OPIC's total commitments in that nine-year period, probably more than 15 percent.

A Global Movement to Stop ECA Destruction

Fortunately, a global grassroots movement is growing in both donor and recipient countries to protest ECA irresponsibility. One of the first victories of this movement occurred in 1998 and 1999 when a broad coalition of German development, church, and environmental groups successfully campaigned against the involvement of several major German companies and banks that were seeking financial guarantees from the German ECA Hermes to help build the Maheshwar Dam on the Narmada River in India. The dam would have forcibly displaced as many as 35,000 rural poor from sixty-one villages without adequate compensation. The deal was supposed to be a model for privatization of dam building across India, but allegations of corruption and undue influence plagued it from the beginning. That was not surprising, since the private company chosen to manage the project, S. K. Kumars, was a textile firm with no experience in building and managing large-scale water projects.[19]

In the late 1990s affected local populations near the dam site mounted massive demonstrations, gathering up to 12,000 people, blockading construction sites, undertaking hunger strikes, and demonstrating in front of the German Embassy in New Delhi. Two of the initial German investors in the dam, the utilities Bayernwerk and VEW, withdrew when they became aware of the widespread opposition to and the substandard planning for the project. Still, the German ECA Hermes continued its involvement, expressing readiness to offer government-supported export guarantees for loans from the German Hypovereinsbank to the German multinational engineering and electric firm Siemens and to the German branch of the Swedish firm ABB if they would go ahead. ABB, sensing that the controversy was too intense in Germany, then, through its Lisbon office, turned to the Portuguese ECA COSEC to guarantee a 46 million euro loan by the Hypovereinsbank. However, an advocacy campaign by Portuguese NGOs initiated in 2000 led the Portuguese ECA and Finance Ministry in 2001 to refuse to guarantee the loan because of the social and environmental risks associated with the project. Meanwhile, the NGO campaign in Germany spurred an independent review of the project commissioned by the German International Development Ministry. The review confirmed in June 2000 that the project would lead to unacceptable violations of the human rights of affected populations. The German and Portuguese NGO campaigns finally killed prospective ECA support, and the land of over 35,000 rural poor people was saved from submergence.[20]

The Maheshwar case illustrates both the potential for global civil society to stop ECA support for unsustainable projects and the difficulties such campaigns face. Multinationals with offices and operations in several OECD countries can play one ECA off against another—in this case threatening to move production of turbines from Germany to Portugal if the German ECA refused support. Though it was clear from the plans that Maheshwar was seriously flawed in economic, social, and environmental aspects, it was stopped only by an exceptionally intense and well-coordinated research and advocacy campaign involving scores of civil society groups in India, Germany, and Portugal. In most cases, local communities, NGOs, and civil society simply don't have the resources to coordinate such a campaign.

Nonetheless, furious protests against ECA projects grew in other countries from the late 1990s into the early 2000s. In Indonesia, for example, mass marches of angry villagers called attention to the poisoning of local water supplies by ECA-financed pulp mills. In May 2000, local community and national protests coalesced into a global network when some 350 citizens' groups from forty-six countries joined in endorsing a campaign statement, the Jakarta Declaration, which calls for far-reaching institutional reform of ECAs so that they will halt their violations of basic social, environmental, and human rights norms.[21]

ECAs exist in relatively insulated enclaves within their governments. They usually report to only one agency, typically the trade, economics, or finance ministry, while for the most part operating without effective oversight by the rest of the government—including the legislature. They thus enjoy the benefits of taxpayer support without the accountability that should go with it. Their lack of transparency and accountability is a major factor in the ECAs' disregard for the environmental and social consequences of their activities. Negotiations among ECAs take place in one of the most obscure and least transparent forums in the international system, the Export Credit Group (ECG) of the OECD in Paris. The OECD is both a think tank and a negotiating forum for the twenty-six leading industrialized nations, and all their ECAs are represented in the group. When ECAs meet in the ECG, the sessions are mostly closed, and little information is released on the substance of discussions or the positions of individual ECAs.

The ECAs go so far as to undertake secret negotiations with one another without notifying their own governments. To cite a notorious recent example, in the winter of 2000 the Trade and Industry Committee in the UK House of Commons condemned the "deplorable and counter-productive lack of transparency in the way documentation has been kept from the public on the proposed Ilisu Dam," a controversial project in Turkey under consideration by the UK ECA and others. The committee noted that several ECAs secretly discussed proposals for funding the project for nearly a year before the UK trade ministry even became aware of the project.[22]

The Ilisu Dam project provides an illuminating example of the propensity of ECAs to support ill-conceived schemes that no public agency would consider and no private bank would finance without taxpayer guarantees. The dam will be built on the Tigris River in southeastern Turkey, despite the protests of over 75,000 Kurds, who will be displaced without adequate compensation. It will inundate one of the most important archaeological sites in Anatolia, and it violates five World Bank environmental and social policies on eighteen counts. The Syrian government had protested to Britain about its participation, pointing out that Turkey has refused to sign a UN convention about equitable water use on international rivers like the Tigris. Yet, in 1999 the ECAs of the UK, Germany, Italy, Austria, Sweden, Switzerland, and the U.S. were all at some point considering financial support for the project. Since the project had no environmental assessment, had no resettlement plan, and was in the middle of a militarized conflict zone, international pressure did bring the ECAs to agree on some minimal environmental and social requirements, such as preparing a resettlement plan and consulting the downstream states—Syria and Iraq—about water flows.

But the extra measures required by the ECAs were too little and too late. Field trips by British, Swiss, and German NGOs working with Kurdish human rights groups continued to document problems on the project. For example, the Turkish company preparing the resettlement plan was known mainly as a travel agency specializing in group tours, a grotesque indicator of the seriousness with which environmental and social impacts were being addressed. In 2002 the main British company involved, Balfour Beatty, which was to subcontract much of the construction and equipment to companies in other European countries (bringing in support from their ECAs), withdrew from the project. The company faced growing domestic and international pressure, including a resolution at its annual meeting in which more than 40 percent of the shareholders refused to support involvement in the project. Ilisu appeared to be dead after the lead Swiss bank involved in the financing and key contractors in Sweden and Italy subsequently withdrew.

Thus, after the successful example of Maheshwar, in 2002 the Ilisu campaign appeared to be an encouraging sign of how international civil society could begin to hold the ECAs and their company clients accountable. Unfortunately, the project was revived in 2005–6, after the ECAs *claimed* to have adopted common environment guidelines.

First Steps Toward Reform?

Ironically, while the United States has been a laggard in many international environmental arenas, it has taken the lead over the past decade in pushing other industrialized nations to agree on minimal environmental standards and guidelines for ECAs.

This effort has been extremely difficult, meeting continued opposition within the OECD Export Credit Group—especially from governments such as France and Germany. In Germany the parts of the government responsible for trade and export credits opposed even minimal reforms over most of the past decade, revealing a remarkable hypocrisy that is mirrored in other European countries. In publicly visible areas that have less economic impact than export finance, the governments announce politically correct positions—for example, moralistic calls for increased development assistance in the United Nations. But when the interests of their key multinationals and export benefits are at stake, many European countries have shown a different face, conveniently hidden from the public by restrictions on public access to information.

Several European nations led by Germany rejected initial proposals by the U.S. in the mid-1990s to negotiate an environmental agreement, arguing in the closed meetings of the ECG that the environment was not even a relevant subject for discussion with respect to export credits. Only after President Clinton personally raised the issue at the G8 economic summits in the late 1990s and 2000 did the ECAs of Germany, France, Japan, and other industrialized nations begin to go through the motions of negotiating minimal environmental and social standards for their activities in developing nations—mainly out of fear that they could lose control of the issue.[23]

In December 2003 the OECD ECAs finally signed off on a weak, legally nonbinding agreement, "Common Approaches on Environment and Export Credits." They voluntarily pledged to conduct basic environmental assessments for projects and investments with major impacts and to apply three (only) of ten World Bank environmental and social safeguard policies for such investments.

Even then, the agreement had curious, apparently irrational, lacunae for anyone familiar with basic good practice in environmental assessment of large projects. For example, Germany, supported by a few other countries, had blocked proposals to at least reference a fourth World Bank safeguard policy on protection of natural habitats (which requires not supporting projects that would significantly degrade critical natural habitats and, in cases where some degradation of habitat occurs, providing funds to protect equivalent ecosystems in the host country). The same opposition succeeded in gutting the most basic elements of credible environmental assessment—transparency and sharing of key environmental information with affected populations in advance of project approval. Instead, the document recommended that ECAs "seek" to make environmental impact information publicly available, "e.g. EIAs [environmental impact assessments], summary thereof," a mere thirty days before finally committing to support the project—but not really, since the ECAs can also decide unilaterally not to make any information available, citing "exceptional reasons." And they are not required to publicly report such exceptions but only to notify the other ECAs in the OECD. This very weak agreement appears, not surprisingly, to have had little impact.

On the hopeful side, almost all twenty-six OECD ECAs have issued environmental procedures to comply with the Common Approaches agreement, and almost all have hired environmental staff. But actual implementation of even the very weak criteria of the agreement have been undermined by continued ECA lack of transparency and lack of an independent monitoring process to ensure real improvements over the past ECA record of environmental and social havoc.

One other hopeful development has been the success of the UK—again over the heads of ECAs in the G8—in pressing ECAs to stop export credits for sales of arms and other "nonproductive" items to the very poorest countries (mainly in sub-Saharan Africa). However, OECD ECAs continue to subsidize these very profitable exports to most other developing countries.

The test of the 2003 environmental agreement lies first and foremost in whether the ECAs no longer support projects with potential for egregious violations of human rights, international law, and basic environmental norms. Incredibly, in late 2005 the German, Swiss, and Austrian ECAs all were considering anew the Ilisu Dam in Turkey, surely one of the most controversial and poorly conceived water project proposals of the past two decades. The German Euler Hermes, Austrian Kortrollbank, and Swiss Export Risk Guarantee (ERG) have been asked by the Austrian company VA Tech, the leader of a multinational construction consortium, to provide $660 million in guarantees, loans, and insurance for the $1.464 billion project.[24]

According to VA Tech, an adequate environmental assessment and a resettlement plan for over 75,000 Kurds in 183 villages and towns were finally in place. Yet the same irreparable problems of forced resettlement of an ethnic minority in a conflict zone, violation of the downstream water rights of Iraq and Syria, and flooding of priceless cultural and archaeological sites remained. For example, VA Tech alleged that there had been "100% consultation" with the population to be resettled. But independent inspection visits to the dam area by German, Swiss, and Austrian NGOs revealed that in many cases this consisted of summoning the male head of a family to the police station and telling him that the family would have to move.

The NGO environmental, development, and human rights groups are again protesting the project, which, even under the weak 2003 OECD "Common Approaches on Environment and Export Credits," should not be given serious consideration for support.

Should ECAs Exist?

The growing role of the ECAs shows how increased global competitiveness in the past fifteen years has dramatically reinforced the economic selfishness of rich industrialized nations. Economic globalization has produced the phenomenon of industrialized countries forcing cuts in domestic social programs and safety nets while increasing government subsidies for corporations engaged in foreign trade and investment—all in the name of global competitiveness.

The ECAs' growing financial importance contrasts sharply with much of the official rhetoric about world economic trends over the past fifteen years, which has touted an independent private sector and free markets. For developing countries in particular, the official story has emphasized how private-sector financing, particularly foreign direct investment, has overtaken and even supplanted development assistance. In reality, however, the private-sector funding is less "private" and "free market" than official pronouncements claim. Much of it—and most big private direct investment in developing nations—is indirectly or directly subsidized by ECAs and to a lesser extent by the rapidly growing private-sector affiliates of the World Bank: the International Finance Corporation and the Multilateral Guarantee Agency.

At root, the policy question for the international community is whether ECAs should even exist. Proponents of the free market, such as the Cato Institute, argue that these organizations create market distortions. Environmental and social advocates see them as undermining their governments' commitments to sustainable development and human rights. But simply abolishing them—as the respected British magazine *The Economist* advocated several years ago—is analogous to advocating the abolition of armies: in a climate of greater international competition for markets and exports, no one wants to disarm unilaterally.

The huge export subsidies major governments provide to corporations through ECAs would seem to be a direct contravention of World Trade Organization rules, but the Uruguay Round of WTO talks explicitly exempted the major industrialized country ECAs that agreed to common minimal premiums and interest rates in the OECD Arrangement. In fact, to join the WTO, countries that are not parties to the OECD Arrangement must phase out their export credits unless they agree to the export finance conditions set by the rich countries in the Arrangement. Thus, merely agreeing to minimal financial norms exempts rich country ECAs from WTO enforcement, but developing country competitors are forced to abide by rules they had no role in setting, while the OECD ECAs are free to continue their taxpayer-subsidized depredations. The WTO exemption, commonly referred to as a "carve-out," sums up the free-market hypocrisy of the rich OECD countries: free markets for the poor, subsidies for the rich.

More disturbing, the autonomous, indeed almost autistic, relationship (or lack of relationship) of ECAs to the rest of the public international system raises troubling questions about the effectiveness of international environmental, labor, human rights, and other social agreements, as well as about the political will of the major industrialized countries to honor those agreements. The OECD appears in this saga as a rather dysfunctional body. For years its Development Assistance Committee and its Environment Directorate have been working on common best practices and procedures for environmental assessment. Yet the OECD Export Credit Group might as well be conducting its discussions on another planet: the ECG's ECA representatives are rarely willing to accept input from other parts of the OECD.

To date, major industrialized country governments have not had the political will to make their ECAs accountable. Germany provides a case in point: in 2000, the newly elected Social Democrat–Green Party government pledged in its coalition agreement to reform German export finance "along socially, environmentally, and developmentally sustainable lines." However, strong domestic pressures exerted by major transnational company clients of the German ECA Hermes, and the government ministries they influenced, effectively blocked all reform. The German center-right government elected in 2005 is even less likely to challenge "Germany Incorporated." Similar scenarios (often without even pretenses of reform) are common in most industrialized exporting nations, as well as in emerging industrial exporting countries such as China, Brazil, and India.

Through 2006, the OECD ECAs are reviewing and revising both the 2003 "Common Approaches" environmental agreement as well as a hitherto toothless 2000 OECD "Action Statement on Bribery," which in typical ECA fashion was more a declaration of inaction than of action. So far the signs are not good. The veil of secrecy behind which the ECAs negotiate was broken by London's *Financial Times* in February 2006. Citing leaked ECA documents, the paper reported that Germany and Japan were leading an effort to block proposals to fight corruption and bribery, particularly a proposal that ECAs start to make public the commissions and fees their private-sector clients pay to "agents" in developing countries.[25] (These agents are local consultants who typically are hired to pass through bribes and facilitate the transfer of stolen funds from developing country officials to offshore accounts.) Several major ECAs, again including Germany and Japan, also oppose requiring the private companies they support with taxpayer funds to disclose whether they have had any prior convictions (for example, in other countries) for bribery and corruption. Negotiations were reported to be at a standstill.

Over the past decade and a half, the ECAs and their corporate clients have formed a perverse partnership that has subsidized trade through the export of destruction. Reform is long overdue. The political will to ensure change will come about only through increased public awareness and public pressure, exercised in major industrial countries through civil society organizations, national parliaments, and the press. It is nevertheless a sign of hope that for several years NGOs in major OECD countries, and in developing nations such as Indonesia and Brazil, have been building an international ECA reform campaign, a campaign whose relevance and importance can only grow.

Notes

1. *Global Development Finance 2002: Analysis and Summary Tables* (Washington, D.C.: World Bank, 2003), p. 108.

2. True, there remains a great discrepancy between the rhetoric of many development agencies, including their stated purpose of helping the poor in an environmentally sustainable fashion, and their practice—a gap often highlighted in nongovernmental groups' criticisms of the World Bank. But, as the eighteenth-century French moralist la Rochefoucauld noted, hypocrisy is the tribute that vice pays to virtue. Indeed, it is often the first step in institutional reform, and bilateral and multilateral aid institutions now at least have policies to which they can be held accountable.

3. "Business Volumes up 21% to $788 billion for Berne Union Members—Record Year for Export Credit and Investment Insurers," press release (London: Berne Union, October 6, 2005); Stephanie Fried and Titi Soentoro, *Export Credit Agency Finance in Indonesia* (Washington, D.C.: Environmental Defense Fund, December 2000), pp. 3, 10.

4. James Harmon, Crescencia Mauer, Jon Sohn, and Tomas Carbonell, *Diverging Paths: What Future for Export Credit Agencies in Development Finance?* (Washington, D.C.: World Resources Institute, 2005), p. 13.

5. Jasper Becker, "Dam Official Flees with $930 Million," *South China Morning Post*, May 3, 2000; *Human Rights Dammed Off at Three Gorges: An Investigation of Resettlement and Human Rights Problems at the Three Gorges Dam Project* (Berkeley, Calif.: International Rivers Network, January 2003). See also Audrey Topping, "Ecological Roulette: Damming the Yangtze," *Foreign Affairs*, September–October 1995.

6. Crescencia Mauer and Ruchi Bhandari, *The Climate of Export Credit Agencies* (Washington, D.C.: World Resources Institute, May 2000), p. 4.

7. Christopher Barr, *Profits on Paper: The Political Economy of Fiber, Finance, and Debt in Indonesia's Pulp and Paper Industries* (Bogor, Indonesia: Center for International Forestry Research, 2000).

8. Peter Waldman and Jay Solomon, "Power Deals with Cuts for First Family in Indonesia Are Coming under Attack," *Wall Street Journal*, December 23, 1998.

9. Inge Altemeier and Harald Schumann, "Der Ueberfluessige Strom," *Der Spiegel*, May 29, 2000.

10. See ECA Watch, "Corrupt Power Projects and the Responsibility of Export Credit Agencies in Indonesia," www.eca-watch.org/problems/corruption/bosshard6_indon_nov2000.html; Hideka Yamaguchi, "Whose Sustainable Development? An Analysis of Japanese Foreign Aid Policy and Support for Energy Sector Projects," *Bulletin of Science, Technology, and Society* 23, no. 4 (August 2003), pp. 302–10, 306; "Paiton Coal-Burning Power Plant, Indonesia," *Unfarallon.info*, www.unfarallon.info/paiton.asp.

11. Will Marshall, "Australian Firms Plunder Papua New Guinea," 2003, www.mines andcommunities.org/ Country/png3.htm; *Putting the Ethic in EFIC* (Sydney, Australia: Aidwatch and Mineral Policy Institute, 1999), pp. 21–26.

12. Ibid. *Guardian* (Australia edn.), December 6, 2000; Melanie Quevillon, coordinator of the NGO Working Group on the EDC, "Export Development Canada–Backed Mine Leaves a Sea of Cyanide," media release (Ottawa: Halifax Initiative, April 10, 2002), www.ecawatch.org/problems/americas/canada/JHalifaxInitPR_G8_20002.html; and Coalition for Public Awareness, *Export Credit Agencies, Corporate Welfare, Lack of Accountability*, www.cpa.org.au/garchives3/102/1028aid.html.

13. Jennifer Lanston, "Quest for American Justice on South Pacific Island," *Seattle Post-Intelligencer*, July 19, 2004, available at http://seattlepi.nwsource.om/local/182687_

bougainville19.html; Marshall, "Australian Firms Plunder Papua New Guinea"; see also this press release at www.hagens-berman.com/frontend;jsessionid=akgbaP5_MP5?command=PressRelease&task=viewPressReleaseDetail&iPressReleaseId=215.

14. Nicholas Gilby, *Arms Exports to Indonesia* (London: Campaign against Arms Trade, October 1999), at www.caat.org.uk/publications/countries/indonesia-1099.php; Rob Evans, "Taxpayers Paid £400m to BAE for Failed Arms Deals," *Guardian*, December 20, 2004, www.guardian.co.uk/indonesia/Story/0,,1377390,00.html#article_continue. See also www.eca-watch.org/problems/arms/.

15. Martin Broeck, "Paper on Export Credit Agencies and Arms Trade" (Amsterdam: Campagne tegen Wafenhandel, March 28, 2003), p. 4, available online at www.caat.org.uk/publications/countries/indonesia-1099.php.

16. Dieter Frisch, *Export Credit Insurance and the Fight against International Corruption*, working paper (Berlin: Transparency International, 1999).

17. James V. Grimaldi, "Enron Pipeline Leaves Scar on South America: Lobbying, U.S. Loans Put Project on Damaging Path," *Washington Post*, May 6, 2002.

18. *The Enron Corporation: Corporate Complicity in Human Rights Violations* (New York: Human Rights Watch, 1999).

19. See Heffa Schücking, "The Maheshwar Dam in India" (Sassenberg, Germany: Urgewald, March 1999), www.narmada.org/urg990421.html; Shirpad Dharmadhikary and Patrick McCully, "Villagers Capture Dam in India," *Earth Island Journal* (Spring 1998), www.earthisland.org/eijournal/spring98/sp98f_wn.htm.

20. Peter Bosshard, *Power Finance: Financial Institutions in India's Hydropower Sector* (Delhi: South Asia Network on Dams, Rivers, and People; Sassenberg, Germany: Urgewald; and Berkeley, Calif.: International Rivers Network, January 2002), pp. 7–11, available at www.irn.org/programs/india/power%20finance-inside-16.pdf; V. Venkatase, "A Moral Victory for the NBA," *Frontline* 17, no. 15 (July 22–August 4, 2000), www.hinduonnet.com/fline/fl1715/17151150.htm; Narmada Bachao Andolan, "Portuguese Guarantee to Maheshwar Project Refused," press release, March 15, 2001, www.narmada.org/nbapress-releases/march-2001/portuguese.guarantee.refused.html.

21. For the Jakarta Declaration, and other information on the international campaign to reform export credits, see www.eca-watch.org.

22. UK House of Commons, Session 1999–2000, Trade and Industry Committee, Sixth Report, "Application for Support from ECGD for UK Participation in the Ilisu Dam Project" (London: HM Stationery Office, February 28, 2000), pp. vii, x.

23. James Harmon, "Ensuring that Subsidized Foreign Projects Are Green," *Environmental Forum* 18, no. 5 (September/October 2000), p. 41.

24. Daniela Setton, Heike Drillisch et al. *Der Ilisu Staudamm: Kein Erfolgsprojekt: Zum Hintergrund un adktuellen Stand des groessten Staudammprojekts im Suedosten der Turkei* (Berlin: Weltwirtschaft, Economy, Ecology, und Entwicklung [World Economy, Ecology, and Development—WEED], November 2005).

25. Edward Alden, David Pilling, and Hugh Williamson, "Export Credit Agencies' Graft Crackdown Stalls," *Financial Times*, February 15, 2006.

11 *G8 debt relief programs will cut less than 1 percent of the $3.2 trillion that developing countries still owe—and their harsh terms will exact additional hardship. What's next for the debt relief campaign?*

The Mirage of Debt Relief

James S. Henry

We should have known that it was high time to study the fine print when veteran rock stars Bono and Bob Geldof, film stars Angelina Jolie and George Clooney, liberal comedian Al Franken, U.S. Treasury Secretary John Snow, World Bank President Paul Wolfowitz, and the UK's Gordon Brown and Tony Blair all lined up on the same side of the field to cheer the G8's July 2005 decision to provide "$40 billion of debt relief" to poor, heavily indebted developing countries.

One might have expected self-effacing politicians like Brown and Blair to hail the agreement. Indeed they did, calling it "an historic breakthrough. . . . The most comprehensive statement that finance ministers have ever made on issues of debt, development, health, and poverty." But while many activists were more restrained, Sir Bob and Bono, the debt-relief campaign's most prominent leaders, were also quick to declare victory. After months of mass mobilization by the Live 8 / "End Poverty Now" campaign—including ten free concerts, 3 billion viewers, 30 million e-mails and faxes, and 250,000 marchers in Gleneagles, Scotland—they seemed unwilling to acknowledge the huge gap that remains between the G8 accord and the amount of debt relief and aid actually needed to "end poverty now."

This turns out to be part of a long-standing pattern. Indeed, Third World debt relief has become a little like Boston's Big Dig, the Middle East peace process, and the cure for cancer—long anticipated, endlessly discussed, and perpetually just around the corner.

After decades of effort, the fact is that very little Third World debt relief has actually been achieved. There is also mounting evidence that even the paltry amounts of debt relief that have been achieved have not done very much. This is partly because debt relief sometimes reinforces questionable policies and bad habits that got developing countries into hock in the first place. It is also because debt relief has tended to reinforce the power of IMF/World Bank econocrats, whose policies have often been disastrous for developing countries. Finally, debt relief is a very poor substitute for other forms of aid and development finance.

Meanwhile, most of the costs of debt relief have been borne by ordinary First and Third World taxpayers, while the global banks and Third World elites that profited enormously from all the lousy projects, capital flight, and corruption that were financed by the debt have escaped scot-free.

This is not to suggest that the entire debt-relief campaign is utterly point-less. It has provided a bully pulpit for scores of entertainers, politicians, econo-mists, religious leaders, and NGOs. It has reminded us of the persistent prob-lems of global poverty and inequality. It has also provided us with an excuse for some pretty good free concerts.

From the standpoint of actually providing enough aid to improve living conditions in debt-ridden countries, however, debt relief has been a disap-pointment. In the immortal words of Bono, "We still haven't found what we're looking for." Fortunately, there is an alternative strategy that would have a greater impact. But it would require a much more combative stance on the part of debt-relief activists, and it would almost certainly not gener-ate as many convivial joint press conferences with the self-effacing leaders of the Free World.

"Fact Check, Please"

Surprisingly, there have been few efforts to take stock of debt-relief efforts to date,[1] to see whether this game has really been worth the candle.

It is high time to take a closer look. After all, it is now more than thirty years since Zaire's bilateral debts were rescheduled by the Paris Club (an association of First World export credit agencies) in 1976, twenty-seven years since the UN Conference on Trade and Development's $6 billion write-off for forty-five developing countries in 1977–79, twenty-three years since the climax of the so-called Third World debt crisis in 1983, and more than a decade since the

Figure 1   Developing Country Foreign Debt and Debt Service, 1970–2006
(Billions of Dollars)

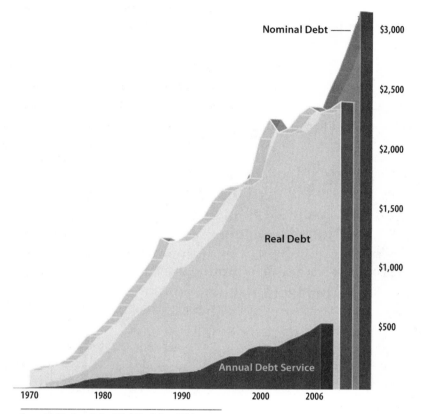

Source: Author's analysis of World Bank data, 2006.

IMF/World Bank's debt-relief program for Heavily Indebted Poor Countries (HIPCs) was inaugurated in 1996.

On the debt-relief campaign side, it is two decades since the formation of the UK Debt Crisis Network, eight years since the 70,000-strong "Drop the Debt" demos at the G8's May 1998 meetings in Birmingham, and nearly two years since the Live 8/Make Poverty History fiesta at Gleneagles.

Along the way, there have been Brady Plans, Mitterand Plans, Lawson Plans, Mizakawa Plans, Sachs Plans, Evian Plans, and more than 200 debt reschedulings by the Paris Club on increasingly generous terms—Toronto terms (1988–91), London terms (1991–94), Naples terms (1995–96), Lyon terms (1996–99), and Cologne terms (1999–). Most recently, in the wake of Live 8, the G8, the World Bank, and the IMF launched their Multilateral Debt

Relief Initiative (MDRI) with a great deal of fanfare, declaring that it will be worth at least "$40 to $50 billion" to the forty or so countries that are eligible.

Realities

Despite all this activity, developing country debt is now greater than ever before, and is still increasing in real terms. For most countries, the debt burden—as measured by the ratio of debt service (interest payments on principal and fees paid on the debt) to national income—is even higher than in the early 1980s, at the peak of the so-called Third World debt crisis (see Figure 1). [2]

By my estimates, as of 2006, the nominal stock of developing country foreign debt outstanding stood at *$3.24 trillion.* This debt now generates about $550 billion of debt service a year for foreign creditors—mainly First World banks, bondholders, and multilateral institutions. That $550 billion includes $41 billion a year paid by the world's sixty poorest countries, whose per capita incomes are all below $825 a year. Even after twenty-five years of debt relief, the annual debt service paid by these countries still almost entirely negates the $40 billion to $45 billion of annual foreign aid they receive. Their debt burden is now a higher percentage of their national income than it was in the early 1980s. [3]

Most heavy debtors also have very little to show for all this debt. These payments are, in effect, a "shark fee" paid to First World creditors for funds that have long since vanished into the ether, or into offshore bank accounts.

Present Value

Since most Third World debt was contracted at higher interest rates than now prevail, the *present value* (PV) of the debt—a better measure of its true cost—is even higher—*nearly $3.7 trillion* (see Table 1). [4]

China and India alone account for about $500 billion of this developing country "present value debt." Both countries have been careful about foreign borrowing, and they have also largely ignored IMF/World Bank policy advice. The result is that their foreign debt burdens are small relative to national income. Both countries—partly because they refuse to follow orthodox neo-liberal policies—now have high-growth economies and large stockpiles of foreign reserves.

Of the other $3.2 trillion of PV debt, however, about $2.6 trillion is owed by twenty-six low-income and forty-nine middle-income countries that pursued "high debt" growth strategies. [5]

Table 1   Estimates of Third World Debt
(Billions of 2006 Dollars)

Debt Projections	Number of Countries	Population, 2004 (Billions)	Low-Income Countries	Middle-Income Countries	Total Debt Estimate
India	1	1.08	135.0		135.0
China	1	1.30		323.5	323.5
All Other Developing Countries		2.91	336.1	2,337.0	2673.1
High-debt/low-income	25	0.35	131.0		131.00
High-debt/middle income	47	1.12		1,874.0	1874.0
High-Debt Countries	72	1.46	131.0	1,874.0	2,005
Other low-income	31	0.87	205.1		205.1
Other middle-income	43	0.58		463.0	463.0
Adjustments to World Bank list[a]	7	0.14	18.4	111.7	112.1
Nigerian debt deal			−18.0		−18.0
Total Nominal Debt Stock			471.5	2,777.9	3,237.1
Total Present Value Third World Debt	155	5.45	412.6	3,277.4	3,690.0
India alone	1	1.08	139.0		139.0
China alone	1	1.30		363.0	363.0
High-debt/low-income	26	0.427	147		147
High-debt/middle-income	49	1.164		2,408	2,408
Total High-Debt Countries	75	1.59	147	2,408	2,555
Other low-income	32	0.90	127		127
Other middle-income	46	0.59		507	507

[a] These countries are Afghanistan, Cuba, Iraq, Namibia, North Korea, Suriname, and Turkmenistan.
Source: World Bank data for 2006; author's analysis.

These heavily indebted countries have about 1.6 billion residents—over a quarter of the world's population, a share that is steadily increasing. After decades of debt relief, their ratios of present value debt to national income are all relatively high: 60 to 90 percent. Debt service still consumes 4 to 9 percent of national income each year, more than they spend on education or health, and far more than they receive in foreign aid (see Table 2). Finally, these countries have had little choice but to accept World Bank/IMF policy advice—despite the fact that, in case after case, such advice has failed them.

Table 2   The Impact of Debt

	Number of Countries	Per Capita Income[a]	Real Per Capita Growth, 1994–2004	PV Debt/ GNI, 2004[b]	Debt Service/ GNI, 2004	Aid as % of GNI, 2004	Education Spending/ Income[c]
High-Debt Countries							
Low-income[b]	26	$1,345	1.7%	89.8%	4.2%	3.9%	3.7%
Middle-income	49	$6,795	1.8%	61.7%	9.0%	0.4%	2.8%
Lower-Debt Countries							
China	1	$5,419	7.9%	14.5%	1.2%	0.1%	n.a.
India	1	$2,885	4.2%	18.4%	2.8%	0.1%	4.1%
Other low-income	32	$1,506	2.0%	31.9%	2.8%	5.5%	3.6%
Other middle-income	46	$6,677	2.5%	25.0%	5.5%	0.3%	5.3%
Developing world	155	$4,417		39.0%	5.4%	1.0%	
World	226	$8,187					

[a] In 2004 dollars at purchasing power parity rates. [b] GNI = gross national income. [c] Average spending for 2000–2004.
Source: World Bank data for 2006; author's analysis.

Where's the Relief?

These debt numbers and ratios suggest some obvious questions. What have all the professional debt relievers been up to all these years (the World Bank, the IMF, and the Paris Club,[6] not to mention those activists who favored focusing on debt relief)? How much debt relief have they actually secured, who has received it, and how helpful has it been?

To begin with, measuring debt relief is not easy. The definitions of debt relief employed by countries and creditors vary significantly, and the reported data on debt and payment flows are subject to huge discrepancies. This helps to account for the fact that only a handful of systematic attempts have ever been made to measure debt relief.[7]

However, some things can be said. This chapter provides the most comprehensive estimate of debt relief to date, based on careful review of all these data sources and my own independent analyses of alternative debt measures.[8]

Overall Relief

My first key finding is that the amount of debt relief provided to developing countries has been pretty modest. From 1982 through 2005, in 2006 NPV dollars, the total value of all low- and middle-income developing country debt that was "relieved"—rescheduled, reduced, or canceled—was $310 billion— just 7.8 percent of all outstanding debt (see Table 3).

Low-Income Relief

The percentage of relief given to the world's sixty poorest countries was higher—about 28 percent of their prerelief debt. These countries have received $161 billion of present value debt relief—more than half of all the debt relief granted. At current interest rates, this relief will save these poor countries about $15.3 billion per year of debt service.[9]

Table 3 Measures of Debt Relief (Billions of 2005 NPV Dollars)			
	Low-Income Countries	Middle-Income Countries	Total Debt Relief
Pre–Debt Relief	$574	$3,426	$4,000
Debt Relief	$161	$149	$310
Post–Debt Relief	$413	$3,277	$3,690
Percent of Debt Relief	28.1%	4.3%	7.8%

Source: World Bank data for 2006; author's analysis.

This is nothing to sneeze at. But it is a far cry from the extra $50 billion to $100 billion per year of cash aid that leading development experts agree is needed if developing countries are to reach the (rather modest) "Millennium Development Goals" that were set back in 2000 by the UN, with a target date of 2015.

It is also important to remember that low-income countries have had to wait a long time for even this modicum of debt relief, most of which did not arrive until the late 1990s. By then, several new countries had joined the ranks of the "heavily indebted."

Sources of Debt Relief for Low-Income Countries

Just 30 percent of all this debt relief for low-income countries came from the World Bank/IMF's HIPC and MDRI programs (discussed later). Another 30 percent came from Russia, which forgave a huge load of bilateral debt owed by Nicaragua, Vietnam, and Yemen when Russia joined the Paris Club in 1997. In February 2006, Russia also wrote off about $5 billion debt owed by Afghanistan.

Another $65 billion in debt relief for poor countries came from the Paris Club, an association of First World export credit agencies (ECAs) such as the U.S. Ex-Im Bank. Their generosity is not surprising—all these agencies have a

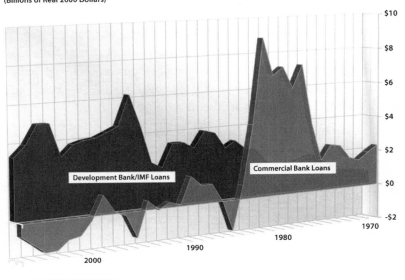

Figure 2 Commercial versus Development Bank Loans
to Low-Income Countries, 1970–2004
(Billions of Real 2000 Dollars)

* Does not include India.
Source: World Bank 2006 data; author's analysis.

very strong clientele among First World exporters, contractors, and engineering firms. These ECA clients all received significant business from projects funded by the earlier loans in the form of project orders, and are now eager to have the ECAs forgive still more loans, at taxpayer expense, to clear the way for yet another round of large projects.

In contrast, leading global commercial banks like Citigroup, UBS, JPMorganChase, Goldman Sachs, Deutsche Bank, BNP, ABN-Amro, and Barclays have provided a grand total of just *$1.5 billion* of debt relief to low-income countries, mostly through the World Bank/IMF's HIPC program.

In the 1970s and early 1980s, these same commercial banks led the way in syndicating loans to developing countries (see Figure 2). Many of them also became pioneers in "private banking," the dubious business of helping Third (and First) World elites park their capital in tax havens free of annoying taxes and regulations.

Ironically, the same banks that promoted debt and wealth flight from poor countries now focus most of their activities in the developing world on more lucrative debt-free countries, like China and India, as well as on First World private banking and investment banking.

While the foreign loan business was booming in the late 1970s and early 1980s among middle-income developing countries, leading international private banks became deeply involved in stashing abroad a large share of the funds that had been loaned to these countries by the banks' own syndicates.[10] In low-income countries, these "pirate" bankers were more often called on to recycle the proceeds of loans from the World Bank and other development banks, the IMF, and ECA project loans, as well as the proceeds of state asset rip-offs.

Overall, therefore, from the standpoint of debt relief, it is hard to say that First World financial giants have done their share—in light of the enormous profits they reaped from Third World lending and private banking. In the wake of the debt crisis, they also scooped up undervalued banks, pension funds, and insurance companies at low prices in countries like Brazil, the Philippines, Argentina, Indonesia, and Mexico. In good times and in bad, they have contrived to prosper, while helping their clients borrow over their heads, launder money, evade taxes, and conceal their ill-gotten gains.

I will return to these financial giants later, because the history of their involvement in this story suggests one interesting possible antidote for our "debt-relief blues."

Middle-Income Relief

So-called middle-income developing countries such as Brazil and Mexico have received $149 billion of debt relief—just 4.3 percent of their $3.4 trillion of prerelief outstanding debt.[11] As discussed later, most of this debt relief was granted by the early 1990s, under the Brady Plan restructuring and by the Paris Club.

High priority was given to these larger, more lucrative, and more heavily indebted countries in the 1980s by First World banks and governments, mainly because the latter had such a large share of their loan portfolios tied up in those markets.[12] Indeed, the true meaning of the Third World debt crisis for most First World bankers, central bankers, officials, and journalists was a crisis for themselves and their shareholders. Over time, as they managed to reduce their Third World exposure, the crisis disappeared from the headlines—although most countries remained in deep trouble.[13]

Sources of Debt Relief for Middle-Income Countries

Overall, private banks provided $75 billion of debt relief to middle-income debtors, about half of all debt relief. Most of this was achieved through debt

Figure 3   Foreign Debt Service Burden, 1970–2004
(Debt Service as a Percentage of Gross National Income for 155 Low-
and Middle-Income Developing Countries)

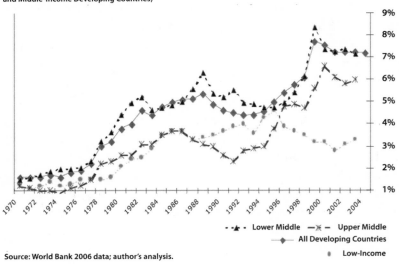

- -▲- - Lower Middle   —✕— Upper Middle
         ◆— All Developing Countries
                        ●   Low-Income

Source: World Bank 2006 data; author's analysis.

swaps and buybacks. The Paris Club added another $28 billion, mainly by way
of traditional bilateral debt rescheduling.

The U.S. Treasury offered $47 billion of net debt relief through the Baker
Plan (1985–89) and the Brady Plan (1989–95). On its own, however, the Baker
Plan actually *increased* middle-income country debt by $77 billion while con-
suming $45 billion of U.S. taxpayer subsidies in the process. It took the more
effective Brady Plan to offset this increase.

From 1995 to 2002, the U.S. Treasury, World Bank, and IMF also provided
short-term financial relief to several major debtors, such as Argentina, Brazil,
Mexico, and Indonesia. These were supposed to be pure debt reschedulings,
with all loans eventually paid back with interest. In theory, then, they should
have had no net impact on PV debt levels.

In practice, however, several of these short-term bailouts were also completely mismanaged by the IMF and the World Bank. For example, Indonesia,
Mexico, and Argentina were all permitted to use emergency dollar loans to
bail out dozens of domestic banks and companies that were owned by influential members of the local elite, many of whom were "not unknown" to First
World bankers and even U.S. treasury secretaries.[14] So a large share of these
bailout loans went to outright graft. But the countries were still expected to
service the loans, often at very high interest rates. Given their governments'

reluctance to raise taxes, especially on local capital, most countries repaid the bailout loans by boosting their *domestic* debts—in effect, by printing money. For example, Mexico's bailout in the mid-1990s ended up costing its taxpayers more than $70 billion, while Indonesia's bailout cost at least $50 billion. In that way, the bailouts ended up actually *increasing* country debt levels, just like the Baker Plan. My estimates of debt relief have generously omitted the impact of these mismanaged bailouts, which would make the aggregate amount of Third World debt relief to date sharply lower.

Overall, during the 1970s and 1980s, middle-income countries like Argentina, Brazil, Indonesia, Iraq, Mexico, the Philippines, Russia, Turkey, and Venezuela became the world's largest debtors. Since they also received little debt relief since the early 1990s, their debt service soared to all-time highs after 2000 (see Figure 3). Recent debt-relief programs have focused almost entirely on low-income countries, ignoring the heavy burden and the illegitimate roots of debt in these middle-income countries. This focus is an important strategic choice that debt-relief campaigns may want to reconsider.

The Political Economy of Debt Relief

So what's gone wrong with debt relief? Why has so little been achieved after all these years? Whose interests have been served, and whose intent have been ignored or gored? And where should debt-relief campaigners go from here?

The Roots of the "Debt" Crisis

To understand the debt-relief track record, it is helpful to review the origins of the so-called Third World debt crisis. This prolonged crisis has its roots in the fact that, from the early 1970s to 2003, developing countries absorbed more than $6.8 trillion in foreign loans, aid, and investment, much more foreign capital than they had ever received before.[15]

As noted, a few developing countries managed this enormous capital influx more or less successfully—mainly Asian countries like South Korea, China, India, Korea, Malaysia, and Vietnam. For a variety of historical reasons, they were able to resist the insidious influence of First World development banks and private banks. Today, they account for almost all the real winners in the globalization sweepstakes, ranking among the world's fastest-growing economies and the First World's most important suppliers, customers, and potential competitors.[16]

Our focus here should not be on this handful of winners, but on the vast majority of the world's 150 developing countries.[17] In general, compared with the handful of winners, the losers have been much more open to unrestricted foreign capital investment and trade since the 1970s, as well as policy advice from the World Bank and the IMF (the so-called Bretton Woods Institutions, or BWIs). For many countries this close encounter with global capitalism has proved troublesome, if not disastrous.[18]

In effect, for several decades these countries conducted a very risky policy experiment. By now the results are clear. Across widely varying income levels and institutional settings, middle-income countries all paid a very heavy price for unfettered access to loans from and dependence on foreign banks. Indeed, I am hard-pressed to find a single exception to the miserable track record of this "wide open, debt-heavy, pro-bank" growth strategy. Most paeans to "globalization" simply gloss over it by focusing on the non-neoliberal winners.

Corrupt Regimes and Unproductive ("Dubious") Debts

Overall, I estimate that more than a trillion dollars—at least 25 to 35 percent—of the $3.7 trillion foreign debt that was compiled by low- and middle-income countries from 1970 to 2004 either disappeared into poorly planned, corruption-ridden development projects or was simply stolen outright.[19]

For several of the largest debtors, like the Philippines, Indonesia, Mexico, Brazil, Venezuela, Argentina, and Nigeria, the share of the debt that was wasted was perhaps even higher. Indeed, one of the most important patterns underlying the debt crisis was the fact that overborrowing, wasteful projects, capital flight, and corruption were all concentrated in about twenty countries. As I will argue, those who seek to revitalize the debt-relief movement must understand this crucial fact, because it implies that the interests at stake here may be far more influential than the ones that have surfaced so far in the struggle for "low-income" debt relief.

Low-Income Heavy Borrowers

A similar pattern of waste and corruption emerges among the forty-eight low-income countries that eventually qualified for debt relief under the World Bank/IMF HIPC and MDRI programs (discussed later). In the early 1980s, the value of these countries' debt increased by 70 percent in just six years;[20] by the time the World Bank/IMF got around to launching HIPC in 1996, this debt had increased another 7–10 percent. Just eleven of the forty-eight—Bolivia, Congo Republic, Democratic Republic of Congo, Ethiopia, Ghana, Ivory Coast, Mozambique, Myanmar, Nicaragua, Sudan, and Zambia—accounted for 68 percent of the group's debt increase from 1980 to 1986.

All eleven top borrowers were not only desperately poor to begin with[21] but also weak, wide-open states run by kleptocratic dictators and/or caught up in bloody civil wars.[22] Sometimes the causality flowed both ways: excess debts exacerbated political instability. But the dominant factor responsible for heavy debts was an unsavory combination of weak states, corrupt leaders, wide-open capital markets, and seductive relationships with foreign bankers. Extending this analysis to the key middle-income debtors noted earlier, we find a similar long-term conjunction of misgovernment, weak states, and wide-open banking.

The evidence thus suggests that the heaviest debtors got into trouble for reasons that were only superficially related to the usual villains in the orthodox account of debt crises—"exogenous shocks," "policy errors," "liquidity crises," and—when pushed to acknowledge the existence of corruption and capital flight—a "lack of transparency." Those countries that are deepest in debt and most in need of relief today are those that have long been among the most consistently misgoverned, the most open to foreign capital and influence, and the most "mis-banked." While natural resource wealth such as minerals or oil has often contributed to economic mismanagement, its presence alone does not cause mismanagement: the decisive factor is the relationship between foreign and domestic elites.

From the standpoint of debt relief, this pattern of weakness, corruption, and debt presents a dilemma. Simply providing countries with debt relief may accomplish little unless deep political reform occurs and relations with external agents are made more transparent. Otherwise, the countries are likely to dig themselves right back into a hole. After all, dictatorships like the Central African Republic have been continuously in arrears on their foreign debts since 1971!

The Debt/Flight Cycle

Servicing huge unproductive debts[23] took a large bite out of poor countries' export earnings and government revenues, draining funds that were badly needed for health, education, and other forms of public investment, and helping to produce crisis after financial crisis. Growth, investment, and employment were throttled by the continuing need—enforced by First World creditors—to generate enough foreign exchange to service the loans. Meanwhile, even as all this foreign capital was rushing in, an unprecedented quantity of flight capital—including a substantial portion of the loan proceeds themselves—headed for the door.

Of course, Third World capital flight is an old story, associated with long-standing factors like individual country risk, unstable currencies, bank secrecy, the rise of offshore tax havens, and the absence of global income tax enforcement.[24] But the *dramatic increase* in poorly managed financial inflows to the developing world in the 1970s and early 1980s—especially foreign loans and aid—boosted Third World capital outflows by an order of magnitude. They basically overwhelmed existing political and economic institutions in many countries, producing the largest tidal wave of capital flight in history while revolutionizing the world's offshore private banking market.

We simply cannot account for the sharp increase in capital flight and offshore haven activity unless we take into account its close relationship to all this "lousy First World lending and loose aid."

Poorly controlled lending and foreign aid contributed to the rise of global capital flight in a purely mathematical sense, by providing the foreign exchange required to finance the flight. But that doesn't explain why all the new "loanable funds" didn't become productive net investment in the borrowers' economies. In most countries, the tidal wave of foreign loans also stimulated additional capital flight in several other ways:

1. The loans destabilized the economies of newly indebted countries, providing more capital than the economies could productively absorb in a short period.

2. They provided a huge source of government revenue that was not directly under taxpayer oversight and was not even accurately measured. This generated enormous opportunities for corruption and waste, partly in poorly planned projects with weak financial controls and partly just by providing finance ministers, central bankers, and other official insiders with dollars to line their pockets and use to speculate against their own currencies.

3. The debt flows laid the foundations for a new, highly efficient, global offshore banking network, which made it much easier and cheaper for corrupt elites to spirit funds to places like the Cayman Islands, Panama, and the Isle of Man and stash them in anonymous, tax-evading investments.

It is no coincidence that this network was dominated by the same global banks that led the way in syndicated lending to the Third World. All three factors combined to encourage Third World officials and wealthy elites to move a significant share of their private wealth into offshore foreign assets, even while

Figure 4 Flight Wealth versus Foreign Debt, 1975–2003
(Billions of Dollars, Low- and Middle-Income Countries)

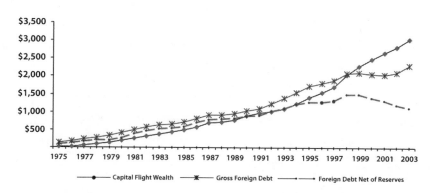

Source: Author's analysis.

their own governments were borrowing more heavily abroad than ever before (see Figure 4).

Part of the resulting flight wave took the form of large amounts of "mattress money" hoarded by residents of Third World countries in strong currencies and large denominations—especially dollars, Swiss francs, Deutschmarks, British pounds, and, after 2002, 100, 200, and 500 euro notes. By 2006, for example, the total stock of U.S. currency was $912 billion, at least two-thirds of which was held offshore, especially in developing countries with a history of devaluations. The demand is reflected in the surge of $100 bills compared to other U.S. denominations.[25]

An even greater amount of capital flight occurred in private elite funds that were spirited to offshore tax havens—often with the clandestine assistance of First World banks, law firms, and accounting firms.

The outflows resulting from this "debt-flight" cycle were massive—by my estimate, an average of $160 billion per year (in real 2000 dollars) from 1977 to 2003.[26] Most of this flight capital was permitted to accumulate offshore in tax-free investments, especially bank deposits and government bonds owned by nonresidents, which were specifically exempted from taxation by First World countries. By the early 1990s, the total amount of untaxed Third World private flight wealth exceeded the value of all outstanding Third World foreign debt![27] Indeed, for large debtors like Venezuela, Nigeria, Argentina, and Mexico—the same countries that dominated borrowing—the value of their elites' private flight wealth was several times the value of their outstanding foreign debts (see Figure 5).

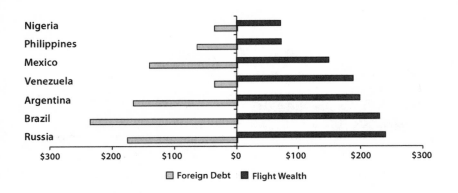

Figure 5   Flight Wealth versus Foreign Debt
(Billions of Dollars, 1977–2003)

For many debtor countries, therefore, the real problem they confront is not a "debt" problem but an "asset" problem—the problem of collecting taxes, controlling corruption, managing state-owned resources, and recovering all this foreign loot. A huge share of "private" wealth—much of it financed by foreign loans or rip-offs of state-owned companies—had simply flown the coop under the watchful eyes of the World Bank/IMF, Wall Street, and the City of London.

Meanwhile, these countries' public sectors—and ultimately their ordinary taxpayers—were stuck with servicing huge unproductive debts, while their legal systems, banking systems, and capital markets became riddled with corruption.

Orthodox economists have not ignored these phenomena completely. But they have tended to compartmentalize them into so-called institutional problems like "corruption" and "transparency," regarding them as endogenous to particular countries.[28] In this narrow-minded approach, the individual country is the unit of analysis. In fact, all these *local* problems have been greatly exacerbated by a *global* problem—the structure of the transnational system for financing development, on the one hand, and for stashing vast quantities of untaxed private capital abroad, on the other.

Human Capital Flight

This underground river of financial flight has been accompanied by an increased outflow of "human capital" as well. As large parts of the developing world have become jobless and unlivable, a significant share of its precious

The Debt Relief Tradition in U.S. History

Since the late eighteenth century, many influential private and public borrowers in the United States, including industrial companies, banks, municipalities, and large farmers, have been permitted to escape debt servitude by way of bankruptcy proceedings, debt moratoria, write-offs, "lender-of-last resort" deposit insurance, and quite a few outright bailouts. For example:

- Former U.S. Presidents Jefferson, Monroe, and Madison—all of whom were Virginia tobacco growers and slave-owners who were mortgaged up to their eyeballs—allowed their London private bankers to twist in the wind, struggling to collect their loans in U.S. courts.
- In 1841–42, eight U.S. states and the Territory of Florida defaulted on all their debts—twice the size of the federal government's debt at the time. As in the case of Third World debt, most of the proceeds turned out to have been borrowed abroad and invested in lousy projects—for example, land banks controlled by big plantation owners. This produced one of the first "emerging market" debt crises in history.
- In 1933, under the influence of companies that were desperate to survive the Great Depression, the U.S. Congress unilaterally abrogated the "gold clause" for all corporate bonds listed on the New York Stock Exchange. This move slashed the real value of all U.S. corporate debts by 31 percent overnight.
- Since the 1970s, there have been many state and federal bailouts of U.S. corporations that were considered "too big to fail," including Conrail, Chrysler, Continental Illinois, Citibank in the late 1980s, and Long-Term Capital Management in 1998. On the horizon, we should anticipate a similar "non-free market" response if Ford or General Motors are threatened with bankruptcy.
- As for sovereign country borrowers, in 1953, under the impact of the Cold War and the desire to see Western Europe recover, the U.S. helped to arrange a generous debt restructuring for West Germany, including a 50-percent debt write-off and a thirty-year repayment schedule for the balance owed.

In short, when it comes to debt relief—"sanctity of contract," "moral hazard," and other neoliberal canons notwithstanding—if the borrowers in question are large enough and have enough political influence, they have usually qualified for exceptional treatment.

skilled labor has decamped for First World labor markets. My own estimate of the net economic value of this displaced Third World "human flight wealth" is $2.5 to $3 trillion as of 2006.[29]

This offshore labor force sends home a stream of remittance income now estimated at up to $250 billion each year. But much of this money is wasted in high transfer costs and misspending. Clearly, depending heavily on labor exports—as the Philippines, El Salvador, Mexico, Haiti, and Ecuador are now doing—is not the best policy; it is a poor substitute for generating jobs and incomes at home.

Summary: The Roots of the Crisis

Overall, the impact of the debt patterns just described on Third World incomes and welfare has been devastating. Except for the handful of globalization winners that managed to avoid the debt trap and neoliberal nostrums, real incomes in the Third World basically stagnated or declined from 1980 to 2005 (see Table 4).[30] While growth has revived since then, especially among exporters of energy and other natural resources, large parts of the developing world are still struggling to regain their pre-1980 levels of consumption, social spending, and domestic tranquility. Very few countries have managed to follow the examples of China and India, diversifying into manufacturing and exportable services.

In addition to prolonged economic stagnation, many debt-ridden developing countries have also experienced sharp increases in unemployment, poverty, inequality, environmental degradation, insecurity, crime, violence, and political instability, all of which were exacerbated by debt and capital flight. Ironically, some degree of instability has occasionally been beneficial—in Argentina, Bolivia, Brazil, Chile, Guatemala, Indonesia, Kenya, Mexico, the Philippines, and South Africa, financial crises helped to undermine autocratic regimes. But democratization should have been possible without so much hardship.

These Third World troubles provided a striking contrast to the First World's relative prosperity. To be sure, there were brief hiccups from oil price spikes in 1973 and 1979, and recessions in 1982–83, 1990–91, and 2001–3. Japan stagnated during the 1990s, and France and Germany have experienced prolonged doldrums. But these were the exceptions. Overall, a large share of the world's poor have become poorer or treaded water since the early 1980s, while the majority of First World countries—and their financial institutions—have continued to prosper.

"Can't Get No Relief!"

Whatever one thinks of globalization and other neoliberal nostrums, it is very hard to make the debt track record look like an achievement. This perspective should help us see "debt relief" in a different light.

Given this sordid track record, First World governments, BWIs, and even the global private banking industry might be expected to at least acknowledge their responsibility, pitch in, and offer to share a significant portion of the bill. But obviously this hasn't happened. As the sidebar discusses, this is not because of any principled opposition to debt relief per se. Indeed, debt relief turns out to be a venerable capitalist institution, at least if the debtors in question have political clout.[31]

Nor has it been possible for the debtor countries themselves to agree on a unilateral moratorium on debt service. Only a handful of countries—Argentina in 2001–2, Russia after World War I, and Cuba in the early 1960s and 1980s—have had the courage to declare unilateral moratoriums on their own, and they have paid a high price for it. Third World debtors as a whole have never been able to marshal the collective will to take this step.

The sole alternative so far has been to rely on voluntary actions by First World creditors, enhanced by debt-relief activists' appeals to conscience. Only modest results have been achieved by this approach.

Table 4   A Balance Sheet: Twenty-Five Years of Development, 1980–2005

	China	India	49 Poorest Countries	All Other Developing Countries (105)	High-Income Countries (54)	World (210)
Percentage of World Population						
1980	22.1%	14.4%	8.1%	33.0%	22.5%	
2005	20.3% (1.3 Billion)	17.1% (1.1 Billion)	11.4% (740 Million)	35.8% (2.3 Billion)	15.3% (980 Million)	
Percentage of World Real Income[a]						
1980	3.2%	3.5%	1.9%	29.3%	62%	
2005	13.6%	6.3%	1.9%	24.5%	54%	
Real Income Per Capita, 2005[a]	$4,972	$2,752	$1,249	$5,123	$26,191	$7,428
Real Average Annual Growth, 1980–2005	8.1%	3.8%	0.7%	0.8%	1.9%	1.6%

[a] In 1995 dollars, purchasing power parity basis.
Source: World Bank 2006 data; author's analysis.

Several political and economic factors have combined to limit the amount of debt relief achieved:

Sticks. Most developing countries believe they are far too dependent on trade finance and aid to risk outright defiance of international creditors.

Carrots. Many members of the Third World elite have in effect been bought by the global financial industry. One common reward is the opportunity to participate in international ventures and receive foreign loans and investments. Beyond that is a whole range of other incentives, including offshore accounts, insider profits, and outright bribes and kickbacks. More subtle rewards include Dow Jones board seats (Mexico's Salinas), positions at prestigious universities, banks, and BWIs (Mexico's Zedillo at Yale, Argentina's Cavallo at New York University, Bolivia's ex-Finance Minister Juan Cariaga and any number of other former officials at the World Bank/International Finance Corporation), participation in other exclusive organizations (the Council of the Americas, the Council on Foreign Relations, the Inter-American Dialogue), and more subtle forms of ideological influence. Meanwhile, social and political networks within the developing world have been relatively weak.

The Banking Cartel. The global financial services industry is much better organized than are debtor countries. Country specialists at leading banks and BWIs have dealt with the same debt problems over and over again, while negotiators for the debtor countries come and go by the dozens.[32] Specialists like Citigroup's William Rhodes and Chase's Francis Mason became adept at isolating the more militant countries and exploiting rivalries among countries. Boilerplate language in standard loan and bond contracts—for example, cross-default clauses—have also helped to perpetuate the power of the creditor cartel.

Declining Political Competition. After 1990, the Soviet bloc ceased to be a serious competitor for Third World affections. From that point on, the real value of First World aid to developing countries fell sharply until the late 1990s. Meanwhile, First World banks completed their write-downs of Third World loans; and the BWIs and other official institutions displaced private banks as the principal source of new loans to low-income countries. With credit risk effectively transferred to the public sector, and the largest debtor countries focused on implementing the neoliberal reforms that the BWIs demanded in exchange for debt relief, support for Third World debt relief atrophied.

With debtor countries so fragmented, "small-scale" debt relief became just another instrument of neoliberal reform. Meanwhile, the cause of large-scale debt relief was relegated to the NGO community and lacked much country involvement. The resulting "movement" was a well-intentioned, loosely run coalition of First World NGOs and celebrities. Lacking a strong political base, the movement worked hard and succeeded in mounting a series of intermittent global campaigns. Perhaps inevitably, the movement assumed a supplicant position of appealing to the "better selves" of politicians like Tony Blair, Jacques Chirac, and George Bush, as well as central bankers, private bankers, and BWI bureaucrats—a hard-nosed bunch if ever there was one.

The Best-Laid Plans . . .

The First World policy establishment has offered no shortage of clever proposals to achieve debt relief for developing countries. Indeed, ever since Third World borrowing took off in the 1970s, schemes have been devised for "international credit commissions," "debt facilities," debt buybacks, debt–equity swaps, and "exit bonds." In the last decade, as frustrations with HIPC grew, proposals have also emerged from the academic community, the IMF, and the World Bank for a new "sovereign debt-restructuring agency," global bankruptcy courts, and modifications to the boilerplate loan contracts noted earlier.

These proposals provided grist for a steady stream of academic articles and conferences, but none has so far made any practical difference. The overall pattern has been cautious incrementalism—a series of modest proposals, each just slightly more ambitious than its predecessor, and all doomed to be ineffectual—with the saving grace that no powerful interests would be offended.

The Baker Plan

The majority of today's Third World population was not even born in October 1985, when President Ronald Reagan's second treasury secretary, James A. Baker III, announced his "Baker Plan" for debt relief. The plan acknowledged that the market-based debt-rescheduling approach that had been pursued by commercial banks since 1982 wasn't working. Indeed, traditional debt rescheduling was aggravating the problem, because banks had ceased to provide new loans while continuing to roll over back-due interest at ever-higher interest rates.

The Baker Plan hoped to change this vicious circle by offering a combination of new loans funded by U.S. taxpayers and the MFIs, plus some private bank loans, in exchange for "market reforms" in recipient countries. It was motivated by the prevailing myth that the 1980s debt crisis was basically a short-term "liquidity" problem, not a reflection of deeper structural flaws and interests. Supposedly a fresh round of (government-subsidized) loans, conditioned on reforms, would allow leading debtor countries to "grow their way" out of the "temporary" crisis.

By 1989, the Baker Plan had produced about $32 billion of new loans,[33] mainly to fifteen middle-income countries like Mexico and Brazil. This inefficient program actually cost First World taxpayers more than $45 billion, mainly by way of the U.S. Treasury. By comparison, the gross external debt of all developing countries at the time was about $1 trillion, so the amount of overall debt relief provided was tiny. Indeed, as noted earlier, the plan actually provided *negative* debt relief because of increased PV debt levels. Finally, of course, the Baker Plan omitted almost all low-income countries. This was partly because First World private banks had made only limited loans to such countries—and partly because writing down the value of development loans was anathema to the World Bank and the IMF.

"Market-Based" Debt Relief

While everyone waited for the Baker Plan to work in the late 1980s, private banks retired about $26 billion of country loans on their own, by way of so-called market-based methods, including buybacks and debt swaps. Some of these methods had very harmful consequences for the countries involved. They also reinforced the de facto "nationalization" of the Third World debt problem by the BWIs and other official lenders. They did, however, succeed in offsetting part of the Baker Plan's harmful effect on country debt levels.[34]

The Brady Plan

When the Baker Plan and market-based methods failed to make much of a dent in the debt problem, former Wall Street investment banker Nicholas Brady, James Baker's successor at the U.S. Treasury, introduced a more aggressive debt-swap plan in March 1989. The key motivator was not generosity. In February 1987, Brazil had introduced a moratorium on interest payments, which had threatened to create a dangerous precedent. Brazil's move was followed by Mexico's rigged presidential election in mid-1988. Mexico's huge debt overhang, declining oil prices, the potential for political instability in Mexico, and Brazil's moratorium all suggested that much more widespread debt defaults might occur unless more aggressive debt-relief measures were taken by the First World.

Under Brady's plan, which was first implemented by Mexico in July 1989, private foreign banks agreed to swap their loans at 30 to 35 percent discounts for a menu of new bonds, whose interest and principal were secured by bonds issued by the U.S. Treasury, the World Bank, the IMF, and Japan's export credit agency—backed up, in turn, by debtor country reserves.

By the end of the Brady Plan in 1993, this semi-voluntary scheme had provided another modest dose of relief, mainly to middle-income Latin American countries like Argentina, Brazil, and Mexico, plus a few U.S. favorites elsewhere like Poland, the Philippines, and Jordan.[35] With the help of taxpayer subsidies, the Brady Plan also succeeded in virtually wiping out the debts of a handful of smaller countries—Guyana, Mozambique, Niger, and Uganda. By 1994, just before Mexico's "Tequila Crisis," the Brady Plan had yielded about $124 billion (in 2006 NPV dollars) of debt relief, at a cost of $66 billion in taxpayer subsidies. Today, the Brady Plan remains the largest and most costly debt-relief initiative.

Some analysts have argued that the Brady Plan also had an *indirect* beneficial effect on the quantity of new loans and investments received by debtor countries in 1989–93 because of its impact on equity markets and direct investment. However, any such gains were temporary and were more than offset by increased capital flight, generating net benefits to developing countries that were clearly less than the First World taxes that paid for them.

Furthermore, even this initial benefit from the Brady Plan was wiped out by subsequent financial crises in Mexico, Argentina, Brazil, Nigeria, Peru, and the Philippines in 1995–99. These crises were actually abetted by the brief surge of undisciplined borrowing that the Brady Plan facilitated.[36] Overall, while the early 1990s produced some reduction in debt service relative to exports and national income for the sixteen recipient countries, by the end of the 1990s most of the "Brady Bunch" had seen their debt burdens return to pre-Brady levels.

So here we have a graphic illustration of the fundamental point noted earlier: Without basic institutional reform—and not just "market" reform within individual countries but general reform of development finance—debt relief in one period may just lead to increased borrowing and renewed debt crises in the next.

"Traditional" Bilateral Relief—Low-Income Countries
Early debt-relief initiatives focused on the world's largest debtors, although a few low-income countries also managed to take advantage of them. By the late 1980s, there was growing recognition that the debts of very low-income countries were exploding and needed more attention.[36]

These countries were paying astronomical debt-service bills, despite the fact that they qualified for "concessional" terms. By 1986, nineteen out of the (future) thirty-eight HIPC low-income countries were devoting at least 5 percent of national income to servicing their foreign debts, and many were paying much more. On average, debt service consumed over a third of their export revenues, compared with less than one tenth a decade earlier.[38] Furthermore, the present value of low-income country debt had continued to grow throughout the Baker/Brady Plan period. By 1992, it was three times the 1980 level and more than a third above the 1986 level.[39] Finally, from 1985 on, private bank lending to low-income countries had been greatly exceeded by development bank lending—another indication of "market failure."

One of the first senior officials to recognize the need for more focus on low-income country debt was Nigel Lawson, the Conservative UK chancellor of the exchequer. In 1987 he proposed that the Paris Club refocus its negotiations with debtor countries on trying to reduce their "debt overhang," as measured by the present value of expected future debt-service payments. This was a striking contrast to conventional debt relief, where the goal of rescheduling had always been to avoid write-downs and to preserve the loans' present value by stretching out repayment. As noted earlier, that approach assumed that the key problem was illiquidity and that the nasty random shocks that had created the crisis would soon reverse themselves. As Lawson and others had come to recognize, these shocks were systemic, not random, and in the absence of serious intervention the "debt overhang" might well be permanent.

Lawson launched the Paris Club on a prolonged series of debt restructurings. In the next decade the group conducted ninety bilateral restructurings with seventy-three countries, on increasingly generous terms.[40] By 1998, this effort—supplemented by assistance from the World Bank's International Development Association Debt Facility for debt swaps—had produced another $95 billion of debt relief.

HIPC

In September 1996, the BWIs established the HIPC Initiative, their first comprehensive debt-relief program ever, targeted at "heavily indebted developing countries." Once again, this initiative was not motivated by generosity—the BWIs were responding to increasing pressure from NGOs, debt activists, and debtor countries. These advocates complained that existing debt-relief programs did not do enough for the world's poorest, most insolvent countries, and that it was also time for wealthy multilateral lenders like the BWIs to finally share the costs.

Qualifications

The World Bank's first list of eligible HIPCs in 1994 included forty-one countries. The list was supposed to have been determined by objective criteria, including factors like real income and the sustainability of projected debt-service levels relative to exports. But such criteria are of course anything but objective, especially where foreign policy is concerned. The original list of countries included those with

- Per capita incomes below $695 in 1993, *plus*
- *Either* PV debt-to-income ratios of at least 80 percent,
- *Or* debt-service-to-export ratios of at least 220 percent.

These criteria would have included such large low-income debtors as Angola, Nigeria, Kenya, Vietnam, and Yemen. They would have omitted such countries as Malawi, Guyana, and Gambia. As of 1996, the countries on the original HIPC list would have accounted for $244 billion of foreign debt and 672 million people—almost two-thirds of all low-income country debt and more than a third of all low-income country residents.

For a variety of reasons—including the desire of the BWIs to contain the cost of debt relief, and sheer geopolitics—the initial list of HIPC countries was altered substantially. Seven countries, including Kenya, Nigeria, and Angola, were eliminated from the list, while nine tiny countries suddenly qualified for relief.[41] When the dust settled, precisely forty-one countries still qualified for HIPC. Compared with the original list, however, the new group accounted for only 39 percent (not 63 percent) of all low-income country debt—just 6 percent of low- and middle-income developing country debt—and only 23 percent (not 34 percent) of all low-income country residents.

This downsizing was partly due to BWI self-interest. The World Bank is a self-perpetuating bureaucracy that is funded in part by its own long-term bond sales as well as by contributions from First World governments. One of its top priorities is therefore to secure its own cash flow and maintain its debt rating. Although in principle contributions from the BWIs' First World member countries can always make up any shortfalls, in practice the World Bank likes to avoid having to solicit such contributions from its members—and thus avoid embarrassing congressional hearings where Bank officials have to explain where Togo is and why this corrupt African country deserves assistance.

Initially the BWIs had proposed to fund HIPC debt relief by liquidating part of the IMF's huge 3.22 metric tons of gold reserves, whose market value had increased to several times its book value.[42] Indeed, in 1999–2000, the IMF had conducted a sale and buyback of 12.9 million ounces with Brazil and Mexico, using the profit to fund its share of HIPC's initial costs. Now, however, another powerful set of institutional self-interests intruded. The IMF/World Bank proposals for a much larger gold sale were scuttled by lobbyists from the World Gold Council (twenty-three global gold mining companies, including Newmont Mining, AngloGold, and Barrick Gold Corporation).[43]

So it turned out that the BWIs had to fund debt relief on a "pay as you go" basis through bond sales and periodic pledges from their First World members. The larger the amount of debt relief, the smaller the World Bank's loan portfolio, and the more it feared that its own bond rating and financial independence might be jeopardized. The Bank thus had a built-in bias in favor of less debt relief.

In the list of qualifying countries, there was no shortage of anomalies. For example, as of the mid-1990s, Angola, Kenya, Nigeria, and Yemen all had higher debt burdens and lower per capita incomes than many of the countries on the final HIPC list, but they were excluded.[44] In contrast, reportedly at the behest of France, HIPC analysts fixed the rules so that Ivory Coast would be included, despite the fact that it had a higher per capita income and lower debt burden than many other countries on the list.[45] Another odd addition was Guyana, a bauxite-rich former British colony in northeastern South America, that in 1996 had a population of just 750,000 and a real per capita income of $3,600—clearly a middle-income country compared with others in HIPC.

Meanwhile, HIPC excluded twenty-nine middle-income countries that the World Bank itself had classified as "severely indebted," including leading countries with "dirty debt"—loan funds that had been used for repression, war, and elite enrichment. These included such countries as Argentina, Ecuador, Indonesia, Pakistan, and the Philippines. In many cases their debt burdens were heavier than those of countries admitted to the HIPC club.[46]

These exclusions were important, because it turned out that, while the final thirty-eight HIPC countries did reduce their debt-service payments by about $2 billion a year from 1996 to 2003, debt-service payments by *non-HIPC* low-income countries actually *increased*—by several times that amount.[47] Overall, therefore, the BWIs' filters with respect to "sustainable debt" and income were inconsistently applied. They seem to have been intended to contain the size of the debt-relief effort and focus it on tiny, more malleable countries.

The Long March

Debt critics were naturally a little disappointed at HIPC's modest scope, relative to the size of all outstanding Third World debt. But they thought they could at least count on the BWIs to provide speedy relief. Even for those countries that were deemed worthy, however, the debt-relief journey usually proved to be a very long march. The World Bank and the IMF imposed a tortuous, drawn-out process before countries actually got any relief, conditioning it on a long menu of their favorite neoliberal reforms, including privatization, tariff cuts, and balanced budgets.

These demands were especially hard to justify in light of the fact that HIPCs on the final list were hardly prime prospects for First World banks, contractors, or equipment suppliers. Fully half had populations smaller than New Jersey's, with per capita incomes averaging less than $1,100, and average life expectancies of just forty-nine years. Offering this group of countries debt relief was not likely to set a dangerous "moral hazard" precedent.

Nevertheless, under the original 1996 HIPC I scheme, all these countries expected to spend three years implementing such reforms under the BWIs' watchful eye before they reached a "decision point." Then a debt-relief package would be assembled and a modest amount of relief would finally be approved.

Countries were *then* supposed to continue their good behavior for another three years before reaching the "completion point," at which point they'd finally see a serious reduction in debt service. Even then, they wouldn't receive a total debt write-off but only a partial subsidy, reducing debt service to a level that the BWIs considered "sustainable" relative to projected exports. Along the way, countries were also expected to draft a BWI-approved "Poverty Reduction Strategy Paper," negotiate a "Poverty Reduction and Growth Facility," and engage the IMF and the World Bank in regular, rather intrusive "Staff Monitoring Programs."

To some extent, all this policy paternalism was justified by the fact that, as we've seen, many of these countries were unstable, poorly governed, and wartorn. The old "more sand, same rat holes" foreign aid dilemma applied—the countries most in need of assistance were often precisely those with the least ability to use it wisely. Furthermore, under the influence of neoliberal policies, state institutions in many of these countries had become even weaker.

From the standpoint of delivering debt relief in a timely fashion, however, the BWIs' strictures clearly went beyond the pale. BWI technocrats adopted a kind of righteous, almost creditor-like stance toward HIPC countries—perhaps because, after all, the BWIs *are* substantial creditors. Slowly rationing out a trickle of debt relief also preserves their control. All the resulting demands and delays were a poor substitute for the more constructive neutral role that, say, a trustee in bankruptcy would typically play in bankruptcy proceedings.

Combined with country backwardness, the BWIs' creditor-cum-neoliberal-reformer mentality had predictable results. Indeed, if HIPC's true goal was to *avoid* giving meaningful debt relief, it almost succeeded. By 2000, just six countries—Bolivia, Burkina Faso, Guyana, Mali, Mozambique, and Uganda—had managed to reach "completion," and zero debt relief had been dispensed. Eventually, HIPC I afforded a grand total of $3.7 billion of debt relief[48] to these six countries.[49] Even this pittance was not distributed immediately, in most cases, but instead was spread out over decades. For example, Uganda's debt-service relief from the World Bank was stretched over twenty-three years and Mozambique's for over thirty-one years. Guyana will still be collecting $1 million per year in 2050!

Would that First World creditors and the BWIs had been as circumspect about making loans to developing countries as they have been about administering debt relief!

HIPC II: The HIPC Sweepstakes

In June 1999, following massive "Drop the Debt" rallies at the May 1998 G8 meeting in Birmingham, the World Bank and IMF launched HIPC II, which was supposed to be a faster, more generous version of HIPC I. But this sequel also proved to be embarrassingly slow. By 2006, of the thirty-eight countries on the HIPC list back in 1996, just eighteen had reached the "completion point." Eleven others had reached "decision points," after a median wait of forty-nine months, but five of these were reporting "slow progress."[50] Of the other nine, just one was both ready to qualify and interested in participating.[51]

To fill out the ranks, in 2006 the BWIs identified six more low-income countries that might still be able to qualify for HIPC relief before final enrollment closed in December 2006. However, only two were both ready and willing to try for this deadline.[52] All told, compared with the original target group of countries, HIPC had been able to provide debt relief to countries that accounted for just 18 percent of outstanding low-income debt and 13 percent of the world's low-income population.

Those countries that managed to navigate all the HIPC hurdles did finally receive some debt relief—a total reduction in debt service of $832 million per year for 2001–6 relative to their debt payments in 1998–99. This sum was shared by the twenty-seven countries that had reached their completion or decision points.[53]

Some countries did much better than others. For example, middle-income Guyana progressed quickly through the program, qualifying for debt relief to the tune of $937 per capita from HIPC I and II. In comparison, the relief provided by HIPC was just $75 per capita. Indeed, Guyana became something of a pro at debt relief—by 2006, it had achieved a record total of $2,971 for each of its citizens, from all debt-relief programs.[54] São Tome, Nicaragua, Congo Republic, Guinea-Bissau, Zambia, Mauritania, Bolivia, Burundi, Democratic Republic of Congo, Sierra Leone, Mozambique, and Ghana also did relatively well on a per capita basis, all realizing more than $100 per capita of HIPC relief.

In terms of the share of all HIPC relief received, the clear winner was Democratic Republic of Congo, Mobutu's old stomping ground, which commanded an astounding 18.2 percent of all HIPC relief and nearly 8 percent of all First World debt relief to low-income countries to date. Other winners included Nicaragua, Zambia, Ethiopia, Ghana, Tanzania, Bolivia, and Mozambique. Indeed, Mozambique, a favorite of World Bank neoliberals, alone swallowed 55 percent of HIPC I's $3.7 billion in total benefits.

Compared with our original list of "war-torn heavy-heavy dictatorships," there is a striking overlap with the debt relief hit parade: The top ten low-income borrowers in 1980–86 accounted for more than half of HIPC relief and all First World debt relief distributed from 1988 through 2006.[55] Many other indebted low-income countries have received much less debt relief, in both per capita and absolute terms.[56]

This per country per capita debt relief analysis, presented here for the first time, underscores several of the most serious problems with using debt relief as a substitute for development aid:

- First, it is difficult to ensure that reductions in debt service (or the increased borrowing that may occur in the aftermath of debt reductions) will actually be applied to worthy causes—the "control problem."
- Second, the amount of relief available varies wildly across countries, according to factors that have little to do with development needs—the "correlation problem."

The BWIs in charge of the HIPC program tried to salve the control problem by insisting on country poverty-reduction programs and policy reforms and by monitoring government spending. Whether this has worked is a matter of much dispute; there is a strong case that this conditionality was counterproductive. Clearly the requirements succeeded in slowing down the distribution of relief.

But there is nothing that HIPC could do about the "correlation" problem—the lack of proportionality between debt relief and development needs. Relying heavily on debt relief for development finance, in other words, inevitably means that some of the worst-governed, most profligate countries in the world will reap the greatest rewards.

Overall HIPC Results

HIPC does appear to have reduced *foreign* debt-service burdens somewhat for the eighteen countries that managed to complete the program—although *domestic* debt service is another story. However, eleven of the original thirty-eight HIPC countries still had *higher* debt-service-to-income ratios in 2004 than in 1996. Poor Burundi is still laboring under a ratio of PV debt to income of 91 percent!

Furthermore, the fact is that debt-service ratios had already declined for twenty-five of the thirty-eight countries from 1986 to 1996, *prior to* HIPC's existence. Debt-service burdens had also declined for many low-income countries that didn't enroll in HIPC, as well as for the nine countries that haven't yet reached the HIPC "decision point" and have thus received no HIPC relief. So it is not easy to call the HIPC program a success, even for the handful of countries that have been able to reach the finish line.[57]

What *is* indisputable is that the total amount of debt relief achieved by HIPC has been extremely modest (see Table 5). While press accounts often refer to HIPC as providing "$50 billion to $60 billion" of relief to developing countries, a more accurate estimate is at most $41.3 billion by 2006. This is only about 10 percent of low-income countries' total outstanding debt.[58] Of this debt relief, $7.6 billion was awarded to the original six countries in the HIPC I program, and another $33.7 billion may eventually go to the other twenty-three countries that have reached the "decision point."[59] The potential cost of providing relief to the remaining nine to fifteen countries that might still qualify for HIPC is estimated at $21 billion, but the reality is that little of this will ever be granted.[60] Indeed, the timing and levels of relief are still highly uncertain even for half of the eleven "decision point" countries.

Table 5   Debt Relief by Country, 1988–2005

	HIPC I & II Relief per Capita (2005 Dollars)	All First World Relief per Capita (2005 Dollars)	All Relief as a Percentage of per Capita Income[a]	Total HIPC Relief (Billions of 2005 Dollars)	Percent of All HIPC Relief
Guyana	$937	$2,971	72.8%	$0.7	1.7%
Saõ Tomé	$753	$3,416	284.7%	$0.1	0.4%
Nicaragua	$731	$2,623	78.5%	$3.9	9.5%
Congo Rep.	$514	$698	77.6%	$2.0	4.8%
Guinea-Bissau	$321	$582	87.7%	$0.5	1.2%
Zambia	$259	$557	64.3%	$3.0	7.2%
Mauritania	$248	$545	30.5%	$0.7	1.8%
Bolivia	$172	$603	42.1%	$1.5	3.7%
Burundi	$135	$376	60.3%	$1.0	2.4%
DR Congo	$134	$183	28.3%	$7.5	18.2%
Sierra Leone	$134	$510	98.9%	$0.7	1.7%
Mozambique	$124	$452	39.8%	$2.4	5.8%
Ghana	$120	$215	10.4%	$2.6	6.3%
Honduras	$94	$274	10.4%	$0.7	1.6%
Cameroon	$93	$102	5.1%	$1.5	3.6%
Rwanda	$93	$120	10.3%	$0.8	2.0%
Guinea	$70	$149	7.4%	$0.6	1.6%
Tanzania	$64	$115	18.5%	$2.4	5.8%
Malawi	$61	$70	11.9%	$0.8	1.8%
Niger	$58	$149	20.8%	$0.8	1.8%
Madagascar	$55	$141	17.9%	$1.0	2.4%
Gambia	$54	$297	16.2%	$0.1	2.4%
Burkina Faso	$51	$88	8.2%	$0.7	1.6%
Senegal	$51	$375	23.8%	$0.6	1.4%
Mali	$49	$110	12.0%	$0.6	1.5%
Uganda	$43	$380	27.9%	$1.2	2.9%
Benin	$39	$107	10.6%	$0.3	0.8%
Ethiopia	$34	$102	14.7%	$2.4	5.7%
Chad	$21	$375	19.5%	$0.2	0.5%
Ivory Coast	$0	$380	26.6%	0%	0%
Haiti	$0	$16	1.0%	0%	0%
HIPC I Six	$86	$258.3	21%	$7.1	
Completion (18)	$88	$235.4	21%	$26.3	
Decision (11)	$122	$240.3	27%	$15.0	
Pre-Decision (9)	$0	$57.0	4%	$0.0	
Old HIPC	$0	$79.9	5%	$0.0	
HIPC (38)	$75	$194.0	17%	$41.3	

[a] Based on annual per capita incomes for 2004.
Source: HIPC program reports; IMF (1999), World Bank (Sept. 2005); author's analysis.

Once again, all figures refer to the *present value of expected future debt service relief,* spread out over decades in many cases, not to current cash transfers. As of 2006, only a third of HIPC I relief and less than a fifth of HIPC II relief had actually been "banked"—an average of less than $1 billion of cash savings per year, to be divided among all these very poor countries.

Even these modest savings were not cost-free to the countries involved. To comply with the BWIs' demands, developing countries often had to implement neoliberal reforms that had perverse political and economic side effects.[61]

The Multilateral Debt Relief Initiative

Our final stop on the debt-relief train is the Multilateral Debt Relief Initiative (MDRI), announced with great fanfare at the July 2005 G8 meetings in Gleneagles. On close inspection, this debt relief plan turns out to be even less impressive than HIPC.

MDRI had its roots in the fact that by 2004 most debtors and NGOs had simply had it with HIPC. The UK chancellor of the exchequer, Gordon Brown, saw a chance to earn some political capital, make up for the UK's own lagging foreign aid contributions, and heal some of the bad feelings generated by UK support for the Iraq War, all at very little cash cost. With HIPC set to expire,[62] and with so much low-income debt still outstanding, Brown decided to work closely with the Live 8/"Make Poverty History" alliance and its free concerts. This collaboration was facilitated by the fact that one of Brown's closest advisers, a former UBS banker, was an Oxfam board member, while Tony Blair's senior adviser on debt policy was Oxfam's former policy director.[63] These connections no doubt smoothed the reception of Brown's proposals in the NGO world, but they ultimately failed to achieve very much incremental debt relief.

The actual cash value of the debt relief provided by MDRI will be far less than the nominal $40 billion to $50 billion widely touted in the press. The face value of the debts owed to the development banks by the forty-two low-income countries that *may be eligible* for cancellation adds up to $38.2 billion.[64]

But MDRI's debt relief, like HIPC's, will not be distributed in one fell swoop. Given the lower interest rates that already apply to most of the loans, and the fact that most are already in arrears, the actual debt-service savings that these countries may reap from the program averages just $950 million per year distributed over the next thirty-seven years among forty-two countries.

This may appear to be a modest sum to First World residents who are used to seeing much larger sums spent per week on agricultural subsidies, long-range missiles, and highways—and invasions of distant countries. But it is a large share of the $2.9 billion a year spent on education and the $2.4 billion spent on public health by the nineteen low-income countries likely to qualify for the program.

Still, the G8 debt cancellation gets us just 6 percent of the way home toward the $25 billion to $30 billion per year of increased aid for low-income countries in Africa proposed by Blair and Brown's Commission for Africa. It also compares rather unfavorably with the $1.8 billion per week that the Iraq War cost in 2006.[65]

Furthermore, to qualify for MDRI relief, countries will have to go through many of the same hoops that HIPC put them through. At least eight of the forty-two countries—including large debtors like Somalia and Sudan—may never meet these qualifications. Even the top nineteen that are likely to qualify will still have $23.5 billion of unrelieved, higher-priced bilateral government debt and private debt outside the MDRI program—with annual debt service of $800 million a year. Once again—the point bears repeating—the countries have very little to show for all these debts.

A Good Deal for the Bank

Even assuming—optimistically—that MDRI's potential beneficiaries would otherwise pay the $0.7 billion to $1.3 billion of debt service owed to the BWIs and the African Development Bank over the next thirty-seven years without arrearages or defaults, the net present value of the debt cancellation is not $40 billion, but at most *$15 billion*. In fact, given the likelihood that some debtors may never meet the program's requirements, the present value of expected MDRI debt relief is really closer to just *$10 billion*.

World Bank and African Development Bank bondholders may actually prefer to have the G8 member countries take them out of what are, in bond market terminology, "dog countries." Indeed, this could even be a very profitable deal for the World Bank, since its cost of funds is not the 3 to 3.5 percent interest paid—if and when they do pay—by low-income debtors, but at least 4.7 to 5.5 percent.

Assuming that the member countries represented on the World Bank's executive board honor their pledges, trading a stream of highly uncertain debt-service payments from debt-ridden poor countries for $10 billion to $15 billion of cold hard cash from its members may look like a pretty good deal for the Bank. Certainly it is better than having to play bill collector in all those nasty hellholes.

And I bet you thought that debt relief was all about generosity!

A Modest Proposal

What are the key lessons for would-be debt relievers from this saga? And where should debt-relief activists and NGOs focus their energies now?

Lesson 1: Beyond the BWIs

As I've argued, it is no accident that, twenty-five years after the debt crisis, some of the poorest countries on the planet, as well as many middle-income countries, continue to be struggling with foreign debt. If we accept the basic premise of debt relief—that debtors who have become mired in debt deserve a chance to wipe the slate clean, once and for all, then the conventional approach to debt relief, as administered by the IMF, the World Bank, the U.S. Treasury, and the Paris Club, has clearly been a failure. Not only has it failed to deliver the goods, but it has also had very high operating costs, in term of delays, administration, and excessive and destructive conditionalities.

In particular, the huge World Bank and IMF bureaucracies have proved far better at rationing debt relief than at making sure that impoverished countries don't sink up to their eyeballs in debt in the first place.

If we are really serious about providing substantial amounts of debt relief, we have to *design new institutions to administer that relief.*

Lesson 2: Beyond Narrow Debt-Relief Campaigns

Perhaps we should not be surprised that First World governments and the BWIs have tended to side with international creditors—after all, governments have long sided with landlords, enclosers, gamekeepers, slave owners, and other propertied interests.

What *is* surprising is that, despite the very high stakes for developing countries, and so much potential popular support for a fairer solution, the debt-relief campaign has been so ineffective. This is partly because it is difficult to sustain a global not-for-profit campaign across diffuse communities of activists and a range of NGOs. It is also because the campaign faces powerful entrenched interests.

But another key difficulty is arguably of our own making. Compared with the dire needs of many countries and the sheer volume of "dubious debt" and capital flight, the debt-relief movements' demands have simply been far too modest. To make a real difference, we need to focus attention on two closely related but necessarily more contentious aspects of the debt/capital flight problem:

1. *Dubious debt,* which was contracted by nondemocratic or dishonest governments and wasted on overpriced projects, shady bank bailouts, cut-rate privatizations, capital flight, and corruption. My own rough estimate is that dubious debt may account for a third of the $3.7 trillion of outstanding developing country debt. Since the mid-1980s, debt campaigners like Jubilee, Probe International's Odious Debt Web site, myself, and other debt critics have been calling for a resurrection of the basic legal principle that such debts should not be enforceable in international courts of law.[66]

2. The huge stock of anonymous, untaxed Third World *flight wealth* that now sits offshore—much of it originally financed by dubious loans, as well as by resource diversions, privatization rip-offs, and other financial chicanery. Most of this wealth—estimated at up to $5 trillion for the Third World alone—has been invested in First World assets, where it generates tax-free returns for its owners and handsome fees for the global private banking industry.

The sums at stake with respect to dubious debt and flight-haven wealth are much larger than those debt-relief campaigners have tackled so far. Dubious debt and wealth flight affect middle-income as well as low-income countries. And these issues address the ongoing responsibility of the leading *private* global financial institutions, law firms, and accounting firms that built the pipelines for Third World flight capital and continue to service it. Since the 1980s, several of these institutions have grown to become many times larger and more influential than the World Bank or the IMF.[67]

If the debt-relief movement has the will to tackle these larger problems, much could be done about them. Among the possible steps:

1. Systematic debt audits and a global asset-recovery institution that helps developing countries recover stolen wealth.

2. Revitalization of the "odious debt" doctrine,[68] which specifies that foreign debts contracted by dictatorships or diverted for personal enrichment are unenforceable.

3. Stronger international tax cooperation and information exchange between First and Third World tax authorities—perhaps including creation of a Tax Department at the World Bank, which still doesn't have one!

4. Codes of conduct for transnational banks, law firms, accounting firms, hedge funds, and corporations to curtail the active facilitation of dubious lending, money laundering, and tax evasion.

5. Enactment of a uniform, minimum, multilateral withholding tax on offshore "anonymous" capital—the proceeds of which could be used to fund development relief. (Even a 1 percent annual assets tax on anonymous bank deposits might bring in $10 billion to $20 billion a year, with OECD country support.)

Many other ideas along these lines are conceivable. Obviously a great deal of organization and education across multiple NGOs are needed to tackle even one such measure. But the most important requirement is *political nerve*—the willingness to move beyond the debt movement's hitherto narrow focus.

Lesson 3: Transcending the Limits of Debt Relief

Earlier I expressed doubts about the "more sand, same rat holes" approach to ending poverty—most of the prime candidates for debt relief simply have great difficulty managing it. This skeptical viewpoint has recently received even more support: there are disturbing reports that the corrupt leaders of resource-rich countries like the Democratic Republic of Congo are squandering the money saved by debt relief on renewed dubious borrowing and arms purchases.

The fundamental problem, glossed over by some debt-relief campaigners and conventional "end poverty now" economists, is that combating poverty is not just a question of providing malaria nets, vaccines, and drinking water, or incremental increases in education, capital, technology, and aid. Ultimately, as China's example shows, long-term poverty reduction requires the promotion of deep-seated structural change. This implies the redistribution of social assets like land, education, technology, and political power. These are concepts that BWI technocrats may never understand—or may recoil from in horror. But they are at the root of every major development success story that we know.

Meanwhile, of course, poor people in debt-ridden countries are in dire need of short-term relief from dire hardship. Even a tiny amount of debt relief may do much good, even after allowing for corruption. I am not for abandoning debt relief entirely, but for putting it in context and augmenting it with new demands.

In that spirit, I would be delighted to see the debt-relief movement, the G8, and the BWIs join hands one more time and finally deliver on their long-standing rhetorical commitment to deliver truly substantial debt relief.

As we've seen, at least 40 percent of the world's population—the 1.6 to 2 billion people who still reside in heavily indebted developing countries—are still waiting for it.

Notes

1. NGOs like Jubilee have also been critical of the paltry amounts of debt relief provided so far. However, this chapter is the first attempt to pull together aggregate estimates of debt relief for all low- and middle-income countries and evaluate how much has been achieved by debt-relief campaigns over the past thirty years.

2. Debt estimates are based on the latest (2006) World Bank data for 155 low- and middle-income developing countries (defined by the Bank), adjusted for countries like Cuba, Iraq, Namibia, North Korea, Suriname, and Turkmenistan that are omitted from World Bank data. The real deflator used to standardize estimates is that for world gross domestic product in year 2000 dollars.

3. Estimates are from 2006 World Bank data on "official development assistance and official aid" (ODA/OA) and debt service by country group. Note that much foreign aid is tied to donor purchase requirements (demands that the poor country buy goods from the donor country with the aid), or is consumed by aid administration. For 2004, for example, the Bank reported that $85.4 billion of ODA/OA was granted to low- and medium-income developing countries, but that only $63.9 billion was actually received by those countries. The gap is partly due to accounting and timing issues, but it also reflects the very high expenses for administration. Creditors, in contrast, are usually very efficient at debt-service collection.

4. In 2006 net present value (NPV) dollars. The estimates presented here rely on the World Bank's 2004 estimates of the ratio of present value to national income for developing countries, supplemented by my own analysis for missing countries.

5. All these seventy-five countries have ratios of PV debt to national income of 50 percent or more, compared to the 15 to 18 percent ratios of China and India. A high ratio implies that the country is much more vulnerable to external shocks and fiscal and currency crises: borrowing usually costs at least 5 percent per year, domestic taxes yield 10 percent or less of national income, and demands for spending on education, health, and defense are at least 10 percent, so developing countries with ratios above 50 percent are financially squeezed.

6. The Paris Club is an "informal association" of official bilateral lenders from First World countries, including export credit agencies like the U.S. Export-Import Bank.

7. Two previous surveys of debt relief are Christina Daseking and Robert Powell, "From Toronto Terms to the HIPC Initiative: A Brief History of Debt Relief for Low-Income Countries," IMF Working Paper no. 99/142 (October 1999); and Aart Kraay and Nico-

las Depetris Chauvin, "What Has 100 Billion Dollars Worth of Debt Relief Done for Low-Income Countries?" World Bank/IADB, September 2005. These two articles limit their attention to the relief provided to low-income countries in 1988–98 and 1988–2003, respectively. Thus they leave out the Multilateral Debt Relief Initiative, post-2003 Heavily Indebted Poor Countries relief, the Baker and Brady Plans, debt swaps, and several large bilateral deals—all told, at least two-thirds of debt relief so far. Attempts to generalize about the overall impact of debt relief on the basis of such incomplete numbers should be taken with a grain of salt.

8. My analyses include the combined value, in 2005 NPV dollars, of the relief already delivered by (1) so-called market-based debt rescheduling (1982–85); (2) the Baker Plan (1985–89); (3) the Brady Plan (1989–95); (4) the debt swaps and other debt reductions negotiated by commercial banks (1989–present); and (5) the so-called traditional debt relief provided by the Paris Club and the World Bank's International Development Association (IDA) Debt Facility (1988–98). It also includes the expected value (only a quarter of which has already been delivered) of (6) the HIPC program (1996–2006); (7) the MDRI program; and (8) large bilateral debt-relief deals by the World Bank, the IMF, the African Development Bank, and multilateral lenders, such as the recent Paris Club/Russia/U.S. relief provided to Iraq (2005), Afghanistan (2006), and Nigeria (2006).

9. It is important to note that this is the *expected future value* of debt relief—in terms of actual cash flow, most of it still lies in the future.

10. For one glaring example, see my book *The Blood Bankers* (New York: Four Walls, Eight Windows, 2003, 2005), chap. 3, "The Philippines."

11. In comparable 2006 NPV dollars.

12. U.S. Treasury Secretary Nicholas Brady, author of the 1989 Brady Plan, and Robert Rubin, his successor under President Clinton in 1993, had both been prominent Wall Street investment bankers. U.S. Treasury Secretary James Baker had served as a corporate lawyer with Baker Botts, a prominent Houston law firm. Baker subsequently helped to form a new, and extremely well-connected, investment bank, the Carlyle Group.

13. The priority given to middle-income countries also reflected the fact that public lenders like the ECAs and the multilateral development banks (MDBs)—whose lending focused on poorer countries—face different accounting rules than private banks, which in theory are supposed to value their loan portfolios at market rates. Daseking and Powell, in "From Toronto Terms to the HIPC Initiative," suggested that accounting rules explained the comparative sloth of debt relief for low-income countries. In my view, the influence of accounting rules is easily exaggerated. First, despite the accounting rules, private banks were also slow to write down and restructure their Third World loans—partly because of "earnings illusion," weak enforcement of accounting standards, and the impact of reported earnings on senior manager compensation. Second, while institutions like the World Bank may be concerned about the impact of debt relief on their debt-financing costs, most ECAs—unlike, say, U.S. savings and loan banks in the 1980s—are fully funded by taxes and don't have to worry about the impacts of writing down debt.

14. For example, Mexico's leading banker, Robert Hernandez, purchased Banamex, the country's second largest bank, from the Salinas government in 1991 for just $3 billion. Over the next decade, he received about $5 billion of financing from the Mexican government that was supposedly invested in the bank. Meanwhile, during the 1994–95 "Tequila Crisis," former Goldman Sachs partner and U.S. Treasury Secretary Robert Rubin helped to assemble a $30 billion bailout package for Mexico from the World Bank, the IMF, and the U.S. government. Mexico, in turn, used a large share of the money to bail out banks

such as Banamex. In theory, these banks should have become the property of the Mexican government again. In practice, owners like Hernandez were permitted to retain their ownership interests without repaying the funds. In 1998, Rubin left the U.S. Treasury to join Citigroup, which purchased Banamex from Hernandez in 2001 for $12.5 billion. Hernandez reportedly paid no taxes on the transaction, nor has the bank repaid Mexico the $5 billion financing. Rubin is now vice chairman of Citigroup.

15. More precisely, $6.82 trillion of loans, aid, and investment from 1971 to 2003, in constant dollars. Of this amount, foreign loans provided $2.97 trillion. Source: My analysis of 2006 World Bank data.

16. Of course, several of these "market-guided" countries leave much to be desired from the standpoint of human and political rights. Nor are they likely to avoid financial crises forever—no capitalist economy has ever done so. Korea and Malaysia experienced serious turbulence in the late 1990s, and China may eventually do so. But—like Japan before them—they demonstrate how much can be achieved with just a few decades of controlled-debt development. Unfortunately, we cannot look to the World Bank and IMF for much guidance on political rights. Their tolerance—indeed, apparent preference—for corrupt, autocratic regimes, from Argentina's military junta and China's Politburo to Marcos and Suharto, is legendary. Except for a handful of regimes like North Korea and Cuba, they have almost never conditioned debt relief on *political* reforms, as opposed to neoliberal *economic* policies.

17. Excluding China, India, Vietnam, Malaysia, and Korea, the projected 2006 population for the world's low- and middle-income countries is 3.1 billion.

18. I tell the remarkable story of the thirty years' "debt-flight" crisis in detail in several recent books: *Blood Bankers*; *The Pirate Bankers* (forthcoming 2007); and *Banqueros y Lavadolares* (Bogota: Tercer Mundo, 1996). For the original story on the debt-flight cycle, see my cover story "The Debt Hoax," *New Republic*, April 1986.

19. See Figure 2: nominal foreign debt for 2006 projected from 2006 World Bank data on foreign debts outstanding for all low- and middle-income countries.

20. The amounts are in real 2000 dollars. In nominal terms, these countries' foreign debt levels nearly doubled from 1980 to 1986, from $63 billion to $123 billion. They accounted for 58.4 percent of the population of the forty-eight low-income countries in 1986.

21. In 1980, real per capita annual incomes in the top ten low-income debtor countries were all below $1,150.

22. In 1980, all eleven of these countries were governed by dictators. Afghanistan and Bangladesh were two other dictator-led low-income countries whose debts expanded significantly during the 1980s. Afghanistan, Democratic Republic of Congo, Ghana, Ethiopia, Mozambique, Nicaragua, Sudan, and Zambia were also engaged in civil wars or prolonged armed conflicts with their neighbors.

23. For this purpose, *unproductive* is defined as failing to earn the *social* marginal cost of capital. This hurdle rate may be above or below the market cost of capital, depending on the kinds of projects contemplated. Environmentally damaging projects, for example, should have a hurdle rate *above* the market cost of capital. Rarely were environmental impacts taken into account in development project planning. Indeed, many projects seem to have been cooked up solely to justify the loans. See Henry, *Blood Bankers*.

24. For a systematic historical analysis of the rise of offshore and onshore havens, and their relationship to private banking, flight capital, and debt, see my books *Banqueros y Lavadolares* and *Pirate Bankers*.

25. I first called attention to this in a May 1976 *Washington Monthly* article, "Calling in the Big Bills."

26. See Henry, *Pirate Bankers*, for a discussion of alternative estimation methods and findings. This estimate, derived from the discrepancy between "sources and uses" in official balance-of-payments data, omits any adjustment for misinvoicing of exports and imports. It also assumes that the "official" statistics for foreign debt and reserves reported by the IMF and the World Bank are accurate. Both assumptions are conservative.

27. My own conservative estimate for the total value of all offshore flight capital owned by the residents of low- and middle-income countries was just over $3 trillion as of 2003. This compares with the $2.55 trillion of their gross foreign debt for that year, and their net foreign debt—net of all foreign reserves—of $1.25 trillion. There is a strong case for removing India and China from these numbers because they account for a disproportionate share of reserves, and, in China's case, capital flight estimates are distorted by a substantial amount of "round-tripping" through Hong Kong (capital flight to Hong Kong that returns to China as "foreign" investment capital). However, even after removing those two countries, the flight wealth from developing countries turns out to be at least $1 trillion greater than their net debt.

28. See, for example, Andrei Shleifer and Daniel Wolfenzon, "Investor Protection and Equity Markets," *Journal of Financial Economics* 66, no. 1 (2002), pp. 3–27; and Rafael LaPorta et al., "Legal Determinants of External Finance," *Journal of Finance* 52 (1997), pp. 1131–50. Interestingly, in September 2000, Shleifer, a tenured Harvard economics professor and program director at Harvard's Institute for International Development in Russia, was one of several key defendants named in a $100 million lawsuit filed by the U.S. government. The suit alleged that, while managing a USAID-funded economic reform effort in Russia during the 1990s, Shleifer had engaged in the "unauthorized use of inside information to commit securities fraud, use of public money for private gain, tax evasion and submission of phony bills . . . a garden-variety, free-market scam." See *U.S. v. President and Fellows of Harvard College, Andrei Shleifer, Jonathan Hay, Nancy Zimmerman, and Elizabeth Herbert* (U.S. District Court of Boston, Civil Action 00119977, September 26, 2000). The suit was settled in July 2005 with a $26.5 million payment by Harvard and a $2 million payment by Professor Shleifer.

29. See Henry, *Pirate Bankers*.

30. For the world's forty-nine poorest countries, by UN designation, real per capita incomes, adjusted for purchasing parity (PPP) differentials, grew an average of just 0.7 percent yearly from 1980 to 2005, and for the rest of low- and middle-income countries—excluding China and India—incomes grew an average of just 0.8 percent yearly. Since higher-income countries continued to grow at an average of 1.9 percent, while China and India grew even faster, the share of income commanded by this lagging 3.1 billion people declined from 30.2 percent in 1980 to 26.4 percent in 2003. Source: My analysis of 2006 World Bank data.

31. For other important historical examples of debt relief, see J. J. Wallis, Richard E. Sylla, and Arthur Grinath III, "Sovereign Debt and Repudiation: The Emerging-Market Debt Crisis in the U.S. States, 1839–1843," NBER Working Paper no. 10753 (Cambridge, Mass.: National Bureau of Economic Research, September 2004); and Timothy W. Guinnane, "Financial *Vergangenheitsbewaltigung*," Discussion Paper no. 880 (New Haven, Conn.: Yale University, Economic Growth Center, January 2004), on the 1953 London Debt Agreement with respect to Germany's debts.

32. One glaring exception was Mexico's Angel Gurria, who handled Mexico's foreign debt negotiations for more than a decade. But eventually even he was co-opted—in 2006, he became secretary-general of the Organisation for Economic Co-operation and Development (OECD).

33. All these figures are in 2006 NPV dollars. The actual original cost of the Baker Plan to the U.S. Treasury in the 1980s was $15 billion for fifteen countries, while the original cost of the Brady Plan was $32 billion.

34. For example, debt–equity swaps required countries to issue new currency, which was then used to buy back foreign loans at discounts from face value. But the increase in currency could have a negative impact on domestic debt and inflation.

35. The Brady Plan's focus clearly reflected U.S. foreign policy priorities at the time. Of the sixteen countries in Brady Plans from 1989 to 1993, Nigeria and Bolivia were the only low-income countries, and the only non-Latin countries were Nigeria, Jordan, Bulgaria, Poland, and the Philippines. The weighted-average real per capita purchasing-parity-adjusted dollar income of these sixteen countries in 1989 was $5,514, compared with just $2,957 for all low- and middle-income countries. They accounted for just 13 percent of the developing world's population.

36. See, for example, Serkan Arslanalp and P. B. Henry, "Helping the Poor to Help Themselves: Debt Relief or Aid?" Stanford University Center for International Development, Nov. 2003. Using World Bank data, the authors found a cumulative "net resource transfer" (net long-term debt disbursements plus foreign direct and portfolio investment, minus interest on long-term foreign debt, minus profits on investments) of $210 billion for all sixteen Brady countries during the five years after 1989, and attributed all this to the impact of the plan. Recalculating the figures using the latest (2006) World Bank numbers, the total is $218.5 billion for 1989–94. However, this estimate ignores the $199.6 billion of capital flight from these countries during the same years, as well as the substantial amount of capital flight that took place by way of "misinvoicing/mispricing."

37. For the forty-eight low-income countries shown, the ratio of external debt to gross national income increased from an already-high average of 49 percent in 1980 to 80 percent in 1986. Debt growth for the group as a whole averaged 12 percent a year, but for war-torn countries like Nicaragua, Mozambique, and Ethiopia, it averaged 20 to 35 percent a year.

38. In 1986, Zambia's foreign debt service was 28.5 percent of its national income; Congo's was 19.8 percent; Gambia's 19.3 percent; Ivory Coast's 15 percent; and Bolivia's 6.9 percent. Source: My analysis of 2006 World Bank data.

39. Daseking and Powell, "From Toronto Terms to the HIPC Initiative."

40. For a synopsis and discussion of the Paris Club's "traditional" efforts, see Daseking and Powell, "From Toronto Terms to the HIPC Initiative."

41. By 2000, Angola, Equatorial Guinea, Kenya, Nigeria, Vietnam, and Yemen had been removed from the initial 1994 HIPC list, and Comoros, Gambia, and Malawi had been added; Myanmar was disqualified because of inadequate data in 2006; and Eritrea, Nepal, Haiti, and Kyrgyzstan were declared eligible in 2006. Sri Lanka and Bhutan were also considered eligible, but declined participation. Countries were reexamined for eligibility in 2006, based on their debt burdens and per capita incomes at the end of 2004. The final deadline for enrolling in the program was extended to December 2006.

42. As of March 2006, the IMF held 103.9 million ounces of gold at depositories around the world, worth $60 billion at current market prices. See "Gold in the IMF," IMF, April 2006, at www.imf.org/external/np/exr/facts/gold.htm.

43. See the membership list at www.gold.org.

44. In Nigeria's case, this was because most of its debt was not multilateral.

45. Ivory Coast had otherwise failed to qualify on the objective grounds of its ratio of PV debt to exports. Ghana, Bolivia, and Uganda also received favorable treatment: they all had higher per capita incomes, lower debt-service ratios, and lower debt-to-gross-national-income ratios than Kenya, for example.

46. For example, Angola, Nigeria, Indonesia, Kenya, the Philippines, and Yemen all had heavier debt burdens—even controlling for income levels. The relative debt burden measure is the product of nominal debt/national income and debt service/national income, weighted by the reciprocal of the log of real purchasing-parity-adjusted dollars per capita income. This measure shows that at least fifteen of the countries that qualified for HIPC help at that point had relatively low debt burdens when adjusted for income.

47. The amount of non-HIPC-country debt service gradually increased from $20.4 billion in 1996 to $29.8 billion in 2003, and then fell to $29.53 billion in 2004. For "former HIPCs" like Kenya and Nigeria, debt service also increased, from $4.83 billion in 1996 to $5.83 billion in 2004.

48. In 2006 NPV dollars.

49. Eventually the six countries did qualify for a grand total of $3.118 billion under the original HIPC I program. Ivory Coast also reached its "decision point" in 1998 before it fell apart in a brutal civil war.

50. See Mark Allen and Danny Leipziger, "Heavily-Indebted Poor Countries (HIPC) Initiative—Statistical Update," IMF/World Bank, International Development Association, March 21, 2006.

51. This was the Central African Republic. The large debtors Liberia, Sudan, and Somalia, as well as Comoros, had not had IMF- or IDA-supported programs in place since 1996 and only had until December 2006 to start them. They accounted for almost 75 percent of the outstanding foreign debts of this group. Laos had qualified but declined to participate. Ivory Coast and Togo qualified but were experiencing "different degrees of difficulty in implementing macroeconomic policies." Myanmar was unable to qualify because its foreign debt data were too uncertain, according to the IMF; of course, it was a brutal military dictatorship.

52. The six new qualifiers, on the basis of their December 2004 incomes and debt burdens, were Bhutan, Eritrea, Haiti, Kyrgyzstan, Nepal, and Sri Lanka. Sri Lanka and Bhutan declined to participate, Eritrea lacked an IDA program, and Nepal had had "protracted interruptions in program implementation"—it was in the middle of a civil war.

53. A different measure of HIPC's impact contrasts the twenty-seven countries' median debt service of $2.5 billion per year in 2004–6 with their median service of $3.1 billion per year for 1998–2002, yielding a $500 million per year saving for the group as a whole.

54. My estimates, based on HIPC I, HIPC II, and the other debt-relief programs.

55. The exact ratios are 50.3 percent of HIPC relief and 51.3 percent of all First World low-income country debt relief, excluding MDRI and "big bilateral" debt relief.

56. For example, Togo received nothing from HIPC and $68 per capita from all other debt-relief programs. Haiti has received nothing from HIPC and $16 per capita from all other programs.

57. The ratio of aggregate debt service to national income for the eighteen "completers" declined from 5.7 percent in 1996 to 3.3 percent in 2003. However, for the nine "pre–decision point" countries, the ratio declined from 5.9 percent to 1.8 percent, while for low-income countries as a whole, it fell from 3.8 percent to 3 percent.

58. The outstanding debt was $412.6 billion in 2006 NPV dollars.

59. See Allen and Leipziger, "Heavily-Indebted Poor Countries (HIPC) Initiative."

60. Three of the countries, Bhutan, Laos, and Sri Lanka, have declined to participate in the program. The three largest potential candidates for relief, Sudan, Liberia, and Somalia, are still subject to domestic turmoil.

61. Interesting examples of the pathologies arising from BWI debt-relief conditionalities include Burkina Faso (water privatization); Cameroon (failed water privatization); Chad (water privatization); Gabon (failed water privatization); Guinea (water privatization); Ivory Coast (failed water privatization); Mozambique (many dubious privatizations; a disastrous World Bank–imposed cashew strategy); Niger (water privatization); Sierra Leone (water privatization); Tanzania (failed water and electricity privatization); Uganda (corrupt bank privatization); Zambia (2004 wage freeze); and Bolivia (water privatization, gas privatization).

62. Initially in December 2004; later extended to December 2006.

63. Shriti Vadkra was the adviser to Brown; Justin Forsythe was the adviser to Blair.

64. Unlike HIPC, MDRI has no Paris Club component.

65. Congressional Budget Office estimate, August 25, 2006.

66. In the Philippines, for example, at least half of the country's public foreign debt was simply stolen by Marcos and his cronies. See Henry, *Blood Bankers*, chapter 3.

67. Just to give one example, Citigroup's total assets at the end of 2005 were $1.5 trillion, compared with the World Bank's $250 billion.

68. This controversial doctrine, originally applied by the U.S. government to debts that had been contracted by Cuba from Spanish lenders in the 1890s, basically holds that, for purposes of international contract law, foreign debts contracted by dictators without popular approval are null and void. This doctrine is really just a logical extension of good old-fashioned neoliberal contract theory, according to which a basis requirement for enforceability is voluntary consent to contractual obligations.

There are *alternatives—and people around the world are helping to*
12 *build them every day. Antonia Juhasz finds an agenda for hope in the global justice movement.*

Global Uprising: The Web of Resistance

Antonia Juhasz

Elvira, a garment worker in the Philippines, shares her dream of a better life with Ellen Augustine in chapter 9 of this book. Elvira imagines "a society where basic needs are provided, there is enough food, there is housing for everyone, all children can go to school, hospitals are for everybody, and there is a job for everyone—a job that helps people to develop their potential as human beings."

Thus far our authors have largely focused on uncovering the many obstacles placed in front of Elvira, and all of us, in our quest for these basic necessities of life. They have also exposed the people and institutions committed to constructing and maintaining those obstacles. But knowledge truly becomes power only when you, the reader, feel inspired to take action for both Elvira and yourself. This concluding chapter is dedicated to spotlighting the many people, movements, and institutions that are not only eliminating obstacles but actually helping establish the just and equitable society of Elvira's dream.

An Insider Confesses

In November 2004, John Perkins published *Confessions of an Economic Hit Man.* One reason for its overwhelming success was that it appeared just when the debate about corporate globalization was being transformed worldwide.

Instead of asking how fast corporate globalization could be advanced, people wanted to know whose interests were being served and at what cost to the rest of us.

Public protest and opposition had been rising for decades in countries on the receiving end of economic hit men like Perkins and the organizations they worked for, including the World Bank, International Monetary Fund (IMF), World Trade Organization (WTO), and dominant financial institutions and multinational corporations. These concerns were increasingly heard, addressed, and shared by people in the Global North. Affected communities and their supporters were screaming out their suffering at the hands of economic hit men, but few hit men were willing to acknowledge the web of control and exploitation they had helped create.

Enter John Perkins.

Perkins was not the first corporate globalization whistle-blower, but he gave a respected Global North insider's validation of the critiques many people had heard for years but were unsure whether to believe. And Perkins did so in a highly engaging and uniquely informative book. It didn't hurt that the book also had a great title. *Confessions* opened a door through which hundreds of thousands of people could peer into the dark side of corporate globalization—a door that *A Game As Old As Empire* has now busted off its hinges. However, in the chapters of both books, the movement against corporate globalization, or, as we call ourselves, the global justice movement, has remained largely in the shadows.

An understanding of the history and ongoing achievements of the global justice movement—including its contribution to the near collapse of the WTO and the sidelining of the World Bank and IMF—can provide direction, empowerment, and—what is most important—hope that we can overcome the many challenges presented in the preceding chapters.

John Christensen may provide the best description of those challenges in chapter 3. While his analysis refers to corporate tax havens, it applies to corporate globalization broadly: "This creates an uneven playing field, favoring multinational businesses over nationally based businesses, which in almost all cases means favoring large businesses from the Global North over their domestic competitors in developing countries." I would add that corporate globalization also favors large multinational businesses over smaller competitors within their own nations and favors the interests of multinational businesses over virtually all other concerns, including those of workers like Elvira, consumers, the environment, and democracy.

Christensen's description of the problem helps us define the winners in the global economy, answering the questions In whose interests? and Why? the policies described in this book, which are so obviously destructive, continue to be implemented.

But while the game may be as old as Empire, the resistance and alternatives to it have an equally long, important, and instructive history.

Birth of a Movement

The movement against modern (post–World War II) corporate globalization is as old as the institutions created to advance the corporate agenda. From the outset, the loudest criticism against the World Bank and IMF and ideas for alternatives to them emerged from the countries that would be forced to live under their policies—the developing world. The peoples of those nations argued instead for rules to direct the terms of trade among nations within the context of democracy, health, labor rights, equality, stability, and alleviation of poverty. They successfully established international bodies within the United Nations to address these issues, such as the UN Conference for Trade and Development (UNCTAD), the World Health Organization, the International Labor Organization, the Food and Agriculture Organization, and the UN Development Program.

Rather than support developing country demands for a strengthened UN, the United States and other Global North countries chose increasingly to turn their money, time, and political attention to the World Bank and IMF, institutions where they maintained dominant and unequal control. A split emerged between developing nations who felt that getting something at the World Bank and IMF was better than nothing at the UN and those who wanted to hold out for more. This split, combined with the drain of money and attention from the North, led to the eventual demise of some programs and the weakening of many others envisioned at the UN, while the World Bank and IMF steadily gained power and influence.

As the web of control described by Steven Hiatt in chapter 1 tightened on developing countries with the 1970s debt crisis, the subsequent introduction of structural adjustment programs (SAPs), and the crushing burden of debt, so, too, grew the global struggle against these institutions.

By the late 1980s, more than seventy countries had been subjected to World Bank and IMF SAPs. Protest movements emerged virtually simultaneously in almost as many nations. Because the institutions have such a profound impact on the most basic areas of people's lives, from the cost of bread to the availability of electricity and water, people in loan-recipient nations become World Bank and IMF experts from an early age (I personally received one of my most illuminating lessons on World Bank policy from a seventeen-year-old boy in Cochabamba, Bolivia). They learn that, to bring about change, they must challenge not only their governments but also the international financial institutions behind them.

As my colleagues and I at the International Forum on Globalization detailed in our report "Does Globalization Help the Poor?" movements against corporate globalization have a long and proud global tradition.[1] For example, in Jamaica in 1985, protests took place across the country denouncing a World Bank SAP requirement to raise fuel prices. Two years later in Zambia, months of protests over increased food costs brought on by an IMF SAP eventually led the government to suspend the program. In Ecuador in 1987, student protesters clashed with riot police, and workers held a one-day general strike, in opposition to a new IMF SAP. In Algeria in 1988, more than 200 people were killed in protests against price increases and unemployment in the wake of a World Bank SAP. In 1989, protests erupted throughout southern Jordan against an increase in food prices brought about by new IMF demands. In 1989 in Nigeria, dozens of people were killed and hundreds were arrested in protests against a new IMF SAP. In response, the Nigerian government offered a new welfare program called the "SAP Relief Package." In 1993 in India, half a million Indian farmers converged on Bangalore in opposition to negotiations to establish the WTO. The list goes on, and the resistance spans the globe.

People in loan-recipient nations not only protested but also made demands, including the end of SAPs, the cancellation of debt, and the introduction of fairness to the international economic system. The demands reached people in lender nations, many of whom joined forces with those in recipient countries and became part of a burgeoning global justice movement.

However, while both government officials and citizen activists in developing countries, and some of their allies in the North, were saddled with the day-to-day battle against the World Bank and IMF, they were less able to address a potentially even more devastating beast growing in their backyard: the World Trade Organization.

Like the World Bank and IMF, the WTO emerged not through some inevitable policy evolution but rather in competition with more equitable alternatives put forward by developing countries.

Corporate Globalization Hits the North: NAFTA, WTO, and MAI

You have probably never heard of the International Trade Organization (ITO), the forerunner to the WTO. That is because it never actually came into being, because the U.S. Senate refused to ratify it. The ITO charter was established at the 1948 UN Conference on Trade and Employment held in Havana. Representatives of fifty-six nations, almost all from developing countries, attended. In the ITO, trade was treated as just one tool among many to achieve economic development. The ITO also included agreements on full employment; breaking up corporate monopolies; commodity trade agreements to ensure that products of developing countries received fair treatment on the world market; and other protections for domestic markets. While the details of the ITO were being hashed out, a General Agreement on Tariffs and Trade (GATT) was established as an interim international negotiating body for trade until the ITO was completed. However, when the U.S. Congress rejected the ITO, based primarily on its lack of investment protections for U.S. corporations operating abroad, the ITO died, leaving the "interim" GATT as the major arbiter of world trade for nearly fifty years.[2]

Although the ITO died in Havana, the belief in a balanced international trading system did not. In the decades that followed, people across the Global South increasingly advocated for the United Nations Conference for Trade and Development (UNCTAD) as the best forum to create international trade rules. They wanted rules for setting fair prices in commodity price agreements; trade preferences to encourage economic development in the South; preferential treatment for local over foreign investors; the use of trade policy as a legitimate instrument for industrialization; and a program of technology transfer to the developing countries.[3] Instead, they got the WTO.

In 1986, government officials met in Uruguay to launch a new round of negotiations to expand the reach and authority of the GATT. Seven and a half years later in 1994, the Uruguay Round was completed in negotiations in Marrakech, Morocco, as 125 countries signed on to the creation of the World Trade Organization.

Global North countries could afford dozens if not hundreds of full-time negotiators to both monitor and attend talks at every international negotiating venue around the world and to follow the daily developments in arcane trade law; few developing countries could do the same. Once the developed countries had hammered out their differences, those delegates from the Global South who were present in Marrakech were too few, too uninformed, and too disempowered to provide a meaningful negotiating voice. Instead, governments and corporate interests from the North drove the Uruguay Round, as bluntly described in 1997 by David Hartridge, then director of the Trade in Services Division of the WTO: "Without the enormous pressure generated by the American financial services sector, particularly companies like American Express and CitiCorp, there would have been no services agreement and therefore perhaps no Uruguay Round and no WTO."[4]

As the Uruguay Round was taking place, the U.S. and Canada were engaged in trade negotiations, culminating first in the 1989 U.S.–Canada Free Trade Agreement and then, five years later with the addition of Mexico, in the North American Free Trade Agreement (NAFTA).

NAFTA and the WTO represent an entirely new direction for trade agreements. In fact, they might best be described as taking the policies of the World Bank and IMF, expanding their breadth and depth, and applying them equally to the developed and developing worlds. In effect, corporations from the North decided that they might as well get the same advantages at home as they were getting abroad, and then some.

Birth of a Global Movement

Some of the first truly global campaigns *against* corporate globalization were those calling for World Bank and IMF debt cancellation. These activists engaged in grassroots organizing and corporate campaigns exposing the beneficiaries of World Bank and IMF policies. They formed international organizations such as 50 Years Is Enough and Jubilee 2000, which lobbied elected officials, conducted analyses, and released reports. They held public teach-ins, press conferences, and protests not only in their home countries but also at World Bank and IMF meetings and corporate headquarters around the world.[5] The broader global justice movement adopted these techniques.

The big turning point for the movement came when people in *lender* nations were suddenly on the receiving end of globalization policies themselves—that is, when more people in the North began to directly experience the downsides of corporate globalization policy.

Committed networks of activists united against NAFTA and the WTO, particularly from the environmental, faith-based, organized labor, farmworker, and consumer advocacy communities. However, their international ties were limited, their initial numbers were relatively small, and their influence was thus less keenly felt. As the agreements were implemented and their direct costs became felt, awareness spread, and the movement grew. Activists joined efforts across issue areas, borders, and regions of the world.

The power of this global movement was felt for the first time with the defeat of two multilateral investment agreements at the WTO and the Organisation for Economic Co-operation and Development (OECD). The investment agreements were based on new measures new measures included in NAFTA that were a radical departure from traditional multilateral rules. NAFTA granted foreign companies and investors unprecedented rights over governments in all three countries. U.S. and British negotiators hoped to implement these same rules across the 27 nations of the OECD and the more than 130 countries of the WTO.

A Victory: Defeat of the Multilateral Agreement on Investment

The sheer audacity of the rights being proposed for global investors, combined with the increasing number of nations, both North and South, that would be brought under its rules, helped birth a global opposition movement. Activists in developing countries were the first to take both notice and action. They worked with their delegates to successfully sideline the proposed Multilateral Investment Agreement (MIA) at the WTO's 1996 ministerial meeting. Their success led MIA advocates to intensify their push at the OECD, the "club" of the twenty-seven wealthiest nations in the world, where the agreement was revived and renamed the Multilateral Agreement on Investment (MAI).

In response, impacted communities in the North looked to those in the South for education and instruction. In 1997, I attended a strategy meeting in Paris at which experts from developing countries such as Martin Khor of Malaysia's Third World Network gave teach-ins on the potential impacts of the MAI to activists from Europe, the U.S., and other countries North and South, so all could join forces to defeat the new agreement. This information was used back home in traditional education and lobbying campaigns.

For example, in my position as coordinator of the MAI campaign at the Preamble Center for Public Policy in Washington, D.C., I personally made dozens of cold calls to representatives of advocacy organizations focused on the environment, worker rights, women's rights, small businesses, community organizing, economic and social justice, and other issue areas. I explained the current impact of NAFTA and the WTO and the potential impact of the MAI on them and their work. Most people I called had never before considered international trade or investment rules. Across the board, they were shocked and angered by what they learned. The members of Congress with whom we shared our views demonstrated a similar naïveté. My associates at groups such as Public Citizen, Friends of the Earth, the Sierra Club, and the AFL-CIO made the same calls and heard the same reactions, as did our international partners.

As activists increasingly combined their efforts across nations to shine light on the negotiating process, elected officials felt the pressure and were ultimately convinced to reject the MAI at the OECD conference in 1998. Its defeat marked one of the first and most important successful global movements of people and governments against an international trade or investment agreement.

At the same time, the devastating reality of these investment rules was on full display as the East Asian financial crisis took hold and began to spread. From 1998 to 1999, nations that had once been characterized as the "East Asian tigers" because of their thriving economies suddenly crashed when the IMF restricted the ability of their governments to regulate which sectors of their economies received foreign investments and how long and in what quantities the investments had to stay. When foreign investors started playing with these nations' currencies as if they were in a global casino, the governments were powerless to act. As the financial crisis spread to Argentina, fear of a global financial calamity generated a wave of resistance.

A Victory: Collapse of the WTO Seattle Ministerial

Every two years the WTO holds ministerial-level meetings at which high-ranking government officials finalize negotiations on existing and new WTO rules. How shortsighted it was that advocates of the MAI relaunched the investment negotiations at the WTO's 1999 Seattle ministerial. In response, people who had worked to defeat the MAI, people who had suffered the consequences of IMF investment rules in East Asia, and people who had worked against the same policies at the World Bank and IMF united their efforts. They expanded global education and media campaigns, organizing and lobbying efforts, and strategic planning for Seattle. Grassroots campaigns emerged around the world involving public education, theater, art, guerrilla and alternative media, and nonviolent direct action and civil disobedience training, all of which contributed to the historic collapse of the meeting that has since been dubbed the "Battle of Seattle."

Upwards of 50,000 people turned out on the streets of Seattle to oppose the WTO. Thousands took part in a unique strategy of peaceful blockades that literally shut down the opening day of the meeting and plagued negotiators for days. Police in riot gear responded with brutal tactics and an aggressive "show of force" throughout the city, although only a handful of protesters had thrown bricks into a few store windows. While the people protested in the streets, developing country delegates stood up as a bloc and said they would no longer simply rubber-stamp the demands of the United States and the European Union. As a result, the meeting collapsed.

In fact, many of those in the streets had also spent years acting as advisers to the delegates from developing countries providing detailed lessons on international trade law and information on day-by-day trade negotiations taking place around the globe.

The public displays of opposition to corporate globalization continued to grow in the months and years after Seattle, mirroring what was happening inside the negotiations: government leaders the world over were rejecting the onrush of corporate globalization.

Global Uprising

Five months after WTO talks collapsed in Seattle, some 30,000 people demonstrated in April 2000 against annual fall meetings of the World Bank and IMF in Washington, D.C. In January 2001, over 10,000 people gathered in Porto Alegre, Brazil, for the first annual World Social Forum, an event organized solely to discuss meaningful alternatives to corporate globalization. Annual participation at the World Social Forum now regularly tops 100,000 people, and regional and national Forums are being held annually around the globe.

In April 2001, 60,000 people protested against the Free Trade Area of the Americas (FTAA) in Québec City, Canada. The FTAA was a dream of three consecutive U.S. presidents: George H. W. Bush, Bill Clinton, and George W. Bush. But opposition to the agreement brought about its ignoble death in 2005. In July 2001, 200,000 people gathered in Genoa, Italy, to express their opposition to corporate globalization, as the Group of Eight industrialized countries (G8) held its annual meeting. The event is remembered, however, for the tragic death of twenty-three-year-old Carlo Giuliani, who was shot by police while participating in a protest.

In March 2001, hundreds of farmers and students protested outside a WTO meeting in the Thai city of Chiang Mai. They dumped potatoes, garlic, onions, and soybeans in the lobby to demonstrate how the WTO Agreement on Agriculture has harmed them. In November, more than 1,000 people—including the Union of Farmers, gathered in Beirut, Lebanon, for the World Forum on Globalization and Global Trade held in opposition to the 2001 WTO ministerial held in Doha, Qatar.

In 2003, tens of thousands of marchers led by farmers from across Mexico, Central America, and as far away as South Korea, protested the Cancún, Mexico, ministerial meeting of the WTO. One South Korean farmer, Lee Kyung Hae, committed suicide in Cancún to protest the Agriculture Agreement. I was among thousands of WTO protestors who looked on in horror as Lee, with a sign across his chest declaring "The WTO Kills Farmers," took a Swiss Army knife from his pocket and stabbed it into his chest—puncturing his heart and one lung. Lee's was an act in protest of WTO agricultural policies that had bankrupted his farm, impoverished his family, and devoured his community. He left a note that read, "It is better that a single person sacrifices [his] life for ten people, than ten people sacrifice their lives for just one."[6]

The WTO Agreement on Agriculture has been implemented in stages. As implementation has advanced, so too have the devastating impacts on farmers worldwide. Via Campesina (Small Farmer's Way) and Movimento dos Trabalhadores Rurais Sem Terra (Landless Workers' Movement) in Central and South America, the Slow Food movement across Europe, the National Family Farm Coalition and the Coalition of Immokalee Workers in the United States, and other national and international farmer networks united in calling for trade policy that favors small, local, and sustainable agriculture rather than large, multinational industrial agriculture corporations.

The birth of the North American Free Trade Agreement was marked by one of the most important indigenous and farmer movements in history: the Zapatistas of Mexico. Farmers, peasants, workers, and citizens of Chiapas, Mexico, who formed the Zapatista Army of National Liberation, specifically chose January 1, 1994, the day NAFTA came into effect, to issue the First Declaration of the Lacadon Jungle and seize six municipal seats in Chiapas, Mexico. According to a Zapatista spokesman, "To us, the free-trade treaty is the death certificate for the ethnic people of Mexico."[7]

Back in Cancún, these farmers were joined by other workers and citizens from around the world who united in the streets. Their efforts supported many developing country negotiators inside the meeting, leading to another ministerial meeting collapse. The 2005 Hong Kong WTO ministerial experienced the same fate.

In fact, the only WTO ministerial that has not collapsed since 1998 was the one in Doha, Qatar, in 2001, held just two months after the September 11 terrorist attacks and located in a country that forbade both political dissent and free entry. Negotiators in Doha were left alone to prove to the Bush administration that they were either with or against the United States. Five years and three failed ministerial meetings later, however, the Doha Round is all but dead, and many believe it is sounding the death knell for the entire WTO as an institution. One reason for its demise is the increasing number of developing countries whose leaders are now opposed to corporate globalization.

Electoral Victories

Across the globe, peoples' movements for global justice have swept in elected officials representing their views. These officials have then brought resistance into the institutions of corporate globalization. Walden Bello of Thailand's Focus on the Global South describes how, in the midst of the East Asian financial crisis, public pressure led Prime Minister Mohamad Mahathir of Malaysia to break with the IMF and impose capital controls, saving the country from the worst effects of the crisis. According to Bello,

> Mahathir's defiance of the IMF was not lost on Thaksin Shinawatra, who ran for prime minister of Thailand on an anti-IMF platform and won. He went on to push for large government expenditures, which stimulated the consumer demand that brought Thailand out of recession. Nestor Kirchner completed the humbling of the IMF when, upon being elected president of Argentina in 2003, he declared that his government would pay its private creditors only 25 cents for every dollar owed. Enraged creditors told the IMF to discipline Kirchner. But with its reputation in tatters and its leverage eroded, the IMF backed off from confronting the Argentine president, who got away with the radical debt write-down.[8]

Similarly, Lori Wallach and Deborah James of Public Citizen in Washington, D.C., have written about the electoral victories sweeping Central and South America:

> There is growing consensus that the clear failure of the model—often called "neoliberalism"—to deliver economic growth or better standards of living for most is translating into electoral victories for leaders who have made rejection of this agenda a staple of their platforms. Nowhere is this more evident than in Bolivia, Argentina, and Venezuela, whose economies all have been decimated under previous neoliberal governments. . . . Even Costa Rica, Peru, and Mexico, traditionally neoliberal strongholds, have experienced presidential elections almost entirely dominated by debate over trade liberalization.[9]

The global justice movement has also matured. For example, under the influence of unions such as Unite! and the Service Employees International Union, organized labor in the U.S. changed from first supporting corporate globalization to then supporting only instances that helped U.S. workers and then to a broader opposition grounded in the reality of the shared sacrifice of workers everywhere. In the U.S., white activists and NGOs have become less dominant, as farmworker, immigrant, nonunionized labor, and youth movements increasingly take the lead.

Victories: Debt Cancellation and the Sidelining of the World Bank and IMF

Many Global North activists were introduced to the World Bank and IMF through their organizing efforts against the WTO, NAFTA, MAI, export credit agencies, and individual corporations and banks. As more people joined the ranks of the global justice movement, fundamental reforms within the IMF and World Bank were demanded and won, including demands for debt cancellation (not just "debt relief").

In February 2005, members of the G8 announced their intention to provide "as much as 100% multilateral debt relief for the 42 Highly Indebted Poor Countries (HIPC)." This was a tremendous victory, although I agree with James S. Henry, who argues in chapter 11 that it did not go far enough: it failed to address commercial debt or the debt of the hundreds of poor nations that do not qualify as HIPC, and it tied cancellation to onerous requirements.

For twenty-five years, the world's poorest nations have demanded debt cancellation. The social movements and elected officials in these nations and their global supporters savored their victory, but they did not then sit idle. Just as they had successfully demanded more from the original HIPC program, so they demanded more from the G8. They will continue to need all the support we can provide in their ongoing struggle.

Decades of criticism, protest, and activism ultimately forced the G8's hand and brought an agreement that the member governments had uniformly resisted. The agreement provides the most significant admission to date that the policies of the World Bank and IMF, and corporate globalization more broadly, have failed to better the lives of people around the world and have in fact worsened them. The discredit brought to the institutions and the policies of corporate globalization cannot be ignored.

Under pressure from social movements, grassroots campaigners, elected officials, and NGOs, governments around the world are reducing their payments to the IMF and World Bank. Countries are refusing new loans and, like Argentina, refusing to pay back old ones. They are denying the institutions' power by refusing to accept their money or return it. The result is that the power of these institutions, like that of the WTO, has been greatly diminished.

But if the global justice movement has helped put the WTO, IMF, and World Bank on the sidelines, what, if anything, do we advocate should take their place? The following proposals are drawn from my recent book, *The Bush Agenda: Invading the World, One Economy at a Time.*[10] They offer a road map for reining in corporate power and igniting support for sustainable, equitable, and just societies like those of Elvira's dreams.

Alternative Policies to Disarm Economic Hit Men and Rein in Corporate Power

The corruption detailed in this book fundamentally rests on the growing power of corporations (and banks) to dominate policy making. The war in Iraq may be the ultimate indicator of that power. It is a war waged for corporate access, oil wealth, and global hegemony.

How then do we disarm economic hit men, rein in corporate power, and establish new rules and institutions that support the pursuit of meaningful alternatives?

The global justice movement has demonstrated the world over that it is far easier to replace corporate globalization policy than its advocates would have us believe. Corporate globalization is a set of policies designed to reduce the ability of local communities and governments to determine the rules by which foreign companies operate in their areas. The alternatives, therefore, are tools that allow local communities and governments to set the terms by which companies (both foreign and local) operate.

Opposition to the rules of corporate globalization often rests on this issue: when a policy decision is made, a wide range of competing interests are ignored, whether they are environmental, labor, human rights, equity, or other interests. Corporate interests trump all others. There is no balance, no debate; in effect (if not in fact), just one group of actors decides the outcome. Their policies simultaneously enrich corporations and increase their political influence, virtually erasing the democratic process and producing the hybrid corporate-government epitomized by the Bush administration. Increased corporate political influence translates directly into influence over government regulation—or lack of regulation—as in the case of offshore tax havens, the catastrophic lending strategies of the world's largest banks, and the economic pillaging facilitated by export credit agencies.

If national policies focused instead on local economic development and restricting multinational corporate power, the current level of international trade and investment activity—as well as the need to regulate it—will likely be significantly reduced. International trade and investment will and should continue, however, so rules to govern it will be necessary.

The World Bank, IMF, and WTO have failed miserably in their agendas. They are creating more poverty, inequality, and instability than they are re-lieving and should therefore be decommissioned. As described earlier in this chapter, developing countries have successfully established international bod-ies within the UN to address both development and the terms of trade. The UN needs reform. It needs to be "decorporatized." It needs more financial resources, greater public attention, greater transparency, more democracy, and more influence. In spite of its considerable flaws, it remains the institu-tion with the broadest mandate, and it is more open and democratic than the World Bank, IMF, and WTO. In practice, it has given much greater weight to human, social, and environmental priorities than they have. When interna-tional trade and investment rules must be written, a reformed UN is the place to do it.[11]

Peoples' Movements and Organizations Creating Alternatives

People the world over are not waiting for institutional reform. They are act-ing now to implement meaningful alternatives to corporate globalization. In Argentina, popular movements have created a model known as *horizontalism*. Among its many important features is the neighborhood assembly, where de-cisions about such matters as trash collection, repair of potholes or road signs, school boards, and even city budgets are made. These assemblies are a form of direct democracy: people participate directly in making political and eco-nomic decisions that affect their daily lives. In addition, a number of Argen-tine factories and other leading businesses are now worker-run cooperatives in which decisions are made through worker assemblies. All workers have equal decision-making authority about pay, production schedules, materials, distribution, and health benefits.

Wisconsin's Liberty Tree Foundation for the Democratic Revolution and media experts SmartMeme in California have worked with local communities and governments to build a new "democracy movement" in the U.S. with a fo-cus on direct democracy. Worker cooperatives are also an increasing presence in the U.S. In 2004, the California-based United States Federation of Worker Cooperatives was formed. Today, it has some thirty member businesses, as diverse as banks, bakeries, and Web site design firms. The federation advocates for businesses in which workers are in control of management, governance, and ownership.

In Bolivia, after a failed World Bank–imposed water privatization measure, the people of Cochabamba established an alternative water system—a government-community-worker hybrid—that has become a model for water systems the world over. The company, SEMAPA (Servicio Municipal de Agua Potable y Alcantarillado), is run by a rotating board of seven directors: three democratically elected from the community, two from the mayor's office, one from the professional schools, and one from the workers' union. Weekly meetings are held in different neighborhoods to assess needs, prices, and overall functioning of the system. The wealthier citizens subsidize those with lower incomes, so that the company has stabilized prices while expanding service to the city's poorest neighborhoods, many of which had never received water before. Evo Morales, Bolivia's new president, was part of this water reclamation movement.

In 2003, city officials in Atlanta ended the largest water privatization deal in the U.S. Mayor Shirley Franklin canceled a twenty-year contract with United Water Company after four years of rising prices, terrible service, broken promises, and public outcry. Groups such as Food and Water Watch in Washington, D.C., are working in global networks to declare water a protected basic human right that must be provided as a safe, affordable, and equitable public service.

In the United States, individual communities and states are stepping in where the federal government has failed to regulate corporations. For example, in 1998 Pennsylvania's Wayne Township passed an ordinance forbidding any corporation with three or more regulatory violations over seven years to establish operations in its jurisdiction. Four years later, another Pennsylvania township, Porter, challenged the constitutional rights of corporations with passage of an ordinance stating, "Corporations shall not be considered to be 'persons' protected by the Constitution of the United States or the Constitution of the Commonwealth of Pennsylvania." In June 2006, California's Humboldt County took this legislation one step farther, passing a resolution that not only directly challenged corporate personhood but also banned all out-of-county corporations from making political contributions in local campaigns.

In 2005, Charlevoix Township in Michigan was one of dozens of cities to approve ordinances giving local government the authority to limit the size of big-box stores. That same year, Maryland passed legislation requiring organizations with more than 10,000 employees in the state to spend at least 8 percent of their payroll on health benefits. The only enterprise affected by this legislation is Wal-Mart. Similar legislation has been proposed in several other states.

There are also strong movements across the U.S. to enforce antitrust legislation on oil and other monopolistic corporations, including Wal-Mart. A campaign led by Washington, D.C.–based Oil Change International, is calling for the "Separation of Oil and State." There are movements to use corporate charters as a means of holding companies accountable for illegal or otherwise unacceptable business practices, whether in the U.S. or abroad, and to make investors liable for harm done by the companies in which they invest.

The peace and global justice movements have united to expose the corporate interests perpetuating the war in Iraq and driving the Bush administration's corporate globalization agenda, including the U.S.–Middle East Free Trade Area. Critics of the Bechtel and Halliburton corporations, working in networks such as the San Francisco Bay Area's Direct Action to Stop the War and the Houston Global Awareness Collective, have repeatedly protested at the companies' headquarters. They have released scathing analyses of the companies' work in Iraq, which have been echoed by the press. Congressional inquiries and investigations have followed. Groups such as United for Peace and Justice in New York, Institute for Policy Studies in Washington, D.C., and Global Exchange and CorpWatch in California have helped put and keep the pressure on.

Unable to endure the constant negative attention from the public, the press, and Congress, Bechtel executives decided not to bid on any new work in Iraq—freeing desperately needed U.S. funds for Iraqi companies. The federal government also canceled at least one Bechtel project in Iraq, a new children's hospital in Basra, after an investigation found it was nearly $90 million over budget and more than a year and a half behind schedule. Dozens of charges against Halliburton are being investigated by government agencies. Most significantly, in 2006, the U.S. army canceled Halliburton's largest government contract, LOGCAP, which covered worldwide logistical support to U.S. troops. Halliburton will finish out its current Iraq contract, but next year LOGCAP will be broken into smaller parts and bid competitively to other companies.

Reclaiming Democracy: What You Can Do

The methods used to advance corporate globalization policy are not static. We must remain vigilant as corporate leaders come up with new strategies. Two of the latest mutations are use of the military to advance corporate globalization aims in Iraq and a return to bilateral trade agreements. The first thing we can do as a movement is to continue to "stop the bad" while simultaneously "supporting the good." Many organizations and people's movements named in this chapter are continuing the vital struggle against the war in Iraq and against new free trade agreements such as the U.S.–Middle East Free Trade Area. On my Web site, www.TheBushAgenda.net, I provide links to many antiwar and global justice networks, including the National Youth and Student Peace Coalition and www.bilaterals.org, the best site for tracking bilateral negotiations.

Because the rules and institutions of corporate globalization have such a broad reach, the movement against them embodies great diversity. People come from all corners of the globe and with a wide variety of specific concerns and needs. The global justice movement is therefore often described as "a movement of movements": different communities resisting corporate globalization who have grown increasingly connected and able to find common purpose in creating change.

When and where do you enter this picture? What can you do? Rather than a list of modes of activism or places to go, here are some guiding ideas that have helped me in my involvement in and support of the global justice movement.

Know Thyself

You exist in many roles in the world, as worker, caregiver, consumer, service provider, service recipient, investor, employer, voter, resident. Each role carries responsibilities, modes of influence, communities within which to organize, and potential alliances you can establish.

As a consumer, for example, you might feel responsible to become informed about the products you buy. Your modes of influence include choosing not to purchase a product because of its harm to the environment or the way in which it's produced or the treatment of the workers who produce it. Or you may decide to buy products that are environmentally sustainable or that are made by unionized workers or cooperatives. The communities within which you can organize include your family, friends, neighbors, and other consumers of the product. Your potential allies include the workers who produce it and those who live where the product is produced and where it is discarded.

In 2005, an alliance between the farmworkers who pick tomatoes for Taco Bell and the people who consume Taco Bell foods led to an amazing victory. On March 8, 2005, the farmworkers won their first pay raise in twenty-five years, the result of a ten-year struggle organized by Florida's Coalition of Immokalee Workers, including a four-year national boycott of Taco Bell and its parent company, Yum! Brands, Inc. Students at some 300 colleges and universities and more than 50 high schools participated in the boycott. They shut down or blocked the chain's restaurants on twenty-two campuses and formed their own network, the Student Farmworker Alliance, making clear the unity between the company's target market and the people who supply their food.

Consumers, producers, and sellers have come together to establish the Fair Trade Certified label. It is the only independent, third-party guarantee to consumers that companies have complied with strict economic, social, and environmental criteria for particular products. Certification helps create a more equitable and sustainable trade system for producers.

Be Informed and Challenge Your Preconceptions

Find out where your pension is being invested, how your products are made and disposed of, why wars are being fought in your name, where your tax dollars are being spent, and who is dodging their taxes altogether. Think you cannot have anything in common with, much less work with, _____? Think you have nothing to learn about _____? Think there isn't anything that can possibly be done about _____? Think you simply don't have the time to _____? Think again.

Be Inspired and Trust the Movement

You do not have to fight every battle—because there are millions of others fighting with you. You are most effective at that which most moves you to act. It might change over time, but you do not have to combat every evil you identify, or take every positive alternative you can imagine, in order for your actions to make a difference. We need not be puritans or perfectionists to be activists and agents for positive change. Know that others are working on debt cancellation, clean energy, oil company corruption, and peace. You can focus on the issue that most touches you and where you feel you can most effectively support others in the struggle; and you can still maintain alliances with those who have chosen other areas to focus on.

Believe in Activism: A Little Does Go a Long Way

Remember the Boston Tea Party, the Suffragists, the lunch counter sit-ins of the civil rights movement, the collapse of the Multilateral Agreement on Investment at the OECD, and the millions of immigrant rights supporters who stopped Congress and the Bush administration in their anti-immigrant tracks. Every thing you do is more than doing nothing. A million small individual acts add up to big actions for change. As Rebecca Solnit wrote in her brilliant book *Hope in the Dark*: "There will always be cruelty, always be violence, always be destruction. . . . We cannot eliminate all devastation for all time, but we can reduce it, outlaw it, undermine its sources and foundations: these are victories."[12]

Push Your Comfort Zone and Expand Your Skills

If you've opposed the war for three years or three weeks, how about discussing your opposition with your family members, your synagogue, and your co-workers? How about writing your first letter to the editor or attending your first vigil or protest? Frustrated by electoral politics? How about introducing yourself to the direct democracy movement? Frustrated by the mainstream media? How about exploring independent media or creating your own? None of these ideas sound effective? Then come up with your own ideas for activism. Push your comfort and skill-set zones, and feel just how comfortable you'll become.

Provide a Service to Those in Long-Term Struggle

Listen to movements of people in struggle. Learn how your actions can best serve their needs, and return to number one, "Know Thyself."

Look Forward with Hope

We have never been, nor are we now, powerless to act against the forces of Empire. The "hit men" in these pages came forward, not to ask our forgiveness, but rather to demand our action. Fortunately, we have a movement to learn from, act within, teach, and expand upon.

Our story is just beginning to unfold. A networked global civil society has given us unprecedented potential to make deep changes and create institutions that can truly serve the global common good. Elvira's dream is universal. That knowledge alone should give us hope.

Notes

1. Jerry Mander and Debi Baker, eds. (Antonia Juhasz, principal researcher and project coordinator), "Does Globalization Help the Poor?" special report, International Forum on Globalization, *IFG Bulletin* 1, no. 3 (August 2001).

2. Daniel Drache, "The Short But Significant Life of the International Trade Organization," (Toronto: York University, Robarts Centre for Canadian Studies, November 2000).

3. Walden Bello in *Views from the South*, ed. Sarah Anderson (San Francisco: Food First Books and the International Forum on Globalization, 2000).

4. David Hartridge, director of the Trade in Services Division, World Trade Organization, "What the General Agreement on Trade in Services Can Do," speech to the conference "Opening Markets for Banking Worldwide: The WTO General Agreement on Trade in Services," organized by British Invisibles and the transnational law firm Clifford Chance, London, January 8, 1997.

5. Mark Engler, "A Movement Looks Forward," *Foreign Policy in Focus*, May 19, 2005.

6. Luis Hernandez Navarro, "Mr. Lee Kyung Hae," *La Jornada*, September 23, 2003.

7. Mander and Bakers, eds., "Does Globalization Help the Poor?"

8. Walden Bello, "The Crisis of Multilateralism," *Foreign Policy in Focus*, September 13, 2006.

9. Lori Wallach and Deborah James, "Why the WTO Round Talks Have Collapsed," *Common Dreams*, April 14, 2006.

10. Antonia Juhasz, *The Bush Agenda: Invading the World, One Economy at a Time* (New York: ReganBooks/HarperCollins, 2006); see also my Web site: www.TheBushAgenda.net.

11. Jerry Mander and John Cavanagh, eds. (Antonia Juhasz, contributing author), *Alternatives to Economic Globalization: A Better World Is Possible*, 2nd edn. (San Francisco: Berrett-Koehler, 2004).

12. Rebecca Solnit, *Hope in the Dark: Untold Histories, Wild Possibilities* (New York: Nation Books, 2004).

About the Authors

Ellen Augustine's passion to create a just, peaceful, and sustainable world has led her to run for U.S. Congress and found/cofound four nonprofits focusing on media violence, mentoring at-risk youth, citizen diplomacy, and environmental restoration. She co-authored (as Ellen Schwartz) *Taking Back Our Lives in the Age of Corporate Dominance* from an optimism that simultaneously recognizes the urgency of our times and the power of intention and conscious action. She currently speaks on "Stories of Hope": profiles of people who are creating businesses that increase profits by being eco-friendly, communities and schools that nurture and sustain us, and initiatives that revitalize our environment (www.storiesofhope.us). She has been a voice for the common good—balancing the present and future needs of people and the planet in all decisions—on numerous radio and television shows, and in magazines such as *Utne Reader*. She has served on several nonprofit boards, including the National Women's Political Caucus and the Sierra Club.

Following a varied career in industry and technical education, **Steve Berkman** joined the World Bank's Africa Region Group in 1983. Hired to provide advice and assistance on capacity-building components for Bank-funded projects, he worked in twenty-one countries. Within a few years, he realized that the Bank's approach to economic development was a failure, but his attempts to convince management of the extent of the problem went unheeded until the arrival of President James Wolfensohn in 1995. Retiring in that same year, he was called back to the Bank from 1998 to 2002 to help establish the Anti-Corruption and Fraud Investigation Unit and was a lead investigator on a number of cases. Since 2002 he has provided assistance to the U.S. Senate Committee on Foreign Relations on legislation calling for reform of the multilateral development banks and Senate consideration of the United Nations Convention Against Corruption. He is currently finishing a manuscript on the World Bank that provides an inside look at the Bank's management, its lending operations, and the theft of billions of dollars from its lending portfolio. He lives in Leesburg, Virginia.

The English novelist Somerset Maugham famously described Monaco, the Mediterranean tax haven, as a "sunny place for shady people." In the mid-1980s, economist **John Christensen** returned to Jersey, a not-so-sunny place for shady people in the English Channel, to investigate how these offshore tax havens work. During the boom years of financial deregulation he worked as a trust and company administrator and as economic adviser to the island's government. Though committed to principles of fair trade and social justice, he became involved in a globalized offshore financial industry that facilitates capital flight, tax evasion, and money laundering. In 1998 he resigned from his post on Jersey, moved with his family to the UK, and became a founder member of a campaign to highlight how tax havens cause poverty. He currently directs the International Secretariat of the Tax Justice Network (www.taxjustice.net).

S.C. Gwynne is executive editor of *Texas Monthly*, having previously been a correspondent for *Time* magazine. After receiving a master's degree from Johns Hopkins University in 1977, he was awarded a teaching fellowship in the writing seminars program under novelist John Barth at Johns Hopkins. But his writing career bracketed a five-year career managing international loan portfolios in the Middle East, North Africa, and Asia, first for Cleveland Trust and later in the Hong Kong office of First Interstate Bank of California. In the 1980s, Gwynne left banking to become a freelance writer, contributing to a number of publications including *Harper's*, the *New York Times*, the *Los Angeles Times*, the *Washington Monthly*, and *California Magazine*. He wrote his first book, *Selling Money: A Young Banker's Account of the Rise and Extraordinary Fall of the Great International Lending Boom* in 1985. In 1991, Gwynne and fellow *Time* correspondent Jonathan Beatty won the Gerald Loeb Award for Distinguished Financial Reporting for their stories on the BCCI scandal for *Time* and the Jack Anderson Award as top investigative reporters of the year. Their subsequent book, *The Outlaw Bank: A Wild Ride into the Secret Heart of BCCI,* was named by *Business Week* magazine as one of the top ten books of the year.

James S. Henry is a leading investigative journalist, economist, and lawyer who has written extensively about economic issues, developing countries, corruption, and money laundering. His news-breaking stories have appeared in the *Wall Street Journal,* the *New York Times,* the *Washington Post, The Nation, Fortune, Jornal do Brasil, Slate,* and *El Financiero.* Henry's investigations yielded documentary evidence that was instrumental in the 1992 conviction of Panama's Manuel Noriega; the tracking of offshore assets stolen by Paraguayan dictator Alfredo Stroessner; identifying the role played by foreign loans to the Philippines Central Bank in the enrichment of Ferdinand Marcos; and documenting the role played by major U.S. banks in facilitating capital flight, money laundering, and tax evasion in developing countries. He is the author of several books, including *The Economics of Strategic Planning* (Lexington Books, 1986) and *The Blood Bankers* (Avalon, 2003), and a contributor to *Of Bonds and Bondage: A Reader on Philippines Foreign Debt,* edited by Emmanuel S. De Dios and Joel Rocamora (TNI, 1992). His new book, *Pirate Bankers,* is forthcoming from Avalon in 2007. He is the author of a leading study of tax compliance by the American Bar Association's Section of Taxation, and has testified several times before the U.S. Senate. Henry is currently managing director of the Sag Harbor Group, a strategy consulting firm. His newsblog, SubmergingMarkets (www.submergingmarkets.com), tracks developing countries and features contributing journalists from around the globe. He and his two children live in New York City and Sag Harbor, New York.

Steven Hiatt is a professional editor and writer—but also has a long history as an activist; he went on his first demonstration, for a city equal housing ordinance, in Des Moines in 1965. He went on to edit an underground newspaper, was active in the movement against the Vietnam War, and then became a community college teacher and teachers union organizer. After moving to California he worked for a number of years at Stanford Research Institute, a think tank and consultancy organization serving multinational corporations and government agencies and closely linked to Bechtel, Chevron, Bank of

America, and other players in the EHM world. There he edited a series of research reports circulated to Global Fortune 1000 companies advocating standard neoliberal nostrums such as public–private partnerships and offshoring. He left SRI in 1987 and has since produced and edited books for Verso, The New Press, and other publishers, working with authors such as Alexander Cockburn, Mike Davis, Lewis H. Lapham, Christian Parenti, and Rebecca Solnit. He is the co-editor, with Mike Davis, of *Fire in the Hearth: The Radical Politics of Place in America* (Verso, 1989). Hiatt lives in San Francisco and is currently president of Editcetera, a nonprofit Bay Area cooperative of publishing professionals.

Antonia Juhasz is a visiting scholar at the Washington, D.C.–based Institute for Policy Studies and author of *The Bush Agenda: Invading the World, One Economy at a Time* (ReganBooks/HarperCollins, 2006), which explores the Bush administration's use of the military to advance a corporate globalization agenda in Iraq and throughout the Middle East (www.TheBushAgenda.net). Juhasz previously served as the project director of the International Forum on Globalization and as a legislative assistant to Congressmen John Conyers Jr. and Elijah Cummings. An award-winning writer, Juhasz appears regularly in the Op-Ed pages of the *Los Angeles Times* as well as numerous other newspapers and publications. She is a contributing author to *Alternatives to Economic Globalization: A Better World Is Possible* (Berrett-Koehler, 2004). She lives in San Francisco.

Kathleen Kern has worked with Christian Peacemaker Teams since 1993. CPT "provides organizational support to persons committed to faith-based nonviolent alternatives in situations where lethal conflict is an immediate reality or is supported by public policy" (see www.cpt.org). However, teams in Haiti, Chiapas, and other locations have found that once the risk of lethal physical violence ends, the economic violence cemented in place by the corporatocracy can cause as much, if not more, suffering. Kern has served on assignments in Haiti, Palestine, Chiapas, South Dakota, Colombia, and the Democratic Republic of Congo. She was a member of a fact-finding delegation to the eastern regions of the Democratic Republic of Congo in autumn 2005, where she gathered information that appears in this book. Kern says that she may be unique among the contributors in that she has never taken an economics or business course, so she recently married someone with a degree in economics who could vet her articles.

Lucy Komisar is a New York–based journalist who traveled in the developing world in the 1980s and 1990s writing about movements to overthrow the despots who were running many of the countries she visited. When she talked to oppositionists in such places as the Philippines, Haiti, and Zaire, they invariably said this about their local dictator: "He's looted the country, stolen everything, and it's all in Swiss banks." The phrase was, as she discovered, shorthand for a parallel international financial system run by the world's largest banks using secret accounts and shell companies in offshore havens like the Cayman Islands and Jersey to hide and move the money of dictators, corrupt officials, drug and people traffickers, terrorists, business fraudsters, stock manipulators, and corporate and wealthy tax cheats—and that their political power kept Western governments from acting against the system. Beginning in 1997, she shifted her focus to reportage about offshore banking. Much of what she has published over the last ten years (see www.thekomisarscoop.com) has never been published elsewhere. Based on her investigations, she is writing a book to be called *Take the Money and Run Offshore.*

James Marriott, artist, ecological activist, and naturalist, has been a co-director of PLATFORM since 1983 (www.platformlondon.org). As part of PLATFORM he brings together individuals from a diversity of disciplines to create projects working for social and ecological justice. Since 1996 his work has focused on the oil and gas industry and its global impacts. He is the co-author, with Andy Rowell and Lorne Stockman, of *The Next Gulf: London, Washington and the Oil Conflict in Nigeria* (Constable, 2005). ·

Greg Muttitt is a researcher at PLATFORM, a London-based organization working on issues of environmental and social justice. He specializes in the impacts of multinational oil corporations of human rights, development, and the environment. Since 2003 he has monitored and worked to expose the hidden plans to open Iraq's oil reserves to Western corporations for the first time since 1972. Muttitt has also researched and campaigned on British Petroleum's Baku-Tbilisi-Ceyhan oil pipeline, including co-authoring the 2002 book *Some Common Concerns,* on Shell's Sakhalin II oil and gas project in Russia's Far East, and on a number of other oil industry activities around the world.

John Perkins currently writes and teaches about achieving peace and prosperity by expanding our personal awareness and transforming our institutions. He founded an alternative energy company that successfully changed the U.S.

utility industry. From 1971 to 1981, he worked for the international consulting firm of Chas. T. Main, where he held the titles of chief economist and manager of economics and regional planning—but in reality was an economic hit man. He continued to keep his EHM role under wraps until the events of September 11, 2001, convinced him to expose this shadowy and secret side of his life. The resulting book, *Confessions of an Economic Hit Man* (Berrett-Koehler, 2004), spent more than twenty-five weeks on the *New York Times* Bestseller List and has sold over 500,000 copies around the world.

Bruce Rich is a senior attorney at Environmental Defense in Washington, D.C. Enjoying improbable challenges, he is involved in research and advocacy to reform export credit agencies, an undertaking that he concedes makes tilting at windmills seem by comparison an undemanding occupation. (See www. eca-watch.org.) He the author of *Mortgaging the Earth* (Beacon Press, Boston, and Earthscan, London, 1994), an environmental exposé and history of the World Bank that was widely acclaimed in reviews ranging from the *New York Times* to *Le Monde Diplomatique*. He has worked as a consultant for numerous international organizations, has testified many times before the U.S. Congress concerning U.S. participation in international financial institutions, and has been awarded the United Nations Environment Program Global 500 Award for Environmental Achievement. His most recent book, *To Uphold the World: War Globalization and the Ethical Revolution of Ancient India's Greatest Emperor*, is being published by Penguin India in mid-2007.

Andrew Rowell is a freelance writer and investigative journalist who has been working for over a dozen years on political, environmental, and health issues. His work has appeared in front-page stories and others published in *The Guardian, The Independent*, the *Village Voice*, and *The Ecologist*. Rowell has also undertaken cutting-edge investigations working with Action on Smoking and Health, Earth Resources Research, Friends of the Earth, IFAW, Greenpeace, the Pan American Health Organization, Project Underground, Transport and Environmental Studies Group, the World Health Organization, World in Action, and the World Wildlife Fund. His book *Green Backlash: Global Subversion of the Environment Movement*, was published by Routledge in 1996. He is the coauthor, with James Marriott and Lorne Stockman, of *The Next Gulf: London, Washington and Oil Conflict in Nigeria* (Constable, 2005).

Acknowledgments

As a companion volume to John Perkins' *Confessions of an Economic Hit Man*, this book owes much to John Perkins for his helpful suggestions, his sage counsel, and—most important—his example in facing difficult truths about the not-so-benevolent global empire of the United States and its First World allies. I would like to thank Steve Piersanti at Berrett-Koehler for his many hours in helping architect this collection; he believed in this book and helped shepherd it along from start to finish. Jeevan Sivasubramaniam of BK was generous with time and help throughout this project, and the staff at Berrett-Koehler proved to be a supportive and talented team with whom it's been a pleasure to work.

My thanks go to Mark Engler, Ted Nace, Scott Steinberg, Chris Tilly, and Jenny Williams, who gave the chapters in this collection the benefit of insightful editorial critiques. Walden Bello, Doug Henwood, Jo Ellen Green Kaiser, Polly Parks, and Joel Rocamora provided crucial information and analysis. Peg Booth, Jan Coleman, Debbe Kennedy, and David Korten played important roles in helping spread the word about *Confessions of an Economic Hit Man*, and they've given generously of their time and talents to help this book as well. Thanks also to Zipporah Collins for her fine copyediting, Tom Hassett for his expert proofreading, and to Stewart Cauley for many assists with the graphics.

I have many intellectual debts to acknowledge: Bruce Clark and Joe Berry helped guide my development as a young activist, and have remained generous comrades over the years. Tariq Ali, Perry Anderson, Dave Alexander, Robin Blackburn, Mike Davis, Roxanne Dunbar-Ortiz, Max Elbaum, Mike Marqusee, Steve Hamilton, Rebecca Solnit, and Richard Walker have contributed enormously to my thinking on these topics. I would like to pay special tribute to Iris Marion Young (1949–2006); I hope that her example of clear thinking and commitment to social justice helps animate these pages.

My work on this book would not have been possible, in so many ways that I cannot count them, without the cogent advice and loving support of my wife, Deirdre Hiatt.

Steven Hiatt
San Francisco,
December 2006

Appendix
Resources of Hope

A Game As Old As Empire is a companion volume to John Perkins' Confessions of an Economic Hit Man (San Francisco: Berrett-Koehler, 2004), which should be your first stop on this list if by chance you've picked up this book without having previously read Confessions. This section lists key resources—books, articles (many available online), Web sites, and radio shows—that you can use to find out more about the issues covered in this book and to learn about new developments. Explore areas that interest you and let these resources of hope guide you to new ones—and to taking action yourself as part of the global web of resistance.

Global Empire and the Web of Control
Ali, Tariq. The Clash of Fundamentalisms: Crusades, Jihads and Modernity. London: Verso, 2002. See his Web site, www.tariqali.org/, for more information.

Bacevich, Andrew J. American Empire: The Realities and Consequences of U.S. Diplomacy. Cambridge, Mass.: Harvard University Press, 2002.

Bello, Walden. Dilemmas of Domination: The Unmaking of the American Empire. New York: Metropolitan, 2005. A volume in Metropolitan's valuable American Empire Project, www.americanempireproject,com/.

Bello, Walden, Shea Cunningham, and Bill Rau. Dark Victory: The United States, Structural Adjustment and Global Poverty, 2nd edn. London: TNI/Pluto Press, 1999.

Blum, William. Killing Hope: U.S. Military and CIA Interventions Since World War II— Updated Through 2003. Monroe, Maine: Common Courage, 2003.

Chang, Ha-Joon. Kicking Away the Ladder: How the Economic and Intellectual Histories of Capitalism Have Been Re-Written to Justify Neo-Liberal Capitalism. Cambridge: Cambridge University Press, 2002.

Chomsky, Noam. *Hegemony or Survival: America's Quest for Global Dominance.* New York: Metropolitan, 2003. Noam Chomsky's Web site is www.chomsky.info/.

Coll, Steve. *Ghost Wars: The Secret History of the CIA, Afghanistan, and Bin Laden, from the Soviet Invasion to September 10, 2001.* New York: Penguin, 2004.

Davis, Mike. *Planet of Slums.* London: Verso, 2006.

Dollars & Sense. *Real World Globalization*, 9th edn. Boston, Mass.: Dollars & Sense, 2007.

Faux, Jeff. *The Global Class War: How America's Bipartisan Elite Lost Our Future—and What It Will Take to Get It Back.* Hoboken, N.J.: John Wiley & Sons, 2006.

Fullbrook, Edward, ed. *A Guide to What's Wrong with Economics.* London: Anthem Press, 2004. Economics as if real-world results, rather than ideology, matter.

Galeano, Eduardo. *Open Veins of Latin America: Five Centuries of the Pillage of a Continent.* New York: Monthly Review, 1997.

Gowan, Peter. *The Global Gamble: Washington's Faustian Bid for World Domination.* London: Verso, 1999.

Grandin, Greg. *Empire's Workshop: Latin America, the United States, and the Rise of the New Imperialism.* New York: Metropolitan, 2006.

Green, Duncan. *Silent Revolution: The Rise and Crisis of Market Economics in Latin America*, 2nd edn. New York: Monthly Review, 2003.

Greider, William. *One World, Ready or Not: The Manic Logic of Global Capitalism.* New York: Simon & Schuster, 1998.

Hall, David, and Robin de la Motte. *Dogmatic Development: Privatisation and Conditionalities in Six Countries.* Greenwich, England: PSIRU/War on Want, 2004. Available at www.waronwant.org/Dogmatic+Development+7540.twl.

Harvey, David. *The New Imperialism.* New York: Oxford University Press, 2003.

Heller, Henry. *The Cold War and the New Imperialism.* New York: Monthly Review, 2006.

Henwood, Doug. *Wall Street: How It Works and for Whom.* London: Verso, 1999.

Hertz, Noreena. *The Silent Takeover: Global Capitalism and the Death of Democracy.* New York: HarperCollins, 2003.

Johnson, Chalmers. *The Sorrows of Empire: Militarism, Secrecy and the End of the Republic.* New York: Metropolitan, 2004.

Kinzer, Stephen. *All the Shah's Men: An American Coup and the Roots of Middle East Terror.* New York: John Wiley & Sons, 2004.

———. *Overthrow: America's Century of Regime Change from Hawaii to Iraq.* New York: Times Books, 2006.

Klare, Michael. *Blood and Oil: The Dangers and Consequences of America's Growing Dependency on Imported Petroleum.* New York: Metropolitan, 2004.

Layne, Christopher. *The Peace of Illusions: American Grand Strategy from 1940 to the Present.* New York: Cornell University Press, 2006.

Madeley, John. *Hungry for Trade: How the Poor Pay for Free Trade.* London: Zed, 2000.

Marable, Manning. *How Capitalism Underdeveloped Black America.* Boston: South End, 1999.

Schlesinger, Stephen, et al. *Bitter Fruit: The Story of the American Coup in Guatemala*, revised edn. Cambridge, Mass.: Harvard/Center for Latin American Studies, 2005.

Shiva, Vandana. *Water Wars: Privatization, Pollution, and Profit.* Boston: South End, 1999.

Sutcliffe, Bob. *100 Ways of Seeing an Unequal World.* London: Zed, 2001.

Wallach, Lori, and Patrick Woodall. *Whose Trade Organization? A Comprehensive Guide to the World Trade Organization*, 2nd edn. New York: New Press, 2002.

West, Cornel. *Democracy Matters: Winning the Fight Against Imperialism.* New York: Penguin, 2004.

Wood, Ellen Meiksins. *Empire of Capital.* London: Verso, 2003.

CorpWatch, www.corpwatch.org. Fights corporate-sponsored globalization through education, network building, and activism.

"Democracy Now!" Daily radio and news program available on over 500 Pacifica, NPR, and other public and community stations in the U.S., as well as on the Internet. Hosted by Amy Goodman and Juan González, "Democracy Now!" includes perspectives from independent journalists and ordinary people from around the world. Schedules and podcasts are available at www.democracynow.org/.

Dollars & Sense magazine, www.dollarsandsense.org. Provides news and analysis of economic justice issues.

Focus on the Global South, www.focusweb.com. A key resource for analysis and commentary on Global South development and trade issues.

International Forum on Globalization, www.ifg.org. Research and educational institution providing analyses of the cultural, social, political, and environmental impacts of globalization.

Mother Jones, www.motherjones.com/. Progressive bimonthly print and online magazine known for its investigative reporting.

New Internationalist, www.newint.org. Originally funded by Oxfam, publishes *New Internationalist* magazine for activists on global justice issues. Eight-time winner of the Independent Press Award for Best International Coverage.

New Economics Foundation, www.neweconomics.org. London-based think tank producing innovative analyses of and practical solutions to economic, environmental, and social issues.

Post-Autistic Economics Review, www.paecon.net/PAEReview/index.htm. Online journal of economics, founded in response to the dominance of mathematical modeling in mainstream economics to the exclusion of real-world economic behavior (which *PAE* refers to as "autistic economics"). Clearly written articles take on many topics relevant to the issues discussed in this book.

Public Sector International Research Unit (PSIRU, www.psiru.org/). PSIRU investigates the privatization of public services around the world. Its research reports assess the performance of these plans—for example, the water privatizations referred to in chapter 1.

The Nation, www.thenation.com. Weekly print/online publication; progressive news and commentary. A radio version, "RadioNation" hosted by Laura Flanders, is available on Air America Radio; www.lauraflanders.com/pages/radionation.html.

TomPaine.com; www. www.tompaine.com. Online public affairs journal of progressive analysis and commentary.

Transnational Institute, www.tni.org/index.htm. Research institute based in Amsterdam; founded in 1974 by scholar-activists to provide intellectual support to democratic and environmental movements. Makes available a wide variety of well-written reports on global issues.

World Development Movement, www.wdm.org.uk. Lobbies decision makers to change policies, and researches and promotes positive alternatives. Networks with people's movements in the developing world.

Dirty Money and Offshore Banking

Baker, Raymond. *Capitalism's Achilles Heel: Dirty Money and How to Renew the Free Market System*. New York: John Wiley & Sons, 2005.

Epstein, Gerald. *Capital Flight and Capital Controls in Developing Countries*. Northampton, Mass.: Edward Elgar, 2005.

Epstein, Gerald, ed. *Financialization and the World Economy*. Northampton, Mass.: Edward Elgar, 2006.

Hampton, Mark, and Jason Abbott. *Offshore Finance Centres and Tax Havens: The Rise of Global Capital*. London: Macmillan, 1999.

Kochan, Nick. *The Washing Machine: How Money Laundering and Terrorist Financing Soils Us*. Mason, Ohio: Thomson, 2005.

Mitchell, Austin, and Prem Sikka. *Taming the Corporations*. Basildon, England: Association for Accountancy and Business Affairs, 2005. Available as a free download from http://visar.csustan.edu/aaba/publications.html.

Murphy, Richard, John Christensen, and Jenny Kimmis, *Tax Us if You Can*. London: Tax Justice Network, 2005. Available as a free download from www.taxjustice.net/cms/front_content.php?idcat=30.

Sikka, Prem, et al., *No Accounting for Tax Havens*. Basildon, England: Association for Accountancy and Business Affairs, 2002. Available as a free download from http://visar.csustan.edu/aaba/publications.html.

Association for Accountancy & Business Affairs, http://aabaglobal.org. Publishes *Accountancy Business and the Public Interest*, a peer-reviewed free journal. See http://visar.csustan.edu/aaba/aabajournalpage.html.

Bretton Woods Project. Established by British NGOs in 1995, BWP serves as a networker, information-provider, and watchdog to scrutinize and influence the World Bank and International Monetary Fund. Its newsletter, *Bretton Woods Update,* is available at www.brettonwoodsproject.org/update/index.shtml.

Offshore Watch. Web site for researchers into corruption and offshore affairs: http://visar.csustan.edu/aaba/jerseypage.html.

Tax Justice Network, www.taxjustice.net/cms/front_content.php?idcat=2www.taxjustice.net. Publishes the online journal *Tax Justice Focus*: to subscribe, contact info@taxjustice.net. You can also browse TJN's informative blog on tax justice issues at http://taxjustice.blogspot.com/.

Tax Research UK, www.taxresearch.org.uk/Blog/. Richard Murphy covers tax evasion and corporate accountability issues, as well as possible measures to counter the baneful effects of the offshore network.

Bank of Credit and Commerce International

Adams, James Ring, and Douglas Frantz. *A Full Service Bank: How BCCI Stole Billions Around the World*. New York: Simon & Schuster, 1992.

Beaty, Jonathan, and S.C. Gwynne. *The Outlaw Bank: A Wild Ride into the Secret Heart of BCCI*. New York: Random House, 1993.

Briody, Dan. *The Iron Triangle: Inside the Secret World of the Carlyle Group*. New York: John Wiley & Sons, 2003.

Cockburn, Alexander, and Jeffrey St. Clair. *Whiteout: The CIA, Drugs and the Press*. London: Verso 1999.

McCoy, Alfred W. *The Politics of Heroin: CIA Complicity in the Global Drug Trade*. Brooklyn, N.Y.: Lawrence Hill, 1991.

Potts, Mark, Nicholas Kochan, and Robert Whittington. *Dirty Money: The Inside Story of the World's Sleaziest Bank*. Washington, D.C.: National Press Books, 1992.

Scott, Peter Dale. *Drugs, Oil, and War: The United States in Afghanistan, Colombia, and Indochina*. Lanham, Md.: Rowman & Littlefield, 2003.

Truell, Peter, and Larry Gurwin. *False Profits: The Inside Story of BCCI, the World's Most Corrupt Financial Empire*. New York: Houghton Mifflin, 1992.

Unger, Craig. *House of Bush, House of Saud: The Secret Relationship Between the World's Two Most Powerful Dynasties*. New York: Scribner, 2004.

Kerry committee full report: www.fas.org/irp/congress/1992_rpt/bcci/.

Investigative journalism by Lucy Komisar: The Komisar Scoop: www.thekomisarscoop.com/.

Congo: Coltan, Civil Strife, and Human Rights

Drohan, Madeleine. *Making a Killing: How and Why Corporations Use Armed Force to Do Business*. Guilford, Conn.: Lyon's Press, 2004.

Feeney, Patricia, ed. *Five Years On: A Review of the OECD Guidelines and National Contact Points*. Amsterdam: OECD Watch, 2005. Available at www.oecdwatch.org/.

Human Rights Watch, "The Curse of Gold: IX. International Initiatives to Address Resource Exploitation in the DRC." New York: Human Rights Watch, 2005. Available at http://hrw.org/reports/2005/drc0505/12.htm#_Toc102992181.

Montague, Dena. "Stolen Goods: Coltan and Conflict in the Democratic Republic of the Congo." *SAIS Review* 22, no. 1 (Winter-Spring 2002).

Montague, Dena, and Frida Berrigan. "The Business of War in the Democratic Republic of Congo." *Dollars and Sense* (July/August 2001).

Onana, Charles. *Les Secrets du génocide rwandais: Enquête sur les mystères d'un président* (The Secrets of the Rwandan Genocide). Paris: Duboiris, 2002.

Tegera, Aloys, Mikolo Sofia, and Dominic Johnson. "The Coltan Phenomenon: How a Rare Mineral Has Changed the Life of the Population of War-Torn North Kivu Province in the East of the Democratic Republic of Congo." Goma, Congo:

Pole Institute, January 2002. Available at www.pole-institute.org/documents/coltanglais02.pdf.

United Nations. "Report of the Panel of Experts on the Illegal Exploitation of Natural Resources and Other Forms of Wealth of the Democratic Republic of Congo," 2001. Available at www.un.org/Docs/sc/letters/2001/357e.pdf.

Nigeria, Oil Reserves, and Mercenaries

Avant, Deborah. *The Market for Force: The Consequences of Privatizing Security.* Cambridge: Cambridge University Press, 2005.

Lang, Karen. *Corporate Warriors: The Rise of the Privatized Military Industry.* Ithaca, N.Y.: Cornell University Press, 2004.

Maier, Karl. *This House Has Fallen: Midnight in Nigeria.* New York: PublicAffairs, 2000.

Okonta, Ike, and Oronto Douglas. *Where Vultures Feast: Shell, Human Rights, and Oil in the Niger Delta.* San Francisco: Sierra Club, 2001.

Rowell, Andy, James Marriott, and Lorne Stockman. *The Next Gulf: London, Washington and Oil Conflict in Nigeria.* London: Constable, 2005.

Saro-Wiwa, Ken. *A Month and a Day & Letters.* Banbury, England: Ayebia, 2005; www.ayebia.co.uk.

OilChange International: http://priceofoil.org/. Up-to-date Web site on the economic, social, and environmental costs of oil.

PLATFORM: www.platformlondon.org/carbonweb/. Information on oil-related and other resources issues, especially the exploitation of oil reserves and related environmental and economic issues in the Global South.

Remember Saro-Wiwa Web site: www.remembersarowiwa.com/. More information on the Remember Ken Saro-Wiwa coalition and issues that he championed.

SpinWatch. www.spinwatch.org. UK watchdog organization that monitors the PR industry and provides information on corporate manipulation of information.

Stakeholder Democracy Network: www.stakeholderdemocracy.org/main. Information on the oil industry in the Delta: works with communities in Nigeria and the Gulf of Guinea region who live alongside oil, gas, and mining facilities.

Iraq, PSAs, and the Occupation

Aburish, Saïd. *A Brutal Friendship: The West and the Arab Elite.* New York: St. Martin's Press, 2001.

Ali, Tariq. "Re-Colonizing Iraq," *New Left Review* 21 (May–June 2003); available at http://newleftreview.org/A2447.

Alnasrawi, Abbas. *Iraq's Burdens: Oil, Sanctions, and Underdevelopment.* Westport, Conn.: Greenwood Press, 2002.

Arnove, Anthony. *Iraq: The Logic of Withdrawal.* New York: New Press, 2006.

Chomsky, Noam, and Gilbert Achcar. *Perilous Power: The Middle East & U.S. Foreign Policy: Dialogues on Terror, Democracy, War, and Justice.* Boulder, Colo.: Paradigm, 2006.

Cockburn, Patrick. *The Occupation: War and Resistance in Iraq.* London: Verso, 2006.

Fisk, Robert. *The Great War for Civilisation: The Conquest of the Middle East.* New York: Knopf, 2005.

Muttitt, Greg. *Crude Designs: The Rip-off of Iraq's Oil Wealth.* London: PLATFORM, 2005. Available at www.globalpolicy.org/security/oil/2005/crudedesigns.htm.

Parenti, Christian. *The Freedom: Shadows and Hallucinations in Occupied Iraq.* New York: New Press, 2004.

Phillips, Kevin. *American Theocracy: The Peril and Politics of Radical Religion, Oil, and Borrowed Money in the 21st Century.* New York: Viking, 2006.

Rutledge, Ian. *Addicted to Oil: America's Relentless Drive for Energy Security.* London: I. B. Tauris, 2005.

Simmons, Matthew. *Twilight in the Desert: The Coming Saudi Oil Shock and the World Economy.* New York: John Wiley & Sons, 2005.

Yergin, Daniel. *The Prize: The Epic Quest for Oil, Money, and Power.* New York: Free Press, 1993.

General Union of Oil Employees: www.basraoilunion.org.

Iraq Occuaption Focus, www.iraqoccupationfocus.org.uk/. Hub for news and analysis of the occupation of Iraq; publishes a free e-newsletter.

The World Bank and Corruption

Caufield, Catherine. *Masters of Illusion: The World Bank and the Poverty of Nations.* New York: Holt, 1996.

Fox, Jonathan A., and L. David Brown, eds. *The Struggle for Accountability: The World Bank, NGOs, and Grassroots Movements.* Cambridge, Mass., MIT Press, 1998.

George, Susan, and Fabrizio Sabelli. *Faith and Credit: The World Bank's Secular Empire.* Boulder, Colo.: Westview, 1994.

Pincus, Jonathan R., and Jeffrey A. Winters. *Reinventing the World Bank.* Ithaca, N.Y.: Cornell University Press, 2002.

Stiglitz, Joseph E. *Globalization and Its Discontents.* New York: Norton, 2003.

Asian Development Bank/OECD Anti-Corruption Initiative for Asia-Pacific. Issues a quarterly newsletter with information on developments and upcoming events in the region's fight against corruption: www.oecd.org/corruption/asiapacific.

Ethics World. Provides news and developments in the fields of business ethics, governance and corruption: www.ethicsworld.org.

No Bribes. Newsletter published by the Anti-Corruption Gateway for Europe and Eurasia. Links to major information sources for anticorruption campaigners and analysts working in Eastern Europe and countries of the former Soviet Union: www.nobribes.org.

Transparency and Accountability. Quarterly newsletter focusing on anticorruption activities in Latin America. Sponsored by the USAID/Accountability and Anti-Corruption Project: www.respondanet.com.

World Bank Institute. Puts out newsletters on its governance and anticorruption activities: www.worldbank.org/wbi/governance.

The Philippines and World Bank Development Strategy

Bello, Walden, David Kinley, and Elaine Elinson. *Development Debacle: The World Bank in the Philippines*. San Francisco: Institute for Food and Development Policy, 1982. This book gives a detailed picture of the economic, social, environmental, and political devastation brought upon the Philippines by World Bank policies and loans from the late 1960s to 1982.

Bello, Walden, and Shalmali Guttal. "Programmed to Fail: The World Bank Clings to a Bankrupt Development Model." *Multinational Monitor* 26 (July 2005).

Bello, Walden, Mary Lou Malig, Marissa de Guzman, and Herbert Docena. *The Anti-Development State: The Political Economy of Permanent Crisis in the Philippines*. London: Zed, 2006.

Danaher, Kevin. *10 Reasons to Abolish the IMF and World Bank*, 2nd edn. New York: Seven Stories, 2004.

Danaher, Kevin, ed. *Fifty Years Is Enough: The Case Against the World Bank and the International Monetary Fund*. Boston: South End, 1994.

Henwood, Doug. *After the New Economy*. New York: New Press, 2003.

Peet, Richard. *Unholy Trinity: The IMF, World Bank and WTO*. London: Zed, 2003.

Woods, Nqaire. *The Globalizers: The IMF, the World Bank, and Their Borrowers*. Ithaca, N.Y.: Cornell University Press, 2006.

Action for Economic Reforms. Founded in 1996, AER is an independent public interest organization that conducts policy analysis and advocacy on key economic issues. Documents are available on AER's Web site, www.aer.ph.

Akbayan Citizen Action Party. Akbayan was launched in 1998 as a progressive political party built on social movements and programs, not personalities. Akbayan has three members in the Philippine Congress and now has roots in most provinces. Its goal is for government to enact redistributive reforms, deliver more basic services, and craft safety nets. See www.akbayan.org .

Focus on the Global South. Nongovernmental organization established in 1995 with staff in Thailand, the Philippines, and India. Focus combines policy research, advocacy, and grassroots capacity building to generate critical analysis and encourage debates on national and international policies related to corporate-led globalization and neoliberalism. Papers and news available online: www.focusweb.org .

Left Business Observer. Doug Henwood's newsletter addresses the world's financial markets, income distribution and poverty in the U.S. and elsewhere, the globalization of finance and production, Third World debt and development, the World Bank, and the IMF. Henwood also has a radio show on WBAI in New York City. See LBO's Web site: www.leftbusinessobserver.com.

Philippine Center for Investigative Journalism. PCIJ is an independent, nonprofit media agency that specializes in investigative reporting on current issues in Philippine society. Its articles are lively and poignant: www.pcij.org.

Co-op America. To find out where to get sweatshop-free clothing, household, and office goods, fair-trade coffee, chocolate, and more, join Co-op America to get its National Green Pages: www.coopamerica.org, or call 800-58-GREEN.

Export Credit Agencies

The Jakarta Declaration. A call of 347 NGOs from 47 countries to reform the abusive lending of export credit agencies: available at www.eca-watch.org/goals/jakartadec.html. A variety of other articles and correspondence concerning ECAs are archived on the Environmental Defense Web site: see www.environmentaldefense.org/documents/2495_ECAArticles.htm.

Bosshard, Peter, et al. "A Trojan Horse for Large Dams: How Export Credit Agencies Are Offering New Subsidies for Destructive Projects under the Guise of Environmental Protection." Paris: ECA Watch, 2005. Available at www.eca-watch.org/problems/fora/oecd/ECAW_reportondams_2sept05.pdf.
Goldzimer, Aaron. "Worse Than the World Bank?: Export Credit Agencies—the Secret Engine of Globalization." Oakland, Calif.: Institute for Food & Development Policy, 2003. See www.foodfirst.org/pubs/backgrdrs/2003/w03v9n1.html.
————. "Globalization's Most Perverse Secret: The Role of Export Credit and Investment Insurance Agencies." Paper presented at the conference "After Neoliberalism: Economic Policies That Work for the Poor," Washington, D.C., May 2002. Available at www.environmentaldefense.org/documents/2487_Globalizations_Secret.pdf.
Rich, Bruce, Korinna Horta, and Aaron Goldzimer. "Africa: Indebtedness for Extractive Industries, Corruption and Conflict." Washington, D.C.: Environmental Defense, 2000; www.environmentaldefense.org/documents/638_ACF666.pdf.
World Resources Institute in Washington has published several informative pieces on ECAs. See http://google.wri.org/search?site=WRI_Website&output=xml_no_dtd&client=WRI_Website&proxystylesheet=WRI_Website&q=export+credit+agencies&imageField.x=18&imageField.y=8.

Corner House. The Corner House has published several comprehensive background reports on ECAs, particularly examining corruption. See www.thecornerhouse.org.uk/subject/aid/.

ECA Watch. The umbrella network for the international campaign to reform export credit agencies. Site contains links to all the major ECAs; to the main groups campaigning against ECAs; to major campaigns identified by region, country, and project; numerous articles and references; and updates on current developments. By far the best single reference: www.eca-watch.org.

Environmental Defense International Program. Conducts research and advocacy to promote reforms in ECAs: www.environmentaldefense.org/programs.cfm.

Pacific Environment. Works to promote environmentally responsible finance in Russia. See www.pacificenvironment.org/article.php?list.

International Rivers Network. The California-based organization has conducted extensive research concerning ECA-financed dam projects. See www.irn.org/.

Probe International. Exposes the environmental, social, and economic effects of Canada's aid and trade abroad, including Canada's Export Development Corporation: www.probeinternational.org/pi/index.cfm?DSP=home.

Debt and Debt Relief

Adams, Patricia. *Odious Debts: Loose Lending, Corruption, and the Third World's Environmental Legacy.* Toronto: Energy Probe Research, 1991.

George, Susan. *The Debt Boomerang: How Third World Debt Harms Us All.* London: Pluto/TNI, 1992.

Gwynne, S.C. *Selling Money.* New York: Weidenfeld and Nicolson, 1986.

Henry, James S. *Banqueros y Lavadolores.* Bogota: Tercer Mundo Editores, 1996.

―――. *The Blood Bankers: Tales from the Global Underground Economy.* New York: Avalon/Four Walls Eight Windows, 2003, 2005.

―――. *Pirate Bankers.* New York: Avalon, 2007.

Hertz, Noreena. *The Debt Threat: How Debt Is Destroying the Developing World.* New York: HarperCollins, 2005.

Mandel, Steve. "Odious Lending: Debt Relief as if Morals Mattered." London: New Economics Foundation, 2006. Available at www.neweconomics.org/gen/uploads/v3gdvw45bflbyn55gy1fwr4514092006174700.pdf.

Odious Debts Web site. Covers debt relief issues from the standpoint of corruption and the legal precedent that illegitimate debts should be cancelled: www.odious-debts.org/odiousdebts/index.cfm?DSP=subcontent&AreaID=1.

JubileeSouth: www.jubileesouth.org.

Jubilee USA Network. Jubilee is an alliance of 75 faith communities, environmental, labor, human rights, and community groups. Through Jubilee you can pressure governments, contact World Bank board members before their annual meeting, take part in Advocacy Days, and connect with others in your area. See www.jubileeusa.org; 202-783-3566.

SubmergingMarkets.com: www.submergingmarkets.com. Tracks the global crisis of development and debt; includes reportage and commentary by James S. Henry and other investigators.

The Web of Resistance

Ali, Tariq. *Pirates of the Caribbean: Axis of Hope.* London: Verso, 2006.

Alperovitz, Gar. *America Beyond Capitalism: Reclaiming Our Wealth, Our Liberty, and Our Democracy.* New York: John Wiley & Sons, 2004.

Balanyá, Belén, Brid Brennan, Olivier Hoedeman, Satoko Kishimoto and Philipp Terhorst. *Reclaiming Public Water: Achievements, Struggles and Visions from Around the World,* 2nd edn. Amsterdam: Transnational Institute and Corporate Europe Observatory, March 2005.

Bello, Walden. *Deglobalization: Ideas for a New World Economy.* London: Zed, 2004.

Black, Maggie. *The No-Nonsense Guide to International Development.* London: Verso/New Internationalist, 2004.

Brecher, Jeremy, and Tim Costello. *Global Village or Global Pillage: Economic Reconstruction from the Bottom Up.* Boston: South End, 1998.

Chang, Ha-Joon, and Ilene Grabel, *Reclaiming Development: An Alternative Economic Policy Manual.* London: Zed, 2004.

Engler, Mark. "A Movement Looks Forward." *Foreign Policy in Focus*, May 19, 2005. For additional work by Mark Engler, see his Democracy Uprising Web site, www.democracyuprising.com/.

Folbre, Nancy. *The Invisible Heart: Economics and Family Values.* New York: New Press, 2001.

George, Susan. *Another World Is Possible If ...* London: Verso, 2004.

Henderson, Hazel. *Beyond Globalization: Shaping a Sustainable Global Economy.* Bloomfield, Conn.: Kumarian Press, 1999.

——. *Ethical Markets: Growing the Green Economy.* White River Junction, Vt.: Chelsea Green, 2007. See her Web site, www.hazelhenderson.com/, for more about her work.

Juhasz, Antonia. *The Bush Agenda: Invading the World, One Economy at a Time.* New York: ReganBooks/HarperCollins, 2006; see also her Web site, www.TheBushAgenda.net.

Keet, Dot. *South-South Strategic Alternatives to the Global Economic System and Power Regime.* Amsterdam: Transnational Institute, October 2006; available at www.tni.org/pubs/index.htm.

Korten, David. *The Post-Corporate World: Life after Capitalism.* San Francisco: Berrett-Koehler, 1999.

——. *The Great Turning: From Empire to Earth Community.* San Francisco: Berrett-Koehler, 2006.

Lappé, Frances Moore. *Democracy's Edge: Choosing to Save Our Country by Bringing Democracy to Life.* San Francisco: Jossey-Bass, 2006. See also the Small Planet Institute Web site, www.smallplanetinstitute.org/.

Leite, Jose Correa. *The World Social Forum: Strategies of Resistance.* Chicago: Haymarket Books, 2005.

MacEwan, Arthur. *Neo-Liberalism or Democracy? Economic Strategy, Markets, and Alternatives for the 21st Century.* London: Zed, 2000.

Mander, Jerry, and Debi Baker, eds. Antonia Juhasz, principal researcher and project coordinator. "Does Globalization Help the Poor?" special report, International Forum on Globalization, *IFG Bulletin* 1, no. 3 (August 2001).

Mander, Jerry, and John Cavanagh, eds. Antonia Juhasz, contributing author, *Alternatives to Economic Globalization: A Better World Is Possible,* 2nd edn. San Francisco: Berrett-Koehler, 2004.

Prashad, Vijay, and Teo Ballvé, eds. *Dispatches from Latin America: On the Frontlines against Neoliberalism.* Boston: South End, 2006.

Ransom, David. *The No-Nonsense Guide to Fair Trade.* London: Verso/New Internationalist, 2004. A quick guide to the fair-trade/free-trade debate.

Santos, Boaventura de Sousa. *The Rise of the Global Left: The World Social Forum and Beyond.* London: Zed, 2006.

Saul, John. *The Next Liberation Struggle: Capitalism, Socialism, and Democracy in Southern Africa.* New York: Monthly Review Press, 2005.

Schweickart, David. *After Capitalism.* Lanham, Md.: Rowman & Littlefield, 2002. See also the Solidarity Economy Web site, www.solidarityeconomy.net/; a short account these ideas is available at http://homepages.luc.edu/~dschwei/economicdemocracy.htm.

Sen, Amartya. *Development as Freedom*. New York: Anchor, 2000.

Shiva, Vandana. *Earth Democracy: Justice, Sustainability, and Peace*. Boston: South End, 2005.

Solnit, David, ed., *Globalize Liberation: How to Uproot the System and Build a Better World*. San Francisco: City Lights, 2004.

Solnit, Rebecca. *Hope in the Dark: Untold Histories, Wild Possibilities*. New York: Nation Books, 2004.

Tabb, William K. *The Amoral Elephant: Globalization and the Struggle for Social Justice in the Twenty-First Century*. New York: Monthly Review Press, 2001.

Wallach, Lori, and Deborah James. "Why the WTO Round Talks Have Collapsed," *Common Dreams*, April 14, 2006. See also the Public Citizen project Global Trade Watch, www.citizen.org/trade/, which Lori Wallach heads.

Food First/Institute for Food and Development Policy. Develops analysis and campaigns to address the root causes of hunger, poverty, and ecological degradation in partnership with other movements for social change: www.foodfirst.org/.

Global Exchange. Membership-based international human rights organization promoting social, economic and environmental justice. Projects range from Reality Tours to Fair Trade stores and CodePink: www.globalexchange.org/index.html.

Halifax Initiative. Canadian coalition of development, environment, faith-based, human rights, and labor groups working to transform the World Bank, IMF, and export credit agencies: www.halifaxinitiative.org/.

Positive Futures Network. PFN is an independent, nonprofit organization supporting people's active engagement in creating a just, sustainable, and compassionate world. Best known for its publication *YES! A Journal of Positive Futures*, which spotlights innovative grassroots work in communities around the world: www.yes magazine.org.

Public Citizen. National, nonprofit research and advocacy organization: www. citizen.org/about/.

Third World Network. International network of organizations and individuals involved in issues relating to development, the Third World, and North-South issues. Clearinghouse for a wide variety of books, research papers, and news: www. twnside.org.sg/twnintro.htm.

War Times/Tiempo de Guerras. Web publication serving the U.S. antiwar movement: www.war-times.org/.

Znet. Web site associated with *Z Magazine*; hub of information on a wide variety of issues: www.zmag.org/intro_to_znet.htm.

Index

Abacha, Sani 44, 125
Abedi, Agha Hasan 69, 70, 75, 77, 86, 87
Abu Dhabi 69, 73, 75, 76
Adham, Kamal 75, 86, 87, 88
Afghanistan 26; drug trade in 70; civil war
  in 70–71
African Development Bank 251
Africa Oil Policy Initiative Group 119
Akbayan 192–93
Alamieyeseigha, Diepreye 121, 123
Algeria 15, 200, 266
Allende, Salvador 27
al-Qaeda 77, 89; and offshore banks 24
al-Taqwa Bank 71, 89
Altman, Robert A. 78, 79, 86, 88
American Express Co. 268
American Mineral Fields 99
Amin, Idi 27
Annan, Kofi 126
AngloGold 244
Anglo-Iranian Oil Company 14
Angola 27, 95; foreign debt 243, 244
Aquino, Benigno 26
Aquino, Corazon 190
Arbusto Energy, Inc. 76
Argentina 236; defiance of IMF 273; foreign

debt 228, 230, 233, 241, 244, 273; popular
  movements in 276; World Bank lending
  in 169–73
Asari, Alhaji 121, 123, 128–29
Asian "tiger" economies 21, 229, 257n16,
  258n27
Azerbaijan 200

Bahamas, as offshore banking haven
  45, 89
Baker, Howard 100
Baker, James 239, 256n12
Baker Plan 228, 239–40
Balfour Beatty 211
Banca del Gottardo 71
Banca Nazionale del Lavoro 72
Banco Ambrosiano 71
Bank of America 69–70, 74, 77
Bank of England 84
Bank of Credit and Commerce Interna-
  tional 24; accountants and 83–84, 86;
  arms trade and 72–73, 90; CIA and 69, 70,
  71–72, 73, 76; drug trade and 70, 80, 87,
  90; indictments 86–88; Iran-Contra 72;
  money laundering 69, 79–81, 90; opera-
  tions 73–75, 86; owners 69–70, 75, 76; as

Ponzi scheme 75; terrorism and 70, 72, 73, 88–90; U.S. operations 77–79
Bank of New York–Inter-Maritime Bank 83, 88–89
Barrick Gold Corp. 99, 244
Bath, James R. 76
Bechtel Corp. 3, 99, 138, 278
Belgium 101, 104
Bello, Walden 186–87, 273
Ben Barka, Medhi 26
Benin, foreign debt of 249
Berlusconi, Silvio 54
Bernabe, Riza 191
"big-box" stores, campaigns against 278
bin Faisal al-Saud, Prince Turki 75, 78
bin Laden family enterprises 71–72, 89
bin Laden, Haydar Mohamed 89
bin Laden, Osama 26, 77, 88, 89, 42; and BCCI 71
Binladen, Yeslam 89
bin Mahfouz, Khalid 76, 77, 78, 86, 87, 88, 89
bin Sultan al-Nahyan, Sheikh Zayed 69, 75
Blair, Tony 219, 250
Blandón, José 80
Blum, Jack 79–81, 85–86
Bolivia 236, 273; foreign debt 230, 246, 247, 249; gas industry 154, 208; water privatization in 277
Boro, Isaac 122
Brady, Nicholas 80, 256n12
Brady Plan 221, 227, 228, 240–41, 259n35
Brazil 18, 27, 130, 208, 216, 236; foreign debt 227, 228, 230, 241, 244
Bretton Woods agreements 63
Bretton Woods institutions *see* World Bank, International Monetary Fund
British Gas 139
British Petroleum 139, 144, 153
British Virgin Islands, as offshore banking haven 54
Brown & Root 99
Brown, Gordon 126, 127, 219, 250
Burkina Faso, foreign debt of 246, 249
Burundi 95, 247, 249
Bush, George H.W., and administration 27–28, 69, 72, 77, 80, 87, 88, 91n10, 100, 138, 206, 271, 272
Bush, George W., and administration 66, 271, 278; and Iraq War 13, 28
Bush Agenda, The (Juhasz) 4, 275

Cabot Corporation 104, 112n32
Cameroon, foreign debt of 249
Canada 99, 101, 201, 268, 271
Canadian Export Development Corp. 201, 202, 203, 204, 206
capital flight 24, 43–44, 231–36, 253, 258n27
Carter, Jimmy 76, 140
Casey, William 70, 82, 90
Cavallo, Domingo Felipe 238
Cayman Islands, as offshore banking haven 65, 72, 73, 74, 75, 86
Center for Global Energy Studies 145
Center for Strategic and International Studies 119, 120
Central African Republic 231
Central Intelligence Agency 3, 5, 15; Afghan rebels and 70–71; BCCI and 69, 70, 71–72, 73, 76, 78, 79–82, 85; Saudi intelligence services and 75
Chad, foreign debt of 249
Chavez, Hugo 3, 25, 273
Cheney, Dick 28, 133
Chevron Oil 135, 138, 139, 144, 153; in Nigeria 123–24
Chile 236; 1973 coup in 27
China 4, 229, 236; foreign debt 222–23; Third World resources and 5, 117–18, 120–21, 124, 126–27, 130
Chomsky, Noam
    Hegemony or Survival 4
Christian Peacemaker Team 96, 106–8
Citibank, Citigroup 75, 100, 130, 138, 226, 238, 268
Clifford, Clark 78–79, 85, 86, 88
Clinton, Bill, and administration 119, 120, 126, 212, 271
Coalition of Immokalee Workers 272, 280
COFACE 201, 205, 212
Cogecom 100
cold war 4; and decolonization 16–17
Colombia, human rights in 107
colonialism, decline of formal 13–14
coltan: efforts to control 5, 26, 95; shortages of 95; uses for 94
Commission for Africa 251
Communism: appeal of 14; fall of 4, 13, 27, 137–38, 238
Confessions of an Economic Hit Man (Perkins) 1–4, 6, 17
Congo, Democratic Republic of (Zaire): civil war in 26, 94–96, 108n3; corruption in 24, 254; foreign debt 220, 230, 247, 249; human rights in 107–8; rape as a weapon

of war in 93, 96–98; Western role in 98–105, 109n4, 111n29; World Bank and 158
Congo Republic 230, 247, 249
cooperatives 276–77
corporations, as legal persons 277
CorpWatch 278
corruption: culture of 51–54; IMF/World Bank and 24–25, 157–74; offshore banking and 44–45, 52–; power and 24; privatization and 24–25, 256n12
COSEC 209–10
Council on Foreign Relations 119–20

dam projects, 209–12
Dar al-Mal al-Islami 89
Daukoru, Edmund 125–27, 128
Davos see World Economic Forum
DeBeers Group 101, 103
decolonization 13, 16–17
debt/flight cycle 231–36, 253, 258n27
debt relief, campaigns for 246, 252–55, 268; in U.S. 235
debt, Third World 32, 35; amount of relief 224–29; banks and 226–27, 229, 232–34; business loans 35–37, 227; cold war strategy and 17; corruption and 230, 231, 232, 253, 254, 257n23; 1982 crisis 39, 55; disunity among debtor nations 237–39; dubious debts and 230, 235, 247, 253, 257n23, 261n68; growth of 18–19, 181, 229–36; as means of control 17, 23, 183–84; payments on 19, 190–91, 223, 228, 231, 247–48, 275; relief plans 220–22, 225–29, 239–52, 274; size of 221–24, 259n37, 260n46; social/economic impacts of 190–91, 231–36, 247–48
democracy: debt crisis and 236; economic reform and 276–79; global justice and 279–81; in Iraq 151–54
Deutsche Bank 226
drug trade 70, 80, 87
Dubai 73
Dulles, Alan 15

Eagle Wings Resources International 104
East Timor 205
economic development strategies: "big projects" and 16–17; debt-led 18–19; state-led 16–17, 19
economic forecasting 3
economic hit men 5; definition 1, 3, 18; John Perkins and 1–4, 17; types of 5, 18
Ecuador 236, 266; foreign debt 244

Egypt 14; Suez Crisis 15–16
Eisenhower, Dwight, and administration 15
elites, wealthy 4, 18, 57, 176, 183, 228, 232, 253; use of tax havens 43–44, 54–56, 65–66, 226, 232–34
El Salvador 26
empire see imperialism
Eni SpA 144, 153
Enron 53, 54, 208–9
Ethiopia 230, 249
European Union 51; agricultural subsidies 22
environment degradation: development projects and 199, 200–211, 257n23; oil production and 115–16
export credit agencies: arms exports and 204–5; campaigns against 209–16; corruption and 200, 202–3, 205, 207–8; debt and 200; environmental effects 199, 200–211; nuclear power and 202, 205–6; operation of 197–201; secrecy of 205, 210–12; size of 201; World Bank and 199, 201, 202, 204
Export Credit Group 210, 215
Export Credits Guarantee Department 201, 205, 211
Export Finance and Investment Corp. 203, 204
export processing zones 178
Export Risk Guarantee 203, 211, 213
ExxonMobil 144

fair trade movement 280
Faisal, Mohammad al- 89
Faux, Jeff
    Global Class War, The 4
Federal Bureau of Investigation 71
Federal Reserve Bank of New York 87
Federal Reserve System 78, 82, 88
Ferguson, Niall 13
First American Bankshares 78, 79, 82, 83, 85, 88
First Quantum Materials 101
First, Ruth 26
Focus on the Global South 187, 273
foreign aid 19; in Congo civil war 99–100
France 236, 244; empire 13; Suez Crisis and 15
free trade 4, 19, 21–23, 268, 271; British development and 21; U.S. development and 21
Free Trade Area of the Americas 271
Friends of the Earth 104, 269

G8 summits 212, 213, 219–20, 221, 246, 250, 271, 275
Gambia 243, 249
García, Alan 74
Gates, Robert 85
Gécamines 100, 104
General Agreement on Tariffs and Trade; agricultural trade 186–87; establishment of 267; TRIPS 23; Uruguay Round 23, 267
General Union of Oil Employees 135–36, 141–44
Georgia 207
Germany 212, 213, 216, 236; export credit agency 201, 202, 203, 205, 206, 207, 209–11, 212, 215–16; Green Party 206, 215
Ghana 16; development projects in 16, 207; foreign debt 230, 247, 249; impact of IMF SAP 5, 22
Giuliani, Carlo 271
Global Awareness Collective 278
Global Class War, The (Faux) 4
Global Exchange 278
globalization 3; alternatives to corporate 275–79; economic 176–79, 230, 236; impacts of 185–90, 234, 236, 263–65; of the financial system 55, 63–66
Globalization and Its Discontents (Stiglitz) 3, 4
Global justice movement: achievements of 276–79; campaigns 269–72, 274–75; in Global North 268–69, 271–72, 274; in Global South 271–74; origins of 268–69; proposals of 275–79; protests by 265–66, 270–71
Global South *see* Third World
Gonzalez, Henry 72, 90
Gorbachev, Mikhail 137
Goulart, João 27
Groupement pour le Traitment des Scories du Terril de Lubumbashi 104
Guatemala 14, 236; Arbenz government 26
Guinea, foreign debt of 249
Guinea-Bassau 26, 247, 249
Guyana: export credit agencies and 203; environmental problems 203; foreign debt 241, 243, 244, 246, 247, 249

Haiti 236, 249; World Bank and 158
Halliburton 3, 133, 278
Hankey, Sir Maurice 145
Harken Energy Corp. 77, 78
Heavily Indebted Poor Countries initiative

221, 225, 226, 230, 242–48, 275; conditions of 243–45; results of 248–50
Hegemony or Survival (Chomsky) 4
Hekmatyar, Gulbuddin 70
Helms, Richard 82
Henwood, Doug 23, 177–79
Heritage Foundation 121
Heritage Oil and Gas 100
Hermes Guarantee 201, 202, 203, 205, 206, 207, 209, 211, 212, 215–16
Honduras, foreign debt of 249
Hope in the Dark (Solnit) 281
Hungary, Soviet intervention in 16
Hussein, Saddam 28, 90, 141–42; and BCCI 72
Hutu people 94–96
Hypovereinsbank 209

Ijaw people 116, 121–23, 128
Illaje people 123
immigrant rights movement 281
imperialism 13–14; coups d'état and 27; divide-and-rule tactics 25, 26, 265; post–cold war changes 4–5; pressure on uncooperative countries 25, 142; resistance to 28, 115–17, 121–30, 143–44, 151–54, 176, 191–92, 265–66; resources and 98–106, 118–21, 133–34, 136, 139–40, 145; as system of control 17–28, 176; use of force 5, 25–28, 111n22, 113–14, 115–17, 123, 111n22
India 16, 119, 229, 236, 266; foreign debt 222, 223; export credit agencies and 206, 208; Maheshwar Dam 209–10
Indonesia 236; corruption in 202–3; export credit agencies and 200, 202–3, 205, 207, 216; foreign debt 228, 230, 244
inequality 44
Institute for Policy Studies 278
International Bank for Reconstruction and Development 157
International Development Association 157, 242
International Forum on Globalization 266
International Monetary Fund 3, 4, 19, 135, 275; conflicts of interest 244; debt relief and 221–22, 224, 226, 237, 240, 243–46, 250–51, 252; Iraq and 151–53; Malaysia and 273; neoliberalism and 176–79, 222; offshore banking and 43, 234; protests against 266; structural adjustment programs 22, 23, 245, 265–66; Rwanda and 100; Uganda and 100

International Tax and Investment Center 134–35, 138–39, 144–54
International Trade Organization 267
Iran 14, 90, 145, 200; coup against Mossadegh 14–15; nationalization of oil industry 14
Iran-Contra affair 71–72
Iraq: BCCI and 72; foreign debt 152; Gulf War and 28, 72, 140, 141, 146; human rights in 105–6; oil production and reserves 135–36, 139–54; production sharing agreements in 147–54; sanctions against 72, 142; social conditions in 135, 142, 143; U.S. occupation of 28, 140, 141–42, 146, 250, 275, 278
Israel: and Suez Crisis 15; Yom Kippur War and 17
Ivory Coast 230; foreign debt 244, 249

"jackals" 25–26
James, Deborah 273
Japan 216, 236
Japan Bank for International Cooperation 201, 202, 203, 241
Jersey 88; banking boom in 46–47; impact on island 46, 51–52, 56–62; as offshore banking haven 43, 45, 56–61
Johnson, Chalmers
  Sorrows of Empire 4
Jordan 241, 266
Jordan, Vernon 100
JPMorganChase 226, 238
Jubilee South 190
Jubilee 2000 268
Juhasz, Antonia; Bush Agenda, The 4, 275
Juma'a, Hassan 135–36, 140, 142–44, 154

Kabila, Joseph 96
Kabila, Laurent 94, 96, 99
Kagame, Paul 94, 98–99; ties to U.S. 99
Kazakhstan 138, 139, 144, 150
Keating, Charles 83
Kenya 236; foreign debt 243, 244
Kerry, John 76; investigation of BCCI 79–83, 87, 89
Kirchner, Nestor 273
Korea, Republic of 229, 272
Korten, David
  When Corporations Rule the World 4
KPMG 52
Krauthammer, Charles 13
Krushchev, Nikita 16

Kurdistan 211–12, 214
Kuwait 133, 141, 146, 152, 154
labor exports 235–36
Lake, Anthony 119–20
Lance, Bert 77
Lawson, Nigel 242
Lawson Plan 221, 242
Lee Kyung Hae 272
Liberia, World Bank lending to 159–67
Liberty Tree Foundation 276
Li Zhaoxing 117–18, 124
Lu Guozeng 117
Lumumba, Patrice 26
Luxembourg, as offshore banking haven 72, 73, 74

Madagascar, foreign debt of 249
Mahathir, Mohamad 273
Malawi 254; foreign debt 243, 249
Malaysia 41–43, 229; defiance of IMF 273
Mali, foreign debt of 246, 249
Marcos, Ferdinand 31, 48, 175, 176, 181–85
markets, corporate domination of 16
Martin, Paul 54
mass media, manipulation of 25
Mauritania, foreign debt of 247, 249
McKinney, Cynthia; hearing on Congo 98–99, 110n11
McLure, Charles 137–39
mercenaries: in Congo 111n22; in Nigeria 5, 25–26, 113–14, 115–17
Mexico 207, 256n14, 273; foreign debt 55, 227, 228, 230, 233, 240–41, 244; labor exports 236; Zapatista uprising 272
Middle East, and struggle for oil 27–28
military-industrial complex 99
military interventions 27–28
Mizban, Faraj Rabat 141
Mitterand Plan 221
Mobutu Sese Seko 24, overthrow of 94
Mondlane, Eduardo 26
Mongolia 207
Morales, Evo 277
Morganthau, Robert 69, 84–87
Moscow, John 58, 87
Mossadegh, Mohammad 3, 14–15, 27
Movement for the Emancipation of the Niger Delta 122–24, 129
Movimento dos Trabalhadores Rurais Sem Terra (Landless Workers' Movement) 272
Mozambique 26, 27, 230; foreign debt 241, 246, 249
Mueller, Robert 87

mujahadeen (Afghanistan): and BCCI 70; and drug trade 70

Mulroney, Brian 100

Multilateral Agreement on Investment 269–70, 281

Multilateral Debt Relief Initiative 222, 225, 230, 250–52

Multilateral Investment Agreement 269

multinational corporations: export credit agencies and 209–11; export processing zones and 178; globalization, pressure for 138, 268, 275; mercenaries, use of 25–26, 111n22, 113–14, 115–17, 123; resources and 101–6, 111n29, 112n31, 112n32; scandals 5; transfer mispricing by 49–51; offshore banks, use of 24, 49–51; patents, control of 23

Museveni, Yoweri 95

Myanmar, foreign debt of 230

Nada, Youssef Mustafa 71–72

Namibia 95; export credit agencies and 207

Nasser, Gamal Abdel 15–16

National Commercial Bank of Saudi Arabia 88–89

National Family Farm Coalition 272

nationalism: pan-Arab 15; Iranian 14

Nehru, Jawaharlal 16

neocolonialism *see* imperialism

neoliberalism 4, 19; critique of 176–79, 190–92, 234, 236; defined 176–77; economic development and 176–79, 232; economic strategies 178–81, 222, 230, 231, 236

Netherlands, overseas empire of 13

Newmont Mining Corp. 244

New World Order 27–28

Nicaragua 207; foreign debt 225, 230, 247, 249; U.S. proxy war against 26, 27, 79

Nicpil, Liddy 190–91, 192

Nidal, Adu 73

Niger, foreign debt of 241, 249

Niger Delta People's Volunteer Force 121, 123

Niger Delta Volunteer Service 122

Niger Delta region: attack on oil platforms 116–17; as "Next Gulf" 118–21; pollution from oil production 115–16; struggle against Shell 115–16, 121–24

Nigeria 200, 266; China and 117–18; colonial rule 115; corruption in 44–45, 230; foreign debt 223, 230, 233, 243, 244; oil production 115–16, 125–27; World Bank lending in 158, 167–69

Nkrumah, Kwame 16

nongovernmental organizations 239, 250

Noriega, Manuel 80; and BCCI 72, 79

North American Free Trade Agreement 4, 268, 272

nuclear power 205–6, 210

Obasanjo, Olusegun 125, 127

Obiang, Teodoro 48

O'Connor, Brian 144–45

OECD Watch 105

offshore banking havens: arms trade and 71–73; campaign against 62–64; central role in world trade 44, 47–48, 64–65; corruption and 24, 44–45, 52–56, 64, 231–33, 253; drug trade and 70; extraction of wealth 43, 54–56, 64–65, 226, 231–33, 253, 258n58; financial centers and 234,; ignored by academia 44, 234; secrecy and 47–48, 53, 66; tax evasion and 43, 48, 49–51, 54, 57–59, 64–65, 226, 232; terrorism and 71, 88

Ogoni people 122–23, 125

Okadigbo, Chuba 116

Okonjo-Iweala, Ngozi 118

Okuntimo, Paul 123

Oil Change International 278

oil price spikes 236

oil production and reserves: future shortages of 28, 140; Indonesia 207; Iraqi 135–36, 144–54; Nigerian 113–14, 128–29; strategies to control 25–26, 27–28, 139–40

OM Group, Inc. 104, 112n31

OPEC 125–26, 128; 1973 oil embargo by 17; dollar deposits in First World 17–18

Organisation for Economic Co-operation and Development 135, 269; "Action Statement on Bribery" 216; export credit agencies and 210, 215; Guidelines for Multinational Enterprises 101, 102, 105–6, 112n31; "OECD Arrangement" 215

Overseas Private Investment Corp. 204, 206–9

Oxfam 43, 62–63, 250

Pakistan 90; Afghan mujahadeen and 70–71; BCCI and 70; export credit agencies and 207; foreign debt 244

Panama 3, 26, 72; as offshore banking haven 73, 74

Papua New Guinea: export credit agencies and 204; mining and environmental problems 204

Paris Club of creditors 220, 225–26, 227, 228, 242, 252

Peru 74; foreign debt 241; impact of IMF SAP 22

petrodollars, recycling of 17–18

Perkins, John 19; *Confessions of an Economic Hit Man* 1–2, 17

Pharaon, Ghaith 76, 77, 86, 87, 88

Philippines, the 31–34, 35–36; corruption in 181–82; democratic movements in 182–85, 236; economic decline in 187–89; emigration from 189, 236; foreign debt 181, 190–91, 230, 241, 244; Marcos regime 31, 34, 175, 176, 180–85, 261n61; martial law in 180–85; social conditions in 179–80, 185–86, 189–91; U.S. rule 175–76; World Bank and 158, 178–81

Pinochet, General Augusto 27, 45–46, 48

PLATFORM 140, 156n28

Portugal 209–10

Posada Carriles, Luis 26

poverty reduction strategy programs *see* structural adjustment programs

Price Waterhouse 83–84

privatization 191

production sharing agreements 147–54

protectionism 21, 181, 186–87

proxy wars 27, 70–71

Public Citizen 269, 273

public utilities, privatization of 191, 261n61, 277

Rahman, Masihur 85

Reagan, Ronald, and administration 19, 79, 87, 136–37, 239; Iran-Contra affair 72

Rich, Marc 90

Rights and Accountability in Development 101, 104, 105

Rio Tinto Zinc 204

Ritch, Lee 79–80

Robson, John 138

Roldós, Jaime 3, 26

Roosevelt, Kermit 15

Rumsfeld, Donald 138

rural economic development 183, 186–87

Russia: debt relief and 225; oil industry 154; transition to capitalism 137–39, 258n28

Rutledge, Ian 149

Rwanda 94–96, 98, 249; massacre in 94, 99

SACE 201

Sachs Plan 221

Saleh, Salim 95

Saõ Tomé, foreign debt of 247, 249

Saud al-Fulaij, Faisal 86, 87

Saudi Arabia 3, 88; and BCCI 70, 75

Saro-Wiwa, Ken 125–26

Scholz, Wesley S. 104

Scowcroft, Brent 72

Senegal 16, 249

Senghor, Léopold 16

September 11, 2001, terrorist attacks 71

Shell Oil 144; Nigeria and 113–15, 122, 123, 125–29; at World Economic Forum 127

Shinawatra, Thaksin 54

Sierra Club 269

Sierra Leone 247

SmartMeme 276

Solnit, Rebecca *Hope in the Dark* 281

Somalia 251

Sorrows of Empire (Johnson) 4

South Africa 236; military interventions 27; Truth and Reconciliation Commission 26

Soviet Union 13, 14; de-Stalinization 16; Hungary, intervention in 16; influence in Third World 14; U.S. and 137

Stephens, Jackson 76, 77

Stiglitz, Joseph 24; *Globalization and Its Discontents* 3, 4

structural adjustment programs (SAPs) 19, 229–30; in Ghana 5, 22; in Peru 22; in the Philippines 176–79, 183–85, 190–92; in Zambia 22

Sudan 230, 251

Suharto 200, 202–3

Syria 211

Switzerland, as offshore banking haven 45, 65, 72

Taco Bell, boycott of 280

Tanzania, foreign debt of 247, 249

tax evasion 43, 48, 49–51, 54, 57–59, 64–65

Tax Foundation 137–38

tax havens *see* offshore banking havens

Tax Justice Network 63

Tax Reform Act of 1986 138

Tenke Mining 99

terrorism: as EHM strategy 26, 72; financing of 42, 88–89; inequality and 44; Islamist 71–72, 89; Palestinian 73

Thatcher, Margaret 19, 138

Third World: as commodity producers 17, 23; conditions in 5, 96–97, 106–8, 116, 179–80, 185–90, 234, 236; development strategies 176–79; divisions among coun-

tries 265–68; elites in 25, 28, 43–44, 176, 226, 232–34; emergence of 14; lack of development in 232, 237; terms of trade and 22, 178–79
Third World Network 269
Tidewater Inc. 113
Torrijos, Omar 3, 26
Total S.A. 144, 153
trade unions 135–36, 141–44, 180, 186, 269, 274
transfer mispricing 49–51; cost to Third World 50
Transparency International 45
Turkey: export credit agencies and 206; Ilisu Dam 211–14
Turkmenistan 200

Uganda 94–96; foreign debt 241, 246, 249
Union Bank of Switzerland 57, 58, 77, 226, 250
United Arab Emirates 69, 73
United Fruit Company 15
United Kingdom 213; NCP for Congo 102–3; empire 13–14, 115, 129, 145; Iran 14–15; Iraq occupation and 146, 151, 152; offshore banking and; Suez Crisis and 15
United Nations: trade issues and 265, 276; Panel of Experts, Congo 100–106, 112n32
United Nations Conference on Trade and Development 220, 265, 267
United States: agricultural subsidies 22; aid 98; as empire 13, 28; cold war strategy of 16, 17, 24, 26; in Congo 99, 104, 105; debt-led development strategy of 176–79; Iran coup and 14–15; Iraqi oil and 133–34, 136, 139–40; Iraq wars 72, 133, 141–42; Islamists and 26; Nigerian oil and 118–21; Philippines and 175–76, 180; strategic doctrines 27–28, 118–19; support of Contras 72; trade deficit 23; trade policies 267
U.S. Drug Enforcement Administration 73
U.S. Export-Import Bank 201, 203, 205, 206–7; environmental standards and 212
U.S. Internal Revenue Service 82
U.S. Justice Department 82, 85, 88–89
U.S.–Middle East Free Trade Area 278, 279
U.S. National Security Council 70, 79
U.S. Office of Naval Intelligence 129–30
U.S. Treasury Department 88, 240, 252
Uzbekistan 200

VA Tech 23–14
Venezuela: Chavez government 273; coup attempt in 3, 25; foreign debt 230, 233; oil industry 154
Vietnam 229; foreign debt 225, 243
Volcker, Paul 78, 82

Wälde, Thomas 147
Walker, Peter Lord 138
Wallach, Lori 273
Watson-Clark, Nigel 113–14, 115–17, 121–22, 124, 127–30
When Corporations Rule the World (Korten) 4
Williamson, Craig 26
Witt, Dan 134–35, 136–39, 144–45
Washington consensus *see* neoliberalism
Wolfowitz, Paul 27, 126
World Bank 19, 23, 135, 253, 275; Argentina and 169–73; Congo and 100; conflicts of interest 243–44; culture of lending 157, 158, 173–74; debt relief and 221–22, 224, 226, 237, 240–41, 242–46, 250–51; dictators and 158, 159; export credit agencies and 199, 201, 202, 204, 212, 213, 214; investigations of fraud 158, 162–73; Iraq and 151–52; Liberia and 159–67; Nigeria and 167–69; offshore banking and 43, 234; Philippines and 175–84; privatization and 100, 191, 277; protests against 266; structural adjustment programs 191–91, 265–66
World Economic Forum 126–27
World Forum on Globalization and Global Trade 271
World Gold Council 244
World Social Forum 271
World Trade Organization 4, 188, 189, 275; Agreement on Agriculture 271–72; agricultural trade and 186–87, 271–72; Doha Round 272–73; establishment of 267–68; export credit agencies and 200, 215; foreign sales corporations and 51; protests against 266, 270–73; Uruguay Round 215

Yamani, Sheikh Ahmad Zaki 145
Yemen, foreign debt 225, 243
Yergin, Daniel 139

Zaire *see* Congo
Zambia: foreign debt 230, 247, 249; impact of IMF SAP 22
Zapatista Army of Liberation 272
Zedillo, Ernesto 238
Zeng Peiyan 126–27